PARISI

THE

THE PARISI

BRITONS AND ROMANS
IN EASTERN YORKSHIRE

PETER HALKON

Front cover
Top: The head of Spring from the Rudston Charioteer mosaic.
(Photo: M. Park courtesy Hull and East Riding Museum: Hull Museums)

Bottom: Iron Age chalk figurines from eastern Yorkshire.
(Photo: M. Park courtesy Hull and East Riding Museum: Hull Museums)

Back cover
The so-called 'goddess' painted wall plaster from Malton.
(Photo: M. Park courtesy Malton Museum Trust)

First published 2013

The History Press
The Mill, Brimscombe Port
Stroud, Gloucestershire, GL5 2QG
www.thehistorypress.co.uk

British Library Cataloguing in Publication Data.
A catalogue record for this book is available from the British Library.

ISBN 978 0 7524 4841 1

Typesetting and origination by The History Press
Printed in Great Britain

CONTENTS

ACKNOWLEDGEMENTS

A book of this kind would not be possible without the contribution of many people. I would like to thank all those who have shared their ideas on Iron Age and Roman East Yorkshire with me, particularly Lindsay Allason-Jones, John Collis, John Creighton, Peter Crew, John Dent, Peter Didsbury, Melanie Giles, Ian Armit, Ian Haynes, Martin Henig, Yvonne Inall, Jim Innes, Rod Mackey, Peter Makey, Terry Manby, Martin Millett (my collaborator in the Foulness Valley project), Tom Moore, Patrick Ottaway, Mark Pearce, Rachel Pope, Jenny Price, Dominic Powlesland, Steve Roskams, Steve Sherlock, Bryan Sitch, Ian Stead, Jeremy Taylor, Steve Willis and Pete Wilson. I am grateful to many past and present students from the University of Hull, especially those who undertook research in the territory of the Parisi; their work is acknowledged in the text and bibliography, and also my archaeological colleagues there, Helen Fenwick and Malcolm Lillie.

I am very grateful to all those members of ERAS and YAS and CBA Yorkshire who have participated in fieldwork and listened to reports on work at various stages. I would like to thanks Dave Evans, Ruth Atkinson, Trevor Brigham and Ken Steedman from Humber Archaeology Partnership and the North Yorkshire Historic Environment Record and to John Oxley, York City Archaeologist, for supplying much data and information. Paula Gentil and Caroline Rhodes of Hull Museums allowed access to finds for photography and research and generously gave of their time. David Marchant of the East Riding Museums Service and Andrew Morrison of the Yorkshire Museum also kindly supplied access to finds and other information. Ann Clark and Malcolm Barnard of Malton Museum were very helpful in allowing access to finds. Jody Joy kindly supplied images from the British Museum and valued comment.

Special thanks must go to John Deverell and Mark Norman who helped me compile the database behind the distribution maps, putting in much work. Naomi Sewpaul, John Dent and Pete Wilson kindly read and commented on the text. Big thanks go to Mike Park, photographer at Hull University, who has provided some stunning images, and to Tom Sparrow and Helen Woodhouse for spending a great deal of time and effort on maps and other drawings for which The Marc Fitch Fund kindly provided some funding.

The book benefitted from several periods of research leave provided by the History Department and Faculty of Arts, University of Hull. I am very grateful to the various editors from The History Press, particularly Emily Locke, Ruth Boyes and Glad Stockdale, who have been very patient and helpful. Finally many thanks to my family for all their support during the writing of this book.

Figures and plates are acknowledged in the captions. Figures 2, 8, 9, 11, 15, 24, 32, 34, 49, 56, 71, 77, 79, 84 and Plate 17 are © crown copyright/database right 2013. An Ordnance Survey/EDINA supplied service, for the background topographical data.

LIST OF ILLUSTRATIONS

LIST OF PLATES

INTRODUCTION

'Εβόρακον
Λεγίω ϛ‾ Νικηφόρος
Καμουλόδουνον
Πρὸς οἱς περι τον Εὐλιμενον κολπον Παρισοι και Πολις Πετουαρια

Eboracon (Eboracum)
Legio VI Victrix (Victorious)
Camulodunum
Near a bay (gulf) suitable for a harbour (are) the Parisoi and the town (city)
Petuaria.

— Ptolemy *Geographia* 2.3.17.

(Stückelberger and Graßhoff 2006, 154; Rivet and Smith 1979, 142.)

This is the first surviving reference to the Parisi. It was made by the ancient geographer
Claudius Ptolemaeus, or Ptolemy as he is better known, who was working in Alexandria,
Egypt, during the AD 140s. Writing in Greek, Ptolemy aimed to provide a description
of the world as he knew it at the height of the Roman Empire. His account gives the
names of its peoples and significant places in their territories across the Roman Empire
and its fringes, listing the major features along coastlines such as gulfs, estuaries and
promontories and their geographical position as closely as he could (Strang 1997). Like
so many ancient texts, Ptolemy's original no longer exists, and the book was handed
down through various transcriptions, one of the oldest surviving versions dating from
the late thirteenth century AD preserved in the Satay Library of the Topkapi palace in
Istanbul, which was used in the most recent full translation into German (Stückelberger
and Graßhoff 2006). Ptolemy's account became better known through various Latin
versions, hence the use here of 'Parisi' rather than 'Parisoi'.

There are various meanings given for the word itself which is of Celtic origin: 'the rulers' or 'the efficacious ones', derived from *paro,* 'the people of the cauldron' which comes from *pario* 'cauldron' or 'the spear people', relating to the Welsh *par* meaning spear (Falileyev 2007, 164).

Ptolemy places the Parisi in what is now eastern Yorkshire. The last definition is particularly interesting as this region possesses an Iron Age burial ritual which involves the throwing of spears at bodies in graves (Stead 1991) which will be discussed in more detail in later chapters.

It is generally presumed, largely due to their geographical coincidence, that there is a direct relationship between Ptolemy's Parisi and the earlier Iron Age people whose burials were placed under low mounds surrounded by small square ditches or 'square barrows', as the densest concentration of these features in Britain is also in this region (Stead 1979; Cunliffe 2005). Although Stead identified the Parisi with square barrows in his *La Tène cultures of eastern Yorkshire* (Stead 1965), he was more circumspect about this and any connection with the Parisii of Gaul mentioned by Julius Caesar (*Gallic Wars* 6:3) in his later books (Stead 1979; 1991).The dead in some of these monuments were accompanied by the remains of two-wheeled vehicles which are usually referred to as chariot burials, and again these are at their densest in East Yorkshire. The first reported excavation of a chariot burial was at Arras near Market Weighton 1815–17 (Stead 1979), hence the 'Arras culture', a label attached to these people by the archaeologist V.G. Childe (1940) because of the distinctive nature of their material remains and its restricted distribution (Fig. 1). It was presumed by a number of scholars such as Hawkes (1960) that the culture was brought in to eastern Yorkshire through an invasion from the Marne region of northern France because of the similarity between the burials in both areas, and the discovery of artefacts decorated in a style which takes its name from a middle Iron Age site at La Tène in Switzerland.

According to Hawkes (1960) this incursion followed an earlier Iron Age invasion from the European continent in the so-called Hallstatt period, named after the lake-side village in Austria associated with salt-mining, where a large cemetery with burials containing artefacts decorated in distinctive styles was excavated. The excavations by the German archaeologist Bersu (1940) on an Iron Age settlement at Little Woodbury in Wiltshire demonstrated continuity with the indigenous Bronze Age material culture, rather than continental invasion, based on the shape of houses, which were round in Britain as opposed to their mainly rectangular counterparts on the European mainland, and other aspects of material culture. When Hodson was writing in 1964, insufficient excavation had been undertaken to match square barrows to roundhouses until Brewster (1980) and Dent (1982, 456) encountered them both at Garton-Wetwang Slack. Despite this Hodson (1964) still saw the Arras culture as originating on the continent along with the Aylesford culture of south-east England.

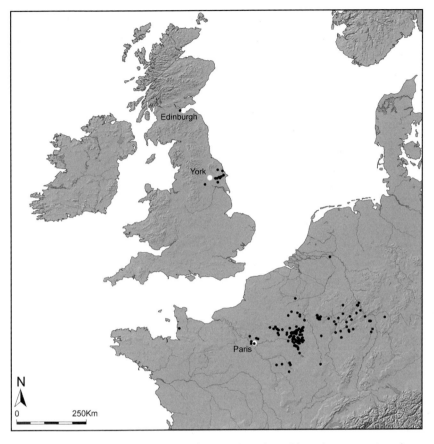

Fig. 1 Europe showing distribution of chariot burials and key places mentioned. Based on Stead (1979) and Anthoons (2011). (H. Woodhouse)

Stead (1979, 93), in comparing burials in East Yorkshire with those on the continent, still advocated some migration:

The arrival in Yorkshire of artefacts from west-central Europe could be explained away by trade, the arrival of ideas – complex burial rites must surely mean the arrival and settlement of people. They could have been tribes but they need not have been numerically strong: perhaps they were adventurers, merchants, evangelists or a few farmers.

He also highlighted the differences, with crouched burials predominating in East Yorkshire and extended ones on the European continent, noting the great contrast in opulence between the French vehicle burials and those of East Yorkshire. By 1991,

15

however, in the light of much excavation, especially his own at Kirkburn, Garton Station, Rudston and Burton Fleming, and those of Dent (1985) at Wetwang Slack, his hypothesis is moderated further: 'Direct continental influence on the Arras culture amounts to two aspects of the burial rite, cart-burials and square barrows – their arrival points to at least one immigrant ... a powerful – well connected evangelist?' (Stead 1991, 228).

The impact of continental contact has therefore been progressively downplayed. Dent (1995, 65) also continued this trend: 'Excavations of Bronze Age and Iron Age settlements have shown that there was a continuous insular cultural tradition in the region. The architecture through this period had more in common with other parts of Britain than the continent.'

Examination of the archaeological evidence on both sides of the English Channel and North Sea, however, suggests that continental links are more complex and traits regarded as 'indigenous' or 'continental' are not mutually exclusive. It has been clear for some time that there are roundhouses in France (Harding 1973; Jacques and Rossignol 2001) and further examples are still being found around Arras (France) (pers. comm. Dimitri Mathiot). Stead (1979, 38) himself points out that there are crouched burials, though very much in the minority, in the Champagne region, which also has vehicle burials and square burial enclosures. Conversely the skeleton in the 'Kings barrow' at Arras (East Yorkshire), buried with two horses, which is itself a unique trait in East Yorkshire vehicle burials, is not crouched but lies on his back with legs flexed (Stillingfleet 1846). Dent's (1995, 52) and Stead's (1991, 179) Type B burials, often accompanied by weapons and pig bones, were also extended and with the head to the east or west rather than north.

The origins of Celtic peoples and even the term 'Celtic' itself have become both topical and contentious in our own era of large-scale immigration and preoccupation with identity and origins (James 1999; Collis 2003). The collating and plotting of the linguistic and archaeological evidence across Europe in the comprehensive volume *An Atlas for Celtic Studies* (Koch 2007), provide what the writer claims is an opportunity to examine the evidence 'free from arbitrary and passing modes of preferred analysis' (Koch 2007, 2).

A different and still controversial approach was taken by Oppenheimer in the *Origins of the British* (2006) and Sykes' *Blood of the Isles* (2006), who used genetics, largely the Y- chromosome of present peoples to remap past populations. Miles (2005) states on the back cover of his book, *The Tribes of Britain*, that 'the English, the Irish, the Scots and the Welsh (are) ... a ragbag of migrants, reflecting thousands of years of continuity and change'. A further scientific approach to determining provenance is based on the measurement of various isotopes, particularly oxygen and strontium in the bones from ancient burials (Montgomery 2010) which will be referred to in subsequent chapters of this book.

Giles, in her recent review of the Iron Age archaeology of the Yorkshire Wolds (2007(a) 105), provides a more detailed account of the various hypotheses concerning the Arras culture than that presented here and goes so far as to write that:

> Even if genetic analyses were to demonstrate links between the communities in East Yorkshire and the Champagne region, we would be left to debate the meaning of and significance of such affinities … I want to suggest that this question is a non-question; that its time has passed.

However difficult it is to answer, this question is surely too important to be dismissed; attempting to understand the cause and effects of movements and interconnections of people is one of the fundamentals of history. The classical sources, for example, provide clear accounts of Iron Age diasporas such as the Helvetii, whose migration in 58 BC from what is now southern Germany to Switzerland created severe disruption (Caesar, *Gallic Wars* 1:1–29), with 368,000 people, including women and children, involved. The number, according to Caesar, was written in Greek script on a list found in the Helvetian camp after their defeat. Although the necessity of treating such numbers from ancient texts with great caution is obvious, even half this amount represents a considerable population.

Caesar (*Gallic Wars* 4:3) also provides further corroboration of a supposed French connection with East Yorkshire, as there is an obvious resemblance of the name 'Parisi' to the 'Parisii' who are placed by Caesar as living in the area around what is now Paris.

In his famous description of Britain (*Gallic Wars* 5:12) he also states that:

> the maritime portion (is inhabited) by those who had passed over from the country of the Belgae for the purpose of plunder and making war; almost all of whom are called by the names of those states from which being sprung they went thither, and having waged war, continued there and began to cultivate the lands.

The suitability of the term 'tribe' to describe the complex and disparate populations of Iron Age and Roman Britain is also worthy of some scrutiny. It has been argued (Moore 2012) that the familiar tribal model owes much to nineteenth-century notions, not always supported by archaeological evidence or classical sources and that the names of the peoples in classical accounts should be considered as reflecting the emergence of new social and political groupings in the later Iron Age. Defining precise territorial boundaries is very difficult and they are likely to have oscillated through time; a combination of natural features, especially rivers, such as the Derwent and Humber, or the North Yorkshire Moors may have served as demarcation. Concentrations of particular traits in material culture extending across what are now the modern counties of the East Riding of Yorkshire, North Yorkshire and the City of York unitary authority, seem, however, to indicate a distinctive identity in the Iron Age and Roman periods.

One of the most obvious cultural signatures for the region is the concentration of chariot burials within it. Research based principally on the typology of iron tyres from chariots also provides interesting similarities between the material culture of the Paris basin and East Yorkshire regions in addition to those outlined above (Anthoons 2007,146). In both areas the buried vehicles had flat wide tyres with no nails present, and although the detail of decoration is different, attention has been paid to the terrets (rings through which reins pass to the yoke) and in both areas there are dismantled chariots and crouched burials. The explanation given for these similarities (Anthoons 2007, 149) was the existence of elite networks linking both areas, a hypothesis which is also discussed by Cunliffe (2005). Cunliffe's model of constant two-way contact between 'zones of influence' including an Eastern Zone, allowing for regional developments, provides one of the neatest explanations for obvious cultural similarities. Although Cunliffe highlights the importance of the Thames estuary, the Humber estuary deserves greater attention as there is much evidence for cultural exchange via this route extending backwards into the Bronze Age and beyond (Manby *et al.* 2003(b); Wright *et al.* 2001).

This volume aims to examine the origins of the Parisi and their relationship to the Iron Age Arras culture in the light of an enormous amount of diverse evidence, ranging from the results of the application of various scientific techniques referred to earlier such as isotope analysis on human bone (Jay and Richards 2007) to large-scale study of ancient landscapes revealed in growing crops (Stoertz 1997). It goes on to consider the impact of Rome on East Yorkshire against the background of recent interpretations of Roman Britain (e.g. Millett 1989; Mattingly 2006) and to assess human-landscape interaction within this region in the Iron Age and Roman periods, taking account of palaeo-environmental studies which have provided much new information on sea level transgression and regression, coastal and climate change, and their effects on human activity across both eras, which are again issues of great relevance today.

Apart from the seminal fieldwork and publications of Tony Brewster, Ian Stead and John Dent, and the discoveries of past antiquarians and archaeologists, whose contributions will be outlined in Chapter 1, the information presented here has been drawn from many sources, particularly the Humber Archaeology Sites and Monuments Register, the Hull and East Riding Museum, the North Yorkshire and City of York Historic Environment records and the work of a large number of colleagues who have generously shared the results of their work and who will be acknowledged below.

This is the first single authored book on Iron Age and Roman eastern Yorkshire since the publication of *The Parisi* by Herman Ramm (Duckworth, Peoples of Roman Britain Series) in 1978, the only other volumes being the proceedings of two conferences organised by the present author (Halkon 1989 and 1998). Since then much new knowledge has accrued due to the enormous amount of fieldwork undertaken. Much of this has been as a result of the various changes in planning regulation, requiring developers to fund archaeological investigation prior to construction. Many of these excavations are yet to be published in full and I am most grateful to colleagues from the various archaeological contractors working in this region for providing their results.

Finds of national and international significance have also been made through research projects undertaken by the voluntary sector and other bodies, especially the East Riding Archaeological Society in some cases collaborating with universities, such as those undertaken in the Foulness Valley since 1980 (Halkon 1983; 1989(b); Halkon and Millett 1999; Halkon 2003; Halkon *et al.* 2000; Halkon and Millett 2003; Millett 2006; Halkon 2008; Halkon *et al.* forthcoming), which have generally focussed on the southern part of East Yorkshire. In the north of the region two remarkable long-term landscape research projects carried out at West Heslerton (Powlesland 2003(a) and (b)) and Wharram Percy (Hayfield 1988) have continued to provide an insight into the archaeology of the Yorkshre Wolds and the Vale of Pickering in the Iron Age and Roman periods. One glance at the maps prepared by Ramm (1978) show an absence of Iron Age and Roman activity in Holderness and the Hull Valley. Research initiated by Peter Didsbury (1990) in the lower Hull Valley has totally transformed our knowledge of this much ignored area and has been followed by research projects at Arram (Wilson *et al.* 2006) and Baswick (Coates 2007). The Humber Wetlands project (Van de Noort and Ellis 1995, 1997, 1999, 2000; Van de Noort 2004) undertook field walking and palaeo-environmental surveys with some excavation yielding important results in the wetlands of easternYorkshire. Other dissertations and projects prepared as part of archaeology courses at Hull University such as those of Hyland in Holderness and Robinson and Coates in the Hull Valley, are particularly important in collating evidence for Roman activity.

Finds have been made by members of the public purely by chance or through metal detecting. The creation of the Portable Antiquities Scheme (PAS) has led to an enormous growth of the number of finds being reported by metal detector users and I am grateful to Dan Petts for allowing access to the PAS database.

Perhaps the most significant contribution to the extension of our knowledge of this period, especially in terms of the wider landscape, has been the National Mapping Programme undertaken by English Heritage and the Royal Commission on Historical Monuments (England) (RCHM (E)) before them, collating and plotting thousands of archaeological sites revealed in growing crops and captured in vertical and oblique aerial photographs. The most impressive of these covered the Yorkshire Wolds (Stoertz 1997), the well-drained soils of which are particularly sensitive to showing up archaeological features. The detailed maps of cropmarks reveal a remarkable palimpsest of settlement patterns from the Neolithic onwards, stretching from the River Humber to Flamborough Head. A similar scheme was undertaken in the Vale of York, though detailed mapping of this has not been fully published (Kershaw 2001) and mapping of the Chalk Lowland and Hull Valley by English Heritage and through the National Mapping Programme is almost completed at the time of writing. The dry summer of 2010 resulted in the appearance of many cropmark sites unknown hitherto, although it has not been possible to fully integrate this information here.

In order to provide as up to date a distribution of Iron Age and Romano-British sites and finds as possible, a new database was compiled using the sources of information listed above. I am greatly indebted to John Deverell, Richard Green, Mark Norman and Helen Woodhouse for their assistance. This database was used to generate distribution maps using Arc Map v.10 (ESRI) to provide greater understanding of the past activities of the people of Iron Age and Roman Eastern Yorkshire within their landscape.

CHAPTER 1

THE SEARCH FOR THE PARISI

BEGINNINGS

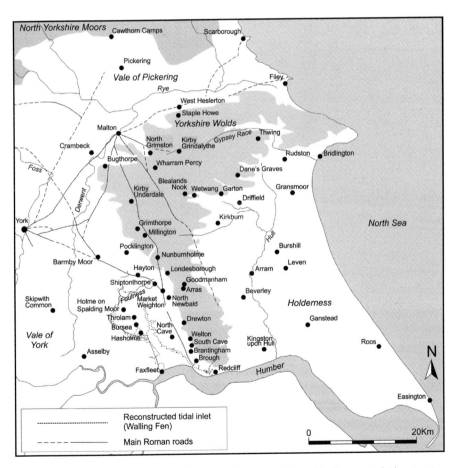

Fig. 2 Eastern Yorkshire showing the main places mentioned in the text of Chapter 1. (H. Woodhouse)

The investigation of Iron Age and Roman eastern Yorkshire began in the sixteenth and seventeenth centuries, following the trend for antiquarian exploration elsewhere in Britain (Gaimster *et al.* 2007). Before that the remains of Roman buildings encountered were treated with little respect and used as a resource. According to Hull Chamberlain's Roll No. 1, payment was made between 1321 and 1324 for the carting of stone from Brough for the refurbishment of the city defences (Corder and Richmond 1942). Roman structures were quarried for the construction of churches as a number in eastern Yorkshire contain reused Roman stone, such as Kirby Grindalythe (Buckland 1988, 295). Indeed in his appendix to Burton's account of the discovery of the circular Roman temple at Millington, Drake remarks that: 'it had been the custom for the inhabitants of their village, time out of mind, to dig for stones in this ground when they wanted.' (Drake 1747, 14).

At Kirby Underdale the possible altar of Mercury (Ramm 1978, 103; Tufi 1983, no.19, Pl 4), which will be discussed in Chapter 10, had a complex history. Originally found in the 1870 refurbishment of the church, it was placed in the rectory garden before being reinstated in the church wall (Kitson Clark 1935, 95).

Although the Tudor antiquarian Leland travelled along the main roads through East Yorkshire (1540–46) which followed the routes of Roman predecessors, he makes little reference to anything other than medieval antiquities. His account, however, does provide interesting topographical observations, including a description of the Walling Fen as, 'so large that fifty-eight villages stand in or abutting it ... the fen itself ... is sixteen miles around its perimeter' (Chandler 1993, 537).

One of the earliest references to Roman coins in the region is a letter from William Strickland of Boynton Hall to Sir William Cecil in 1571, then Secretary of State to Elizabeth I, which refers to a hoard of at least sixty Roman coins dating from Vespasian to Antoninus Pius (AD 69–161), found when a house was swept away by the sea at 'Awburn' (Auburn) near Bridlington (Lemon 1856, 406; Kitson Clark 1935, 63). This example also provides a reminder of the vulnerability of the Holderness to coastal erosion.

It was not until William Camden (1551–1623) that the history and topography of Roman York and eastern Yorkshire was recorded in any systematic way. Camden (Holland 1610, 35) was one of the first to equate the settlements listed by Ptolemy, and other Roman documents such as the *Antonine Itinerary*, the *Notitia Dignitatum* and *Ravenna Cosmography* (Ramm 1978; Rivet and Smith 1979), with towns within the East Riding of his day: 'Under the Roman Empire, not farre from the banke, by Foulnesse a River of small account, where Wighton, a little Towne of Husbandry well inhabited is now seen stood, as we may well thinke in old time *Delgovitia*.'

The debate about the location of *Delgovitia* and other places mentioned in these documents is still ongoing (Creighton 1988; Millett 2006) and will be addressed later in this book.

In 1699, Abraham De La Pryme (1671–1704), Curate of Holy Trinity church in Hull (Jackson 1870, 200), without knowing the full implications of his observation, noted the following in his diary: 'I saw on my journey to York many hundreds of tumuli which I take to be Roman at a place called Arras on this side Wighton not mentioned in any author description thereof which I intend to digg into...'

De La Pryme's enthusiasm for the study of the past is beyond doubt, expressed in this extract of a letter to Dr Gale, Dean of York: 'Thank you for your encouraging me to prosecute these studdys, than which nothing is more sweet, nothing more pleasant to me ... I do already find that there are a great many old antiquitys monuments and inscriptions ... in many parts of this country' (Jackson 1870, 200).

De La Pryme never did carry out this intention and it was not until 1815–17 that the mounds at Arras were opened by Stillingfleet, Hull and Clarkson and found to be Iron Age in date, an event which will be discussed in more detail below.

De La Pryme was also the first to recognise the significance of Roman antiquities at Brough-on-Humber (Jackson 1870, 219). Another antiquarian, Horsley, also described the ramparts and foundations of Roman Brough and their setting, observing that 'The Humber formerly came just up to it, and it still does at high spring tides' (Horsley 1732, 314 and 374).

In the late 1970s Peter Armstrong (pers. comm.) recognised curves of ancient shorelines, fossilised within field boundaries to the west of Brough. Herman Ramm (1978, 111) also noted the changes that had taken place in the shape of the Humber shore in the Walling Fen area based on eighteenth-century maps. It was not until the research of the present author that the full significance of Horsley's remark was recognised (Halkon 1987; 2008; Halkon and Millett 1999). From study of soil maps (King and Bradley 1987) it was realised that Roman Brough was at the edge of the tidal inlet into which the Foulness flowed, later becoming the Walling Fen, described by Leland. This observation also provided a context for the inscribed Roman lead pigs found in this vicinity, traded from Derbyshire through the Humber estuary, which were first recorded in the later eighteenth century (Gough 1789; Kitson Clark 1935).

Horsley's contemporary, the great York antiquarian Francis Drake, disputed the former's equation of Brough with Petuaria in his attempt to place the Roman settlement names of East Yorkshire (Drake 1736) and to trace the routes of the Roman roads around York (Plate 1). At Barmby Moor, Drake (1736, 63) cites the perceptive observation of Dr Martin Lister, made around 1700, one of the first recorded 'scientific' fabric descriptions of the pottery which he found there, rightly presuming it to be Roman:

There are found in York in the road or Roman Street out of Micklegate and likewise by the river side ... urns of three different tempers viz.- 1. Urns of a blewish gray colour having a great quantity of coarse sand wrought in with the clay 2. Others of the same colour being either a very fine sand mixed with it full of mica or 'cat silver' or made of clay naturally sandy ... The composition of the first kind of pot did first give me occasion to discover the place where they were made. The one about midway between Wilberfoss and Barmby on the Moor ... in the sand hills on rising ground where the warren now is – where I have found scattered widely up and down, broken pieces of rims, slag and cinders. (Lister 1681–2, in Hutton *et al.* 1809, 518).

The pottery described is very similar to that produced at Holme-on-Spalding Moor (Halkon and Millett 1999), and the 'sand hills on rising ground' are very like the location of most of the Roman settlements and kiln sites around Holme.

Drake (1736, 33) adds that: 'It is to be observed that the present road to York goes through this bed of sand, cinders &c [etc] but the Roman way lies as I suppose a little on the right of it.'

One of the first Roman mosaics to be found in the East Riding was ploughed up at Bishop Burton near Beverley (Thoresby 1715, 558) and described in more detail by Gent (1733, 77) as being of red, white and blue stones (see Chapter 8). It is only recently that the precise find spot has been located (Williamson 1987). In the north of possible Parisi territory, the Roman forts near Pickering, usually known as Cawthorn camps were first noted by Robinson in a letter to Gale in 1724, which subsequently became the focus of much later research.

To the west of the Wolds, near the source of the River Foulness at Londesborough, Drake (1736, 32) reported the discovery of a Roman road during the construction of the Great Pond, one of a series of lakes and canals created by Knowlton, the chief gardener to Richard Boyle, 3rd Earl of Burlington and 4th Earl of Cork (1694–1753) at Londesborough Park. Burlington, a great patron of the arts, must take credit for supporting this important burst of activity (Henrey 1986, 78).

The discovery of the road renewed the efforts of antiquarians to locate the Roman settlements listed by classical authors, for Drake was in correspondence with the Revd William Stukeley, the doyen of English Antiquarians of the time, concerning his discoveries. Stukeley visited 'Lonsburrow' and Goodmanham on 1 July 1740 and the newly discovered Roman road was exposed for him to examine (Lukis 1887, 386). Lord Burlington commissioned John Haynes of York to draw a map showing the route of the Roman road through his estate and beyond. The document, dated 1744, was entitled *'An accurate survey of some stupendous remains of Roman antiquity on the Wolds in Yorkshire ... through which some grand military ways to several eminent stations are traced'* (Henrey 1986, 205) and it is a testament to Haynes' map-making skills that it was possible to correlate the buildings illustrated in his map to those revealed in recent survey work (Halkon *et al.* 2003; Halkon 2008, 198).

In a letter to Mark Catesby read at a meeting of the Royal Society on 6 March 1745–46, Thomas Knowlton described the discovery (Philosophical Transactions Royal Society, March/April 1746, 100):

Many foundations (were found) in a ploughed field … discovered by one Mr Hudson, a farmer at Millington, as he formerly tended his sheep on one side of the hill, and on the opposite side had perceived in the corn a different colour for some years before: which led him this summer to dig … there were many other foundations which had Roman pavements within them … by which I imagine after the dissolution of the temple became a Roman station, then called *Delgovicia*, which has been so uncertainly fixed at Goodmanham, Londesborough, Hayton &c.[etc].

This extract is particularly interesting because it is one of the earliest references from the East Riding to cropmarks being used for the recognition of archaeological features. It is also a reminder that Hayton, which has been the focus of recent fieldwork (Halkon and Millett 2003; Halkon *et al.* forthcoming), was even at this date perceived to be a possible location for a Roman settlement of some significance.

The discovery of the Millington remains caused some excitement as Drake and his colleague John Burton (Burton 1745; 1753) carried out survey work there as well. Ramm (1990) highlights some contradictions between the accounts of Knowlton and the other two writers, though Burton and Drake both endorsed Knowlton's conclusion that Millington was *Delgovicia*. In the manuscript version, Drake points out an interesting hazard to archaeological survey at this time:

Whilst we were on the spot directing the survey, in the year 1745, a year in which the House of Stewart again did attempt to recover the British Crown, some people observing us, gave an information at York, that we were marking out a camp in the Wolds; which had like to cause us some trouble to contradict. (Drake 1746, cited in Ramm 1990, 13).

The remains at Millington and the location of *Delgovicia* will be discussed below, but the impact of these discoveries remained in local memory for some time afterwards as they are reported in the diary of John Wesley:

Mon. July 1, 1776. I preached at about eleven to a numerous and serious congregation at Pocklington. In my way from hence to Malton, Mr C- (a man of some sense and veracity) gave me the following account: his grandfather Mr H-, he said about twenty years ago, ploughing up a field, two or three miles from

Pocklington, turned up a large stone, under which he perceived there was a hollow. Digging on he found at a small distance, a large magnificent house. He cleared away the earth; and going in to it, found many spacious rooms. The floors of the lower storey were of mosaic work, exquisitely wrought. Mr C- himself counted sixteen stones within an inch square. Many flocked to see it from various parts, as long as it stood open, but after some days, Mr P- (he knew not why) ordered it to be covered again and he would never suffer any to open it, but ploughed the field all over. (Curnock 1938, 113).

Surprisingly Drake paid little attention to Malton, the main Roman centre in the north of the territory of the Parisi, other than noting the presence of its fortifications (Kitson Clark 1935, 99). He was, however, involved with the discovery and exhibition to the Royal Society in 1755 of the tombstone inscription to Macrinus, a cavalryman in the imperial bodyguard found there which will be discussed more fully in Chapter 6 (*RIB* 714; Kitson Clark 1935, 100). John Walker, a Fellow of the Society of Antiquaries of London, lived in Malton and noted some finds. He corresponded with Thomas Hinderwell who copied much material into a 1798 edition of his *History of Scarborough* (Hinderwell 1798). It is thanks to this remarkable book that so much information about Roman Malton and district is preserved. The *Malton Messenger* newspaper also provided detailed accounts of discoveries, many of them reported by the antiquarians Captain Copperthwaite, George Pycock and Charles Monkman during the period of rapid development which followed the arrival of the railways from the 1860s onwards (Kitson Clark 1935). The foundations were therefore laid for the important fieldwork around Malton undertaken in the 1920s to 1940s by the Roman Malton and District Committee of which Philip Corder, John L. Kirk and the Revd Thomas Romans were the luminaries. Their work, which expanded to include other areas of North and East Yorkshire, became the main archaeological effort in the region between the nineteenth-century barrow diggers and the excavations backed by the Ministry of Works in the 1960s and later. The contribution of this group will be considered more closely in the next section.

As far as the Iron Age is concerned, the first recorded excavations of square barrows in East Yorkshire were at Danes Graves near Kilham in 1721 (Stead 1979,16) when several mounds were dug into after they were observed by a group who were beating the bounds of the parish, an event which was recorded in a parish register. Antiquarian exploration resumed at Arras from 1815 to 1817, where Barnard Clarkson, of Holme House, Holme-on-Spalding Moor, the Revd Edward Stillingfleet, vicar of South Cave and an active antiquarian, with Dr Thomas Hull of Beverley, supervised the excavation of many of the barrows, which had been noted by De La Pryme. They identified the burials as being of 'Ancient British' origin, the discovery of several chariot burials causing Stillingfleet (1846) to equate them to classical descriptions of chariot-fighting Britons. It is important to note that the so-called 'King's Barrow' and 'Queen's Barrow' are described as being circular.

The only contemporary account of the find is a manuscript plan drawn up by William Watson, a mapmaker of Seaton Ross, which is dated August 1816 (Stead 1979, Plate 1, 109). The first published reference appears in Oliver's *History of Beverley* (Oliver 1829), which includes a letter from Thomas Hull to the Scarborough antiquarian Hinderwell. A fuller account was given by Stillingfleet (1846), published thirty years after the discovery. Presumably inspired by the publication of the above, the Yorkshire Antiquarian club carried out further excavation at Arras in 1850 (Proctor 1855; Davis and Thurnam 1865; Stead 1979), as well as on the contrasting lowland square barrow cemetery at Skipwith Common (Stead 1979).

The indefatigable Canon Greenwell excavated further Iron Age burials, some furnished with chariots at Arras and Beverley (Greenwell and Rolleston 1877; Greenwell 1906, Kinnes and Longworth 1985, 142, PL un. 64), and finally aged seventy-seven, with his old arch rival Mortimer (then aged seventy-two) at Danes Graves, in 1897–98, with the comparatively youthful drainage commissioner and antiquary Thomas Boynton FSA of Bridlington, aged sixty-five (Fig. 3a, b, c).

The details of these and later excavations are described by Stead (1979) and will be discussed in Chapter 4.

Apart from the route of the Roman roads and the location of named Roman settlements, the focus of antiquarians, especially on the Yorkshire Wolds, had been on burials, which they hoped would supply artefacts for their collections. However, Stillingfleet (1846) made some observations about the landscape of the area around the Arras cemetery. He was one of the first to suggest that the nearby 'Double Dykes' were contemporary with the burials, and similar to the linear earthworks of the North Yorkshire Moors, studied by Spratt (1981; 1989). Drake and Burton had mapped the entrenchments around the temple site at Millington, wrongly attributing them to the Romans, assuming that they were part of the 'Roman Station' of *Delgovitia*. Some antiquarians had confused the linear earthworks with roads, an error highlighted by the Revd Maule Cole (1899), who published the first systematic account of the roads since Drake. This survey is of particular importance, for according to Kitson Clark (1935, 33), the Ordnance Survey maps at 6 inches to the mile were based on his paper.

The most important work on the so-called 'British entrenchments', which travel long distances across the Yorkshire Wolds and will be discussed below, was by John Robert Mortimer (Giles 2006; Harrison, 2011), a Driffield-based corn-merchant whose *Forty years Researches...* remains one of the most important books to have been written on the archaeology of East Yorkshire (Mortimer 1905, 381–385). The linear earthworks were almost the only non-sepulchral monuments to receive attention (Plate 3).

Fig. 3a Boynton, Mortimer and Greenwell excavating at Danes Graves, 1898. **b** Drawing of the Danes Graves chariot burial. (Mortimer 1905, 359) **c** Copper-alloy pin decorated with coral from Danes Graves, now in the Yorkshire Museum, York. (Mortimer 1905, 364)

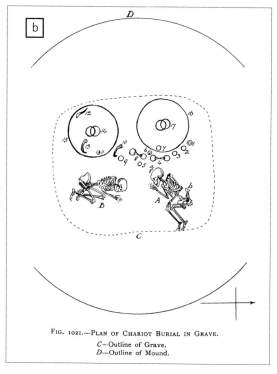

FIG. 1021.—PLAN OF CHARIOT BURIAL IN GRAVE.
C—Outline of Grave.
D—Outline of Mound.

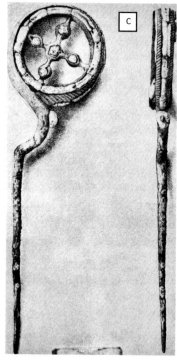

Mortimer (1905, lxxxii) expressed his disappointment in not finding more Roman remains, although he did find pottery and other material in enclosure ditches at Blealands Nook, as well as several corn driers, or malting ovens which he wrongly identified as hypocausts. He also misidentified the important Iron Age burial accompanied by fine swords at North Grimston in 1902 as Roman, although he recorded and illustrated the finds with his usual thoroughness.

Roman coins were one of the most frequent discoveries made by nineteenth-century antiquarians such as those found '... about 25 chains (500m) north-east of Ludhill Spring, Hunger Hill closes', near Nunburnholme (Kitson Clark 1935, 136) reported on by the great Victorian antiquarian and landowner Lord Albert Conyngham (Denison) 1st Baron Londesborough (1806–1860). Less than half a kilometre away and possibly related, a very large hoard of coins was found in a pot at Methill Hall, Nunburnholme, which consisted of at least 3,000 coins (Kitson Clark 1935, 136). These were presented by Lord Londesborough to the museums of the Yorkshire Philosophical Society and Leeds Literary and Philosophical Society. Further Roman activity was found at Nunburnholme by the Revd M.C.F. Morris (1907), whilst attempting to locate the nunnery. He excavated the foundations of a Roman building with pottery and a coin of the Emperor Caracalla (AD 211–217).

The Nunburnholme discoveries provide an example of continued antiquarian interest on the Yorkshire Wolds. Its practitioners, who were largely clerics or gentry, present a microcosm of developments elsewhere in Britain. Most discoveries were sporadic chance finds made during agricultural activities or as a result of the development of the region's infrastructure. At Rosehill, Goodmanham, for example, a Roman site was found in 1888, during the construction of a railway cutting and viaduct. Here 'A quantity of Roman pottery was disinterred from the surface soil consisting of ... samian ware; thin smooth light grey ... and coarse black pottery with particles of Chalk in it. Some beads, ornaments of jet, iron spearheads and Roman coins were also found' (Maule Cole 1899, 44), discoveries followed up by the present author.

Away from the Yorkshire Wolds, on the lowlands of the Vale of York, more Roman finds were reported. In 1853, the Revd R. Whytehead gave a number of Roman urns to the museum of the Yorkshire Philosophical Society in York discovered at Holme-on-Spalding Moor (*Yorkshire Philsophical Society Annual Report* 1853). Roman pottery is also recorded from Tollingham, in the same parish, in 1873, where a Roman lead coffin was also found, displayed outside the vicarage as an ornamental trough and subsequently stolen! (*Yorkshire Weekly Post*, 14 January 1899.)

FROM ANTIQUARIAN TO ARCHAEOLOGIST

A key figure in the development of a more systematic and academic approach to archaeological rather than antiquarian investigation was Thomas Sheppard, appointed Curator at Hull Museums in 1901 and Director 1921–41, who himself had been introduced to prehistory by Mortimer (Schadla-Hall 1989; Sitch 1993). There is insufficient space here to discuss Sheppard's major contribution in any detail. In terms of Roman archaeology, Sheppard collaborated with Philip Corder, schoolmaster at Bootham School, York, who eventually became Assistant Secretary of the Society of Antiquaries of London and President of the Royal Archaeological Institute. Corder was keen to find opportunities to excavate Roman pottery production sites to provide comparisons with those he had excavated at Crambeck, near Castle Howard (Corder 1928) and so Sheppard and Corder decided to follow up earlier references concerning Roman pottery at Holme-on-Spalding Moor. Sheppard describes his first visit to Throlam as follows:

> There, in a large field arising out of a flat peaty area, was 'Pot Hill' … We picked up as many pieces of earthenware rims, bases, and handles as we could carry. The hill was 100ft across and 6ft high and said to be a solid mass of pottery fragments. On seeing the mound I felt like repeating what the American said when he first saw a giraffe, 'I don't believe it!' (Sheppard 1932, 3).

In May 1930, Corder, together with Dr J.L. Kirk and two 'trained men' from Malton, excavated several kilns there (Corder 1930(a), 6) and Sheppard provides the following account of the first day's work:

> Subsequently … with the aid of a large double-decker bus lent by the Hull Corporation, a party of the Hull Grammar School boys interested in historical work was conveyed to Pot Hill and carried with them a score of spades, shovels and pickaxes, supplied by the city engineer, and some new large tin drums lent by Mr Douglas of the Hull Corporation Sanitary Department. A full day was spent and something like 12cwt of pottery was brought away as a result of the day's digging. (Sheppard in Corder 1930(a), 7)

This excavation was of considerable significance as it identified the source of much of the greyware pottery, ubiquitous on Roman sites in East Yorkshire, which received the generic term 'Throlam Ware'. This name persisted until recently when it was realised that there were many more kilns in the Holme-on-Spalding Moor area (Halkon 1983; Halkon 1987; Halkon 2003; 2008; Halkon and Millett 1999). At the end of his report, Corder stated that knowledge of the history of the fort at Brough might provide a solution to the problem of dating the pottery (Corder 1930(a)). This comment is important as it showed the existence of a research strategy aimed at understanding the Roman sites of this part of East Yorkshire as a coherent entity.

Further opportunities were provided by the foundation of Hull University College, whose Local History Committee instigated a five-year programme of excavation from 1934 at Brough-on-Humber (Wright 1990) co-directed by Corder with the Revd Thomas Romans (Corder 1934; Corder and Romans 1935, 1936, 1937). The work was undertaken with a small team of paid excavators led by Bertie Gott and a number of volunteers, including E.V. (Ted) and C.W. Wright, who would later discover the Bronze Age Ferriby boats, and Mary Kitson Clark, who compiled 'A *Gazetteer of Roman Remains in East Yorkshire*' (1935) which remains a fundamental resource (Fig. 5).

Digging took place over a month-long summer season, and the quality of work was certainly the best that had so far been carried out. The main results of the five years of the Brough Excavation Committee's research were the confirmation of the presence of a conquest period fort, a later fort and civilian settlement complete with a theatre, suggested by the discovery of the inscription recording the presentation of a new stage (*RIB* 707) (Fig. 6).

Fig. 4 Excavation at Pot Hill, Throlam, May 1930. Bertie Gott cuts a trench through the buried dump of Romano-British pottery 'wasters'. (Corder 1930)

Fig. 5 The 'staff' at Brough, 22 August 1936. Standing, right to left: Philip Corder, Thomas Romans Jnr (son of co-director the Revd Thomas Romans who probably took the photograph), Bertie Gott, R. Gilyard-Beer. Seated, right to left: Mary Kitson-Clark, Joan Southan, Richard Harland (identified by Richard Harland). (Hull and East Riding Museum: Hull Museums)

As a spin-off from the above, Corder also published the discovery of a Roman cemetery next to the Roman road running towards South Cave, which was found in 1936. The most spectacular find here was a male skeleton accompanied by a wooden bucket, hooped in iron, and the remains of two iron sceptres, decorated with helmeted bronze heads which will be discussed in Chapter 10 (Corder and Richmond 1938).

Corder's work at Brough was not followed up until 1958–61, when John Wacher, under the auspices of the Ministry of Works (Wacher 1969) resumed excavation there as part of the growing 'professionalisation' of archaeology in the region. Wacher (1995) reassessed his excavations subsequently and the town has been subject to large-scale redevelopment, preceded by rescue excavation and evaluation. These interventions have been summarised by Wilson (2003). In 1977, at Cave Road, Brough, Peter Armstrong with the East Riding Archaeological Society (ERAS) excavated a stone enclosure and roadway overlying first century AD ditches, lying close to the Walling Fen inlet, though the site has not been published. In 1980, at Petuaria Close, to the north of Welton Road, ERAS undertook rescue excavations, which revealed occupation of the late first and early second centuriesAD, including a possible military oven and 'ill-defined' post structures (Armstrong 1981, 6). The footings of a very substantial later Roman limestone wall were also found which, according to Armstrong, may be part of the later town defences. Welton Road was also the focus for an evaluation in 1991 by the Humberside Archaeological Unit uncovering a road and associated features. This was followed up in 1994 by the York Archaeological Trust, who excavated further

Fig. 6 The Brough theatre inscription as found, just to the west of Building 1 in Bozzes Field during the 1937 excavation by Bertie Gott, Corder's foreman. (Hull and East Riding Museum: Hull Museums)

Roman buildings in plots positioned along the Roman road with associated fields, discovering a T-shaped malting oven or corn drier, cremation and inhumation burials and animal burials (Hunter-Mann *et al.* 2000).

Further along the Roman road at North Newbald, M.W. Barley and Corder also carried out an excavation of a Roman villa in 1939, which was furnished with mosaics and painted wall plaster (Corder 1941). Work here was continued by Mr D. Brooks of ERAS in the 1960s but remains unpublished. A further villa was found at Rudston in 1933, when a Mr Robson of Breeze Farm ploughed up tesserae in a field near the parish boundary with Kilham (Stead 1980) which turned out to be from mosaics including one portraying Venus, which remains iconic in the archaeology of Roman Britain and will be the subject of further discussion. Later excavations by Stead during the removal of the Venus mosaic from the sheds which had been erected to protect it from the elements to Hull Museums resulted in the discovery of the spectacular 'Charioteer' mosaic in 1971. Stead also carried out some excavation on the extensive Roman villa at Brantingham in 1961–62 (Stead *et al.* 1973). The site had been discovered in 1941 during quarrying and a mosaic pavement and other artefacts were recovered in 1948 and taken to Hull Museum. A fine geometric mosaic was stolen under mysterious circumstances, but had fortunately been carefully photographed in situ (Neal and Cosh 2002, 325). The location of the Brantingham complex and its relationship to nearby Brough will be discussed later.

By the 1930s, E.V. and C.W. Wright began to explore the Humber foreshore near their home at North Ferriby, under the guidance of Corder, an activity which was to have important implications for the study of Iron Age East Yorkshire as a whole. They recovered late Iron Age imported wheel-made pottery (Corder *et al.* 1939; Wright 1990). A trial excavation was also carried out there, in which more pottery and brooches were found, but little structural evidence. Corder (Corder and Davies Pryce 1938) suggested that the site was a native trading station doing business with the Roman world. As with Brough, there was to be a long gap before further fieldwork was undertaken on this most important site. This subsequent work was largely the result of the continued enthusiasm of Ted Wright and vigilance of Peter Didsbury (Crowther and Didsbury 1988), who continued to examine the eroding cliff. Excavations at Redcliff followed, taking place between 1986 and 1988 (Crowther *et al.* 1990).

Apart from the work at Redcliff and the activities of Greenwell and Mortimer, little attention had been paid to the Iron Age since the excavation of Stillingfleet and his colleagues (Stillingfleet 1846). In 1836 labourers cleaning out a ditch at Roos Carr, near Withernsea came across one of East Yorkshire's most celebrated finds, the Roos Carr figures, along with other wooden objects (Plate 2) (Poulson 1841, 100; Sheppard 1902; 1903). Five male figures survive although Poulson recorded eight. Some of the figures bore round shields and there may have been two boats, one animal head carved from yew, with various other wooden articles 'too much decayed to remove'. The eyes of some of the figures consisted of quartzite pebbles. The figures, which have been conserved and redisplayed, have been radiocarbon dated to Cal BC 770–409 (1 sigma) Cal BC 800–400 (2 sigma) (Dent 2010, 101) and are therefore of early Iron Age date. Much has been written about the Roos Carr figures which most perceive as objects of ritual deposition (Coles 1996; Aldhouse-Green 2004).

At Bugthorpe, a single sword in a sheath was discovered during land drainage (Wood 1860). Thurnham (1871) and Greenwell and Rolleston (1877) refer to a body being found with an iron sword in a bronze sheath and an enamelled bronze brooch here (Stead 1979) and there is some doubt as to whether the two swords from Bugthorpe are the same. Although Stead's main concern is the presence or absence of a barrow mound, he does mention the possibility that there were in fact two swords. It may be that the sword that Wood referred to was a votive offering in a 'watery place' (Bradley 1990) as the fact that it was found whilst draining implies that the ground was wet.

A further Iron Age 'warrior burial' and three burials without grave goods were found 6km away at Grimthorpe in a chalk-pit (Plate 3) (Mortimer 1905, 150–52, Stead 1979, 37) in the contrasting landscape of the Wolds. This discovery was partly the inspiration for Stead's excavation in 1962 of the nearby hill fort at Grimthorpe (Stead 1968), one of the few excavations of an Iron Age settlement on the western escarpment of the Yorkshire Wolds. The landscape context of Grimthorpe will be discussed below. Recent re-calibrated C14 dates (Dent 1995; 2010, 100), however, make it unlikely that the warrior burial was contemporary with the construction of the hill fort and may not have occurred even during its occupation. Stead's main interest at this stage was, however, in the burials of the Arras culture, and he returned to the type-site to carry out further excavation and a geophysical survey in 1959 (Stead 1979) with inconclusive results.

In 1950 the hilltop site of Staple Howe, Knapton, near Malton, was discovered by picnickers who took sherds of pottery that they had found to Tony Brewster, then a teacher at Heslerton School, for identification in a session organised by the Ordnance Survey Archaeology Division (Brewster 1963). This led to the excavation of what has become a type-site for the British early Iron Age. Its lavish publication was also ahead of its time and allowed for re-interpretation by future generations of archaeologists. At the time the site was thought to be the hilltop fortification of early Celtic continental invaders (Hawkes 1963) though most archaeologists today would no longer agree with this hypothesis. Brewster went into archaeology full time and began the fieldwork at Garton Slack, with the East Riding Archaeological Research Committee, prior to large-scale gravel quarrying by W. Clifford Watts. Extensive settlements remains were found there including Iron Age roundhouses and graves, the most important being the first 'chariot' burial to be excavated under modern conditions which will be discussed in greater detail in later chapters.

At Garton Slack, Brewster was following up rescue work by Cecil and Eric Grantham, butchers of Driffield, who had a private museum behind their shop with a collection of thousands of objects, which was the envy of the British Museum. According to Cecil, this activity was inspired by the discovery of stone axes and similar items in the walls of the trenches of the Somme in the First World War (Peter Hopkirk, Dispatch of *The Times*, London, *The Milwaukee Journal*, 1 April 1970, 1 and 3). From 1963 onwards they had been monitoring the gravel extraction clearing burials before their destruction (Brewster 1980, 1; Dent 1983(a)) and their Iron Age finds included chalk figurines and the iron currency bar from Gransmoor which will be considered below.

Meanwhile, Bill Varley, a lecturer from Hull College of Higher Education, carried out an excavation on a Deserted Medieval Village at Ousethorpe, not far from both the hill fort at Grimthorpe and the Roman remains referred to earlier. During this excavation, a pit containing Iron Age pottery was found, though its full implications were not explored (Loughlin and Miller 1979, 119). Work undertaken at Ousethorpe by the present writer will be discussed below.

The foundation of the East Riding Archaeological Society (ERAS) in the early 1960s, under the aegis of John Bartlett of Hull Museum, led to further investigation. The work of ERAS at Brough has been referred to above. On the Humber bank at Market Weighton Lock, Faxfleet a large amount of Roman pottery, building materials and an inscribed lead pig was reported during quarrying by contractors (Bartlett 1967; 1968). Much material was salvaged as a result of a watching brief by ERAS members, especially John Leonard of Lock Farm, though the post-excavation study and the full significance of the site as a possible transhipment point related to the Walling Fen tidal inlet was not carried out until 1987 by Bryan Sitch (Sitch 1987; 1990).

Further upstream at Bursea House, Holme-on-Spalding Moor, Bartlett had already been investigating finds made by Mr A.S. Johnson, including part of a human cranium and Roman pottery. On the next farm, Hasholme Hall, Mr W. Halkon, the present writer's father, had recorded many sherds of Roman pottery in 1957 and subsequently the field became known as 'Pot Field'. Mr J. Williamson of Hasholme Grange, which borders Pot Field, recounted a childhood activity of smashing up pots with a catapult at this location in the late 1940s, not realising that these vessels were Roman!

In 1963, Mr Skinner of Market Weighton School, with the aid of the writer's father and the Johnsons of Bursea House, and accompanied by the young author, excavated a small trench at Pot Field and this discovery was reported to Hull Museum. In 1970 and 1971 to 1972, the ERAS carried out an excavation in which the writer took part, which unearthed several Roman pottery kilns (Hicks and Wilson 1975), providing an impetus for future research with Martin Millett (Halkon 1987; Halkon and Millett 1999). A complex of earlier ditched enclosures was recorded, which contained quantities of hand-thrown pottery in the Iron Age tradition. Evidence for iron working was also found in the form of the base of a furnace and an iron anvil of Roman date (Manning 1975). Later work at Hasholme will be discussed below.

As the first phase of work at Hasholme was finishing, a major excavation sponsored by the Department of the Environment was undertaken at Welton Wold (Mackey 1998). This settlement evolved from a small sub-rectangular Iron Age enclosure into a villa, which, although it continued in occupation throughout the Roman period, never reached the sophistication of the Roman villas at Brantingham and Rudston (Stead 1980). The Welton team also carried out rescue work on an Iron Age and Romano-British settlement at North Cave 16km to the west, during the summers of 1974 and 1976 (R. Mackey pers. comm.).

An important impetus to further exploration occurred in 1974 at Hayton, where Professor J.K. St Joseph photographed the clear cropmark of a Roman fort. Excavation was carried out there in February and October-November 1975, directed by Dr Stephen Johnson under the auspices of the Department of the Environment (Johnson 1978). The fort, which overlay an Iron Age settlement, was interpreted by the excavator as having been founded during the Roman advance into Yorkshire in *c*. AD 71 and occupied for little over a decade. During this time, a watching brief was also kept on the dualling of the York-Hull A1079. A whole complex of cropmark sites was also plotted by the RCHM (E) (Johnson 1978, 59 fig. 2). The significance of this in the context of the work undertaken at Hayton (Halkon and Millett 2003) will be detailed below.

Although the antiquarian and archaeological exploration outlined above is very diverse in nature, certain trends and foci of interest can be determined. With the aid of classical texts, many sought to locate named places within Roman East Yorkshire. Each exceptional find of Roman structures or artefacts led its finder to claim that the site that they had located must be one of the 'lost' Roman settlements in East Yorkshire. In some respects the work of Corder at Brough fits into this category, a trend of investigation within the region which continues today (Creighton 1988; Lawton 1994; Hind 2007). The reliance of the antiquarians on classical texts, however, is hardly surprising given their background and occupation – the East Yorkshire clergy and gentry involved in these first attempts at chronicling the region through its material remains were following national fashions. This makes the career of John Robert Mortimer, a 'tradesman', looked down on by his great rival Greenwell, the more remarkable. The scientific approach of Lister with his fabric descriptions of both the Roman pottery and the physical surroundings of his discoveries proved to be something of a false dawn.

Most interest was concentrated on the Yorkshire Wolds and on the funerary monuments in particular rather than settlements, what Ted Wright called the 'Greenwell-Mortimer syndrome' (Wright 1990, 76), although the Granthams excavated and recorded both with equal enthusiasm. Despite the outstanding importance of Stead's work on the burials of the Arras culture, he was still following in some ways the foundations laid by Greenwell and Mortimer. Where antiquarians and archaeologists did stray on to the lowlands, it was mainly to follow the 'corridors' of Roman roads, but despite these shortcomings, their work also laid the basis for further study.

RESEARCH PROJECTS AND DEVELOPER-FUNDED ARCHAEOLOGY

With the local government reform of 1974 which led to the setting up of the Humberside County Council, there was for the first time a large regionally based archaeology unit, the Humberside Archaeology Unit (HAU). One of the most important actions of the Humberside County Council was to produce the *Survey of Archaeological Sites in Humberside* (Loughlin and Miller 1979), a catalogue of archaeological sites of all periods, combining information from such sources as the Ordnance Survey, Yorkshire Archaeological Society and Hull Museum records and works as well as the Kitson Clark (1935) gazetteer. This formed the basis of the Humberside Sites and Monuments Record. The *Survey of Archaeological Sites in Humberside* followed Herman Ramm's Parisi volume (1978) which was the first substantial work dealing solely with the Roman tribe and its origins, based on the author's encyclopaedic knowledge of the region, particularly its cropmarks, earthworks and excavations drawn from his many years working for the Royal Commission on Historical Monuments: England, based in York.

As far as the scope of the present book is concerned, perhaps the most significant contribution of the HAU was at Garton and Wetwang Slack where John Dent continued the work begun by the Granthams and Tony Brewster, when quarrying provided the opportunity for total excavation of an extensive prehistoric and Roman landscape, including the largest concentration of chariot burials in Britain (Dent 1983(a) (b); 1985; 1998; 2010). Dent (1988; 1989) also undertook excavations at Brantingham and North Cave on Iron Age and Roman settlements prior to mineral extraction.

Large-scale road building such as the construction of the Leven to Brandesburton by-pass (Evans and Steedman 1997, 125) and other developments revealed Roman sites in the Hull Valley and Holderness, especially around Hull itself on sites such as Malmo Road and Gibraltar Farm (Evans and Steedman 1997, 124). The latter followed on from ground-breaking research by Peter Didsbury, then working at Hull Museums, who despite protestations that Hull was under water in the Roman period and that Roman coins found in the city were souvenirs brought back by returning Second World War soldiers, showed without question that periods of sea level change had allowed Iron Age and Roman activity on the alluvium of the lower Hull Valley (Didsbury 1988; 1990).

As a result of further changes to local government in the 1990s, HAU became Humber Archaeology Partnership, with commercial contractors Humber Field Archaeology and the curatorial Humber Sites and Monuments Record. At the same time the county of Humberside was replaced by The East Riding of Yorkshire Council and Hull became a unitary authority. The North Yorkshire County Council and City of York Council also set up what are now known as Historic Environment Records.

Archaeological excavation prior to development carried out after the introduction of Planning and Policy Guidance (PPG16) stipulating that developers should pay for archaeological work to be done prior to construction, also confirmed that the major towns of the region Beverley, Bridington, Driffield, Market Weighton and Pocklington all had Roman activity in and around them. The results of these investigations will be incorporated into the appropriate sections of this book. Since further local government reform in the 1990s introduced competitive tendering and 'contract' archaeology, many organisations have undertaken fieldwork in the East Yorkshire region apart from Humber Field Archaeology, including Ed Dennison Archaeological Services, MAP Archaeological Consultancy of Malton, Northern Archaeological Associates, On-Site Archaeology, The Guildhouse Consultancy, West Yorkshire Archaeology Service and the York Archaeological Trust. Summaries of their work have been reported in the newsletters of the Prehistoric and Roman Antiquities Sections of the Yorkshire Archaeological Society, and the bulletin of the Yorkshire region of the Council for British Archaeology. The *East Riding Archaeologist* (Evans and Steedman 1997; 2001; Evans and Atkinson 2009) also contains regional round-ups of investigations. The Archaeological Investigations project undertaken by the Bournemouth University

Archaeology Department has also enabled better access to information on the results of archaeological interventions by archaeological contractors contained in the so-called 'grey literature' reports.

The construction of long-distance pipelines such as the Tees-side to Saltend Ethylene pipeline in the late 1990s and the Langeled gas pipeline from Norway to Easington in Holderness (Richardson 2011), Asselby to Ganstead (Daniel *et al.* forthcoming) and Ganstead to Easington pipelines all revealed hitherto unknown Iron Age and Roman sites, though the results of some of this fieldwork is yet to be published in full.

It took many years before the example of Philip Corder was followed and focussed research projects established. Some reference has already been made to the landscape survey begun by the author with ERAS in 1980, run jointly with Martin Millett since 1983. Initially an 8 x 8km area around Holme-on-Spalding Moor was examined by a range of techniques including aerial and geophysical survey, systematic field walking and a series of excavations (Halkon and Millett 1999); this was followed up by study of the Roman roadside settlement at Shiptonthorpe (Millett 2006) and a 3 x 3km area around Hayton (Halkon and Millett 2003). From the onset this was a community-based project with volunteers working side-by-side with school and university students. There have been several offshoots associated with these projects (Halkon 2008) including investigation of several Roman villas around Pocklington and the Roman temple site at Millington which has already been referred to above and the western Wolds escarpment around Market Weighton. The results of this work will be referred to when appropriate. Since 2005, fieldwork has also been undertaken by Cambridge University at Thwing under the direction of Martin Millett which has revealed a Roman building and shed more light on the extensive ladder settlement which preceded it (Ferraby *et al.* 2008 and 2009).

In the north of the region at about the same time as the Foulness Valley project began, a remarkable long-term landscape research project commenced at West Heslerton in 1979 (Powlesland 2003 (a) and (b)). Initially aimed at rescuing an extensive Anglo-Saxon cemetery and settlement, it soon became apparent that this could only be understood in the context of the development of the landscape. Most relevant here was the discovery a late Roman temple or shrine complex which may have been the primary focus for the Anglo-Saxon settlement and cemetery and one of the largest geophysical surveys undertaken anywhere in Britain in which an extensive linear enclosure complex was revealed. More details concerning these discoveries will be discussed below.

Perhaps the most significant contribution to the extension of our knowledge of this period, especially in terms of the wider landscape, has been the National Mapping Programme undertaken by English Heritage and the RCHM (E) before them, collating and plotting thousands of archaeological sites revealed in growing crops and captured in vertical and oblique aerial photographs. The most impressive of these surveys covered the Yorkshire Wolds (Stoertz 1997) referred to in the introduction, the well-drained soils of which are particularly sensitive to showing up archaeological features, Neolithic onwards, stretching from the River Humber to Flamborough Head. Stoertz's categorisation and typological analysis of the features revealed also provided essential impetus for a whole range of field-based projects referred to above and also the British Museum East Yorkshire Settlements Project (Rigby 2004) designed to complement the excavation of square barrow cemeteries (Stead 1991) by sampling pits in settlements revealed through aerial photography and provide a better dating sequence for the Iron Age pottery of the region.

A similar scheme was undertaken by English Heritage in the Vale of York (Horne and Kershaw 2002; Kershaw and Horne forthcoming), and at the time of writing in the Hull Valley, though detailed mapping of this has not been published. The plots have, however, already been used in a number of projects including the writer's. In 1994, the English Heritage-sponsored Humber Wetlands project, based at the University of Hull, was set up to carry out field surveys in Holderness, the Hull Valley, the Vale of York, the Humberhead Levels, the lower Trent and Ancholme valleys. Multi-period in scope, some new Iron Age and Roman sites and artefacts were recorded in each of these areas (Van de Noort and Ellis 1995; 1999).

Although primarily aimed at understanding the deserted medieval village, one of the most important and long-lasting research projects in the history of British archaeology was initiated by Maurice Beresford and John Hurst at Wharram Percy (Beresford and Hurst 1990), which soon revealed the presence of earlier activity extending backwards into prehistory. Most pertinent here are the extensive linear enclosure complexes of ladder settlements revealed through aerial photography and investigated by programmes of geophysics, field walking and excavation (Hayfield 1988). A number of Roman villas were also discovered (Rahtz *et al.* 1986; Rahtz 1988) and collaborative research there is still continuing under the auspices of various university departments including those at York, Sheffield and Manchester in the Yorkshire Wolds project.

The setting up of part-time archaeology courses at the University of Hull has also resulted in some important new research by students. Of particular note in terms of fieldwork are excavations carried out on previously unknown Iron Age and Roman settlements at Arram and Burshill in the Hull Valley (Wilson *et al.* 2006; Coates 2007). Mick Carr, who initiated research at Burshill, developed an interest in archaeology as a metal detector and provides an example of how it is still possible for individuals to make an important contribution by the proper reporting of finds made through metal detecting or purely by chance through the Portable Antiquities Scheme, which was established in 1997. Although there is still sometimes acrimonious debate about the pros and cons of metal detecting, it cannot be denied that our knowledge of both the Iron Age and

Roman periods has been greatly enhanced by this scheme. This is certainly the case in the territory of the Parisi, the discovery of hoards of Coriletauvian coins near Beverley and Driffield and the South Cave weapons cache being the most spectacular examples for the Iron Age period, however the various MAs and PhDs being done on the PAS material that represent the collation of less spectacular individual finds is proving to be most illuminating. Collaboration between metal-detectorists and archaeologists has also proved beneficial in enhancing our knowledge of the Roman roadside settlements of Shiptonthorpe (Halkon *et al*. 2006) and Hayton (Millett and Halkon 2003) as many objects (Stratton 2005) and coins have been accurately located using hand-held global positioning equipment, enabling the mapping of artefacts and manipulation through Geographical Information Systems. Sadly, however, there are still those who visit sites illicitly and 'night-hawk' which remains a particular problem along the Roman roads.

A number of university archaeology departments continue to have an active interest in the territory of the Parisi apart from those projects mentioned above. Of particular significance is the research undertaken by Melanie Giles on the Iron Age landscape of the Yorkshire Wolds as a post-graduate student at Sheffield University and lecturer at various institutions (Giles 2000; 2007a and b). Chris Fenton-Thomas (2003) has also provided an interesting overview of the archaeology of the Wolds and Mick Atha (2007) of the University of York undertook a detailed study of the so-called 'ladder settlements' of the Yorkshire Wolds. A new approach to the study of the people of the region in the Iron Age and Roman period has been the scientific examination of human and animal remains, particularly on isotopes, DNA and new approaches to palaeopathology undertaken at Bradford and Durham Universities by Mandy Jay and Janet Montgomery. Their work will be referred to in the rest of this book.

SUMMARY

Throughout the study of Iron Age and Roman East Yorkshire, there has been particular interest in burials, primarily in the grave goods. Since the 1990s, however, scientific advances have enabled the extraction of detailed information about the people themselves from skeletal remains. By comparison, detailed study of settlements is relatively new and the development of aerial photography and other remote sensing techniques, combined with environmental archaeology, is allowing the study of whole landscapes through time, which will be the subject of the next chapter.

CHAPTER 2

THE LANDSCAPE OF EASTERN YORKSHIRE

SETTING THE SCENE

In the days before the mechanisation of agriculture, the geology (Fig. 7), topography of the landscape (Fig. 8), the properties of its soils (Plate 6) and presence of water were fundamental to the livelihood of the people within it. Although there are many differences between the landscape of East Yorkshire today and that of the Iron Age and Roman period, there are basic similarities which helped to shape the relationship between humans and their environment.

The landscape of eastern Yorkshire is made up of contrasting zones. Its most distinctive feature, the rolling Cretaceous chalk hills of the Yorkshire Wolds, run north-east in a crescent from the River Humber in the south to the promontory of Flamborough Head, rising to around 240m in the north, 160m above sea level in the south, and 140m in the east. The open chalk plateau of the Wolds is intersected by sinuous valleys, formed during various phases of glacial activity (Gaunt and Buckland 2003). The soils of the Wolds are generally fertile and freely draining and of varying thickness, created from a combination of loess blown from the lowlands and soils derived from the chalk bedrock (King and Bradley 1987; Ellis 1996). There has been considerable soil erosion caused by modern agricultural activity and natural processes, particularly on the thinner soils of the northern Wolds (Ellis and Newsome 1991).

The western edge of the Wolds forms an escarpment, and here, below the chalk, is a succession of Jurassic and Lower Cretaceous mudstones, oolitic limestones and clays, which form a 'bench' of higher land running parallel to the Wolds escarpment (Kent 1980), forming a 'bench' of higher land at about 40m OD, before dropping away to glacio-fluvial sand and gravel foothills. To the east, the Wolds slope gently down into the plain of Holderness.

On the western escarpment, at the intersection of the chalk and Lias bench, is a spring line, the springs being densest to the north of the village of Millington. In the north-east the Wolds are cut by the Great Wold Valley, formed by the Gypsey Race. The modern source of this stream reflects hydrological change and it seems fairly certain that the source in the Iron Age and Roman periods was at Wharram Le Street (Rahtz *et al*. 1986, 2). In the Neolithic the western end of the Gypsey Race became a

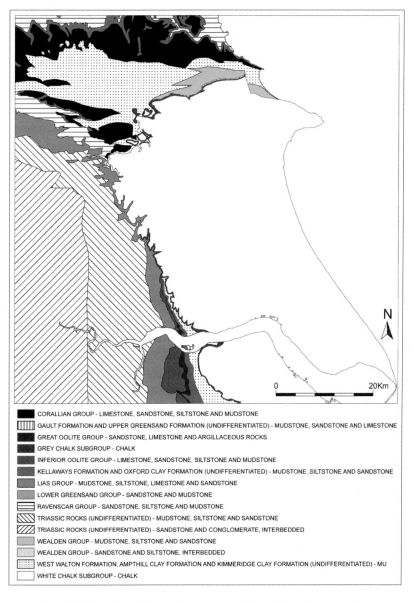

CORALLIAN GROUP - LIMESTONE, SANDSTONE, SILTSTONE AND MUDSTONE
GAULT FORMATION AND UPPER GREENSAND FORMATION (UNDIFFERENTIATED) - MUDSTONE, SANDSTONE AND LIMESTONE
GREAT OOLITE GROUP - SANDSTONE, LIMESTONE AND ARGILLACEOUS ROCKS
GREY CHALK SUBGROUP - CHALK
INFERIOR OOLITE GROUP - LIMESTONE, SANDSTONE, SILTSTONE AND MUDSTONE
KELLAWAYS FORMATION AND OXFORD CLAY FORMATION (UNDIFFERENTIATED) - MUDSTONE, SILTSTONE AND SANDSTONE
LIAS GROUP - MUDSTONE, SILTSTONE, LIMESTONE AND SANDSTONE
LOWER GREENSAND GROUP - SANDSTONE AND MUDSTONE
RAVENSCAR GROUP - SANDSTONE, SILTSTONE AND MUDSTONE
TRIASSIC ROCKS (UNDIFFERENTIATED) - MUDSTONE, SILTSTONE AND SANDSTONE
TRIASSIC ROCKS (UNDIFFERENTIATED) - SANDSTONE AND CONGLOMERATE, INTERBEDDED
WEALDEN GROUP - MUDSTONE, SILTSTONE AND SANDSTONE
WEALDEN GROUP - SANDSTONE AND SILTSTONE, INTERBEDDED
WEST WALTON FORMATION, AMPTHILL CLAY FORMATION AND KIMMERIDGE CLAY FORMATION (UNDIFFERENTIATED) - MU
WHITE CHALK SUBGROUP - CHALK

Fig. 7 Simplified geological map of eastern Yorkshire. (Based on British Geological Survey data © BGS)

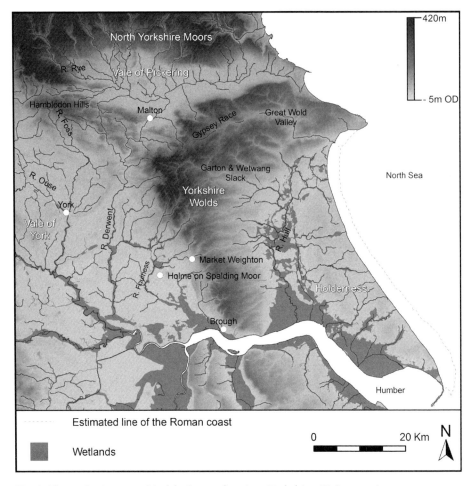

Fig. 8 The major topographical features of eastern Yorkshire. (T. Sparrow)

focus for ritual activity including the great burial mound of Duggleby Howe (Manby *et al.* 2003(b), 73). At Rudston, due to a geological fault, the valley turns sharply to the south before resuming its course, reaching the North Sea in what is now Bridlington Harbour. The point where the Great Wold Valley changed direction became the focus for a concentration of Neolithic and Bronze Age ceremonial and funerary monuments, including the Rudston Monolith and Cursuses (Manby *et al.* 2003(b), 78).

Further to the south the Wolds are cut by what Dent (1995; 2010) calls the Great Slack, slack being derived from *slakki*, the Old Norse for a hollow or valley (Cameron 1961, 225). This feature which runs roughly east-west through the Wolds opens at the head of the Hull Valley. Further south, dry valleys created by glacial melt water and relict watercourses, formed routes running generally east-west through the Wolds, with the most prominent of these being the Goodmanham spillway, which divides the Wolds in two.

The Wolds are surrounded on three sides by lowlands. Above the northern escarpment is the Vale of Pickering, at its centre peaty wetlands derived from the former Lake Flixton, the margins of which were exploited by Mesolithic hunter-gatherers. Evidence for their activities is best known through discoveries made during the famous excavations at Star Carr and more recently Seamer Carr (Clark 1954; Conneller and Schadla-Hall 2003). The main watercourse here is the River Derwent, which unusually flows westwards inland rather than seawards before it turns to flow south, forming the old boundary of the East Riding of Yorkshire and emptying near the confluence of the rivers Humber and Ouse.

To the west of the Wolds is the Vale of York, its flat expanse being largely derived from the former glacial Lake Humber, with soils comprising clay plains and ridges of windblown sand, especially in the area between the River Foulness and the Yorkshire Wolds, which rarely rise to 10m above sea level. The most prominent topographical feature at 46m OD is Church Hill, Holme-on-Spalding Moor, made up of Triassic Mercia Mudstones, topped with gravels and a sand deposit which may date from the Anglian period of the Ice Age (Fairburn 2009).

Apart from the River Derwent and its tributary streams, the main river system in the southern Vale of York is the River Foulness which rises from springs on the Yorkshire Wolds near Goodmanham and flows south-westwards before turning east, forming the boundary of Holme-on-Spalding Moor. At present the River Foulness empties into the Market Weighton Canal, constructed in 1772, but before that it had its outflow into the Walling Fen. Drained and farmed today, palaeo-environmental research has shown that this feature was a tidal estuarine inlet of the River Humber in the Mesolithic/Neolithic period and again in the late Bronze Age to Roman period (Halkon and Innes 2005; Halkon et al. 2009). The significance of this coastal change will be discussed in the sections below.

To the east of the Wolds is the plain of Holderness. Its soils are generally poorly drained and overlie layers of glacial till. In places the landscape undulates, rising to around 30m above sea level. These slight elevations, mainly consisting of glacially derived sands and gravels, are important in providing better drained locations for settlement and agriculture. Topographic and place name evidence betrays the presence of seventy former glacial lakes, the only survivor being Hornsea Mere. Although it is now largely drained and reclaimed, the Humber coast of Holderness was once marshy (Sheppard 1966; Ellis 1996).

The main drainage of Holderness is provided by the River Hull, the valley of which forms a sub-region in its own right (Van de Noort and Ellis 2000). Rising at springs at Elmswell on the eastern edge of the Yorkshire Wolds, and various other locations, the

River Hull flows south, now joining the Humber at the city of Kingston upon Hull. On each side of the river were extensive areas of wetland, now largely drained. As in the Foulness Valley to the west of the Wolds, fluctuations in sea level made these wetlands accessible for activity at some times and flooded at others. This is fundamental to our understanding of Iron Age and Roman activity here (Catt 1990; Valentin 1971).

A major difference between the Iron Age and Roman landscape and that of today is the shape of the coastline, due to the rapid erosion of the Holderness coast. To the south of the high cliffs of Filey Brigg, Bempton and Flamborough Head, the softer clay is particularly vulnerable to the impact of the North Sea. Much has been written about this topic (De Boer 1996(a) and (b)) and English Heritage has completed a Yorkshire Coast and Humber Estuary Rapid Coastal Zone Assessment Survey (RCZAS) (Brigham *et al*. 2011) in order to monitor the extent of erosion and its effect on the archaeology. Estimates as to the loss of land since the Roman period vary between 2.4 and 4km. This factor has an important bearing on our understanding of the region as many sites are likely to have been lost to the sea. Related to this is the changing configuration of Spurn Point (De Boer 1964; 1996(b)). Having provided a general introduction to the East Yorkshire landscape today, the next section will attempt to provide a more detailed insight into the landscape of the Iron Age and Roman period.

CLIMATE AND SEA LEVEL CHANGE

Some reference has already been made to the effect of changing sea level on this region. The Iron Age and Roman periods were probably eras of climatic instability (Lamb 1988), which would have had an impact on the landscape and the people who lived within it. Factors such as temperature and rainfall affect natural vegetation and crop growth. Without adequate methods of food storage and suitable weather for planting, growing and harvesting, past societies which were primarily agrarian would have been vulnerable, as they are today in many parts of the developing world. Exact determination of present climatic variation and the reasons behind it, is very complex (Houghton *et al*. 1990) and it is even more difficult to reconstruct the climate of the past. Various types of evidence such as historical records and so-called 'proxy data', such as plant and animal remains and various types of sediment, can be investigated.

Dendrochronology or tree-ring dating has been used to propose complex sequences of environmental and climatic change (Baillie 1995) which have in turn been used to explain societal change. In Iron Age Ireland for example (Turney *et al*. 2005) there may be parallels with eastern Yorkshire, as in both areas periods of rapid climatic deterioration would have resulted in greater competition for resources, exemplified by the construction of fortifications and division of landscapes. Various scientists (van Geel *et al*. 1996, 454) have linked this climate change with a rapid rise in ground water tables in the Netherlands, and the extension of fens and bogs, which they claimed caused a major impact on human populations. A move to wetter conditions has also been identified in North Yorkshire around 800 BC (Blackford and Chambers 1999).

Research on peat bogs in various parts of Britain seems to confirm the lower relative temperatures of the later Bronze Age, an increase of temperature, with a maximum in the early part of the Roman period with a dip in temperatures at the end of the fourth century AD. Moves to wetter conditions were dated to 560 BC and 60 BC, with drier conditions ensuing in AD 220–360, the so-called Romano-British warm period, which was followed by further climatic deterioration in the fifth century AD (Blundell and Barber 2005, 1273).

Although climate can be a factor in influencing vegetation types or rises in water tables, humans themselves can have an impact through drainage, clearance of trees and grazing of animals. At Thorne and Hatfield Moors in the Humberhead Levels, for example, human influence in peat formation was detected with even a small-scale woodland clearance resulting in a raised water table (Buckland 1979). Pollen data from Thorne Moor also demonstrates clearance of woodland with an increase in herbs and grasses indicating the likelihood of pastoral farming from the middle/late Bronze Age to the early to middle Iron Age (Smith 2002, 51).

A recent study (Macklin *et al*. 2005, 937) concerning the link between climate and flooding in the British Isles during the prehistory, identified sixteen episodes of increased flood occurrence, twelve of which are recorded in most regions. Of these twelve flooding episodes, four at *c*. 2730 BP, (*c*. 780 BC) 2550 BP (*c*. 600 BC), 2280 BP (*c*. 330 BC), 1650 BP (*c*. 300 AD) are within the time period considered in this book.

The European bog-oak record, especially that of Ireland (Macklin *et al*. 2005) also suggests that the onset of more frequent and larger floods coincides with rising ground water levels and wetter climatic conditions, especially those of 2730 and 1950 Cal BC. Paradoxically, Macklin *et al*. argue that the 2550 BP and 1650 BP floods seem to have occurred in warmer climatic periods, and may relate to a greater impact in human activity and land-use changes, and perhaps the adoption of iron technology, which could have increased run-off and erosion, resulting in greater flood-related sedimentation.

In low-lying regions such as Hull and the lower Foulness Valley any change towards a wetter climate would result in an increased risk of flooding. This was also a time of sea level change and the relief of the southern sectors of the Foulness and Hull valleys made them vulnerable to its effects. Coring of underlying deposits along the Foulness Valley (Long *et al*. 1998; Halkon and Innes 2005) indicated high sea levels with marine flooding or transgression in the Mesolithic/Neolithic transition and again between the Bronze Age and Iron Age *c*. 800–300 BC (Plates 6 and 7). Recent coring across the Walling Fen at Hotham Carrs demonstrated the presence of upper marine clays resembling those identified at Hasholme at 0.5 to 0.7m OD (Coles 2010) with marine deposits extended up to 12km northwards from the present Humber coastline towards Market Weighton.

Similar deposits have been identified in the Hull Valley in its upper middle reaches around 12km north of the present Humber shore (Coates 2010). Further down the Humber estuary at Winestead Carrs, marine flood deposits were also identified overlying Iron Age activity, and at various low areas along the Easington to Paull pipeline (Rowland 2012). The effects of such changes on settlement will be discussed below.

In the earlier Roman period in Britain, climate amelioration coupled with phases of marine regression allowed activity on the alluvium of the Hull Valley, especially on the underlying glacial till above -3.8 OD (Didsbury 1990; Valentin 1957), which will be considered in greater detail in subsequent chapters.

THE CHANGING COASTLINE

The rivers Humber and Ouse form the southern boundary of the area of study and probably the frontier between the tribal areas of the Corieltauvi to the south and Parisi. It is clear that without modern flood defences and drainage, the northern shore of this large tidal river would have had a different configuration in the past. The reconstruction of coastlines in the Roman period, and by inference the Iron Age, is, however, difficult, due to various factors (Dark and Dark 1997; Gaunt and Tooley 1974; Tooley 1974).

A major problem is coastal erosion, which particularly affects the North Sea coast in Holderness and relates to the cyclical movement of Spurn Point (De Boer 1964; 1996(b)) referred to above with consequential effects on the Humber estuary and lower reaches of the valleys of the rivers Hull and Foulness. Research by LOIS (Land-Ocean Interaction Study) (Long et al. 1998) estimates the loss of between 1 and 3m per year, with the Roman coastline being some 4km further east than at present, with variations along the coast. This contrasts with Sheppard (1912(a)), who according to De Boer (1996(a), 6), suggests a rate of land loss of 2.16m per annum along the whole coastline, with 4km eroding since the Roman period. This contradicts Sheppard's map from which De Boer extrapolated 2.4km of coastal erosion. De Boer, using estimates of Roman coastal erosion extrapolated from Valentin (1971), projects a Roman coastline largely following the outline proposed by Sheppard's map, with some variation in the north, where De Boer suggests that Bridlington Bay was more deeply recessed. The historical implications of this last reconstruction are worth considering further.

It has been argued that the embayment at Bridlington equates with Ptolemy's Εὐλίμενον κόλπον, 'opportunus sinus' or 'a bay suitable for a harbour' (Geographia II, 3, 10; Stückelberger and Graßhoff 2006, 154; Rivet and Smith 1979, 139 and 433) mentioned in the introduction (Camden 1701, 242). This is thought to match with an earlier entry describing the coastline, which refers to the 'Gulf of the Gabrantovices suitable for a harbour' (Ptolemy *Geographia* II, 3, 4; Rivet and Smith 1979, 137 and 364). The bay at Filey (Cortis 1857) has also been identified as possible locations.

An alternative reading of this section of Ptolemy translated as 'Next to whom, beside the gulf suitable for a harbour, are the Parisi and the city Petuaria' (Ptolemy *Geographia* II, 3, 10; Rivet and Smith 1979, 142; Ramm 1978, 22) may provide another candidate for '*opportunus sinus*'.

If Petuaria is indeed Brough-on-Humber, on which most authorities agree (Rivet and Smith 1979; Wilson 2003; Wacher 1995; Creighton 1988), there appears to be a conflict between the two entries, given the considerable distance between Brough and Bridlington. In what claims to be the most up-to-date translation and interpretation, compiled from all available versions, a slightly different translation is offered: 'Near which on the Opportunum bay are the Parisi and the town Petuaria' (Thayer 2005).

Thayer also states that 'no reasonable emendation will put Petuaria on a bay; and I can't tell whose error this is, either'.

It is possible that there is no error at all here, and the 'Opportunum bay', or Safe-haven Bay as it is translated (Rivet and Smith 1979; Ramm 1978, 23), is the Walling Fen tidal inlet. This would be an apt name for such a 'bay' or inlet, as Brough (Petuaria) is conveniently positioned on the confluence of the River Humber and the inlet, providing access down the rivers Trent and Ancholme to the south and westwards down the River Ouse to York, also referred to by Ptolemy, although a location on the North Sea coast is perhaps more likely.

The geological and soil mapping and other palaeo-environmental evidence mentioned above shows that the Walling Fen tidal inlet extended 12km north of the present Humber coastline, with compelling evidence for its use in the Iron Age. Although periods of marine regression have been recognised (Metcalfe *et al.* 2000), it is likely that the inlet remained in the Roman period (Halkon and Millett 1999).

As we have seen in Chapter 1, the Walling Fen was a 6km-wide salt marsh (Sheppard 1966), which Leland, in his itinerary of Yorkshire in 1539 (Chandler 1993, 537) describes as follows: 'This area of marshland has many Carrs of water, and is known as Walling Fen. It is so large that fifty-eight villages stand in or abutting ... The fen itself ... is sixteen miles around its perimeter'.

In the mid-eighteenth century AD, Gough (1789, 98) describes it as being: 'A lake of about 1 or 200 acres on a large common subject to be over flowed by salt water from the Humber.'

The coring and soil survey referred to above show an extensive area of marine alluvium in the Walling Fen area, which both the archaeological and palaeo-environmental evidence suggests was deposited around 800–500 BC by the marine incursion, creating a tidal inlet of the lower Foulness Valley (Jordan 1987). It has been shown that at this time marine conditions reached their maximum Holocene extent in the Humber estuary (Long *et al*. 1998; Metcalfe *et al*. 2000; Kirby 2001). According to Innes and Blackford (2003, 28), 'Peat beds exposed in the present intertidal zones are the most visible signs of sea level change ... Neolithic and Bronze Age terrestrial and then salt marsh peats are overlain conformably by estuarine clays at Kilnsea and Melton on the Humber.'

Certainly at Hasholme, the transition phases between a Bronze Age woodland environment and marine transgression clays are very marked (Plate 6). From the air, the former coastline can also be seen here as a soil mark and in growing crops. Coring undertaken along the Foulness Valley demonstrated that the marine silts and clays deposited by the Iron Age marine transgression extended westwards to Welham Bridge, covering Bronze Age peat layers, which themselves overlay the clays of a later Mesolithic/Neolithic transgression. This confirmed Jordan (1987) analysis of the marine clays with which the Hasholme logboat, with a dendrochronological date of 321 and 277 BC (Millett and McGrail 1987), was associated.

The coring across the lower end of the Walling Fen (Lillie and Gearey 1999) identified a deposit similar to the upper trangressive unit at Hasholme. The alluvium masked a complex sequence of changing environments and features, including earlier channels. On the southern bank of the River Humber, estuarine sediments were accumulating in the Ancholme Valley 22km inland and in the Aire Valley, 15km upstream from the confluence with the River Ouse (Kirby 2001, 28), which are thought to be contemporary with those at Hasholme. Major floods have been identified in the whole of the Ouse catchment between *c*. 900 and 430 Cal BC (Macklin *et al*. 2000) and in the Trent Valley at Bole Ings, evidence for an abrupt late Bronze Age/Iron Age sediment transition around 25km south of the Humber (Brayshay and Dinnin 1999, 126). Here woody, silty peat is overlain by organic silty clay, though it is not stated whether this is estuarine or not. The entomological evidence does, however, indicate increased wetness rather than an expansion of grassland or cultivation.

SUMMARY

Through a combination of documentary, archaeological and palaeo-environmental research it has been possible to provide a setting for human activity in the Iron Age and early Roman periods. In the later Bronze Age to early Iron Age period there was a major marine transgression which was to have a significant effect on human landscape interaction in the region. As well as those recorded at Hasholme, transgression clays were reported further to the east at Winestead Carrs, Holderness, in an unpublished excavation by the late Angus Smith (Smith 1990, 7) in the 1980s and 1990s. A similar trangressive phase, characterised by grey marine clay dated to 2865 +-75 BP (*c.* 915 BC) has been identified at various other places on the North Sea coast including Hartlepool Bay (Horton et al 1999, 76), which compares well with the date from Sandholme Lodge in the Foulness Valley (Long *et al.* 1998, 231).

Research has shown that sea level rise also affected the Lincolnshire coast (Long *et al* 1998; Simmons 1977), demonstrating that it also had a radically different shape to the present, with an embayment in the area which is now the Wash, making the Roman centres of Lincoln and Horncastle much nearer the coast than at present (Leahy 1993) confirmed by the LOIS project (Brew *et al* 2000, 269). The archaeological implications of the former Humber coastline during the Iron Age and Roman periods will be discussed below.

CHAPTER 3

THE EMERGENCE OF A TRIBAL SOCIETY

THE DIVISION OF THE LANDSCAPE

At what stage in the past is it possible to see eastern Yorkshire as developing a distinctive regional identity? Although certain regional traits can be seen as far back as the Neolithic, it is perhaps in the later Bronze Age that characteristic features emerge. Although present elsewhere in Britain, one of the most recognisable monument types in the landscape of eastern Yorkshire is the network of linear earthworks, 'dykes', or 'entrenchments' which are at their densest on the Yorkshire Wolds. Observed by earlier antiquarians, these systems of banks and ditches were wrongly attributed to the Romans as in the case of the earthworks around Millington (Burton and Drake 1747) or to the Vikings, as is Dane's Dyke, which cuts off the promontory of Flamborough Head from its hinterland. The linear earthworks were first mapped in detail by Mortimer (1905), particularly around the village of Fimber (Plate 4) and regarded by him as of 'Ancient British' origin. Relatively few sections of linear earthworks now survive above ground and their true extent can only be fully appreciated from the various National Mapping Programmes undertaken by RCHM(E) and English Heritage, particularly the aerial surveys of the Yorkshire Wolds (Stoertz 1997) and the Howardian Hills (Carter 1995). The linear earthwork systems of the North Yorkshire Moors and Tabular Hills have also been examined (Spratt 1989).

It is generally agreed that the linear earthwork systems began in the later Bronze Age, succeeding rows of pits (pit alignments) (Stoertz 1997, 18) and continued to be constructed well into the Iron Age and possibly the Roman period (Fenton-Thomas 2003; Manby *et al.* 2003(b)) though direct dating evidence is hard to come by and often difficult to interpret. At Lady's Grave, Fimber, Mortimer (1905, 188) excavated a pit in a linear earthwork and found casting debris from the manufacture of weapons later identified as belonging to the so-called Wilburton metalworking stage (1150–950 BC) (Manby *et al.* 2003(b), 77). At Huggate, W.J. Varley (Challis and Harding 1975, Fig. 65) excavated a section across a single bank and ditch of the dyke system, discovering a sherd of later Bronze Age pottery, associated with earthworks. At Green Lane, between Sledmere and Wetwang, the Granthams found later Bronze Age sherds in the make-up of the chalk bank (Grantham and Grantham 1965).

Much-needed information from modern controlled excavation was provided at Melton during the A63 road improvements between 2004 and 2005. Here a round barrow was used to align three parallel ditches running north-south across the site. There was a slightly meandering pit alignment between the centre and easternmost ditches, which probably held a line of posts (Fenton-Thomas 2011, 360). Both the ditches and the pit alignment were recut at various times. The precise date of the initial creation of the boundary feature is not known, however a date in the earlier part of the first millennium BC is likely. This linear system was in turn used to reference a small inhumation cemetery dating from the eighth to sixth century BC, with nine or so burials extending around 150m along the feature. One of the graves contained hand-thrown pottery probably dating to around 500 BC (Didsbury and Vince 2011, 196). It is interesting to note that the majority of the occupants of this cemetery were children and young adults and palaeo-pathological examination showed they were generally ill-nourished and suffered from the fractures and injuries associated with a hard agricultural life and had surprisingly poor teeth (Caffell and Holst 2011). Their burial positions, laid out north-south in a generally crouched position, are of great interest as they predate the Arras culture tradition of square barrows, of which there are two on the site. The burials were covered with small round barrows, which unusually were marked with a central post (Fenton-Thomas 2011).

Many of the linear earthworks are thought to represent large-scale territorial division which takes place simultaneously in many parts of Britain (Bradley 1994). Although this division of the landscape marks a break with the past, the position of linear earthworks and their relationship with earlier monuments as in the case of Melton, seems to represent a deliberate attempt to link with existing features, especially the round barrows, as in some cases the linear earthworks have been carefully diverted around them (Mortimer 1905; Fenton-Thomas 2003). Once constructed, the linear boundary features eventually became a focus for burial themselves, for example at South Moor, Pocklington, where square barrows and ring ditches seem to have been deliberately aligned on a series of linear ditches observed as cropmarks running parallel to Whiterail and Cocoa Becks. Burial along boundaries may well have been a way of reinforcing territorial rights and again this is endorsed at Melton (Fenton-Thomas 2011).

In eastern Yorkshire there are single, double and multiple linear earthworks. The apparent multiplication of some features may simply be due to realignment of single ditches over a long period of time, producing a multiple effect. This is particularly the case where multiple linear earthworks are associated with droveway banks and ditches (Stoertz 1997). In other places, however, the multiplication of banks and ditches may be intended to emphasise a place within the landscape. The most frequent type of multiple earthworks are those with three banks and ditches. The significance of the number three or 'triplism' in Celtic religion and ritual has been much discussed (Green 1993) and it could be that the tripling of features may also be symbolic in some way. In the Foulness Valley, tripling of ditches in the linear earthwork systems is sometimes associated with what appear to be deliberate gaps or entrances at certain points, as in Sancton parish, where part of a system runs across the head of three dry valleys, appearing to control access. At Tibthorpe and North Dalton a section of multiple earthworks with up to six ditches runs south to the head of the dry valley.

The close relationship between linear earthworks and terrain was identified by Maule Cole (1899), Mortimer (1905) and Dent (1995; 2010) and is evident in many parts of the Yorkshire Wolds, Howardian Hills and North Yorkshire Moors. It is particularly noticeable that many of the longer double and multiple linear features are situated on the southern side of valleys, close to the edge or at the top of dales, which generally run from north-east to south-west. One such example is the linear earthwork which runs for over 26km from Wetwang and Fimber to Millington, and between Millington and Huggate, forming the boundary between these townships. Varying in size and complexity in accordance with topography, it provides 'the only route across the Wolds that avoids the steep sides of the dry valleys' (Fenton-Thomas 2003, 39).

At the end of a valley known as Horse Dale, the linear earthwork reaches a narrow neck of land at the head of a prominent valley and elaborates into a spectacular system of six banks and ditches known as Huggate Dykes (Mortimer 1905; Halkon 1990; 2008). This is the one of most impressive monuments of this type in the East Yorkshire region consisting of six ditches, now partially filled. There are five intermediate banks, some still standing around 2m above ground level, though these too have been eroded. The multiple earthworks remain complete for *c.* 200m and a further 400m remains as a single bank and ditch and 'probably began as a simple earthwork across the watershed, but it was incorporated into a much larger system which crossed the Wolds from below the western escarpment to within 8km of the North Sea' (Dent 1995, 26).

In many ways, the Huggate Dykes system resembles a landscape in miniature, the multiple banks and ditches appearing to replicate the steep valleys and ridges around it (Plate 5). The view looking south from the top of the ridge is striking and from here it is possible to see right down into the Vale of York and a traveller could not fail to be impressed by the elaborate dyke system as they climbed northwards from the lowlands onto the Wolds.

A further reason for the spectacular nature of Huggate Dykes may be their relationship with water (Fig. 9).

According to recent research, non-milking cattle drink around 20 litres per day and lactating cows up to 100 litres of water per animal per day. Calves need less at 5–9 litres (King *et al.* 2006, 25). Although later prehistoric varieties of cattle were considerably smaller than modern livestock and therefore drank less, ensuring regular access to water must have been a major preoccupation. With the exception of a narrow offset in the line at Sylvan Dale, the linear system running south from Huggate Dykes was probably designed to control access to the dense cluster of springs which feed Millington Beck (Fig. 9). Sheep need considerably less water, in the range of 3 to 7 litres depending on lactation and lambs 1.7 litres (King *et al.* 2006, 25).

A Y-shaped system of double linear features and associated droveways in Warter Parish leads down to the springs, which supply the Nunburnholme Beck system.

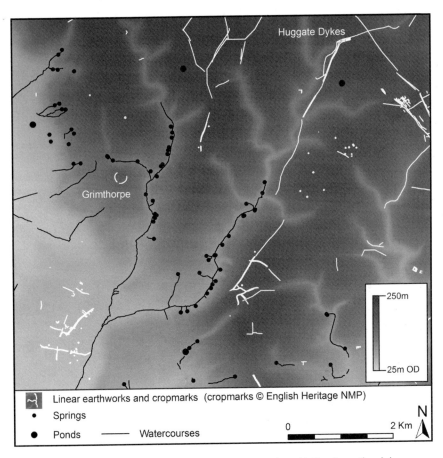

Fig. 9 The area around Grimthorpe and Huggate Dykes. Notice how the dykes appear to control access to the springs and streams to the west. (Halkon 2008, fig. 7.13) (Crop marks after Stoertz (1997))

Further south on the Wolds, a short length of linear earthwork leads to the head of St Austin's Dale, near South Cave, which also contains many springs. The link between linear features and springs seems indisputable. There may also be a strong relationship between linear earthworks and the ponds in the central and northern Wolds, some of which became village ponds (Fenton-Thomas 2003, 42). It seems clear, therefore, that those responsible for the construction of the linear earthworks intended to control routes through the landscape and the resources within it.

There are also linear earthwork systems on the lowlands of the Vale of York, plotted during the English Heritage National Mapping Programme and here also they are related to watercourses. At Thornton for example, a multiple-ditched feature, running for a kilometre, cuts off a loop in the stream later diverted to form the Pocklington Canal. A double-ditched linear feature about 2km long to the south-east of Shiptonthorpe also relates to the course of Skelfrey Beck. Neither of these features has yet been excavated but in the case of Shiptonthorpe, both round and square barrows are aligned on the linear earthwork (Halkon 2008, 159). A similar relationship between boundaries and watercourses has been recognised in Lincolnshire (Boutwood 1998), though here the earthworks are by no means as extensive as they are on the Yorkshire Wolds.

It is possible that the close relationship between linear earthwork systems, watercourses and division of the landscape into territories may relate to large-scale animal husbandry, linear earthworks acting as droveways along which stock, particularly cattle and horses, could be easily driven to water. The presence of so many linear earthworks also implies that like the Tabular, Howardian and Hambleton Hills, large areas of the Yorkshire Wolds were deforested. It has been noted (Manby *et al.* 2003(b)) that few copper-alloy axes and adzes have been found on the Wolds compared with Neolithic stone and flint axes. The implication here is that much of the Wolds were already cleared by the Neolithic. The relatively large numbers of copper-alloy axe-heads on the lowlands of the Foulness Valley may suggest, however, that this area remained wooded, which appears to be supported by palaeo-environmental investigation and rather than representing large-scale clearance for agriculture, the bronze tool distribution there may relate to woodland management, especially in the southern portion of the study area between Everingham Carrs and the River Humber. The 800-year-old tree, felled 322–277 BC, from which the Hasholme logboat was hewn (Millett and McGrail 1987, 83) was probably a product of this closed canopy later Bronze Age woodland.

Dent (pers. comm.) has, however, pointed out that stone and bronze axe distribution may have been affected by the length of time land has been in cultivation, contrasting with much of the Walling Fen area which was eighteenth-century intake, whereas in the medieval open fields of the Wolds, bronze axes noticed during ploughing would have been valuable as scrap, stone ones not. There is also a possibility that axes in wetland locations may be ritually deposited and not chance losses during the clearance of trees.

Apart from the examples referred to above, there are relatively few linear earthwork features in the southern portion of the Foulness Valley lowlands and in the broadly similar topography of South Holderness and the Hull Valley in comparison with the upland areas. Where they do occur they tend to be on slightly better drained land, such as a section of triple dykes near Swine. In general, however, it may be that where and if boundaries are required they are provided by watercourses, changes of soil type and other natural features, making artificial boundaries unnecessary. Another reason for their relative absence in the lowlands may be a difference in land use.

What do the linear earthworks tell us about society at the time? Someone must have instigated their construction and although this may have taken place over an extended time-span, they do represent considerable effort. The question of whether this was an act of communal cooperation or an arrangement between neighbouring elites has been a matter of much discussion (Fenton-Thomas 2003), and depends on the differing opinions of those with a socio-political view of the past with some economic interpretation (e.g. Bradley 1984) and those who believe that their construction was motivated by largely economic factors (e.g. Fowler 1984). Some writers (Barrett 1994) explain the land division of this period as representing a radical break between the ceremonial landscapes of the Neolithic to early Bronze Age, with their greater emphasis on communality, rights of access and ancestral heritage, to agricultural landscapes with carefully defined boundaries, belonging to a particular powerful individual or group.

The fact that many of the Yorkshire dykes respect round barrows and are deliberately aligned on them (Manby *et al.* 2003(b)) suggests some kind of reference to barrow-building predecessors. If prestigious grave-goods are indicative of social elites, then the location of barrows and Beaker burials at the mouths of the valleys which form routes between the lowlands and the southern Wolds, such as those at South Cave and Brantingham (Halkon 2003; Halkon 2008; Halkon *et al.* 2009), may symbolise manipulation of landscapes earlier in the Bronze Age by those responsible for the burials. Was the construction of the linear earthworks formalisation of earlier boundaries associated with the barrow builders, or were the barrows simply convenient markers on which linear earthworks could be aligned?

There is other evidence that the boundaries created by the linear earthworks had a long ancestry as a number of them overlie or respect pit alignments. At Ebberston Common on the North Yorkshire Moors, still visible as surface features, the latest of the sequence of at least six pit alignments appears to predate a round barrow, presumably constructed in the earlier Bronze Age (Oswald 2011, 4).

It has been stressed that some linear earthworks, especially those derived from trackways, may follow routes which were significant even further back to the hunter-foragers of the Mesolithic (Dent 1995, 21; Fenton-Thomas 2003). This reflects the phenomenological approach of Tilley (1994) who sees specific locations in the landscape as holding symbolic and ritual meaning for past people in a similar to the way to native Australians in the modern era. It is interesting to note that a microlith was discovered on top of one of the banks of the Huggate Dykes complex in 2002 during a field visit led by the author. Although this was surely disturbed and re-deposited during construction, its presence may support the idea that the linear earthwork here was constructed on a well-established route way between the lowlands of the Vale of York and the Yorkshire Wolds that had its origins before farming.

In contrast to the massive banks and ditches of Huggate Dykes, there are in some areas relatively short lengths of multiple linear earthworks which are too ephemeral for defence or directing stock. These may also have been used to mark out and emphasise the importance of a particular landscape feature to travellers (Bryant 1997; Fenton-Thomas 2003).

If the spectacular discovery of the skeletons of young men with combat wounds from Tormarton in Gloucestershire (Armit 2001; Osgood 2005) relates to a territorial dispute associated with an unfinished section of ditch, thought to be a linear boundary, then at least some of the dyke systems may have been constructed in circumstances of conflict rather than collaboration. The reacceptance of real rather than ceremonial warfare in the later Bronze Age (Osgood 2005; Bridgford 1997) also provides a possible context for a late Bronze Age socketed spearhead from Elloughton (Elgee and Elgee 1933, 238; Radley 1967, 17) and the clay mould fragments from Fimber (Manby et al. 2003(b), 77) which may provide indirect evidence for a link between the dykes and the manufacture of elite weapons.

One of the most impressive of all the linear earthwork features is the Great Wold Dyke which runs for over 15km, following the southern edge of the Great Wold Valley (Stoertz 1997, 77). Running parallel to this on the northern edge is an 11km-long earthwork. Between them, these two features enclose over 10,000 ha. The southernmost earthwork was found on excavation to contain later Bronze Age pottery (Manby 1980). Why was there a need to enclose such a large area? Between them the northern and southern linear earthworks control access to the Gypsey Race, one of the key water supplies of the region, further reinforcing the idea presented above for a close relationship between linear earthworks and watercourses. There is some debate as to what went on between these long linear earthworks. There are relatively few cropmark features in this area compared to the Wolds on either side and Manby (2003(b); 2007) has argued that woodland remained here for the building of timber structures such as the ring fort at Thwing. Alternatively Fenton-Thomas (2003, 128) proposes that this seemingly empty space may have been an area of common pasture. The management of stock may help to explain the elaborate multiple-linear enclosures with 'funnels' around Weaverthorpe, between the Great Wold Dyke and its northern equivalent, which have been shown from pottery excavated in the ditches to have been in use into the later

Iron Age (Fenton-Thomas 2003). Perhaps there may be truth in both explanations, the 'funnel' features representing a change of land use through time.

It is clear then that linear earthworks performed a variety of functions within the landscape as territorial boundaries and route ways. Although they are found elsewhere in Britain, particularly on the Wessex chalk lands, they do seem to be a distinctive component of the archaeology of the later prehistoric in eastern Yorkshire. They reflect an increasingly complex society in which there was a strong need to divide and control the land. It is very difficult to date them precisely, but it would appear that some remained important well into the Iron Age and beyond and were incorporated into parish boundaries. There is a strong relationship between linear earthworks and topographical features, particularly water sources and route ways, which may be symbolic as well as practical. It is also clear that there is a strong relationship between linear earthworks and hill fort-like enclosures (Powlesland 1988; Manby *et al.* 2003(b)) and it may be that some of these were the centres from which this large-scale landscape reorganisation originated.

HILL FORTS AND CURVILINEAR ENCLOSURES

Hill forts and curvilinear enclosures and the dyke systems make an appearance at around the same time. Both types of monument may be an expression of growing conflict and control over territory in many parts of Europe during the later Bronze Age. According to Harding (2000, 426), 'There are clear signs of the rise of hierarchical settlement structures. This is evidenced most clearly by the fortified sites, especially hill forts. Such sites can frequently be seen to have a fairly regular spacing across a given landscape.'

One of the reasons given for the apparent growth of tension and greater competition for resources within society which led to the construction of linear earthworks and hill forts is the deterioration of climate outlined in the previous chapter. Beetle evidence from Hasholme (Heath and Wagner 2009) and pollen analysis on the North Yorkshire Moors (Blackford and Chambers 1991) provide evidence for this, culminating in a short-lived but very severe cold and wet period around 800–750 BC, which corresponds with the evidence across north-west Europe (van Geel *et al.* 1996). Analyses of pollen, beetle and plant remains gives evidence for increasing wetness throughout the Humber region (Tweddle 2001; Smith 2002; Whitehouse 2004). The dramatic landscape change around 800–500 BC caused by the marine flooding of the Humber estuary which created the Walling Fen tidal inlet has been referred to in the previous chapter, with the head of the tidal inlet extending 12km north of the present Humber bank. The same types of deposit have been located in the Hull Valley and late Bronze Age cultural material has been found within or beneath marine clays at many places in the Humber system, for example the Melton timber trackways (Crowther 1987; Long *et al.* 1998). At Hasholme over a metre of estuarine clay was deposited over the earlier Bronze Age peat. In the upper reaches of the Foulness Valley, water logging and peat formation became widespread as a consequence of this sea level rise. In the short term, such flooding episodes may have had a negative impact on people living within the area, but the creation of the tidal estuarine inlet was eventually to have beneficial effects, by opening up the Foulness system to sea-going networks (Halkon and Innes 2005).

Hill fort-type features can be divided into three broad types, large regular hilltop enclosures or ring-forts, more irregular enclosures and smaller ovoid enclosures (Halkon 2008, 75) (Fig. 10).

Stoertz (1997, 48, fig. 24) identifies these at eleven locations on the Yorkshire Wolds. Their distribution seems to follow the fairly regular pattern of spacing and it is tempting to see the enclosures as corresponding to territories, partly defined by the linear earthworks (Fig. 11).

A good example of this relationship can be seen at Paddock Hill, Thwing where the large circular enclosure lies near the junction of major dyke systems (Manby 1980; Manby *et al.* 2003(b); Stoertz 1997, 78).

A similar close relationship between hill forts and linear earthworks on the chalk downlands of Wessex has been explored through the Danebury Environs project

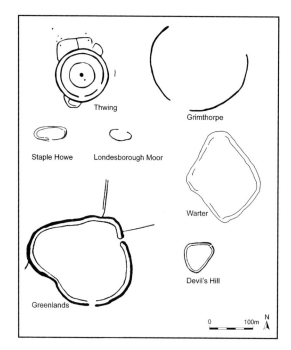

Fig. 10 Comparative plans of curvilinear enclosures and hillforts at Thwing, Grimthorpe, Staple Howe, Londesborough Moor, Warter, Greenlands and Devil's Hill. (Based on Stoertz (1997)). (T. Sparrow)

(Palmer 1984: Cunliffe 2003), which is thought to demonstrate control of the landscape and its economic output by hill fort-based hierarchies. The idea of hill forts as the main centre of elite individuals or groups has, however, been questioned (Hill 1995; Chadwick 1999; Robbins 1999) by those who prefer to see Iron Age society as more egalitarian. Harding (2004) would also caution against comparing the hill forts of the North of England with those of the South. However, the relationship between eastern Yorkshire hill forts and the landscape does seem to some extent to support the idea of control and hierarchy put forward by Cunliffe and his team. Manby (2007, 418), for example, would see the ringwork at Paddock Hill as a 'strategic territorial centre' (Plates 9 and 10). It is also likely that hill forts fulfilled some kind of ritual or symbolic purpose, for example Paddock Hill, built on a Neolithic henge-like monument, with a later central hollow and chalk boss feature which was incorporated into the large central circular building (Manby 2007).

Due to centuries of ploughing, no large East Yorkshire hill forts are as well preserved as the great hill forts of Wessex, such as Danebury or Maiden Castle and those that do survive appear to lack the elaborate defences of these monuments. The relatively good state of preservation of the small hilltop enclosure at Staple Howe (Fig. 12) (Brewster 1963) is due to its topographical setting on a chalk outcrop which would be very difficult to plough.

Until the introduction of aerial survey, few hill forts were recognised in East Yorkshire, and their significance within the region restricted to the earlier Iron Age (Millett 1990, 350; Dent 1995; 2010). Lack of excavation, however, makes it difficult to generalise about the date, length and character of their occupation. Those that have been dug include Grimthorpe (Stead 1968), Paddock Hill, Thwing (Manby et al. 2003(b); Manby 2007), Devil's Hill and Staple Howe (Brewster 1963; Powlesland 1988) and the promontory fort at Scarborough Castle (Smith 1928; Challis and Harding 1975; Pacitto 2004). At Scarborough, pottery from the excavations showed that it was occupied in the later Bronze Age and finds included a fine copper-alloy sword. Geophysical surveys have been undertaken at a number of sites including the 200x240m, 3.5ha Greenlands hill fort (Challis and Harding 1975, 122, Pl 1; Stoertz 1997, 47).

At over 24ha, the hill fort at Roulston Scar, on the edge of the North Yorkshire Moors, is one of largest in the wider region. Although first recognised in 1960 as a large hill fort, it was only after a recent English Heritage survey that its full scale and significance was appreciated. In places the defences survived to more than 2.7m in height and on excavation were found to be of box rampart construction, faced with a timber palisade which possibly stood up to 3.6m high. The earthwork survey revealed no evidence for internal settlement structures and the excavations of the late 1960s did not recover the large amounts of pottery and bone which would be expected if the site was intensively occupied. Commanding extensive views, it would have dominated the landscape. It has

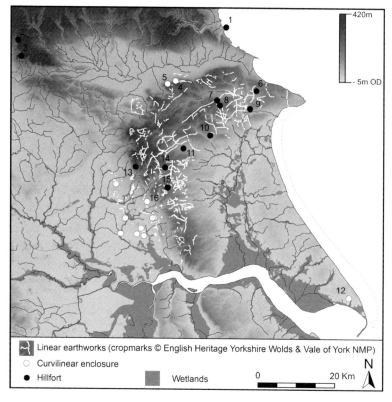

Fig. 11 The relationship between linear earthworks, larger hill forts and curvilinear enclosures on the Yorkshire Wolds and Foulness Valley. (Based on Stoertz (1997) and Halkon (2008)) 1.Scarborough. 2. Boltby. 3. Raulston Scar. 4. Devil's Hill. 5.Staple Howe. 6. Reighton. 7. Thwing. 8. Swaythorpe. 9. Greenlands. 10. Driffield Wold. 11. Wetwang. 12. Skeffling. 13. Grimthorpe. 14. Warter. 15. Kiplingcotes. 16. Londesborough Moor. (T. Sparrow)

been postulated that there may also be a relationship between the hill fort and a square barrow recorded nearby (Oswald and Pearson 2001).

A further hill fort at Boltby Scar (Plate 8), around 4km to the north-west of Roulston Scar, on a west-facing limestone promontory overlooking the Vale of Mowbray, was excavated in 2009 and 2011 (Powlesland 2011). It lies close to the linear earthwork system known as the Cleave Dyke and there may be a close relationship between them. Like the Roulston Scar hill fort it possessed commanding views across the landscape. There was earlier activity on the site in the form of a round barrow, which contained high-status grave goods. The main hill fort was preceded by a palisaded enclosure. The majority of the ramparts had been levelled by bulldozer in 1961, though a section

IMPRESSION OF STAPLE HOWE IN THE LAST STAGE OF OCCUPATION

Fig. 12 Reconstruction of Staple Howe by S. Dove. (Brewster 1963, 10, fig 6)

survives on the edge of the cliff. The entrance, which may have had a timber gatehouse, was flanked by ditches cut 2m vertically into the limestone bedrock.

The lack of excavation makes it very difficult to be certain about their function and chronology, but radiocarbon dates of the East Yorkshire hill forts are tabulated below.

Table 1. Radiocarbon dates of hill forts in eastern Yorkshire

Name	Context	Date	Lab. Ref.	Reference
Grimthorpe	Rubble ditch infill beside causeway	2920±130 BP Cal BC 1372 – 931 (68.2%) Cal BC 1489 – 820 (95.4%)	NPL – 137	Manby 1980 Dent 2010, 100
	Occupation debris upper ditch fill	2640±130 BP Cal BC 969 – 603 (68.2%) Cal BC 1188 – 410 (95.4%)	NPL – 136	
Staple Howe	Charred grain from phase II palisade slot	2400±50 BP Cal BC 753 – 402 (68.2%) Cal BC 765 – 390 (95.4%)	BM-63	Brewster 1963, 140 Dent 2010, 100
Thwing	Pre-rampart charcoal	2910±70 BP Cal BC 1288 – 976 (68.2%) Cal BC 1374– 905 (95.4%) sigma)**	HAR – 1398	Manby 2007, 409 Dent 2010, 100
	Antler from rampart rubble	2590±90 BP Cal BC 1310 – 910 (95.4%) Cal BC 915 – 410 (95.4%)	OxA – 25819	

Continued : . .

Name	Context	Date	Lab. Ref.	Reference
Boltby Scar	Turf at the base of the rampart	2715 ± 35BP Cal BC 924–806 BC (95.4%)	SUERC-37212 (GU26040)	Powlesland (pers comm.)
	The date is from humic fraction extracted from buried turf/peat	Cal BC 896–829 BC (86.2%)		

Reference has already been made to the relationship between the Huggate Dykes system and springs. At Grimthorpe (Stead 1968) for example, the position of the fort makes it well-placed to control access to both springs and streams. A similar relationship can be observed at Mount Airy, overlooking the Humber near South Cave, which is situated on a promontory at the southern end of the Yorkshire Wolds, where aerial photography by English Heritage and the writer revealed the presence of a possible defended site. A geophysical survey was undertaken by English Heritage (Martin 2003), although again little trace of any internal features could be discerned, appearing to support the idea that hill forts need not necessarily have been heavily occupied nucleated settlements, as in the case of the hill fort at Breiddin in the Welsh Marches (Buckland *et al.* 2001). It must be noted, however, that experimental archaeology such as that carried out at Little Butser (Reynolds 1979) has shown that quite substantial houses could leave little trace even on excavation, let alone geophysical survey.

Smaller curvilinear enclosures which may be hill forts were identified at Warter (Stoertz 1997 fig. 24, 6; Manby 2007) and at Kiplingcotes in Middleton Parish, (Stoertz 1997, fig. 24, 7; Manby 2007). Their dispersed distribution which complements and continues that demonstrated by Stoertz (1997 fig. 33) on the Wolds and by Taylor (1999, 32) in the Holme-on-Spalding Moor area, and the relationship between the curvilinear enclosures and linear earthworks appears to support the hypothesis that these features acted as central places for territories demarcated by the latter (Halkon 2008, 160). An analogy may therefore be made with the West Heslerton area where Powlesland (1988, 103), with reference to the sites of Staple Howe and Devil's Hill, states that: 'It is difficult to argue that these are not related elements in a well organised landscape.'

Investigation, including geophysical survey and sample excavation, has been carried out on a large enclosure on the western escarpment of the Wolds overlooking Market Weighton, which has an impressive view over the Plain of York (Halkon and Woodhouse 2010). First recorded as a cropmark in aerial photography by Stoertz (1997) and by the author in 2003, the site lies between shallow dry valleys that lead from the lowlands to the Wold top, close to several ploughed-out Bronze Age round barrows. Although any conclusions must be tentative due to the relatively small size of the trenches, it is possible to suggest a sequence of activity. Two ovoid enclosures were constructed on the crest of the hill, which on the basis of the pottery found in the ditch of one of these, was of early to middle Iron Age date. The ditch also contained bones of cattle, sheep and pig (Sewpaul pers. comm.), probably the remnants of feasting activity of some kind. The ovoid enclosures may then have been surrounded by a 90 x 90m rectilinear ditched enclosure with a single east-facing entrance. The larger enclosure was integral to a linear earthwork system, which extended roughly north-south, visible as a cropmark for around a kilometre.

Typological comparison suggests that a curvilinear enclosure at Londesborough Moor, photographed by the author and Anthony Crawshaw, is similar to excavated sites such as Staple Howe (Brewster 1963) and Devil's Hill (Powlesland 1988) on the northern edge of the Yorkshire Wolds. Many of the curvilinear enclosures seem to be integral to field systems, such as the feature near Tollingham and Forest Farm, Holme-on-Spalding Moor; others would appear to be isolated, like the site at Londesborough Moor where exploratory field walking by the author was unproductive, apart from finds of fire-cracked cobbles.

The Londesborough enclosure resembles the largest of a cluster of four curvilinear enclosures at Market Weighton Common (Ramm 1978, 12; Stoertz 1997; Halkon 2008, 75). Each of these is slightly different in shape, but they all share the same alignment. The largest enclosure contains at least one roundhouse. However there is a roundhouse just outside to the east. The relationship between the short lengths of linear feature and the enclosures is unclear. The paired arrangement of these features is similar in layout to curvilinear enclosures investigated by the Humber Wetlands project at Sutton Common, South Yorkshire (Parker-Pearson and Sydes 1997; Van de Noort *et al.* 2007), dated to the early Iron Age date. Field walking over the Market Weighton enclosures was again unproductive, apart from finds of fire-cracked cobbles. In North Lincolnshire, similar single curvilinear enclosures visible as cropmarks have been dated to the Iron Age (Winton 1998), confirmed by archaeological evaluation prior to development at Kirton in Lindsey (Albone 2002) and North Killingholme (Jordan 2005).

The function of such lowland enclosures is a matter of debate. Some have been interpreted as 'marsh forts' (Van de Noort *et al.* 2007: Whiting 1936). The Londesborough Moor enclosure is indeed well defended by areas of wetland. The Market Weighton enclosure contains a ring ditch, which may either be a haystack stand or small roundhouse and in the Londesborough enclosure there was a sizeable roundhouse and various pits.

At Sutton Common the excavation of 'four post structures', saddle quern fragments and carbonised cereal may relate to some form of cereal storage and processing. Possible granary structures were excavated at Grimthorpe, similar to those at Staple Howe (Brewster 1963) where a deposit of carbonised dwarf or club wheat was found (Manby *et al.* (b) 2003). Dent (1995, 42), however, points out that different interpretations can be made of four-post structures including watchtowers. Some enclosure may have been associated with pastoral agriculture. At Grimthorpe (Jarman *et al.* 1968) the proportion of cattle and sheep suggests both lowland and upland grazing, which the site was well positioned to exploit, although extreme care must be used in making any assumption about animal husbandry here due to the relatively small number of bones recovered. Some caution is also necessary in presuming that sheep can only prosper in such chalk upland landscapes, as Pryor (1999) has successfully farmed Soay sheep, the nearest living relative of Iron Age sheep, in a fenland area and indeed feral sheep survive quite happily on the rocky shore of such islands as St Kilda in the Hebrides. Further to the north at Thwing, analysis of artefacts and palaeo-environmental material shows that the site had access to a wide variety of economic resources with activities on site including stock rearing with a greater proportion of sheep to cattle. Pork seems to have been an important food resource and may be associated with feasting activities (Manby *et al.* 2003(b)). A variety of crafts were undertaken including pottery and textile manufacture, bone and copper-alloy working. The high status of the site is perhaps confirmed by the discovery of a fine late Bronze Age gold penannular ring nearby (Varndell 2003, 19) (Plate 9).

In Holderness, a further lowland ovoid enclosure 90 x 40m, with a controlled entrance, was excavated to the west of Skeffling, prior to the construction of the pipeline between Easington and Paull (Rowland 2012). Located on a slight rise at around 9m OD, daub, pottery, burnt cobbles and other refuse was found on this possible 'marsh fort' particularly in ditches dating from *c.* 540–380 BC. The enclosure contained a number of roundhouses.

Few houses have been excavated inside the hill forts of eastern Yorkshire. The roundhouse at the centre of the Thwing ringwork was 26m in diameter (Manby *et al.* 2003(b)) with a double ring of postholes which would have held uprights to support a massive roof (Plate 10). Staple Howe contained the remains of three houses, belonging to different phases (Fig. 12). The earliest was an oval structure (Hut II) measuring 10 x 6m, probably built around 500 BC, with a stone wall and rammed chalk floor containing a hearth and other features. Around a century later, the oval house was replaced by a pair of timber roundhouses and a granary supported by five posts. Hut I was *c.* 9m in diameter and of post construction containing an oven and a loom. The remains of Hut III were more ephemeral, with a porch and inner ring of posts. Although there were traces of burning within the house, the hearth itself may have been removed by erosion. A large quantity of pottery was recovered from the settlement along with copper-alloy razors and a few small iron objects including an awl. The razors are of particular significance as they closely resemble examples from northern Germany and the Netherlands (Brewster 1963, 115). Once regarded as evidence to support an invasion hypothesis (Hawkes 1963), it has been suggested that the razors may be British in origin, albeit inspired by continental counterparts (O'Connor 2007).

Apart from the Melton inhumations, the whereabouts of the dead in the transition between the Bronze and Iron Ages is problematic as they are virtually absent in the region. In the later middle Bronze Age, a small cemetery was excavated at Catfoss in Holderness (McInnes 1968; Manby *et al.* 2003(b), 67) with cremations in barrel and bucket-shaped pottery vessels, some of which were surrounded by a penannular ditch. The excavator again quoted parallels with burials from the Netherlands. At Staple Howe the remains of three individuals were found in a very fragmentary state of preservation, all perhaps adults. It is possible that these bodies were simply exposed or excarnated with no grave and therefore unlike the later Arras burials very difficult to locate. A large fragment of a skull was found in the packing of a palisade trench which may indicate some form of ritual deposition reminiscent of Danebury.

Although beyond the territory of the Parisi, the Sutton Common enclosures referred to above may provide useful comparisons with the smaller curvilinear enclosures being discussed here. Various aspects of Sutton Common were interpreted as relating to ceremony and ritual, including a causeway linking the two enclosures, thought to be monumental in scale. The two human skulls, animal bone and a bone comb in the ditch terminals of the large enclosure, are also thought to represent 'structured deposition' (Hill 1995) of a similar kind to that found at other hill forts such as Danebury, where special deposits ranging from iron billets to dismembered people were placed into grain storage pits (Cunliffe 2003). Human skulls were also found in the two terminals of a circular enclosure surrounding two roundhouses and a granary at Weelsby Avenue, Grimsby, North Lincolnshire, and the enclosure ditch also contained copper-alloy casting debris (Sills and Kinsley 1978, 1979, 1990).

At Grimthorpe, the male interred with a shield and sword (Mortimer 1905, 150) (Plate 3) may have been buried to align with the hill fort. This may be coincidence as the burial, on typological grounds, is substantially later than the time when the fort is thought to have been abandoned. It could, however, represent deliberate recognition of the symbolic importance of the site and its relationship to the cluster of springs nearby. In a similar way, the secondary deposition of cremated human bones and a strip of hammered gold at Sutton Common, thought to have been deposited in the first century BC (Van de Noort *et al.* 2007), may represent veneration of an older site and/or some kind of offering related to water. Although again probably much later than the hill fort, the spectacular cache of five swords and a bundle of thirty-three spearheads buried in an enclosure ditch at South Cave, which will be considered in more detail in subsequent chapters, could also have been deliberately aligned on the hilltop enclosure at Mount Airy, which like Grimthorpe, appears to be associated with streams and springs.

It may well be significant that the hill forts of eastern Yorkshire include some of the earliest examples of the use of iron in the North of England. As well as the iron items found at Staple Howe, pieces of iron rod were also found with Ewart Park phase

(900–800 BC) copper-alloy objects in pits at the Scarborough Castle hill fort (Smith 1928; Collard *et al*. 2006; Challis and Harding 1975, 46). Iron fragments were also discovered in the fills of ditches at the Grimthorpe hill fort (Stead 1968, 166 nos 5–7). It would seem, therefore, that control of iron at this early stage in its use may have belonged to elites.

SUMMARY

In later Bronze Age and early Iron Age eastern Yorkshire there is strong evidence from the study of environmental remains for climatic instability which may have contributed to the development of an increasingly combative and hierarchical society as resources became scarcer. Sea levels rose, transforming the coastline and flooding the lowlands. The landscape was divided up and controlled through a network of linear earthworks, possibly by a tribal elite based in the hill fort-type features. On the basis of the relationship between the major east-west dyke systems and hill forts it has been argued that the Wolds were divided into two blocks along the watershed with a northern block based on the Vale of Pickering and a southern relating to Holderness and the Vale of York (Dent 2010, 34). Field work and aerial survey over the last few decades has shown some extension of linear earthworks and curvilinear enclosures interpreted as marsh forts in the Vale of York and Holderness.

Excavations at Staple Howe showed that its occupants had at least some contact with the European continent, deduced through similarities in artefact types, though most authorities would argue that the majority of people were of native origin. Both linear earthworks and enclosures may also have had ritual and symbolic meanings closely related to the landscape and its resources.

Very few smaller settlements dating from this period have yet been found, but these may exist amongst the large number of cropmark sites still to be explored. Unenclosed settlements of ring-post-type roundhouses characteristic of this era are almost impossible to spot through any method other than excavation. We know very little about the people of the early Iron Age as burials are all but absent which makes the burials from Melton so important; although few in number, their burial posture and alignment appear to be a precursor to the Arras culture for which this region is internationally significant.

CHAPTER 4

THE ARRAS CULTURE

The much-debated origins of the middle Iron Age Arras culture have been referred to in the introduction to this book and one of its most distinctive features were the square enclosures surrounding burials or square barrows. The precise date of their arrival is problematic, largely due to the plateau in the radiocarbon calibration curve which caused dates of 2540 BP to calibrate to between 800 and 400 BC (van der Plicht 2004, 45). Typological methods, particularly comparison of grave goods such as brooches suggested cemeteries may have begun in the fifth century BC. The application of Bayesian statistical analysis to radiocarbon dates is, however, beginning to provide a tighter chronology suggesting that burial at Wetwang for example spanned the third and earlier second centuries Cal BC, a shorter period than once thought (Jay *et al*. 2012), however it is almost certain that the Wetwang cemetery is not the earliest of its type in the region.

East Yorkshire is unusual in Iron Age Britain as it is one of the few regions where most people were buried, often accompanied by grave goods ranging from a single glass bead, or a pottery jar with a sheep bone, to those containing swords in decorated sheaths or dismantled chariots. Apart from a few exceptions, such as the South West of England, elsewhere the commonest method of disposal of the dead may have been exposure to the elements (excarnation) or deposition in bogs, rivers and streams or caves (Fitzpatrick 2007); however the small amount of direct evidence that survives for it may not justify application to the general population. A few more burials have been found in the developer-funded excavations of the last decade (Jay *et al*. 2012, 161) and the burials from Melton referred to in the previous chapter are of great importance in shedding light on the burial tradition of the early Iron Age in the region and their north-south alignment and crouched posture appears to herald the Arras culture (Fenton-Thomas 2011, 373).

The fact that so many burials survive in East Yorkshire provides us with a detailed insight into its past population. From the grave goods it is possible to infer social status and information about their manufacture and use, trade and fashion. Study of skeletons tells us about age, sex, stature, disease and trauma, and thanks to recent scientific developments aspects of diet and possible geographical origins. These factors will be discussed in more detail below.

SQUARE BARROWS AND CEMETERIES

Square barrows are one of the most familiar and characteristic field monuments of Iron Age East Yorkshire. It is almost certain that this burial tradition was of continental origin, as it extends from the Czech Republic to the east and Dorset in the west, between Lunan Water and the Firth of Forth to the Meuse, Rhine and Elbe rivers. Apart from East Yorkshire, there are concentrations in the Champagne and Marne regions of France and Hunsrück-Eifel areas of Germany (Stead 1979; Anthoons 2011).

Square barrows are also important, as almost alone amongst the Iron Age monuments visible as cropmarks detected during aerial photography, many are directly associated with individuals, though on excavation some secondary burials have also been discovered. Only about 56 per cent of the burials at Wetwang (*c.*250) were primary burials, the remaining 200 or so were secondary (Dent 2010). Secondary burials were also present at Danes Graves though they were rarer at Burton Fleming and Rudston (Stead 1991). In a few places, such as Scorborough (Fig. 13), Beverley Westwood, Danes Graves near Kilham and Skipwith Common, square barrows survive above ground.

They have also been recorded in the North Yorkshire Moors and Howardian Hills further north, but are at their most dense on the Yorkshire Wolds, as well over 2,000 were plotted from aerial photographs (Stoertz 1997). Square barrows are present in the lowland areas of Holderness such as at Swine and Skirlaugh and in the Vale of York around Holme-on-Spalding Moor and North Cave.

Square barrows can be categorised into three main groups (Dent 1995; 2010):

Group 1 – enclosures, usually large, with no surviving central burial, occupying early positions in the cemetery

Group 2 – enclosures of varying size with shallow, medium depth or occasionally deep graves – early and middle stages of the cemetery

Group 3 – enclosures, never large, and sometimes curvilinear, with deep graves (0.6m and over) – latest stages

It is thought that the earliest were of the type that were excavated at Cowlam (Group 1) (Stead 1979), near Driffield, where the burial was placed directly on the ground surface, or in a shallow grave and enclosed by a large, deep rectilinear ditch with rounded corners, the up-cast soil forming a mound, which in intensive arable areas leaves the burial and grave goods vulnerable and thus destroying potential dating evidence.

The majority of this type fall within the range of 12–15m square, though some were considerably larger at over 20m square. The other square barrows were generally smaller than the Group 1 type (8–11m square), and were more regular in shape with

Fig. 13 Scorborough square barrow cemetery from the air. This is one of the few upstanding square barrow cemeteries in the region. (P. Halkon)

sharper corners. In many of these a central grave pit is visible. A link has been suggested between barrow size and chronology, with smaller barrows being later in the sequence and their decrease in size being due to increased population pressure on available land (Dent 1982; 1995; 2010). This change may have taken place during the third and second centuries BC. Group 1 barrows (Stoertz 1997, 39) generally occur as single monuments or in small groups, clustered loosely within the groups. Not all the burial mounds were square, as some burials were enclosed by ring ditches, though the reason for this difference is now lost to us.

The largest cemeteries recorded in the aerial survey of the Yorkshire Wolds (Stoertz 1997) were at Carnaby with over 300 burials, Danes Graves with over 300 and Burton Fleming/Makeshift with 346. At Garton-Wetwang Slack 446 burials were excavated by Brewster and Dent (Jay *et al.* 2012, 161). At Arras, Stead illustrates 100 barrows (Stead, 1979 figs 1, 9), only seventy-nine are recorded as cropmarks by Stoertz (1997) with more photographed there by the present author in 1990 and 2006 (Fig. 14).

The cemetery at Arras seems to have been used for a long time, as there are differences in the distribution pattern of barrows in each class within the cemetery. Group 1 barrows were widely dispersed across the cemetery, with a noticeable cluster at the head of Sancton Dale itself. This positioning may not be accidental, as Sancton Dale forms a route way between the Humber Lowlands and the Yorkshire Wolds. The important early Anglo-Saxon cremation cemetery is situated at the foot of this valley which may indicate some form of territorial statement by incoming people from the European continent. Were the Iron Age burials placed at the head of the valley for similar reasons? At Arras the smaller and later barrows are more tightly clustered, to the extent that some shared ditches. There were also clear alignments of barrows. A similar arrangement can be seen at the much smaller cemetery near Pocklington, with a dispersed distribution of Group 1 barrows and clusters of the smaller, later types. The reasons for the changes in barrow type and distribution may remain difficult to discover, but it is clear that the creation and positioning of each grave represented the choice of the individuals or groups of people responsible for disposal of the dead. It may be that such clusters and alignments reflect family groupings.

At Bell Slack, between Rudston and Burton Fleming, a Group 1 burial formed the nucleus of the cemetery, with seventeen Group 2 burials clustering around them. In the northern part of the same cemetery, there were *c.* forty-six Group 3 barrows in very close and regular rows. Typological analysis of the brooches within the graves suggests the initial slow development of the cemetery from one or two early barrows, with a great many barrows being constructed in a relatively short period, towards the end of the Arras burial tradition. This distribution may have been related to settlement along the droveway and selection of particular areas for burial (Dent 1995, 51).

Within the Foulness Valley study area, eight of the twenty-two square barrow cemeteries appeared to be associated with settlement droveways (Halkon 2008). The Arras cemetery is situated between two droveways or in a gap in the same droveway, with the largest cluster of barrows at its southern end, on a small plateau at the edge of Sancton Dale. At Nunburnholme, a large barrow cemetery is also located at the end of a droveway, but it is not clear which came first. In this case there are no barrows dispersed along the droveway settlement itself.

There is a strong relationship between barrow cemeteries and movement through the landscape (Fig. 15).

Single barrows and cemeteries are positioned at key points in the Great Wold Valley, particularly around Rudston and Burton Fleming, aligned with the Gypsy Race itself and

Fig. 14 The Arras square barrow cemetery from the air. Note the linear feature to the right of the picture. (P. Halkon)

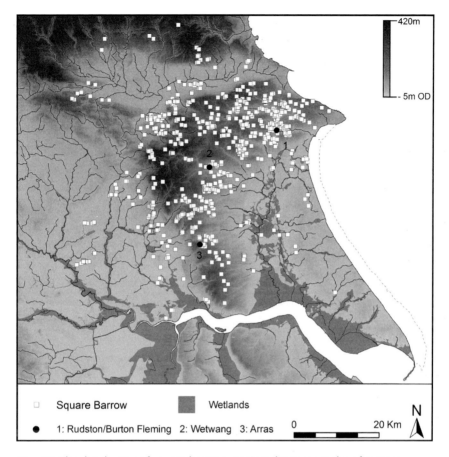

Fig. 15 The distribution of square barrows against the topography of eastern Yorkshire. There would seem to be a correlation between cemeteries, routes through the landscape and features such as water sources. (T. Sparrow)

earlier monuments, such as the Neolithic cursuses (Stoertz 1997, 72). Large cemeteries at Warter and North Dalton all overlook major valleys, which formed routes through the Wolds. The positioning of the clusters of chariot burials at Garton-Wetwang Slack and Arras may not be coincidental as both cemeteries relate to significant routes through the Wolds down to watersheds. Garton-Wetwang Slack leads down to the headwaters of the River Hull near Elmswell (Congreve 1938) where iron smelting took place, probably in the Iron Age. From the cemetery at Arras, Sancton Dale leads down to the Foulness Valley river systems and associated iron industries which will be discussed in the next chapter.

There may therefore have been a similar link of 'control' in the Arras period between square barrow cemeteries, water supply and routes through the landscape as there was between natural features and linear earthworks earlier in the Iron Age noted above. At some locations the two types of monument coincide, with the positioning of burials along the boundaries, implying that their potency continued. This relationship was apparent at Melton, as a square barrow with a central grave was aligned on the north-south triple linear feature referred to in Chapter 3 (Fenton-Thomas 2011, 373). An intriguing find in the ditch fill of the barrow ditch was the copper-alloy core of a contemporary copy of a once gold-plated coin of the Coriletauvi (Sills 2011(a)) dated to the period c. AD 10–40. The use of small items for dating in such contexts is not reliable as the other square barrow from the site which did not have a central grave contained a leaf-shaped Neolithic arrowhead (Fenton-Thomas 2011, 112).

In contrast other square barrow cemeteries seem to have been reabsorbed into working landscapes. In a dispersed cemetery of mainly Group 1 barrows at Warter, to the south of an Iron Age field system, the eastern ditch of one of the barrows was cut by

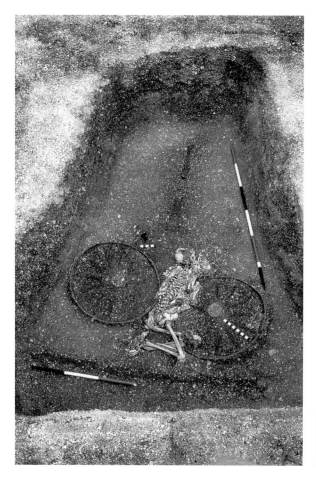

Fig. 16 Garton Slack chariot burial 1971 (NB scales are in imperial measurements). (T.C.M. Brewster ERART)

a field boundary, suggesting that the barrow had lost its significance (Halkon 2008, 84). Similarly palaeo-environmental analysis in the Kirkburn cemetery shows that cattle were grazed over the square barrows here (Thew and Wagner 1991).

The burials themselves have been categorised into three main types (Stead 1991). In Type A, the corpse was crouched or contracted, sometimes in a coffin, with the head at the north end of the grave facing east, often accompanied by a pot and the upper left foreleg of a sheep, with the most common artefact being a brooch. In Type B the body was flexed or fully extended, with the head to the east or west, with a much wider range of artefacts including swords, spearheads, spindle whorls and pork rather than lamb. In Type C burials the same portions of pork were included as in Type B, but their position within the burial was always the same, with the left half of the animal's head near the skull of the person, the right half near the stomach, the left leg on the left side of the human and the right leg on the right side. No brooches were included in Type C burials.

Examination of skeletons at Rudston (Stead 1991) revealed close genetic similarities which may indicate burial in family groups. Features were shared by neighbouring skeletons in Type A and B burials and showed that both forms were used by the same family (Anthoons 2011, 16). What is not clear, however, is the relative dating between these burial types. The recent programmes of radiocarbon dating (Garrow *et al.* 2009; Jay *et al.* 2012) are beginning to clarify the chronology. Burial in family groups has also been identified at Wetwang where genetic abnormalities, including metopism (the retention of the medio-frontal suture of the cranium), Wormian bones (small bones appearing in the cranial sutures) and sacralised 5th lumbar vertebra (fusion of the first sacral vertebra and fifth lumbar vertebra) were found in skeletons from the same part of the cemetery (Dent 1995, 52).

CHARIOT BURIALS

Amongst the most spectacular burials of Iron Age Britain are those containing two-wheeled vehicles, interpreted as chariots or carts, an argument which will be discussed below. In what are now the East Riding of Yorkshire and North Yorkshire, twenty of these have been discovered, with an outlier at Ferry Fryston in West Yorkshire (Plate 16) (Boyle 2004; Brown *et al.* 2007). The only example outside Yorkshire was found at Newbridge near Edinburgh radiocarbon dated to 520–370 BC (Carter and Hunter 2003(a) and (b)). Details of the East and North Yorkshire Chariot burials are tabulated below.

Chariot burials can be divided into two main types: those in which the wheels were removed from the vehicle and laid in the bottom of the grave, and those in which the wheels remained attached. The distribution of dismantled vehicle burials in the central area of East Yorkshire at either side of the Wolds is most interesting, as it seems to

Table 2 Chariot burials in eastern Yorkshire

D- Dismantled   I = Intact   ? unknown   Cu A= Cu alloy

Place	Name	Discovery date	Type	Sex	Death age	Body position	Chariot fittings	Weapons	Other Grave goods	Animal bones	Date	Other
Arras	Kings Barrow W44	1815–17	D	M	Old	Head to N facing E. On back between wheels. Legs crossed. Arms crossed on breast	2 tyres Nave bands 2 bits 2 linch-pins 5 terrets			Horse under each wheel (13 hands) 2 pig skulls either side of head		
Arras	Charioteer W 56–88	1815–17	D	M		Head to N Resting on shield between wheels	2 tyres 2 bits		Cu alloy "case" end of chariot pole? Cu alloy disc	2 boars tusks on body		
Arras	Lady's Barrow	1877	D	F		Head to N Back resting on wheels Head on mirror	2 tyres 2 nave bands		Parts of a whip	2 pigs		Circular grave
Beverley Westwood		1875	D	?		N-S	2 tyres nave band 2 bits Iron linch-pin (all badly corroded)					Oval grave
Cawthorn Camp		1849	I				2 tyres Nave hoops Iron and Cu alloy					Close parallels with Nanterre. Paris

Continued . . .

Place	Name	Discovery date	Type	Sex	Death age	Body position	Chariot fittings	Weapons	Other Grave goods	Animal bones	Date	Other
Danes Graves	13	1897	D	2 M	Adult	NW-SE left side N-S right side	2 tyres 1 nave rings 5 terrets 2 linch-pins 2 bits	Oak shield decorated with Cu alloy binding and face	Iron and Cu alloy brooch	Pig bones		
Garton Slack	GS XI Burial 2	1971	D	M	30	Flexed N-S facing E	5 terrets 2 tyres 2 bits		Cu alloy fittings from a whip Iron pole cap	Pig's head halved between at chest and stomach		Coral decoration on terrets
Garton Station	GS6	1985	D	M	35–45	Flexed N-S facing E	2 tyres 5 terrets Linch-pins		Wheels on side of trench	2 groups of pigs bones to W of skull and in front of chest		Linch-pins, unlike others closest match Jonchery-sur-Suippe, Marne
Hornsea		1904					Tyres Bits	Spears?				
Huggate							Tyres			Many bones		'Howes' flattened and spread
Hunmanby		1906	I	?		Decayed "greasy" soil may indicate burial	2 tyres linch-pins? bit	Oak shield decorated with bronze binding and face		Horse teeth		Large circular grave

Continued . . .

Place	Name	Discovery date	Type	Sex	Death age	Body position	Chariot fittings	Weapons	Other Grave goods	Animal bones	Date	Other
Kirkburn	K5	1987	D	M	25–35	Crouched N-S facing E	2 tyres Nave bands 2 linch-pins 5 terrets	Mail tunic	Decorated lid	2 groups of pig bones to N and W of skull and at knees		
Middleton/ Enthorpe		1888					Linch-pin			Bones		
Pexton Moor		1911 and 1935	I			No bones survive	2 tyres bit					Slots cut for wheels
Seamer		1862	?			Bones removed	2 tyres bit			Horse bones		
Wetwang	1	1984	D	M	26–35	Crouched N-S facing W	2 tyres nave bands 5 terrets 2 linch-pins	Sword 7 spears Shield		Pig quartered between head and knees		
Wetwang	2	1984	D	F	45+	Flexed N-S facing E	2 tyres nave bands 2 linch-pins 5 terrets (worn)		Mirror "Bean tin" Iron and gold pin	Pig forequarters between arms and thighs		
Wetwang	3	1984	D	M	26–35	Crouched (knees up and tight) N-S facing E	2 tyres nave bands 2 linch-pins 5 terrets	Sword Shield fitting				
Wetwang Village		2001	D	F	35–45	Crouched S-N facing W	2 tyres 2 linch-pins 5 terrets		Mirror with bead tassle	Pig bone (at least 1 male) some charred on torso pelvis and forearms	210–195 Cal BC 215–180 Cal BC (Jay et al. 2012).	Strap union

be restricted geographically and may indicate some form of shared identity or tribal grouping. The Yorkshire outliers at Pexton Moor, Cawthorn and Ferry Fryston and the Newbridge find were all buried intact, as are most, but not all continental examples (Anthoons 2011, 69).

The Ferry Fryston burial is particularly interesting as it seems to be a 'hybrid'. Although it was buried intact like the continental examples, the corpse, which was clearly placed within the 'carriage', was flexed in the manner of the dismantled East Yorkshire burials, rather than extended like the majority of continental examples. Carefully positioned pork portions were also arranged on and around him in the East Yorkshire tradition. It is difficult to know whether these similarities are coincidental, or whether the burial might be some kind of link with East Yorkshire in terms of territorial control. The landscape setting of the Ferry Fryston chariot is worthy of note, as it lies near one of the important crossing places of the River Ouse, on the rolling limestone hills between the Pennine uplands and the Vale of York lowlands. This area had been a focus for ritual activity since the Neolithic, for it contains a large henge and other hengiform monuments, Bronze Age burials (some including Beakers) and surprisingly little evidence for settlement until the later Iron Age and Romano-British periods (Roberts 2005). It almost appears that people from each era felt the need to mark the landscape at that point in a special way. Packed tightly into the ditch of the Ferry Fryston square barrow were the bones of 250 cattle, interpreted as the remains of an enormous funeral feast. Remarkably the cattle bones were radiocarbon dated to the second century AD, whilst the chariot burial was dated to 210–195 Cal BC (68 per cent probability) 225–185 Cal BC (95 per cent probability) (Jay *et al.* 2012, 172). There is either an error in the radiocarbon dates, or by design or coincidence the burial mound remained a focus of ritual activity for several hundred years. There are, however, precedents nearby for the revisiting of earlier monuments, as the deliberately broken scabbard of an Iron Age sword was found in the primary ditch fill of the henge at Ferrybridge. At Stanwick, Northants, a Bronze Age barrow was reused as a shrine in the Roman period (Neal 1989). This contrasts greatly with the seeming disregard for the square barrows at Warter and Kirkburn noted above.

The tradition of chariot burial is ancient and widespread, some of the earliest were found in Transcaucasia and southern Russia dating from *c.* 1600 BC which are themselves derived from Near Eastern examples (Pogrebova 2003) and chariots are known from high-status tombs from ancient Egypt and China. As far as the Iron Age is concerned, four-wheeled wagons of the early Iron Age Hallstatt period have been found largely in what are now France and Germany. By the middle Iron Age La Tène period, this tradition had been replaced by the burial of a two-wheeled vehicle.

There is a debate as to whether these vehicles should be called 'carts' or 'chariots'; the former implies everyday transport particularly relating to agriculture, the later conjures up a more exciting image of warriors being driven around battlefields. The excavators of the Arras burials in 1815–17 had no doubt that they were 'British chariots' of the same kind referred to by Julius Caesar and the Roman historian Tacitus, which played a key role in warfare at this time. It is interesting to note that Stead (1991) prefers to use the term 'cart' as did Dent (1985), though a decade later returning to the term chariot throughout his PhD thesis (Dent 1995). Anthoons (2011, 2) is in no doubt as to their nomenclature: 'Chariot is a much more appropriate word, since the term cart does not really do justice to the decorated vehicle parts and colourful harnesses discovered in the burials.'

As most of the organic material has decayed, it is difficult to deduce how these vehicles functioned. Historical descriptions, portrayals in ancient art and sculptures provide some clues. Careful excavation of those found since 1971 (Table 2) has provided a context for the various fittings of metal, bone and antler. It has been possible to reconstruct some wooden elements due to mineralisation where wood has decayed

Fig. 17 Garton Station chariot burial, 1985. Note the wheels stacked at the side of the grave next to the pole. The harness was laid out to the left of the corpse, only the metal fittings such as the terrets survive. (V. Fell)

close to metal items such as iron tyres, or where the voids created by rotting wood have allowed casts to be made. Stillingfleet (1846) identified the wood still adhering to the iron tyres of the 'King's Barrow' (Plate 14) as oak; the felloes (sections that make up the rim) of the wheels from Garton Station (Fig. 17) (Stead 1991), which were found leaning against the wall of the grave, block-lifted and excavated in laboratory conditions, were of ash. Generally the wheels had twelve spokes and were held in place on the axle by a linch-pin made variously of antler, bronze, iron, or iron cased in copper alloy. The terminals of linch-pins were sometimes highly decorated as in the case of Kirkburn, which had a triskele pattern on its cast copper-alloy end.

From excavations at Garton-Wetwang Slack (Brewster 1971; Stead 1991) it was believed that the key structural element of the vehicle was a pole joined to an axle to form a T shape, which supported a box-like superstructure visible as a soil mark, though Mackey (2005) has argued that this superstructure or 'platform' was not fixed rigidly but fastened in some way in front of the axle. It has also been proposed that this box may have served as a coffin or the carriage from which the vehicle was driven. There is some evidence that it was detachable, and at Wetwang Slack (Dent 1985) it was suggested that the box had been removed and inverted tortoise-shell like over the whole burial. More recent excavations at Wetwang village (Plate 13) (Hill 2002; Mackey 2005) and Ferry Fryston (Boyle 2004; Brown et al. 2007) have provided details that had not been observed elsewhere. At Ferry Fryston decayed material, almost certainly leather, showed that in this case, the superstructure had a curved front (Brown et al. 2007, 144). During the excavation of the Wetwang village burial, fittings were found which were interpreted as showing that the vehicle may have been sprung in some way, an idea which was tested in reconstructions for several TV programmes including *Meet the Ancestors* for BBC2. The reconstructions also showed that the vehicles could be easily adapted for various purposes supporting descriptions of the different uses of chariots in early Irish literature (Karl 2003).

Other items of harness were also included in the burials, usually arranged in a set pattern. The organic elements of the yoke had decayed, leaving behind the terrets through which the reins would have passed to the bridles. At Garton-Wetwang the yoke lay north-south on the west side of the grave in all cases, but not in the Wetwang village burial. Unlike the rest of the Wetwang burials, the woman at Wetwang village was not laid over the wheels but on some kind of organic platform to the south of them.

Like the linch-pins, the terrets were often highly decorated, and examples from Wetwang Slack, and Wetwang village embellished with coral from the Mediterranean, which is now white, but was once pinky red. At Garton Slack (Brewster 1971) red chalk was used in imitation of coral and at Wetwang village an inlay of red glass enamel was used to replace one of coral. What was particularly interesting about this example was the use of birch-bark tar as glue to hold the inlay (Stacey 2004). Five of the other chariots also have some evidence for repair, which implies their use for a considerable time before burial.

The horse bits were mainly of three link or double-jointed snaffle type which allows direct control on the horse's mouth, and at Arras, Stillingfleet (1846) commented on their modern appearance, familiar at a time when horse-drawn transport and riding were still the main means of travel. They were generally made of iron encased in copper alloy. Some harness fittings were clearly made as a set by the same craftsman as they share motifs and styles. This is particularly noticeable on the Garton Station terrets and linch-pins (Stead 1991). At Wetwang Slack it is interesting to note that of the three chariot burials the woman's burial has the most highly decorated harness fittings.

Apart from the harness fittings, several chariot burials included unusual objects. At Kirkburn (Stead 1991) a mail shirt which may be one of the earliest in Europe, was draped upside down over the corpse. The woman in Wetwang Slack Chariot burial 2 (Plate 11b) was buried with the so-called 'bean-tin', a canister of copper alloy closed at both ends, decorated with La Tène curvilinear engraving around the cylinder, and red enamel on a roundel on the 'lid' (Dent 1985). It was attached to a chain and was probably worn around the waist, possibly as an item of status, though its precise function remains unknown. There is a close similarity between the engraving on the 'bean-tin' and that on the sword-sheaths in the two male burials which may be the work of a single craftsman.

Other objects found in the female burials at Wetwang in 1984 and 2001 and Arras, also imply that, at least superficially, some women within the region may have possessed an equal or even a higher status to men, if the correlation between high-quality grave goods and a social elite is to be accepted. As well as possessing harness fittings of superior quality in terms of decoration and workmanship, when compared with those accompanying the two males, the woman from Wetwang Slack (Dent 1985) was buried with one of only two gold items yet found in middle Iron Age East Yorkshire, an iron dress pin of involuted type which had been decorated with a piece of coral held in place by a gold strip. The rarity of gold at this time in Britain as a whole has been noted elsewhere (Creighton 2000). The other item was not from a chariot burial, but the burial of a woman, the so-called 'Queen's Barrow' (Plate 15) described by Stillingfleet (1846) as having been under a small round barrow around 90cm high, excavated in September 1816. The grave itself was only 30cm deep. Originally thought to be a ring by the excavators and later by Canon Greenwell, it has been reinterpreted (Jope 1995, 114) as part of an elaborate combined pendant and necklace with festoons of over 100 glass beads with clear continental parallels. A flamboyant brooch also decorated with coral was found in this burial along with a copper-alloy disc with a central sandstone setting surrounded by pieces of coral (Stead 1979).

OTHER BURIALS

The Queen's Barrow at Arras is one of the richest burials from a group who may also represent the upper echelons of society. Close to the Kirkburn chariot burial, surrounded by a small circular rather than a square ditch, was a male (K3) aged seventeen to twenty-five accompanied by what has been called one of the finest swords in Iron Age Europe (Fig.18; Plate 19) (Stead 1991).

The handle of the sword was lavishly decorated with red enamel, and the sheath engraved with a curvilinear design similar to that on the Wetwang scabbards. This was a Type C burial with pig bones which had been carefully arranged on the corpse. Perhaps the most surprising aspect of this burial was the discovery of three spearheads point down, above the lower rib cage of its occupant. This is an example of one of the most bizarre aspects of Arras culture burials, the spearing of corpses referred to above.

This phenomenon had been recognised at Garton Station in burial GS10, where six spears had been driven into the corpse and the other twelve scattered around (Stead 1991). Again in burial GS7, eleven spearheads were found; four had been driven into the waist, one in the chest, with three around the skeleton and three still standing vertically

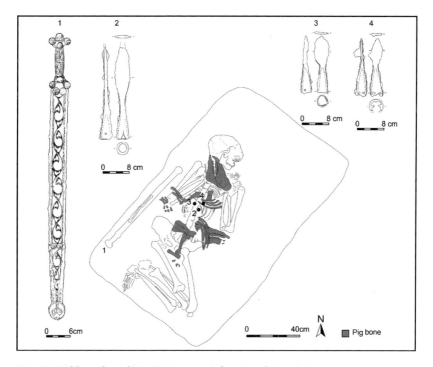

Fig. 18 Kirkburn burial K3. T. Sparrow (after Stead 1991). Courtesy Trustees British Museum)

in the grave fill. It is clear that a graveside ritual had taken place in which spears were hurled at the corpse, a custom repeated at Rudston. In Wetwang Chariot burial 1, seven spears seemed to have been laid, rather than hurled onto the body and some are unlikely to have fitted into the grave with complete shafts. This young man was no stranger to violence as recent examination shows that he had suffered a heavy blow on the head, possibly from an axe which had left a 30.9mm Y-shaped wound on the back of his head, removing some bone, and his right humerus had been broken in several places; both wounds had healed (King 2010, 122).

What did this spear-throwing ritual mean? Is it an example of ritual killing to ensure, Dracula-style, that the corpse would remain dead? Was it a form of tribute equivalent to that in which mourners throw a handful of soil onto a coffin today, with warriors filing past the open grave and hurling in their spears, equivalent to a rifle volley in a military-style funeral today? We will never know the answer, but the identification of this ritual has cast a vivid light on life and death in Iron Age East Yorkshire. Like dismantled chariot burials, the speared corpse ritual seems to have been restricted geographically.

A number of the spears embedded in these corpses were not there as a result of the spearing ritual but of combat, for example Rudston burial R152 had been stabbed from behind. In R94 a spear had penetrated from the back to the right of the spine (Stead 1991). Evidence for violent trauma on the skeletons of the dead of Iron Age East Yorkshire has been found at Wetwang Slack on a number of other individuals including a young man probably killed by a sword cut on the back lower right of his cranium (King 2010, 310) and Acklam where a thirty to forty-year-old male had suffered blows from a sword or similar weapon on the left-hand side and back of his cranium, at or near the time of death (Dent 1983; King 2010, 239). He was buried with a sword that had been ritually bent.

This again raises the issue of warfare in Iron Age society; in the previous decade or so it had become fashionable to play down the warlike nature of the Iron Age society (e.g. Hill 1996) despite copious references to warfare in the accounts of the classical authors. The term 'warrior burial' has also been criticised (Collis 1994), the preferred term being 'burials with weapons', though the balance has to some extent begun to swing towards greater acknowledgement of the violence of Iron Age society (James 2007). Present in all the regional traditions of Iron Age Britain (Fitzpatrick 2007), with eleven to the south of the Humber with the largest concentration in East Yorkshire, the military aspects of weapons burials have also been underplayed. It has been argued for example that chariot burials are little more than the interments of rich farmers (Collis 2004). It is true that much of the wealth and status of the people represented by such burials may have been related to agriculture and landownership in some way, as Iron Age society was primarily agrarian, but this does not prevent at least some of them from being warriors as well. In the later Middle Ages military service and land ownership were closely related, and was indeed a key part of the feudal system. On the other hand it would seem that many of those portrayed on medieval monumental brasses and other tombs in full armour may never have fought a battle, their dress symbolic of their status.

The age profile of those buried with swords is worth noting: of the twelve males with swords from Kirkburn, Garton Station and Rudston with sufficient skeletal material present to determine their age at death, six fell in the seventeen to twenty-five age group, six in the twenty-five to thirty-five range and only one, R107, was over forty-five (Stead 1991). In Britain as a whole, most sword burials where an age is stated (Whimster 1981) were in a similar age range, although the male at Owslebury was aged forty to fifty.

Perhaps an analogy may be made with the so-called 'Warrior burials' of the Anglo-Saxon period in the fifth to eighth centuries AD (Härke 1990). Archaeological and skeletal evidence shows that the rite of weapon burial in the Anglo-Saxon period was probably a symbolic act and the deceased may not always have been a warrior but conferred with 'warrior status' by the inclusion of weapons. Unlike the East Yorkshire examples (Stead 1991) where the occupants of almost all the weapon graves were of an appropriate age to bear arms, the Anglo-Saxons buried with weapons ranged in age from twelve months to sixty years (Härke 1990) and were weak and strong, including spina bifida victims (Härke 1990, 126). Härke did notice, however, that those with swords tended to be taller than average. There is as yet not enough information to make such correlations in Iron Age East Yorkshire.

At Garton Station the average height of males was 1.7m (5ft 7in) and females 1.63m (5ft 4in) (Stead 1991). At Wetwang Slack the average height of adult males was 1.67m (5ft 6in), and adult females 1.56m (5ft 1½in) (Dent 1995, 52). This compares with mean heights Maiden Castle at the 1.65 (5ft 5in) for men and 1.52m (4ft 11in) for women (Stead 1991). The reasons for the greater average height of people in the Yorkshire burials, especially those at Garton Station, may be better diet, as the grave goods here suggested that they were of higher status. They were certainly in a much better state of health than many of the people at Danebury whose skeletons show that they suffered from various vitamin deficiencies (Cunliffe 2003). As would be expected in such societies, there was a peak in female deaths in the age range seventeen to twenty-five in the East Yorkshire burials as a result of complications in childbirth. In a grave at Kirkburn for example, a young woman (K6) was buried with a newborn child below a woman with the remains of a foetus. (Stead 1991, 39). Infant burial in cemeteries was rare in East Yorkshire but are relatively common on Iron Age settlement sites such as Hayton (Halkon and Millett 2003).

Various scientific techniques have revealed fascinating information from examination of skeletal remains. For example at Wetwang (Jay and Richards 2005) analysis of carbon and nitrogen isotopes from sixty-two individuals revealed a high animal protein intake with little evidence for the consumption of seafood. There were no differences between the higher-status burials and the rest of the cemetery population. Some of the older males displayed a trend towards more nitrogen and less carbon, though no explanation is given for this. Two adults also stood out from the rest, though the idea they came from outside the region has been discounted until further research can be done. A combination of the isotope analysis and identification of the animal bones themselves shows that the favoured meat was young pig and the careful positioning of selective joints of meat within burials has already been referred to. Most remarkably, perhaps, analysis of the isotopes in the bones of infants from Wetwang showed that breastfeeding was restricted in comparison with the populations from archaeological sites elsewhere (Jay *et al.* 2008).

Human remains from burials can provide clues as to facial appearance. As far as the author is aware, only the woman in the Wetwang Village burial has had her face reconstructed as part of the *Meet the Ancestors* TV programme for BBC2, but there is some dispute as to what she looked in life. The reconstruction for the TV programme showed the two sides of her face as being unequal and according to one specialist she had a mark on her cheek as a result of ahaemangioma. Others, however (Mackey pers. comm.), disagree and the distortion may be as a result of compression of the earth on the skull after burial. The woman would, however, have been very striking as at 1.75m (5ft 9in) she was one of the tallest people yet found in any burial in Iron Age East Yorkshire. She had injuries to her shoulder and the jaw suggestive of a bad fall, perhaps from a chariot (Hill 2002).

As far as dress is concerned, textiles have been preserved where they have become mineralised by the corrosion of iron objects. On the underside of the folded mail tunic in the Kirkburn chariot burial, textile remains showed that the deceased had been wearing a tunic or a gown down to the knees and some kind of outer garment, possibly a cloak, and both garments were in a fine weave (Crowfoot 1991, 122–23). At Burton Fleming, a fragment of cloth, probably the remains of a stole or cloak, had been wrapped around the iron brooch from a male burial (Crowfoot 1991) which had a border with a diamond twill. Mineralised textile shows that tabby weaves were also used.

Normally the only clues concerning costume are accessories in copper alloy and iron such as ring-headed pins, generally used from the eighth to the third centuries BC, and were then replaced by brooches. Iron Age brooches from Wetwang and other East Yorkshire cemeteries have recently been reassessed (Jay *et al.* 2012). The earliest of these were arched bow brooches, of the so-called Marzabotto type from Cowlam dated to the fourth century BC and a related type from Burton Fleming in a style which developed in Britain. The replacement of the pin of the former has been taken to show that it was an heirloom and may have already been old when it was placed in the grave. Although inspired by continental examples, brooches developed insular forms, becoming progressively flatter through time, possibly indicting that cloth which they held together became thinner or less pleated (James and Rigby 1997). Some brooches were decorated with coral, now white but once red, or with enamel. Strings of glass and amber beads were also worn and may well have been a mark of status, such as the example found in the 'Queen's Barrow' at Arras (Stead 1979) (Plate 15). It has been suggested that colour was important in all dress accessories as well as in decoration of weapons and other items such as the Kirkburn sword, particularly red (Giles 2008).

SUMMARY

Eastern Yorkshire is marked out from the rest of Iron Age Britain as it contains the greatest concentration of square barrows and is also distinctive for its tradition of chariot burials and the speared corpses. The population may also have been slightly taller than the average for other parts of Iron Age Britain, though the reasons for these differences are by no means clear. Square barrows and chariot burials may well have been continental in origin, but seem, like the decoration of artefacts, brooch forms and chariot burials, to have been locally adapted. It is interesting to note, however, that some of the most recent burials with weapons to be found in Iron Age Britain at Brisley Farm in Kent (Stevenson and Johnson 2004) were both surrounded by square ditches, one containing half a pig's head, like those from East Yorkshire. Unlike any of the East Yorkshire examples, however, they contained wheel-thrown pottery vessels of continental origin dating from the late first century BC to early first century AD. Perhaps these were the last in a long line of immigrants, endorsing the comment of Julius Caesar (*Gallic Wars*, 12) referred to in the introduction concerning the origins of Britons in the maritime regions.

The chances of finding a buried immigrant population are slight, but by no means impossible, as the oxygen isotope analysis of the Bronze Age Amesbury archer has shown he was a migrant into the region where he died (Fitzpatrick 2011). It is interesting to note that his burial contained some of the earliest gold and copper artefacts yet found in Britain. His burial also contained some of the earliest Beakers and serves as a reminder that people moved around in prehistory and may have brought innovations with them – perhaps there may be comparisons here with the Arras culture. This is, however, complicated by the fact that the earliest square barrows had no central graves and therefore the chance of finding any dating evidence is slight. The 'Queen's Barrow' at Arras excavated in 1816 was interred in a grave that was only 30cm deep, under a mound less than a metre high, and is unlikely to have survived a modern agricultural regime.

Recent reassessment of the East Yorkshire burials in comparison with the near continent suggests close similarities, particularly in the Paris area. The tyres in East Yorkshire were shrunk onto the wooden wheel felloes, a technique which is standard in the Paris region and never nailed, like earlier continental examples. Unlike the earliest known British chariot burial from Newbridge, which has four terrets, those from East Yorkshire have five, which is also attested in the Paris region (Anthoons 2011). Pottery which is absent in East Yorkshire chariot burials is also very rare in the Paris region, though when it does occur, is impressive in quantity and quality. There are some dismantled chariots around Paris as well, and although generally laid out in an extended posture, many of the burials are aligned south-north (those in East Yorkshire are north-south) rather than the east-west of the Aisne-Marne region (Anthoons 2011). There are, however, differences as well. There are no speared corpse burials anywhere apart from East Yorkshire. Around Paris burials with weapons contain a full set, rather than one or two pieces and perhaps most importantly, the square barrows so common in eastern Yorkshire are absent around Paris, though present in the Champagne and elsewhere in northern France (Anthoons 2011).

Why did chariot burials containing 'shrunken' tyres appear almost simultaneously around Paris and East Yorkshire? One explanation was the emergence of the Parisii in France, who according to Caesar (*Gallic Wars* 6:3) had once been part of the Senones, though the precise date of this split depends on the translation of *patrum memoria* as being a generation (Handford 1976, 163) or forefathers (Anthoons 2011, 156). This flamboyant burial rite has been interpreted as an affirmation of this new regime (Marion 2007, 106). The application of new techniques of radiocarbon dating shows that the Wetwang chariot burials began in 255–195 Cal BC (95 per cent probability) or between 225–200 Cal BC (68 per cent probability) and only lasted for one to seventy years (95 per cent probability) or one to twenty-five years (68 per cent probability), ending around 210–165 Cal BC (95 per cent probability) or 210–185 Cal BC (68 per cent probability) (Jay *et al.* 2012, 181). If *patrum* means father in the literal sense, then there can be no direct relationship between Caesar's account and East Yorkshire radiocarbon dates. This does become possible if *patrum memoria* refers to ancestral memory. The new dating system makes it possible to think in almost historical terms about the meaning and origins of the burials of the Arras culture, though more dates are needed from other burials before firmer conclusions can be reached. There is still a considerable time lag between Newbridge and the East Yorkshire chariots, however.

Reference to Caesar reminds us of the existence of tribes and chiefs. It is tempting to see the richer burials at Arras, Danes Graves and Wetwang as belonging to elite groups. The chariot burial cluster in Garton-Wetwang Slack, contrasts with their absence in the Great Wold Valley, with its wealth of earlier ritual monuments, despite the presence of many square barrows. This may also signify some kind of political change and a break with the past (Dent 1995 and 2010). Unlike Caesar's Gauls, however, we will never know the names of those buried at Wetwang. Having considered the burials and the information that can be gained from studying them, the next chapter will examine the settlements of the Arras period and their relationship to the landscape of eastern Yorkshire.

CHAPTER 5

SETTLEMENT AND ECONOMY IN IRON AGE EASTERN YORKSHIRE

The landscape of East Yorkshire as outlined in Chapter 2 can be divided into distinctive regions, based on topography, soils and drainage and water supply, all key factors within an agriculturally based society. The fertility and drainage qualities of the soil and the topography of the landscape itself determine how the land can be used, either for pastoral or arable farming, or a combination of both, and water is needed to sustain humans and animals. What does the archaeological evidence tell us about where people lived within this landscape and how they supported themselves?

Unlike the upland areas of Britain, where settlements built with stone can still be seen above the ground surface, we are almost completely reliant on cropmark data, or chance discoveries leading to excavation for information about the Iron Age settlements of East Yorkshire, as they were made almost entirely of earth and timber and other organic remains which do not survive today. On excavation, the only traces remaining are ditches, banks, post holes and gullies which have been dug into the subsoil. The settlement types of the late Bronze Age and early Iron Age have been discussed already. In many ways the settlements of the middle Iron Age should be seen as a continuous development from the earlier period, as in the case of Wetwang Slack (Dent 1995; 2010), though there does seem to be an element of change through time in the morphology of settlements and the design of houses.

HOUSES

Iron Age East Yorkshire houses, like their Bronze Age predecessors, were almost always circular, hence 'roundhouses' as they are better known. Houses have been categorised into various types based on their method of construction. Earlier examples such as those from Staple Howe tended to be based on rings of posts, either double or single. Sometimes the posts made up the walls of the building, with an inner ring of posts holding the roof supports. In other cases the houses were constructed with a circular or penannular foundation trench, with various arrangements of postholes for internal features, doorways and porches (Figs 19 and 20).

This type of house tends to be later than those with ring-post construction. Sometimes circular gullies collected water from the conical roofs of the houses, often known as eaves drips. Excavation suggests that those with a double ring of posts are earliest.

Fig. 19 The roundhouse at Burnby Lane, Hayton, under excavation. (P. Halkon)

Fig. 20 Reconstruction of the roundhouse at Burnby Lane, Hayton. (M. Faulkner)

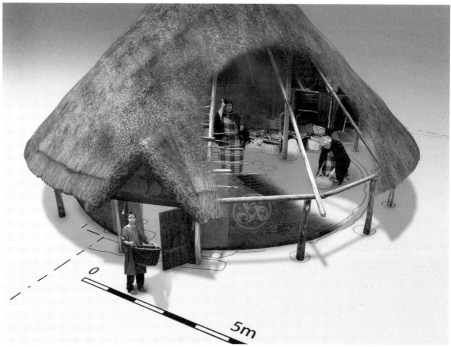

Houses with single rings of posts seem to have made an appearance from the middle of the first millenium BC, though it is clear that double-ringed buildings continued in use. Some of the earliest of these were at Wetwang Slack (Dent 1995; 2010). At Garton and Wetwang the majority of the houses were between 6.5m to 9.5m in diameter and most had their entrance in the south-east. It is probable, as has been explained above, that the Thwing house was of special status or had some ceremonial function. Smaller double-ring houses 7.5m in diameter have been identified at West Heslerton (Powlesland 2003(a) and (b)), dated by Staple Howe-type pottery.

As elsewhere in Britain the houses tend to be built of the most easily available materials, which in the case of East Yorkshire tends to be timber, wattle and daub. Stone was used in the construction of the roundhouses at Staple Howe discussed earlier. Occasionally daub is preserved, especially where it has been burnt and turned ceramic and sometimes the impressions of the wood used in construction are visible. At Sewerby, part of the clay walls of three roundhouses remained intact (Steedman 1991), which is a rare occurrence. It is important to note that one of these had neither a foundation trench, nor postholes for uprights; it would therefore be very difficult to detect the remains of these houses by any method other than excavation. It has been shown by experimentation (Reynolds 1979) that even quite substantial houses can be constructed on the ground surface which would leave little or no trace. This is why so-called open settlements, particularly those comprising roundhouses with post rather than ring-gulley foundations, are much more difficult to find from the air than those with enclosure ditches around them. However, even those houses which had no earth-fast posts would have taken up considerable resources. It has been shown from the reconstruction of Iron Age houses at Little Butser in Hampshire, for example, that to construct a roundhouse with a double ring of posts 12.8m in diameter, such as the Pimperne House, based on an excavation in Dorset (Reynolds 1979, 100), would have needed the timber from 200 trees, the round wood from over eighty coppiced hazel stools to use in the walls and around 4 tonnes of straw for thatch. It is, however, more likely that in the Foulness Valley especially, where there was easy access to wetland resources, reeds rather than straw were used. In the reconstructions of roundhouses built at Castell Henllys, for example, 2,000 bundles of reeds were required to thatch one of the roofs (Bennett 2001). Experimentation has shown that a carefully constructed conical roof will carry a great deal of weight and once constructed the walls can be replaced with no difficulty (Reynolds 1979). In order to sustain such construction, woodland management must have been carried out, if not, large-scale clearance would have had a considerable impact on the landscape. Changes in the style of houses from double to single ring may have been due to the shortage of trees, which would have been further exacerbated by growing populations.

Because of the fact that so few of the floors of Iron Age roundhouses in Yorkshire survive, it is extremely difficult to work out how people lived within them, or indeed whether all roundhouses were inhabited by people rather than animals. There have been various attempts to interpret distributions of finds, post holes and gullies as indicating the location of activities within them, some arguing that it is possible to determine this using largely ethnographic parallels and factors such as the positioning of doorways. Most roundhouses have their entrances facing east or south-east, which would provide some shelter from the westerly wind and allow the morning sun to shine into the house. At Wetwang, for example, discovery of loom weights on the floor immediately to the north of the door suggests that weaving may have been undertaken here, taking advantage of the location in the house with the most light (Dent 1995; 2010). Others have argued that the positioning of doorways was related to cosmography, custom and ritual, with certain parts of houses being reserved for males and females for example (Oswald 1991). This has been suggested in the case of the remarkably well-preserved Bronze Age and Iron Age houses at Cladh Hallan, South Uist in the Hebrides (Parker-Pearson *et al.* 2007), which have provided a fascinating insight into life in roundhouses, although a note of caution is needed in comparing the Western Isles to eastern Yorkshire. It is argued that daily life was influenced by the movement of the sun around the houses, with east-facing doorways, sleeping areas on a low turf platform on the north side, and during the day cooking and other domestic activities were undertaken only on the south side. The houses at Cladh Hallan had remained in occupation for 600 years with the floors being re-laid on eight occasions. Ritual pits with offerings including mummified human bodies and animals were buried beneath floors. A small house with a west-facing door and no hearth was thought to be for ritual purposes.

Out of all the roundhouses at Garton-Wetwang Slack only four were enclosed. A roundhouse containing internal pits in Garton Slack Area 14 was enclosed by a narrow ditch and palisade. Finds included penannular brooches and a glass bead inside the house and a bronze bracelet from a pit outside the enclosure (Dent 1995). At Wetwang Slack in Area 9 there was a double-ring house with associated pits in an enclosure *c.* 31m by 25m which had its entrance on the east side. A later burial was cut into the house. In Area 11 an irregular enclosure *c.* 76m by 70m with a 2m-wide entrance contained two roundhouses and a four post structure with an internal hearth which may be a smithy. The palisade was eventually replaced for most of its length by a ditch. A recut of the enclosure ditch contained Romano-British pottery and earlier material, including mould fragments for chariot and harness fittings (Dent 1995). The fact that these houses were selected for enclosure may have some ritual significance, marking them out from the rest of the settlement, though this would be very difficult to prove and a recent study of roundhouses has shown that some of the ideas about their ritual aspects can no longer be sustained (Pope 2007).

SETTLEMENT TYPES

Many settlements in East Yorkshire probably consisted of unenclosed groups of roundhouses or 'open settlements'. One of the largest yet excavated at Wetwang Slack contained eighty roundhouses extending along the valley for over 1.3km (Fig. 21).

These houses were not randomly situated and the whole settlement appears to have been deliberately laid out in various activity zones, with an area set aside for burial. Many crafts such as the processing of wool, spinning and weaving took place here, as bone combs, spindle whorls and loom weights are common finds. It is likely that some of the post holes associated with roundhouses were the settings for upright looms. The fact that the same types of finds including brooches, metal pins and a glass bead are found in the square barrow cemetery, show that they were contemporary (Dent 1983; 1995; 2010). Pits were found within and around the houses and four and five-post structures which are generally interpreted as granaries with evidence for the burrowing of small mammals around their bases (Dent 1995, 2010).

Open settlements such as Wetwang can be difficult to spot from the air but one such example was recognised at Rillington (Dent 1982). At Garton-Wetwang enclosure was a gradual feature and by the later Iron Age, most of the settlements in Iron Age East Yorkshire were enclosed in some way. One of the classic forms in the north of England (Haselgrove 1982) were single rectilinear enclosures, of which West Brandon, County Durham (Jobey 1962), is a good example. Excavations here revealed two phases of activity; an almost square bank and ditch enclosed the foundations of two roundhouses, the earliest consisting of a ring of posts, while its replacement was constructed with continuous ring-ditch foundations. A further example of such a site is at Bursea Grange, Holme-on-Spalding Moor (Fig. 22) (Riley 1982, figs 28, 34; Halkon and Millett 1999, 67 and 37 illus 2.18).

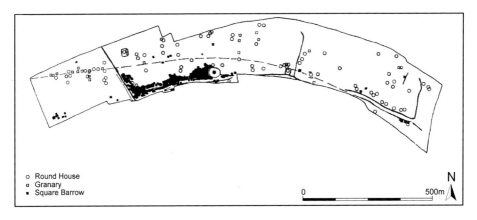

o Round House
□ Granary
▪ Square Barrow

0   500m

N

Fig. 21 Plan of the Wetwang Slack settlement (after Dent).

Two phases of activity were apparent from the aerial photograph and confirmed by excavation (Halkon and Millett 1999). The earlier phase consisted of a large enclosure with a narrow palisade and a sub-rectangular post hole building. This was replaced by an almost square ditched enclosure containing a large roundhouse 17.5m in diameter. The lack of finds here makes dating difficult, though phase 2 may date from the middle Iron Age, with Structure 1 and Ditch 1 representing an earlier phase (Halkon and Millett 1999, 71). Caution is, however, needed in dating all such rectilinear enclosure to this period (Stoertz 1997) as excavation of similar sites on the Yorkshire Wolds has provided evidence of occupation extending well into the Roman period (Mackey, pers. comm.; Dent 1995; Rigby 2004).

There seems to be a close relationship between the form of settlements and the landscape. The biggest concentration of single rectilinear enclosures in East Yorkshire is in the area between the River Foulness and the Yorkshire Wolds, where enclosure ditches were necessary for drainage in an area with a high water table (Dent 1995). At Bursea Grange (Halkon and Millett 1999), the 2.1m-wide and 0.75m-deep ditch and the wide ring gulley around the house were designed principally to keep the interior dry. Where enclosure entrances were visible, they seem to relate to watercourses.

Fig. 22 Crop mark of the Bursea Grange settlement. Note the relict stream channel at the top of the picture. (P. Halkon)

There are slight differences in the shape of the single rectilinear enclosures; an example from Hasholme Hall (Halkon and Millett 1999, 36, fig. 2.17) has more rounded corners, while others were squarer. Enclosures ranged in area from 0.06 to 0.9ha with the majority below 0.5ha. Stoertz, when referring to the Danebury Environs project in Hampshire (Stoertz 1997, 51 quoting Palmer 1984, 27), notes that 'plots of this size would comfortably accommodate a family vegetable garden'. In the Foulness Valley research area, all single rectilinear enclosures were situated on either sand or Brown Earths and those on wider expanses of sandy soil sometimes had associated field systems. In the Hull Valley similar enclosures containing single roundhouses have also been recognised from the air at Burshill near Leven, located on a sand and gravel rise not far from the River Hull itself. Unlike the Bursea Grange site, however, on excavation the enclosure ditch here was found to contain substantial amounts of mid- to later Iron Age pottery (Coates 2007).

Other roughly contemporary Hull Valley settlements (Fig. 23) contain features which are clearly designed to cope with poor drainage, such as the combination of unenclosed roundhouses and those surrounded with curvilinear enclosures, at Creyke Beck, Cottingham (Fig. 23a) (Evans and Steedman 2001).

This settlement consisted of seven roundhouses, some of them having penannular or circular ditches constructed around the houses to provide extra drainage. A number of Iron Age settlements excavated along the route of the Easington to Paull natural gas pipeline, such as Site 6 south of Welwick and Patrington Haven, were clearly designed for wet conditions and palaeo-environmental analysis has confirmed that there was standing water in the ditches at certain times in antiquity (Rowland 2012). Similar landscape constraints affected settlement form and location elsewhere in south Holderness and there were Iron Age settlements with roundhouses at Ellerby, near Burton Constable, Burstwick, Halsham, and Skeffling, discovered during pre-construction excavation for the Asselby to Easington pipeline (Daniel *et al.* forthcoming).

The settlement at Saltshouse Road, Hull (Fig. 23c) (Didsbury 1990; Challis and Harding 1975) had a similar arrangement of features, consisting of curvilinear drainage trenches and three or possibly four roundhouses, which unusually still contained central hearths. Such adaptation for damp conditions can also be seen in the settlement of cellular and open roundhouses at Dryham, North Cave, in the Foulness Valley (Fig. 23b)(Dent 1989). What appeared to be refuse in the form of pottery and bone was thrown into the ends of the ditches nearest to the house door, behaviour which has been interpreted as deliberate deposition relating to some form of ritual (Hill 1995) rather than simply waste disposal, although as we have seen in the case of roundhouses, some authorities are more sceptical. The anaerobic conditions at North Cave (Dent 1989) resulted in the preservation of organic remains, particularly a wooden rake and what is probably part of a yoke. These were found in a waterhole and had been reused as steps.

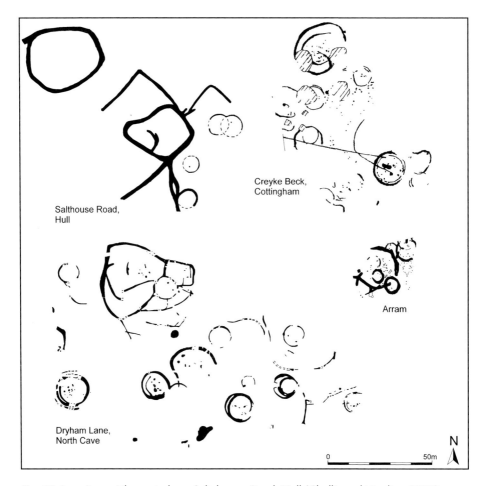

Fig. 23 Iron Age settlement plans. Saltshouse Road, Hull (Challis and Harding 1978) Creyke Beck, Cottingham (Evans and Steadman 2011, 68) Dryham Lane, North Cave (Dent 1989) Arram (Myres 2010). All these settlements were adapted for wet conditions (T. Sparrow)

At Lingcroft Farm, Naburn, also in the Vale of York (Jones 1988), single rectilinear enclosures 1,200m square containing roundhouses, around 15m in diameter, also appear to have been designed with drainage in mind, with broad penannular eaves, drip gullies and enclosure ditches. Although the acidic sandy soil resulted in very poor preservation of bone, charred deposits in Building 1 preserved the remains of club wheat/bread wheat and barley.

The Iron Age settlement discovered at Heslington East (O'Connor *et al.* 2011) during the construction of the new York University campus resembled Bursea Grange, with a roundhouse positioned inside a ditched enclosure, with an associated field system.

A further cluster of ring gullies lay in an enclosure immediately to the south. Located where a number of palaeochannels and springs flowed out of the terminal moraine upon which the present city developed, the site had attracted human activity since the Mesolithic and a series of waterholes dating from the Bronze Age may have had some kind of ceremonial purpose. A headless red deer had been placed in a palaeochannel during the Iron Age and a series of pits had been dug to the north of the main enclosure, one of which contained the skull of a male with the mandible still articulated. Aged twenty-six to forty-five, he had been been hanged and his head carefully severed with a knife and placed in a pit face down. Most remarkably brain tissue was preserved inside his cranium, a very rare survival. Radiocarbon dates of 673–482 BC (OxA-20677) obtained from collagen make this one of the oldest surviving brains in Europe. DNA analysis suggested that he may have been of haplogroup J1d, a branch of the human family tree first seen in modern DNA sequences in just a few individuals from Tuscany and the Near East, not yet found elsewhere in Britain (O'Connor *et al.* 2011, 1643).

Contrasting with the settlement forms of the lowlands are the linear enclosure complexes or 'ladder settlements', as they are usually known, their subdividing ditches resembling the rungs of a ladder (Fig. 24). These are most dense around the Great Wold Valley and eastern slopes of the Yorkshire Wolds (Stoertz 1997, 66, Fig. 34). Dent (1995, 20) calls them droveway settlements, and writes that they appear so comparable to medieval settlements in their composition that the term '"village" would seem to be appropriate'.

Excavation and remote sensing as part of the Heslerton Parish project in the Vale of Pickering has revealed a linear enclosure complex running east-west for many kilometres that may have been continuously occupied from around 500 BC to AD 500 (Powlesland 2003(a) and (b); Atha 2007). It is important to note that although vestigial cropmarks were visible, the full extent of this feature could only be appreciated after extensive geophysical survey. There is, therefore, the possibility of good subsurface preservation in some places.

Within the Foulness Valley linear enclosure complexes range in length from 100m to 2.6km (Halkon 2008) and Dent (1995) records thirteen over 1km in length in the Wolds area. Although superimposition and inter-cutting makes it difficult to count the number of enclosures which go to make up this settlement type, in the Foulness Valley study area the number ranged between one and ninety, with 86 per cent having less than twenty. The enclosures themselves range in area from 0.08ha to 0.53ha with 83 per cent falling within the range 0.08 to 0.2ha. This is very similar to the area of the single rectilinear enclosures. The fact that these complexes ran over long distances shows that large stretches of land were cleared, the rolling chalk countryside allowing settlements to develop uninterrupted. There are some linear enclosure settlements on the lowlands of the Foulness Valley study area, such as at Arglam, near Holme-on-Spalding Moor,

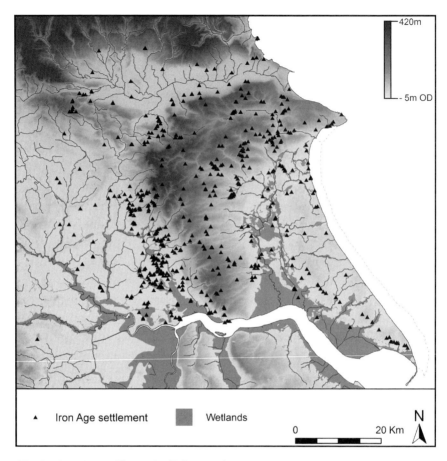

Fig. 24 Iron Age settlements. (T. Sparrow)

where the droveway between the flanking enclosures was almost certainly used to lead livestock up and down to riverside grazing, thus serving as part of a stock management system, though some of the enclosures here contained roundhouses (Halkon 2008).

Linear enclosure complexes might also relate to the intensification of arable agriculture in the later Iron Age (Haselgrove 1984), though Fenton-Thomas (2003), whilst urging the need for caution in interpreting a common function merely from aerial photography, suggests a more theoretical explanation, linking increased land division to transformation in the social and symbolic relationship between people and land. Whilst such ideas are useful in promoting discussion, we do not know what Iron Age people thought. We do know that stock, crops and people need water and the suggestion by Dent (1995) that the enclosures of these settlements may also have been used for keeping stock away from growing crops also seems plausible.

There may be a closer relationship between linear enclosure complexes and square barrows than either the curvilinear or single rectilinear settlement types. A good example of this is at Arras (Fig. 25) where there is a pair of distinctive square barrows and a small round barrow at the northern end of the droveway, with the southern end leading to the centre of the large square barrow cemetery. In North Dalton parish, however, the ditch of an enclosure in a linear enclosure complex clearly cuts a Group1–type square barrow and a sinuous triple linear feature, and is therefore later than both these features. This apparent stratigraphic relationship would seem to confirm Stoertz's (1997) dating of these features to the end of the second century BC continuing throughout the Roman period. A similar sequence can be seen elsewhere such as at Burton Fleming (Stead 1991) where a linear enclosure complex overlies a cemetery of Group 1 and later square barrows.

In the last two decades a number of linear enclosure complexes have been excavated, providing opportunities to establish a better chronology for the development of these settlements. Excavation at Melton (Bishop, 1999; Fenton-Thomas 2011) on the under-explored southern Yorkshire Wolds near the Humber, provided a rare opportunity to disentangle the complex palimpsest of ditched enclosures which form this monument type. Sometime in the mid- to later Iron Age, an east-west trackway leading down towards the Humber cut across the north-south linear earthwork referred to in Chapter 3 (Fenton-Thomas 2011), although the north-south linear boundary retained some significance. A square enclosure was attached to this feature containing a roundhouse, with further roundhouses, pits, and the postholes of other structures to the east of the enclosure (Fenton-Thomas 2011, 346). The square barrow at Melton mentioned previously belongs to this phase of activity, aligned on the north-south linear feature rather than the east-west trackway.

Some linear enclosure complexes display a high degree of uniformity and organisation as at North Dalton, where three square enclosures of the same size are set at regular intervals, on the western side of the droveway. Elsewhere on the Wolds the layout and form of the linear enclosure complexes at Blealands Nook (1.4km), Maiden's Grave Farm (1.0km) and Bell Slack (1.7km) also suggest deliberate planning. Others represent less structured agglomeration of enclosures and despite the equation of linear enclosure complexes with villages, aerial photography reveals few houses within the cropmarks observed. In the Foulness Valley study area, for example, it was possible to identify roundhouses at only five of the forty-six linear enclosure complexes.

At Rudston, however, a ladder settlement predating the Roman villa (Stead 1980) was found to contain roundhouses. The complex at Yapham contained a possible rectilinear building which is likely to relate to Roman phases of occupation, as fieldwork has shown that linear enclosure complexes show intense activity at this period at Wharram Percy (Hayfield 1988), Melton (Bishop 1999) and Wheldrake (Van De Noort and Ellis 1999) for example. It is therefore likely that many of the enclosures which made up

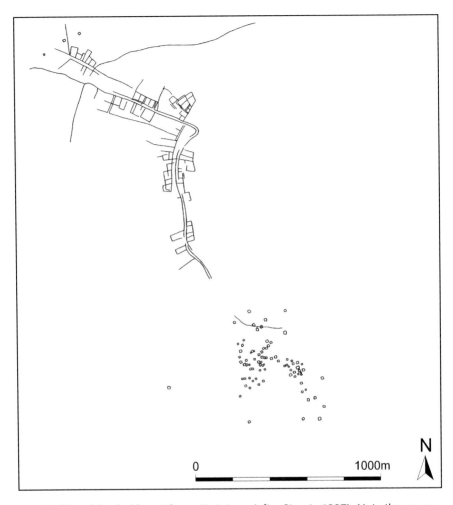

Fig. 25 Plan of the 'ladder settlement' at Arras (after Stoertz 1997). Note the square barrows at each end of the linear enclosure complex.

the linear complexes were for animals. At Wharram Percy Hayfield (1988) suggested that most of the enclosures in the so-called ladders were for agricultural rather than domestic purposes and should therefore be considered as fields, however, excavation of the ladder settlement at Wharram Grange Crossroads showed that pits and ditches contained mid- to late Iron Age pottery and other material associated with settlement (Atha 2007). The evidence from the Wolds and Foulness Valley supports the suggestion that 'some complexes may have been established in a single phase, while it seems that others probably experienced successive periods of expansion, contraction and rebuilding' (Stoertz 1997, 53).

Excavation, geophysical survey and topographical survey have also been undertaken on one of the rare linear enclosure complexes in the Vale of York at Wheldrake 2 (Van De Noort and Ellis 1999) close to the wetlands of the River Derwent and pottery evidence showed Roman activity here from AD 230–370 (Chapman *et al.* 1999, 188).

In the Foulness Valley study area, eight of the forty-six linear complexes appeared to be associated with larger field systems resembling the 'infield-outfield' farming associated with medieval villages (Dent 1995, 23). Good examples of this can be seen at Sancton (Stoertz 1997, 57 fig. 29, 1; Fenn 2002), Middleton (Stoertz 1997, 57 fig. 29, 2) and Londesborough (Stoertz 1997, 57 figs 29, 3). At Londesborough, the droveway of the ladder settlement flares out into a funnel arrangement which may relate to stock management and the movement of cattle. A large complex of linear features and funnelled droveways near Weaverthorpe in the Northern sector of the Yorkshire Wolds featured in the BBC TV programme *Time Flyers* has been interpreted as the remains of:

a highly sophisticated cattle business, rather than small-scale peasant farming. The funnels are thought to have channelled livestock into broad droveways leading down to the settlements along the Gypsey Race, which is still the only reliable water source on the Wolds. The cattle would have been driven back up and out of the funnels to the higher pasture to graze and brought down for water twice a day. We think the funnels are part of a much bigger system stretching over twenty kilometres. (Dave Macleod, English Heritage 2002).

When crop and soil conditions are particularly favourable, there are sites where large numbers of pits have become visible as cropmarks. One of the most remarkable of these is Tuft Hill/West Field Burton Agnes (Rigby 2004) where *c.* 1,000 pits were mainly situated to the south of the Woldgate between two droveway features, covering an area of about 10ha. Woldgate had been the scene of distinctive ceremonial activity since the Neolithic, with two of the Rudston cursuses focussing on a large long enclosure on the south-facing slope and some of Greenwell's richest barrows were also located on this ridge. The pits, therefore, seem to endorse the long-lasting importance of the location (Dent 2010, 55). Twenty-three were excavated and analysis of finds showed that there had been activity on the site since the Neolithic, but was at its most extensive from the early Iron Age into the Roman period (Rigby 2004). Quite why there were so many pits here is not known. No houses could be seen in the immediate vicinity, though they might not have been visible if they were of post-ring construction. The site may have acted as a storage depot for a large area and there may also have been a ritual element involved as it seems likely that structured deposition took place in pits, possibly as some kind of propitiation in return for the safe storage of corn. At Garton Slack, for example, a set of smith's tools (Fig. 28) were found in a pit (Brewster 1980, Halkon 2012) comparing well with the Danebury hill fort (Cunliffe 2003) in Hampshire, where many of the large number of pits contained animals, objects and even parts of humans, which have been interpreted as special deposits.

It is clear that certain locations remained favourable for settlement throughout the Iron Age and these sites appear as palimpsests of cropmark features, which can be categorised as enclosure complexes (Taylor 1999; Halkon 2008). These tend to be more concentrated than the linear enclosures and in the Holme-on-Spalding Moor area appear to be constrained by landscape factors such as soils (Halkon and Millett 1999). The densest concentration of these features is on the sand and gravel to the west of the Yorkshire Wolds, between Market Weighton and South Cave. Excavation here prior to quarrying of sand and gravel has shown almost continuous activity from the Bronze Age to the Roman period (Dent 1989; Halkon 2008; Brigham *et al*. 2008). These settlements enjoyed the benefits of slightly better drainage provided by the sandy soils, but were still close enough to benefit from the wetland resources of the Walling Fen, such as reeds for thatching and wildfowl.

AGRICULTURE

Most settlements in Iron Age eastern Yorkshire related to agriculture in some way and livestock played a very important part in the economy. We have already seen from isotope analysis of human bone from Wetwang Slack that the meat from cattle, sheep and pigs dominated Iron Age diets with avoidance of fish and sea food. Droveways and enclosures were designed to ease the movement of livestock across the landscape, especially to water. In Chapter 3 it was noted that sheep need less water than cattle and drier upland pastures would have provided ideal grazing, however, sheep can be kept successfully in lowland areas (Pryor 1999) such as Foulness Valley (Halkon 2008) and Holderness (Rowland 2012) as well as the Wolds. Mutton or lamb played a more important part of the diet of the poorer members of East Yorkshire society as it is noticeable that Type A burials, the least richly furnished, contain sheep bones (Stead 1991). Pork may have been more favoured by the upper echelons of society, as selected cuts appear in graves of Type C and most of the chariot burials (Chapter 4). It is not clear whether the pigs were wild, semi-wild or completely domesticated, but it is likely that boar hunting took place. Boars are regarded as important in Celtic mythology (Green 1993). Although antler is used in the manufacture of linch-pins for chariots and other items for grooming and domestic use, venison, or indeed wild mammal resources of any kind, appears to have formed a very small component of the Iron Age diet in the region, although it is possible that the number of deer bones have been underestimated (Hawkes and Browning 2004, 80). Alternatively shed antler could have been used for the manufacture of various items.

Horses were certainly important for pulling vehicles including chariots and a pair of complete horse skeletons was found in the King's Barrow at Arras. At Kirkburn two horses were buried in separate graves in their own circular barrows, within a Neolithic long enclosure some way from the chariot burials, immediately east of an Iron Age square enclosure. The horses were small compared to modern standards, akin to the Welsh cob of today, standing at between 13 and 14 hands. The Kirkburn horses showed signs of wear on the teeth and jaw relating to the use of iron bits and pathology associated with hard riding on solid ground and overwork (Legge 1991). Some the droveways and enclosures detected during aerial photography may have been designed for the management of horses, though this would be difficult to prove without excavation.

The British Museum East Yorkshire Settlements Project (Rigby 2004) provided an opportunity to sample pits from sites appearing as cropmarks on aerial photographs. In all a large quantity of bone was recovered and detailed analysis undertaken on two of the twelve sites investigated, the main focus of activity on the pits site in Burton Agnes referred to above being 900–600 BC and at North Dalton, 600–400 BC. Analysis of the animal bone (Hawkes and Browning 2004) showed a shift from cattle to sheep between the two periods and evidence of thorough exploitation of all parts of the animals. Standing at 1.20m at the withers the cattle were taller than the Roman average of 1.14m, the sheep were also noticeably larger. The presence of large tracts of open grassland for grazing this stock is apparent in the analysis of the molluscs (Wagner 2004) which show a preponderance of species which prefer this habitat. Further evidence for the grazing of cattle is the remains of the dung beetle *Onthophagus* preserved at Skelfrey Beck, Shiptonthorpe (Wagner 1999).

The Hasholme logboat had been carrying meat when it sank in a creek of the Walling Fen tidal estuarine inlet and the presence of droveway settlements along the River Foulness has already been noted above. Amongst the bone assemblage associated with the boat was half of the skull of a castrate (bullock) of short horned variety, aged about twenty-four to thirty months. The impact point of the pole-axe used to kill the beast is clearly visible in the centre of the forehead. The fine disarticulation marks from a knife on a young cattle femur are typical of the Iron Age butchery method which involved cutting the carcass at joints with smaller slices rather than chopping, as might be seen with a cleaver (Stallibrass 1987; Seetah 2004). The age of the Hasholme cattle tended to indicate culling for meat in contrast to the pits site at Burton Agnes where the cattle were older when they died, implying that dairying was more important there, though the small sample size of the Hasholme assemblage must be considered. Some of the bones from Hasholme were cracked open to extract marrow. The people on this Iron Age settlement were clearly trying to make the best use of their resources by extracting all the nutrition they could from the bone cavities themselves. Sheep bones were also found around the boat. Cattle, sheep, horse and fowl were also found at Arram in the Hull Valley in a similar landscape (Fig. 23) (Wilson *et al.* 2006).

Further south in Holderness, the excavations undertaken at Winestead Carrs provided evidence for the keeping of cattle in the form of ditch features and the footprints of trampling of stock were preserved under a layer of estuarine clay (Angus Smith 1990). Along the Paull to Easington pipeline, there was further evidence from the Iron Age settlements for animal husbandry, mainly of cattle and sheep, including the remains of dung beetles preserved in wetland deposits (Rowland 2012).

In terms of arable farming, charred grain has been found on a number of sites in the region including Garton Slack Area 9: Grain Silo 1, where a deposit which contained mainly barley had a radiocarbon date in the fourth entury BC (Dent 1995). Reference has already been made to grain storage at Staple Howe and Grimthorpe in the earlier Iron Age. Finds of querns for cereal processing are relatively common, especially on the Wolds, with concentrations in the Great Wold Valley and at Garton-Wetwang. These are generally of the saddle type for the earlier period, with beehive rotary querns making an appearance later in the Iron Age. Research by the Yorkshire Quern Survey has shown that the beehive querns of the East Yorkshire region were distinctive in form with a smaller bun-shaped top stone than those found elsewhere (Cruse forthcoming).

Querns (Fig. 26) are generally associated with the processing of cereals for food, but it is not always clear whether the grain itself was grown in the vicinity of the settlement or brought in from elsewhere. The calcareous soils of the Yorkshire Wolds, especially those in the Panholes and Andover soil series (King and Bradley 1987), are easily worked and ideal for growing cereals as the underlying chalk allows for free drainage, yet the soil itself retains some moisture. The Garton-Wetwang settlement was therefore ideally placed to exploit such conditions.

In contrast the settlement excavated at Chapel Garth, Arram is situated on the gently undulating glacial till of the Holderness soil series, on the edge of the wetlands of the River Hull, yet querns including pieces of 12 querns of beehive type and the remains of cereals, mainly spelt wheat and barley, were found during the excavations here (Wilson *et al.* 2006; O'Brien and Elliott 2005). The plant macrofossils also included indicators of open and disturbed wasteground with damp areas. Suitable ground for growing cereals would appear to be limited and it is likely that the crops were grown in the immediate vicinity of the settlement, although they may have been brought to the site for cereal processing.

In south Holderness, palaeo-environmental analysis on deposits from the Paull to Easington pipeline showed very little evidence for trees and spelt wheat and barley were grown on the better-drained land away from the wetland such as Site 6 south of Welwick/Patrington Haven. Unlike Arram and sites on the Wolds, there were remarkably few querns (Rowland 2012). In the Foulness Valley, a pollen core from Hasholme (Turner 1987, 85–88) showed an increase in cereal-type pollen around 850–530 Cal BC, though there is little evidence for cereal production in the form of querns or charred grain recovered from excavated deposit in neighbouring settlements.

CRAFTS AND INDUSTRY

Pollen, beetle and preserved organic material (Heath and Wagner 2009; Halkon and Innes 2005) show that considerable woodland remained in the lower Foulness Valley to fuel a iron industry of at least national significance, for during field survey nineteen iron-smelting sites presumed to be of Iron Age date were found within an 8 x 8km landscape block. Almost all of the smelting sites were situated on the sand ridges close to the River Foulness (Halkon 1997(b); 2003, Halkon and Millett 1999; Halkon 2012). At Moore's Farm, Welham Bridge (Plate 17), a slag heap was excavated which contained 5,338kg of slag, the second largest from Iron Age Britain and was, according to Crew (pers. comm.), enough for the manufacture of *c*. 800 bars of trade iron, or currency bars as they were once known. The heap was dated from the charcoal in the slag to 450–250 Cal BC (2 sigma) (HAR-9234) and 600–380 Cal BC (2 sigma) (HAR 9235) (Halkon 1997(b); Halkon and Millett 1999).

Due primarily to the experimental archaeology undertaken by Peter and Susan Crew (Crew 1991; Crew 2013) it is possible to estimate the quantities of raw material and output resulting from the smelting process. The heap would have required 9,120kg of ore and *c*. 3,360kg of charcoal, which Millett calculated (based on Rackham 1980) was equivalent to the

Fig. 26 Iron Age querns from the Rudston area. These are of the rotary 'beehive' type which probably appears in the middle Iron Age. (P. Halkon)

annual product of 47.3ha of woodland. The radiocarbon dates suggest that smelting was carried out over a relatively long time-span (Halkon and Millett 1999) and so it is not clear how much wood was taken at any one time. The presence of closed canopy woodland is implied by the parent tree of the Hasholme log boat (Plate 18, Fig. 27) with a felling date of 321–277 BC (Millett and McGrail 1987), which was contemporary with the Moore's Farm slag heap, and indeed Iron Age smelting was carried out on the rectilinear enclosure settlement at Hasholme referred to above, which overlooked the creek into which the log boat sank.

Iron smelting was also carried out at Dryham Lane, North Cave (Fig. 23) (Dent 1989) on the opposite side of the Walling Fen tidal inlet. Here furnaces and large quantities of slag from iron smelting were excavated, some of which closely resembled that from Moore's Farm. No direct dating evidence was available but typology, stratigraphy and pottery suggests a date contemporary with other sites in the Foulness Valley. Around 1km to the west a further logboat was found at South Carr Farm (Halkon 1997(a)), which may be contemporary with the Hasholme boat. It is possible that both vessels could have been involved in transporting products along the river systems. More evidence for smelting has been found at various sites in the Vale of York including Barmby Moor (Cowgill et al. 2003) and Allerthorpe Common (pers.comm. Dave Macleod), though this was of small scale compared with the Moore's Farm site.

Despite large-scale field walking as part of the English Heritage Humber Wetlands project in the lowlands of Holderness and the Hull Valley (Van De Noort and Ellis 1995; 2000) and Peter Didsbury (1990) in the Lower Hull Valley, and the construction of major pipelines, very little evidence for iron production or even working in the form of slag has been reported. A key factor in the location of iron production was the availability of raw materials. Fieldwork and analysis shows that bog iron ores were utilised in the Foulness and Hull valleys, both regions having plentiful supplies of timber for the production of charcoal and clay for furnace building.

However, in recent years iron slag has been found in Iron Age contexts at several sites around Beverley, including Arram (Wilson et al. 2006) and Thearne (Campbell 2008; Halkon 2012) where furnace bottoms resembling those from Moore's Farm and North Cave have been found on the surface of the field. These may relate to a furnace discovered during tree planting and partially excavated. Neither location yielded as much iron slag as the important settlement at Elmswell, at the head waters of the River Hull (Congreve 1938). Here a heap of what the excavator described as bloomery slag weighing about 1.5 tonnes was found. There was smithing slag across the site and a number of pits which contained burnt clay and ash.

The location of Elmswell is significant as it lies at the head waters of the River Hull at the mouth of Garton and Wetwang Slack with its large Iron Age cemeteries, including the seven chariot burials referred to above. The chariot burials contained many objects of copper-alloy and iron and a link between those buried in the richer graves, some of which contained objects decorated with gold and coral, and control of iron production and other resources has been discussed in Chapter 4.

Reference has already been made to the blacksmith's tools including tongs, a poker and what is described as a 'paddle' deposited in a former grain storage pit at Garton Slack (Fig. 28) (Brewster 1980). At Rudston (Stead 1991) a pair of blacksmith's tongs and a hammer were found in Grave 154, the burial of a male aged around twenty. The tips of two spears had been jammed between the arms of the tongs and a short sword were also found in the burial. It is not known whether or not the deposition of these tools in his grave reflected his status in life as a smith or warrior. Possible craftsman burials are rare in Britain and include an example from Whitcombe in Dorset (Stead 1990 and pers. comm.).

An iron 'currency bar' found by the Granthams near Gransmoor, with Iron Age pottery and querns early in the 1960s (Dent 1995, pers. comm. P. Makey; Halkon 2012) is of major importance, as it is the only example known from the East Yorkshire region (Fig. 29). The upper part, including the handle, was welded to another bar. The Granthams also reported fragments of the burnt clay walls of a 'kiln' which may be fragments of a furnace or hearth, though there are no reports of any iron slag.

More iron objects are known from the burials of Iron Age East Yorkshire than anywhere else in Britain, partly because more burials have been excavated here. A total of 418 iron artefacts were recorded from 856 burials. Cemeteries with chariot burials such as Wetwang contained the most iron artefacts. The most frequently occurring objects were brooches (30 per cent) and spearheads (16 per cent) with weapons almost exclusively in male burials and objects associated with personal adornment more common with females. There seems to be a strong correlation between the amount of iron in burials and social rank, if those buried with vehicles and weapons are indeed the top of the hierarchy. Estimates based on experimental smelting show that the production of 1kg of fully refined bar iron would have needed a total of between eight

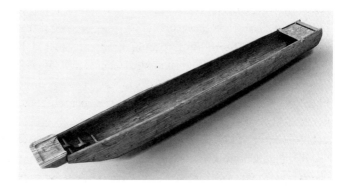

Fig. 27 Reconstruction of the Hasholme logboat. (M. Faulkner)

and twenty-five person-day's work, depending on the ore type and the technology used (Crew 2013). Replica iron tyres made for the Yorkshire Museum, York, by Don Barker, weighed 12kg and a total of 36kg of iron was needed for all the chariot fittings (http://www.yorkshiremuseum.org.uk/Page/CPArchSub6.aspx). The production of this amount of iron would have taken *c*. 288 days of labour at the lowest estimate using Iron Age methods. The chariot burials discussed in Chapter 4, such as Kirkburn, which contained a mail tunic (Stead 1991), represent a considerable investment in time and materials. In contrast some Type A burials contain only a single iron brooch.

It may be that the people buried with chariots not only controlled the production of iron, but were also the patrons of some of the best craftsmen of Iron Age Britain, proficient in the manufacture of copper-alloy objects and techniques of embellishment, using enamel, coral and other materials. The swords from Wetwang and Kirkburn (Plate 17), the 'Bean Tin' from Wetwang Slack and the highly decorated bit from Rise in Holderness are good illustrations of their expertise. The distinctive styles with which objects, especially the sword sheaths are decorated, demonstrate strong regionality (Stead 2006) and evidence for Iron Age copper-alloy working, combined with that for iron production and smithing, make it possible that swords and other items were produced in eastern Yorkshire.

So far evidence for working of copper alloys has been found at twelve sites in East Yorkshire (Fig. 14) (Wilson 2006). In the Hull Valley at Elmswell a piece of crucible found in a pit indicated that copper-alloy casting had been carried out there and the very fine decorated copper-alloy panel covered with a flowing embossed 'Celtic' decoration now in Hull Museum (Corder 1940, Plate 16) could have been made on site. At Kelk, seventy-three fragments of material associated with copper-alloy casting were excavated, including moulds for casting objects including bridle rings, during the Humber Wetlands project survey of the Hull Valley (Van de Noort *et al.* 2000). Over ninety fragments of ceramic material relating to copper-alloy working were excavated at Arram (Wilson 2006) and on the Saltshouse Road settlement, fragments of mould discovered. A number of settlement sites on the Wolds also have evidence for copper-alloy working, including Wetwang, Tuft Hill, Burton Agnes, Hanging Cliff, Kilham and Rudston. The finds at Kelk and Wetwang, the currency bar at Gransmoor, and evidence for the working of both iron and copper-alloy at Elmswell raise the possibility that the finds from the Wetwang burials were made in the surrounding area, especially as the metalworking debris from Elmswell included parts of moulds for terrets and linch pins (Wilson 2006; Dent 2010). In the Foulness Valley and Vale of York evidence for copper-alloy working has been found at North Cave (Mackey 2001) in late Iron Age and Roman contexts, and in later Iron Age features at Burnby Lane, Hayton (Mortimer forthcoming).

After animal bone, one of the most frequent finds on Iron Age sites in East Yorkshire is pottery. Detailed analysis of Iron Age pottery was undertaken by a team from the

Fig. 28 Iron working tools from Garton Slack (length of tongs 67.3 cm). (M. Park courtesy Hull and East Riding Museum: Hull Museums)

British Museum to accompany the study of settlements referred to above (Rigby *et al*. 1999; 2004). Pots are frequent finds in Type A square barrows of the Arras culture, though none have been found in the chariot burials. Pottery was used for the storage, preparation and cooking of foodstuffs and finer vessels may have been exchanged as gifts. Scientific study of pottery has enabled the identification of organic materials soaked into the fabric of pottery which provides a guide to the function of the vessel and diet of the people.

The fabric of the pottery can also be analysed to provide clues as to the location of its manufacture from geological examination of the clay itself and the inclusions such as calcite, shell, flint and other crushed rock which were deliberately mixed with the clay to facilitate the escape of water during the firing process, which was undertaken in a bonfire or clamp. In East Yorkshire, flint, calcite, shell and crushed glacially derived rocks or erratics were the most usual types of temper. Some of the erratic tempered wares were better finished, carinated at the shoulder and of a finer fabric (Rigby *et al*. 1999; 2004). It used to be thought that most pottery was made within or close to the site, but petrological analysis shows that either vessels or raw materials may have travelled up to 20km. One explanation for this may be itinerant potters. The pottery from the Rudston/Burton Fleming cemeteries, however, seems to have been produced locally (Rigby 2004). At Melton at least eleven fabric types were identified by microscopic and chemical analysis (Didsbury and Vince 2011, 195). Some with shelly inclusions originated in North Lincolnshire, a few sherds containing calcite temper were from the Vale of Pickering and the majority were made locally. Crushed iron slag has also been identified in the pottery from the Iron Age settlement and iron production site at

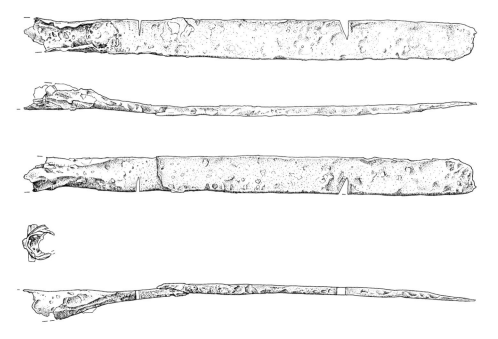

Fig. 29 The Gransmoor currency bar (length 42 cm). (J. Marshall)

Hasholme and a number of other locations. The colour of the pottery was generally determined by the quantity of oxygen in the kiln during the firing process, which could partly be determined by the dampness of the fuel, black or grey where the fuel was damp and there was little or no oxygen present (reduced), or light in colour when more oxygen was present (oxidised). Most pottery was handmade and pots were built up from slabs or coils of clay luted together. It was not until the end of the period that the potter's wheel was introduced.

The shape or form of the vessel was generally dictated by its function: wide-mouthed bowls for mixing and similar processes and taller narrower neck jars for storage. Sooting on the outside of pots and analysis of the fabric for lipids and other substances which have been absorbed into the fabric can determine what was being cooked or kept inside the vessels. Various simple decorative techniques were used, such as frilling, finger-nail impressions and cordons in the earlier Iron Age at the time of Staple Howe (Brewster 1963) and the end of the period when wheel-thrown vessels were introduced from south of the River Humber, which will be considered in the following chapter. One of the main purposes of the British Museum East Yorkshire Settlements Project was to try to work out a typology of the vessels based on artefacts found with the various vessel forms (Rigby 2004, 46–47):

900–600 BC	Plain jars and bowls with carinated shoulders
850–600 BC	Wide mouthed carinated bowls and jars. Finger nail and slashed decoration
600–400 BC	Plain round-bodied jars with lid seat, convex and everted rims
400–100 BC	Shapeless jars
100 BC–AD100	Handmade high shouldered globular vessels – wheel-thrown cordoned bowls

For much of the Iron Age, including the Arras period, therefore, the most common forms were rather shapeless straight-sided jars with very simple outward-turned rims, which tended to be in fabrics with calcite inclusions. The apparent crudity of the pottery compared to the sophistication of the metalwork is striking (Fig. 30).

A further heat-based industry for which there is evidence generally in the south of the region is the production of salt. In the days before refrigeration salting was an important method of food preservation. There is evidence for the extraction of salt from sea-water

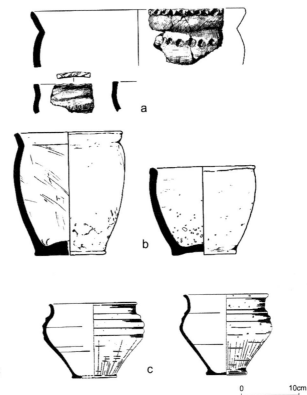

Fig. 30 Early middle and later Iron Age pottery from eastern Yorkshire. a. Staple Howe (after Brewster 1963); b. Rudston/Burton Fleming (after Stead 1991); c. Brantingham (after Dent 1989).

by evaporation in the form of the clay superstructure known as briquetage at Faxfleet A, an Iron Age site on the banks of the Humber (Sitch 1989). Briquetage has also been identified on a late Iron Age and Roman site near Black Dike close to the Walling Fen inlet, excavated prior to the construction of the Asselby to Easington pipeline (Daniel *et al.* forthcoming), and North Cave, were it was initially confused with clay material from working copper-alloys.

SUMMARY

Most people in Iron Age East Yorkshire lived in roundhouses, either in single dispersed enclosures or in villages comprising strings of enclosures arranged along the networks of trackways especially across the Wolds. Soils, drainage and topography had an important effect on site location and activity and there is evidence for both arable and pastoral farming. Areas of better soils were intensively exploited, yet areas of woodland remained, especially in the Foulness Valley which provided fuel for the production of iron and wood for the construction of log boats and other items. Waterways were very important for communication, especially the rivers Foulness and Hull.

Although inspired by continental designs it is clear that there were metal workers of great skill operating within the region, exemplified by the objects from Arras culture graves. The quality of metal objects is in great contrast to the contemporary pottery dominated by relatively crude hand-built straight-sided jars.

CHAPTER 6

LATER IRON AGE EASTERN YORKSHIRE AND THE COMING OF ROME

By the end of the first century BC it is likely that much of East Yorkshire was heavily occupied, although some lowlands, such as the lower Foulness Valley, remained wooded. Palaeo-environmental evidence shows that climate amelioration and regression in sea level extended into the second century AD, allowing for encroachment of activity onto the alluvium in the Humber Wetlands. This may account for the growth of settlements along the Hull Valley such as those at Arram and Burshill and Faxfleet site A in the Foulness Valley referred to in the previous chapter. Faxfleet A was situated either on an island or peninsula of the Walling Fen tidal inlet and may initially have been associated with the production of salt as briquetage and related material was discovered there (Sitch 1989). This site was a precursor to Faxfleet B, which developed in the Roman period and will be considered in more detail below.

In the Hull Valley sea levels had dropped sufficiently to allow some occupation at -3.8m OD, where the alluvium overlies rises in the underlying boulder clay, activity which intensified during the Roman period (Didsbury 1990). The layout of some of these settlements has been described above and many of them were positioned to occupy grazing land close to the river, exploiting the new opportunities which the fall in sea level and improvement in climate presented. These settlements were ideally placed to benefit from waterborne trade and communication networks. The rural settlements in the Roman Hull Valley will be discussed in Chapter 8.

The clearest evidence for the existence of late Iron Age cross-Humber trade is wheel-thrown continentally influenced Gallo-Belgic type pottery, especially the fineware cordoned vessels, most closely paralleled in ceramic stages 10 and 11 at Dragonby in Lincolnshire (Elsdon 1989: 37, 1996a cf. fig. 19.38 no 340, 473). Thin sectioning suggests that some of this pottery was manufactured on the north bank of the Humber (Rigby 2004). Over the last few decades the number of East Yorkshire sites where this type of vessel has been identified is increasing, generally close to river systems. Dragonby-style pottery has been found in the Foulness Valley at Bursea House, Holme-on-Spalding Moor (Halkon and Millett 1999) and Brantingham (Dent 1989) and Risby (Didsbury 1988) Creyke Beck, Cottingham (Evans and Steedman 2001) and Arram in the Hull Valley (Wilson *et al.* 2006). Wheel-thrown pottery has been found on sites further north in the Great Wold Valley away from the coast at Hanging Cliff, Kilham, Argam and Rudston (Rigby 2004), though only in small quantities with little impact on local pottery styles.

The settlement at Brantingham (Fig. 31) is positioned on the limestone ridge below the Wolds escarpment, overlooking the Humber and the Walling Fen tidal inlet. Though little survived of the internal features, it consisted of at least three adjoining enclosures with wide ditches arranged in a ladder formation. As well as the wheel-thrown pottery described above, finds included coarse pottery, triangular loom weights and bone tools (Dent 1989; 2010). A gold coin, a stater inscribed VEP CORF (van Arsdell 1989, type 930), the name of one or perhaps two tribal leaders of the Corieltauvi, whose territory lay south of the Humber in an areas equivalent to Lincolnshire and Leicestershire, was found later during metal detecting (Oliver 1995). The Brantingham area, which has a cluster of Corieltauvian coins, could therefore have been important for other than geographical or economic factors and may have been a place of ritual significance since the Neolithic as there is a group of henge-like monuments and various other ritual structures to the east of a large enclosure which may be of Iron Age or Roman date.

As well as the arrival of wheel-thrown pottery and Corieltauvian coinage, new burial rites appeared which may also have been the result of influence from the south. At the ladder settlements of Sherburn and East Heslerton discussed above (Powlesland 2003(a)), so-called 'barrowlets' have been identified, which on excavation were found to contain cremations surrounded by a small circular ditch in contrast to the crouched inhumations of the Arras culture. It is not known whether this change in burial rite is due to an influx of people or influence from southern Britain where cremation was generally the favoured method of disposal of the dead (Fitzpatrick 2007).

There has been a considerable increase in the number of finds of Iron Age coins in East Yorkshire, largely due to the growth of metal detecting and the subsequent reporting of finds through the Portable Antiquities Scheme. These discoveries include hoards from the Walkington and North Dalton areas. The Walkington hoard of around 100 coins was found between 1999 and 2008 (Plate 22). It comprised Corieltauvian gold staters of the South Ferriby type and Kite and Domino types dating from the late first century BC (Barclay 2000, 100; Barclay 2004,152; Williams 2002, 126; 2004, 152). The former was named after the location at which this type was first recognised and the latter from the shape which the motifs on them resemble.

A hoard of over fifty coins found in the vicinity of North Dalton contained many of the same types as that from Walkington, but also included a few bearing the names of Corielatuvian rulers VEP CORF, ESUPRASU and DUMNOVELLAUNOS, the latter

Fig. 31 Plan of the Brantingham settlement. The large ditches of the tripartite Iron Age enclosure are overlain by Roman buildings (after Dent 1989).

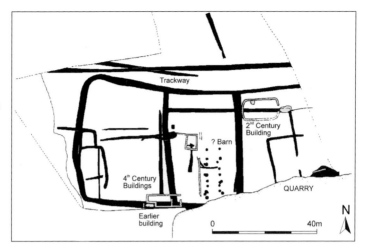

struck about AD 43 (Williams 2002, 126; 2004, 152). It has been suggested that the two hoards were once part of the same large payment to the Parisi, perhaps in return for some kind of military service associated with the Roman invasion, or may relate to changes in the balance of power across the Humber resulting in an influx of people escaping Roman control (Sills 2011(b)).

In the 20 x 30km Foulness Valley study area (Halkon 2008) it was noted that of the fourteen single Iron Age coins, which were mainly gold staters of the Corieltauvi, all but one were found on the best-quality soil, which may not be coincidental and may relate to elite control of the best farmland. There also seems to be a correlation between coins and watercourses for which a range of explanations can be offered, including waterborne communications or some form of structured deposition (Fig. 32).

Coriletauvian coins have also been found at Redcliff, North Ferriby referred to above (Plate 23). The site was first recognised by Ted Wright in the 1930s and excavation was eventually undertaken there in the 1980s (Crowther and Didsbury 1988; Crowther *et al*.1990) though by this time much of the settlement had been lost to the River Humber through erosion and the surviving features difficult to interpret. What is remarkable about the site was the disproportionate amount of imported fineware pottery and other artefacts dating from the period AD 43–70, the time between the invasion of the Emperor Claudius, or slightly earlier, and the Roman take-over of the region in AD 71. Finds included fine tablewares from Gaul, such as Terra Nigra, Terra Rubra, early decorated samian pottery and Italian wine amphorae (Willis 1996). Sherds of Terra Rubra were also discovered on late Iron Age settlements excavated along the Easington to Paull pipeline (OA North 2011; Rowland 2012).

The arrival of such vessels may represent a move towards a Gallo-Roman style of dining which the tribal elites of southern Britain had already adopted, with a change

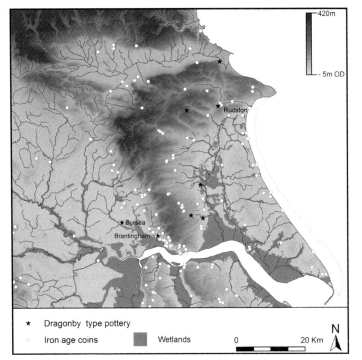

Fig. 32
Distribution
of later Iron
Age coins and
'Dragonby style'
pottery activity.
(T. Sparrow)

of cuisine (Cunliffe 2005; Creighton 2000), and highlights the continued significance of the Humber in trading networks at this time. Redcliff probably served as a place through which prestige goods were traded with the as yet unconquered lands north of the Humber. In what is now North Yorkshire at around the same time, imported pottery, glass and Roman roof tile were arriving at the late Iron Age high-status complex at Stanwick, near Scotch Corner, interpreted (Haselgrove 1990; Haselgrove *et al*.1991; Turnbull and Fitts 1988) as belonging to Cartimandua, Queen of the Brigantes. Much has been written about the portrayal of Cartimandua by Tacitus and the negative way in which she was perceived by the Romans (e.g. Braund 1996; Hanson and Campbell 1996; Howarth 2008) but her story provides one of the only written accounts of the events leading up to the Roman conquest of what is now Yorkshire.

According to Tacitus (*Annals* 12:32), after initial unrest in AD 48 the Brigantes, under Cartimandua and her husband Venutius, enjoyed client status, a scenario which would fit the archaeological evidence from Stanwick with its imported pottery and glass. When the defeated British resistance leader Caratacus sought sanctuary in AD 51, Cartimandua handed him over to the Romans (*Annals* xii, 36). Following the divorce of Cartimandua and Venutius in AD 55/56, there was further unrest and Venutius and his war-band attacked his former wife, who according to Tacitus (*Annals* xii, 40) had to be rescued by Roman cohorts. It is possible that the foundation of some of the

Roman military installations in western and southern Yorkshire may relate to the above historical events as a vexillation fortress was founded at Rossington Bridge, 7km south of Doncaster AD 52–57 (Buckland 1986) and at Templeborough near Rotherham (May 1922; Buckland 1986) at around the same time (Ottoway 2003).

Finally in AD 69/70 Cartimandua's replacement of her husband by his armour bearer Vellocatus (Tacitus *Histories* 3:45) provoked a further revolt and another attack by Venutius, again necessitating Cartimandua's rescue by a detachment of Roman troops, which in turn provided the pretext for full-scale invasion under Governor Q. Petillius Cerealis (*Agricola* 12:1) in AD 70/71. Although today archaeologists tend to be much more cautious than their predecessors in equating archaeological finds with historical events too closely, most archaeologists agree that the forts at Malton, Brough and Hayton were established at this time (Hartley 1988). It has, however, been proposed that there was some earlier military activity (Wilson 2009).

We do not know precisely what the relationship was between the Brigantes, whose territory according to Ptolemy's *Geographia* extended from the North Sea to the Irish sea, and probably between the northern frontier and the River Don, and their smaller neighbour the Parisi, but it is clear that Roman control of their territory was a prerequisite to the take-over of Brigantian territory. The sketchy evidence concerning the Parisi and their attitude to Rome is ambiguous:

They are usually regarded as pro-Roman because of their receptiveness to Roman goods, their position between the Brigantian kingdom and the conquered province, and the limited number of forts located within their territory. But whatever their inclination towards Rome, the knowledge that the Roman troops were in the area may have served either to reassure them that the problems further north were in hand, or to warn them not to consider participation (Hanson and Campbell 1986, 83–84).

There has been a presumption that the later Iron Age peoples of East Yorkshire were peaceful, but the chalk figurines in the form of warriors, some of which may have been ritually decapitated, a number of later warrior burials and the remarkable South Cave weapons cache would suggest otherwise. The chalk figurines (Stead 1988) probably date from the first centuries BC and AD, range in size from 70–170mm in height and generally have a sword slung down their back (Fig. 33).

Like the earlier speared corpse burials, their distribution is restricted to the area around Garton-Wetwang Slack, with outliers at Malton and Withernsea. There is some doubt as to the original context of the latter, which may have been included in a load of gravel from the Clifford Watts quarry at Garton-Wetwang. The Withernsea figure is also the most realistically portrayed and has a phallus carved off-centre on its front, perhaps emphasising his masculinity. A chalk figurine similar to those from East Yorkshire was found in a shaft in the Iron Age and Roman cemetery at Deal in Kent (Parfitt and Green 1987, Parfitt 1995) which is thought to have fallen from a niche in the side wall, in a context thought to be Roman in date. The Deal cemetery also contained a burial furnished with weapons and wearing the remains of a headress comprising decorated copper-alloy bands which is probably of middle Iron Age date (Harding 2007).

Though precise dating is difficult, burial with weapons may have continued into the later Iron Age as the east-west burials from the Rudston/Burton Fleming cemeteries are thought to be the latest in the sequence there. A further problem of typological dating is the probability that weapons may have been handed down through generations. For example the burial of a male from North Grimston (Plate 20) discovered in 1902 (Mortimer 1905) contained a long sword of middle La Tène date and a short sword with an anthropoid hilt with parallels from Ireland to Hungary, which on stylistic grounds may date from the later second century BC (Harding 2007)). This particularly fine example has a well-depicted human head with a curly fringe and straight combed long hair down his neck, a moustache and lentoid eyes. Whether or not these swords were involved in rituals including human sacrifice (Green 2001) remains a subject of speculation.

The most important example of late Iron Age weaponry yet found in the region, and one of the most significant in Europe, is the remarkable cache of five swords in scabbards and thirty-three spearheads found near South Cave (Plate 21) (Evans 2006; Marchant and Halkon 2008; Powell *et al.* forthcoming), concealed in a settlement ditch under sherds of Dressel 20 amphora (Didsbury 2003). Roman greyware pottery, probably from Lincolnshire, dating to the later first century was also found in the same context as the cache (Didsbury 2003). The highly ornate decoration on the scabbards is suggestive of a 'northern style' of Iron Age art (Ian Stead pers. comm.) broadly similar to the sword from Bugthorpe (Stead 1996, 11) and the larger of the swords from Grimthorpe (Plate 3) (Mortimer 1905, 150 and frontispiece).

Although analysis of one of the copper-alloy chapes shows that it was made of metal from France, the remainder of the evidence makes it likely that the

Fig. 33 Chalk figurines from eastern Yorkshire. Above, left to right: Garton Slack, Wetwang Slack, Garton Slack, Withernsea (height 110mm) Wetwang Slack, Garton Slack. Below: Malton (right figure height 88mm). (M. Park courtesy Hull and East Riding Museum: Hull Museums)

swords were manufactured in the region. Copper alloy was worked here at this time, iron production continued and the mastery of combining different materials is demonstrated in earlier objects such as the Kirkburn sword and metalwork from Wetwang discussed above (Marchant and Halkon 2008). The decoration on the sheaths is exceptional and organic materials including horn, antler, elephant and whale ivory as well as enamel and glass were utilised (O'Connor 2008; Powell *et al.* forthcoming). Although the elephant ivory was traded, the whale bone, probably from the teeth of a sperm whale, may have been taken from an animal beached on the Humber foreshore or North Sea coast.

The burial spot may have been deliberately aligned on the hilltop enclosure at Mt Airy and the fragmentary double-ditched enclosure in a direct line between the cache and Mt Airy (Carr 2005) could have also been significant. Although no Iron Age coins were found with the South Cave weapons cache and there appeared to have been no evidence for feasting in the form of animal bones, the deposition of the swords may be analogous in some ways with the East Leicestershire or Hallaton hoard (Priest *et al.* 2003, Faulkner 2006; Score 2011), which occurred at roughly the same time. This consisted of 5,500 Iron Age, Roman Republican and early Imperial coins and a highly decorated Roman cavalry parade helmet, associated with the entrance of a ditched feature. The Iron Age coins were mainly Corieltauvian, dating from the first half of the first century AD, but also included one of the earliest known British coins. The burial of an unmistakeably Roman object such as the helmet with Iron Age coins echoes the deposition of the South Cave weapons cache which was buried with amphorae and other early Roman pottery types. The possible ritual context of the swords is not as clear, however, as the East Leicestershire hoard. Perhaps they were buried at distinguishable place in the landscape as an aid to their future recovery, or a final act of structured deposition in recognition of the ending of a passing era with the advent of Rome, when the carrying of arms was forbidden by the *lex Julia Vi publica* (*Digest* 48:6, 1)? The swords and spears may have armed a group of warriors and if so, it would be fascinating to know how they interacted with the invading Roman army.

SUMMARY OF IRON AGE EAST YORKSHIRE – TOWARDS A TRIBAL IDENTITY?

Although in general terms Iron Age East Yorkshire followed developments in Britain as a whole, the material evidence does show the emergence of a distinct regional identity by the later Iron Age and perhaps a tribal name. These differences have been confirmed by recent detailed surveys of the archaeology of the neighbouring regions of West and South Yorkshire (Roberts *et al.* 2010) and North Yorkshire and Teeside (Sherlock 2012) in terms of settlement types, burial and other aspects of material culture. In the earlier period, the landscape was divided by linear earthworks, perhaps more concentrated on the Yorkshire Wolds than anywhere else. Regional styles of pottery developed and in the middle Iron Age, East Yorkshire possessed the biggest concentration of square barrows in Britain, though the mechanism by which they arrived is still a matter of speculation. Apart from a few outliers, the region also contains the largest concentration of burials with chariots, and many of the metal objects contained within them are decorated in a regionally distinctive style. Linear enclosure complexes or ladder settlements are far more frequent here than in neighbouring regions as are the speared corpse burials and chalk warrior figurines.

In the introduction to this book, comment was made on the tribal name Parisi. An old Welsh word for spear is 'par' (Pughe 1832, 396) and Parisi has been interpreted as 'the spear people' (Falileyev 2007, 164). Although place name evidence from the ancient world must be treated with care and is often disregarded by archaeologists, the East Yorkshire region contains other place names relating to spears such as Delgovicia listed in the *Antonine Itinerary*, derived from 'delgo' meaning a thorn, or spear (Isaac 2004), hence 'the town or settlement of the spear fighters' (Jackson 1948, 57). The remarkable speared corpse burials of the region confirm the significance of this weapon in Iron Age rituals associated with death. Although burials of this kind do not appear around Paris, and there spears in graves are deposited in the conventional manner, they are clearly important weapons (Marion 2009). In the Aisne-Marne region, the quantity of spearheads in elite male burials of the middle Iron Age is greater than those lower down the social hierarchy. In the Paris region some large highly decorated spears may also have accrued a symbolic meaning (Anthoons 2010, 163) and with this in mind it is interesting to note that the South Cave weapons cache contains a large spear with continental parallels which would have not have been a very practical weapon (Inall pers. comm.; Brunaux and Rapin 1988, 124–126).

By the end of the Iron Age new influences were apparent in the form of coinage and pottery from the south bank of the Humber, some of which may have entered through the short-lived site at Redcliff, North Ferriby and square barrow and chariot burial may have been in decline or ceased. One of the catalysts for these changes is likely to have been the Roman conquest of Britain south of the Humber.

THE ROMAN CONQUEST AND THE ARMY

Around AD 70 when Roman forces consisting of Legio IX Hispana and unknown auxiliary regiments under the command of Q. Petillius Cerealis moved into the region, forts were established in the Foulness Valley at Hayton and Brough-on-Humber, Hayton being roughly half way between Brough and the legionary base at York

(Fig. 34) (Ottaway 2003; 2004). Both were strategically sited within the landscape. Brough was ideally positioned to control both the river system and routes into the Wolds, at the confluence of the Walling Fen tidal inlet and the River Humber directly opposite the Ancholme Valley. The tidal inlet itself would have provided a sheltered harbour in this difficult tidal estuary. The possibility that this sheltered harbour was the 'Safe Haven Bay' of Ptolemy has been argued above. The Hayton fort was carefully located on rising ground between two areas of alluvial soil. Hayton Beck flows through the westernmost 'finger' of alluvium and it is possible that a stream, now partially drained and culverted, ran through the eastern alluvium in the Roman period. From its position on rising ground at the foothills of the Wolds the fort at Hayton controlled access to the chalk uplands and the valley of Hayton Beck.

The first fort at Brough was excavated by Corder 1935–37 (Fig. 35) (Corder and Romans 1936) to the south of Welton Road, although its full plan is by no means certain. At 1.8ha in area, it was slightly larger than Hayton. Sections were excavated across the defences and the ramparts were found to consist of layers of turf, built around a wooden frame comprising upright timbers slotted into a sleeper beam. The carbonised remains of the wood were plainly visible. Wacher (1969), who excavated at Brough 1958–1961 suggests that the fort was built on the site of a temporary camp associated with a stores depot, occupied for around a decade. Several internal buildings were found. In the 1980 excavations at Petuaria Close, however, the remains of a clay oven of military character, together with other features, were recorded which provided evidence of later activity in the form of coins of the emperors Domitian (AD 81–96) and Nerva (AD 96–98) which were found immediately above the oven (Halkon 1980). There is some dispute as to whether this activity may be associated with the stores depot, which Wacher argues remained in use after the fort was abandoned, or alternatively may be associated with an annexe that projected northwards across Welton Road, or even a further fort on a slightly different alignment. In 2004 and 2009, pre-development evaluation at 3 and 5 Burrs, found further evidence in the form of a ditch containing food debris, subsequently sealed by a building and gravel street. It has recently been suggested that this site may lie in the area of the *praetorium* of the early fort (Evans and Atkinson 2009, 280).

According to Wacher (1969; 1995), the fort was briefly reoccupied in the Hadrianic period around AD 125 with some refurbishment of the defences and new internal buildings. The so-called '*vicus*' or civilian settlement developed *c.* AD 125–200. The theatre (see below) may be associated with this phase. Wacher (1969; 1995) suggests that a rampart and ditch enclosed a supply depot or detachment of the Roman navy. This and other aspects of later Roman Brough will be discussed in Chapter 11.

First recognised as a cropmark by St Joseph in 1974, the fort at Hayton was excavated the following year and shown to be Flavian in foundation (AD 71–72) (Plate 24). It was originally thought to have been occupied for a relatively short time,

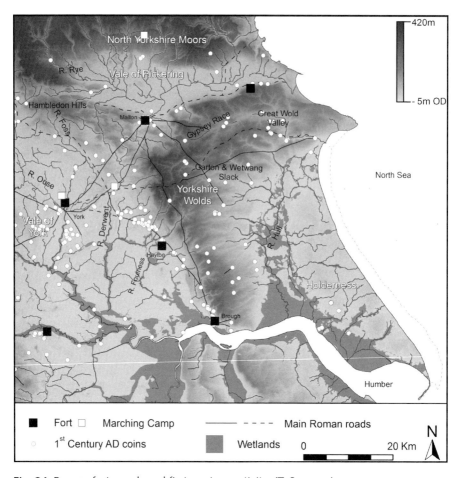

Fig. 34 Roman forts roads and first-century activity. (T. Sparrow)

perhaps being abandoned by the mid-'80s AD (Johnson 1978; Breeze and Dobson 1985, 7). Re-assessment of the coins found by metal detectorists in the area of the fort, however (Millett pers. comm. and Halkon *et al.* forthcoming), whilst confirming a Flavian foundation, also show a peak in the reign of Domitian (81–96) with a few coins between AD 96 and 217, followed by a gap until the second quarter of the third century peaking again in the early fourth century AD, which complements the evidence from pottery found during field walking, showing that there was later occupation on the site of an uncertain nature.

The same aerial photography which located the Hayton fort, also revealed later prehistoric activity visible as the cropmarks of droveways, fields, enclosures and hut-circles. Dense Iron Age activity, around the fort and on the gravel terraces bordering

Hayton beck has been confirmed by further aerial photography and fieldwork undertaken as part of the Foulness Valley project (Halkon 2008; Halkon and Millett 2003; Halkon *et al.* 2000 and forthcoming). It has been postulated that a particularly prominent enclosure to the north of the fort containing a large roundhouse, might represent the deliberate relocation of a chieftain to be close to the Roman fort (Halkon and Millett 2003), which would fit with the idea of local elites taking advantage of the benefits of collaboration (Millett 1989) though this is by no means certain. Alternatively the cropmarks may show that the fort was placed directly over Iron Age features and this is certainly the opinion of the excavator (Johnson 1978). Johnson also suggests that a human skull, albeit fragmentary, in the primary fill of the fort ditch may have belonged to an opponent, implying that the incorporation of the 'natives' here may not have been as quite as easy as supposed. The skull fragment may, however, derive from an earlier disturbed burial.

Little is known of the interior of the fort due to plough damage since the medieval period and the relatively small area of the interior excavated. Parts of the foundations of barracks were found and it is possible that the garrison was a *cohors quingenaria equitata* (Bidwell and Hodgson 2009, 182) comprising around 120 auxiliary cavalry

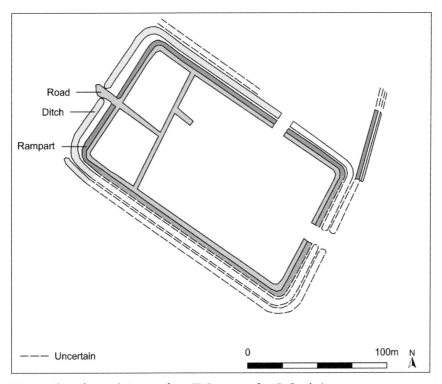

Fig. 35 Plan of Brough Roman fort. (T. Sparrow after P. Corder)

and 480 infantry. Constructed largely of timber the fort at Hayton would have had a major impact on the landscape. Calculations based on the excavation of a similar-sized fort at Carlisle have shown that *c*. 137,000 4m lengths of timber and nearly 4ha of turf would have been needed for its construction. Whilst some timbers would have been brought in, it is likely that the majority were harvested from the locality. Examination of the Carlisle timbers showed that there had been a pre-Roman system of woodland management based on coppicing and pollarding (McCarthy 1985). The need to feed the 500 or so troops and their horses stationed here would also have had a significant impact on the local community.

A fort which may be contemporary with Hayton was identified in 2008 both from geophysics and from the air at Staxton, at the foot of the northern escarpment of the Yorkshire Wolds. Like Hayton the fort was as one would expect strategically located to control a dry route through the Vale of Pickering towards the coast. As no gates were found, the fort could cover 4ha (Bidwell and Hodgson 2009, 164). This may also account for features, thought to belong to a farmstead (Ramm 1978, 78) excavated at nearby Newham's Pit (Brewster 1957), for amongst the finds was terminal of a penannular brooch, almost certainly originating in Gallia Belgica (Netherlands, Belgium, Eastern France, Luxembourg, western Germany) closely paralleled at the south Welsh fortress of Caerleon (Galliou 1981, 289). To the original excavator, the samian and enamelled fittings implied that there was a strong military connection, yet the published plan shows two concentric sub-rectangular enclosures and internal huts. The best explanation is that the site began to be occupied in the Iron Age and was remodelled at various points in the Roman period. There was evidence for Anglian activity there as well.

A further temporary camp, probably contemporary with Hayton, was discovered from the air at Buttercrambe (Horne and Lawton 1998; Lawton 2000). Almost equidistant between Hayton, Malton and York, located on the eastern bank of the Derwent near Stamford Bridge, excavation showed that it had only been occupied for days or weeks.

The military installation at Malton (Fig. 36) was constructed around 12km to the north of Buttercrambe on slightly raised ground overlooking the River Derwent, controlling an important route along the Vale of Pickering and the northern extremities of the territory of the Parisi, particularly the eastern approaches to the Legionary fortress at York. The earliest fort may date to the governorship of Cerealis and therefore contemporary with Hayton and Brough (Wilson 2006). It has been suggested that the earliest construction was a vexillation fortress containing a detachment of a legion (Bidwell and Hodgson 2009). In the Agricolan period (AD 77–83) this was reduced in size to an earth and timber fort covering 3.4ha, the ramparts of which still survive above ground. The north-east gateway had a double entrance (Wilson 2006).

The replacement of the earth and timber defences at Malton in stone and construction of the annexe occurred sometime during the reign of the Emperor Trajan (AD 98–117)

(Wenham and Heywood 1997), which coincides with the building of a stone gate by the IX Legion at the fortress at York, commemorated by an inscription found at King's Square (Ottaway 2004, 17, fig. 4).

New ditches were cut and the north gate rebuilt with a single entrance (Wilson 2006). It is thought that like many of the forts in northern Britain, the garrison was reduced in the Hadrianic period (Wilson 2006, 38) with reoccupation in the late AD 150s. It seems unlikely, however, that the whole fort was abandoned as there is evidence for Hadrianic period construction outside its south-east corner.

Further remodelling of the defences with wider walls took place in the late third or early fourth century AD (Bidwell and Hodgson 2009, 165–166; Wilson 2006), with the rebuilding of the northern gate. This may be associated with the Emperors Carausius and Allectus or perhaps Constantine I. Little of the fort interior has yet been excavated; however, a geophysical survey in 2007 detected rows of possible barracks or stables, granaries and other large buildings (Horsley 2007). Perhaps the most interesting discovery being a 30cm-thick deposit of charred grain, not the result of enemy attack, but the cleansing by fire of a granary due to an insect infestation (Buckland 1982). Fragmentary remains of the principia (HQ building) have been located. Further aspects of the later occupation of the fort will be discussed in Chapter 11.

We know the name of one of the regiments stationed at Malton from an inscription on a limestone slab found in 1970 amongst building debris, which may commemorate the dedication of a bath house (Wright and Hassall 1971, 291):

I... CANDID PRAEF ALAE PICENTIAN D D
(I. (Julius??) Candidus Prefect of the *Ala Picentiana* made this gift)

This cavalry regiment (*ala* – meaning wing – refers to the traditional position of the cavalry in the line of battle at the outside of the infantry also appears on an inscriptions and military diploma dated to AD 122 and 124 as *ala Gallorum Picentiana* and therefore originally raised in Gaul. The unit had served in Upper Germania in the AD 70s and 80s (Jarrett1994) (Plate 25). Various items of military equipment have ben discovered in excavations around Malton (Fig. 38, Plates 26 and 27).

The tombstone referred to in Chapter 1 found at Pye Pits near the fort at Malton in 1753 but now lost, is particularly interesting; it reads:

D (is) M(anibus) AVR(elius) MACRINVS EX EQ(uite) SING(ulari) VIXIT.

This is usually translated as: 'To the spirits of the departed, Aurelius Macrinus, formerly a cavalryman in the emperor's bodyguard'.

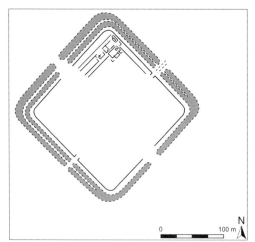

Fig. 36
Malton Roman fort. (T. Sparrow after Robinson (1978))

Fig. 37 Excavating the defences of Malton fort in Orchard Fields. (Malton Museum Trust)

There is some dispute as to how a cavalryman who had served in Rome came to be buried in Malton and it has been argued instead that Macrinus served in the bodyguard of the Governor of Britain (Davies 1976).

The presence of troops from other parts of the Roman Empire in East Yorkshire may be indicated from various finds. At Hayton a brooch of Kraftig profilierte type originating from Pannonia (modern Hungary) (Bayley and Butcher 2004) was identified (Stratton 2005) dating from the first and early second century AD, coinciding with the occupation of the fort. Pannonian troops are attested from various diplomas from the east and north of Britain (Tully 2005; Marsden 2003; Burn 1969; *CIL* XVI, 65). A remarkable pot in the shape of a head found near Church Hill, Holme-on-Spalding Moor (Fig. 39) with a pointed chin, bulbous eyes and pierced ears (Halkon 1992; Halkon and Millett 1999; Halkon 2008) is very similar to examples from Austria and Hungary along the Danube (Braithwaite 1984).

SUMMARY

The discovery of the South Cave swords and the presence of Flavian forts at Hayton, Brough, Malton and Staxton, and the marching camp at Buttercrambe, can be interpreted as demonstrating that relations between the indigenous population of the region and

Fig. 38 Roman artillery ammunition from Malton. Stone balls and a ballista bolt. (M. Park courtesy Malton Museum Trust)

Rome may not have been as peaceful as has been thought. All the forts are situated at strategically important locations and, apart from Hayton, lie on the possible boundaries of the tribal territory, in this case between the Parisi and Brigantes, following a pattern noted elsewhere in the province (Millett 1989). Recent reassessment of the coin evidence from Hayton suggests that the garrison remained for several decades longer than supposed. Peaks in military activity can be inferred from the evidence at Staxton/ Newham's Pit in the period AD 70–80 and AD100–120 and the fort at Brough, probably garrisoned into the AD 120s, though its later history is more problematic. Malton seems to have retained its importance as a military centre for a longer period of time and one of its last garrisons may have comprised the *numerus supervenientium Petueriensium* listed in the *Notitia Dignitatum* who were transferred from Brough in the late fourth century. This and other aspects of later Roman East Yorkshire will be discussed in Chapter 11. The next chapter assesses the impact of Rome and the development of the larger settlements of Roman East Yorkshire.

CHAPTER 7

THE IMPACT OF ROME – THE LARGER SETTLEMENTS

INTRODUCTION

There has been much debate in recent years as to exactly what it was to be 'Roman' in Britain. Some writers see the introduction of Roman culture as an imposition heavily directed by military conquest and centralised control, contrasting the way the different communities, groups and individuals that comprised Roman Britain perceived themselves (Mattingly 2006). Others have stressed the importance of competition between tribal elites to gain access to Roman goods and vie with each other to show off their status by the adoption of new lifestyles (Millett 1989). The latter seems to be well demonstrated in the south-east of England where late Iron Age elite burials such as those at Welwyn Garden City (Niblett 2004) contained wine amphorae and dining equipment from the Roman world. Numismatic evidence (Creighton 2000) also supports comments by classical authors (Strabo IV. 5. 3) that the sons of British chiefs went to Rome to be educated in the later decades BC during the Augustan period. Can similar processes be observed in the region of the Parisi? We have seen that at around the same time as Cartimandua of the Brigantes was enjoying the luxuries contained in the Roman

glassware and pottery at Stanwick (Haselgrove *et al*. 1991), Redcliff may have been operating as a port through which similar goods were being imported into the territory of the Parisi. The South Cave weapons cache discussed in the previous chapter may indicate some resistance to the Roman conquest of this region,

Fig. 39 Head pot from Holme-on-Spalding Moor. Note the pierced ears. The closest parallels to this pot are in the Balkans. (A. Arnott)

128

but the fact that the weapons were hidden under sherds of Dressel 20 amphora which had probably contained olive oil from Spain or Portugal demonstrates some form of contact with the Roman Empire.

At the time of the invasion of East Yorkshire, the Roman Empire stretched from Britain to North Africa and Egypt, from the Iberian Peninsula to the Black Sea, and on the European mainland, as far north as the rivers Rhine and Danube, including almost fifty modern states. It encompassed an enormous diversity of ethnic groups and the contrast in lifestyles between the peoples of southern Europe and the East who had resided in cities for millennia in some cases and those of north-west Europe, many of whom lived in dispersed settlements of timber houses, was great. In the West Latin was the official language and in the East Greek, but it is likely that many would have continued to speak in the vernacular in their everyday lives. Apart from a few exceptions, people within the Roman Empire worshipped more or less as they wished and in many cases local deities were conflated with Roman ones, which were themselves of Greek origin. Britain maintained a garrison of three legions; only two other provinces, Syria and Moesia Inferior (parts of Bulgaria and Romania), had as many and the troops were drawn from provinces including those equivalent to the former Yugoslavia, France, the Netherlands and Spain. Study of material culture such as pottery and dress accessories shows that even after incorporation into the Empire, elements of regional identity were maintained amongst both newcomers and the indigenous population.

Although the idea of invading Romans bringing 'civilisation' into these islands is now regarded as a gross oversimplification and there is much debate about the nature of urbanism at this time, it is clear that the development of larger towns and cities was a direct result of this – after all the term civilisation is derived from the Latin *civis* – a town. The development of town life has sometimes been taken as a measure by which provinces were absorbed into Roman *mores*. According to Tacitus (*Agricola*, 21), during the governorship of Agricola Britons keenly took on the trappings of Roman society and in the next century attempts were made in the reign of Hadrian to bring the towns of Britain 'up to scratch' as evidence such as the inscription (*RIB*288) found at the forum of Wroxeter shows:

IMP(eratori) CA[es(ari)] DIVI TRAIANI PARTHI / CI FIL(io) DI[vi] NERVAE NEPOTI TRA / IANO H[a]DRIANO AVG(usto) PONTI[fi] CI MAXIMO TRIB(unicia) POT(estate) XIII[I CO(n)S(uli)III P(atri) P(atriae)] / CIVITAS CORNOV[iorum]

For the Emperor Caesar Trajan Hadrian Augustus, son of the deified Trajan, conqueror of Parthia, grandson of the deified Nerva, Pontifex Maximus, in

Fig.40 Brough from the air. The former coastlines can be seen in the curved field boundaries to the right. Cave Road in the centre of the photograph follows the line of the Roman road. (P. Halkon)

the fourteenth year of tribunician power, thrice consul, father of his country, the civitas of the Cornovians (erected this).

The Cornovii who occupied what are now the West Midlands and Welsh borders, erected this inscription in the fourth largest city in Roman Britain, as an expression of civic pride in the construction of a suite of municipal buildings. The impressive remains of the basilica and baths still stand today. The next section considers the extent to which such ideas were taken up within the territory of the Parisi, beginning with the larger settlements.

BROUGH ON HUMBER

East Yorkshire lacked the large late Iron Age centres or oppida of southern Britain, many of which like Silchester, Colchester or Verulamium (St Albans), rose to prominence as important centres during the Roman period. The two largest settlements in Roman East Yorkshire, Brough and Malton, developed from forts and were largely new foundations, though there is evidence of some Iron Age activity in and around both locations. Brough lay on the eastern shore of the Walling Fen tidal estuarine inlet, on a crossing point of the River Humber between the Foulness Valley lowlands and the Yorkshire Wolds; it was therefore ideally situated to function as a port, though so far there is a lack of large-scale port installations (Fig. 40) (Evans and Atkinson 2009, 279) though recent excavations have provided some information about the changing sequence of sediments, demonstrating the rise and fall of sea level around Brough Haven (Fraser and Brigham 2009).

Fig.41 Lead pigs from East Yorkshire. The majority of these were found around Brough and are inscribed SOC.LVT.BRIT.EX.ARG, 'Product of the Lutudariensian partners: From the British lead silver works'. Length *c*. 590mm, weight *c*. 85kg each. (M. Park courtesy Hull and East Riding Museum: Hull Museums)

There is good evidence for trade around Brough including a cluster of lead 'pigs', some inscribed SOCIOR LUT BR EX ARG, 'the product of the Lutudariensian partners: British lead from the lead silver works' (Fig. 41). Lutudarum in Derbyshire was a major production centre of this valuable resource and the lead pigs would have been loaded onto boats and transported up the River Trent to the Humber and beyond. Four lead pigs found at Elloughton near Brough were buried under almost 1.5m of blown sand. At Ellerker, a lead pig was discovered at a depth of 1m in a mortar floor, and a further inscribed example was found in 1967 during an excavation at Faxfleet B near Broomfleet, across the tidal inlet (Sitch 1989). At South Cave the lead pig found in 1980 was located at the edge of a spring. The context of several of the lead pigs seems unusual and although some may be casual losses, others could represent evidence of ritual deposition continuing into the Roman era; alternatively the lead may have been stolen and hidden for later retrieval!

Brough became part of a trading network which included Faxfleet B on the western shore of the estuarine tidal inlet which may also have served as a transhipment point for goods as well as a location from which pilots guided shipping through the difficult waters of the Humber to and from the legionary base and later provincial capital at York (Sitch 1989), where M. Minucius Audens, a gubenator (river-pilot) of Legio VI, dedicated an altar, now in the Yorkshire Museum, York, to the Mother Goddesses of Africa, Italy and Gaul (Ottaway 2004, 61, fig. 29). At Adlingfleet (Fenwick *et al.* 1998) immediately to the south-west of the confluence of the rivers Ouse and Trent with the old course of the River Don, there was also extensive evidence for riverside activity including unusually large quantities of samian pottery. This site may have also served as some form of trading centre associated with military sites further along the river system.

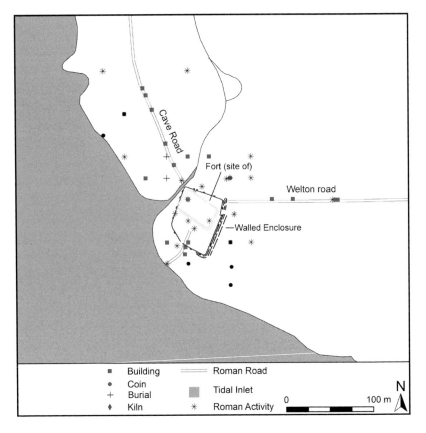

Fig.42 Roman Brough. Note the concentration of activity along the Roman roads. (T. Sparrow)

An altar from Bordeaux in south-western France also provides clues concerning trade along the Humber estuary and beyond. Found during the demolition of a wall constructed in the later third century, it commemorates the fulfilment of a vow by Marcus Aurelius Lunaris, a *servir augustalis* or priest of the imperial cult in both York and Lincoln (Ottaway 2004, 84). On his journey to both places it is very likely that the ships he used would have travelled along the Humber and its associated rivers perhaps bringing in consignments of samian pottery and wine.

Good communications were also provided by the road network, as Brough was situated at the beginning of the main Roman road to York, which skirted round the wetlands on the drier land at the foot of the Yorkshire Wolds, to the east of the Walling Fen inlet. The density of finds along the roads out of Brough, especially on Welton Road which runs eastwards (Hunter-Mann *et al.* 1994) and Cave Road to the north, provides evidence for ribbon development, confirmed by excavations which revealed long narrow plots fronting onto the road itself. It is clear that the settlement was not confined to the area which was later to be enclosed by defences. Recent research including questionnaires of householders in Brough and Elloughton (Clarke 1998; Hanson 2006) has shown that material is still regularly found in gardens, adding to our knowledge of the size of Roman Brough (Fig.42).

The precise status of the Roman civilian settlement at Brough has been a matter of considerable debate (Wacher 1995; Wilson 2003), though it is presumed to be Petuaria, the tribal or 'civitas' capital of the Parisi. Much of what we know has been inferred from an inscription (*RIB* 707) now in the Hull and East Riding Museum, found by Bertie Gott at the west end of Building I in the Bozzes's excavation led by Corder in 1937 (Figs 6 and 43). According to Corder, the stone was found 'lying on end, as if it had fallen from the building when it collapsed, and showed no signs of having been re-used.' The inscription reads:

OB. HONOR[EM]	For the honour
DOMVS DIVI [NAE]	of the Divine house
IMP CAESSTALH [ADRI]	of the Emperor Caesar Aelius Hadrianus
ANT ANTONINIA[VG]	Antoninus Augustus
P P COS	Father of his country, consul
ET NUMINIB A[VG]	and to the spirits of the Augusti
M VLP IANVARIV [S]	Marcus Ulpius Januarius
AEDILIS VICI PETV[AR]	Aedile of the Vicus of Petu(aria)
PROSCAEN	(gives) a stage
DE [S]VO	at his own expense

On the left side of the inscription in a pelta pattern, there is what could be a letter C. This is generally taken to be an abbreviation of *Civitas* (county or tribal area) and it is presumed that there was a matching letter P for *Parisiorum*, of the Parisi, to the right of the inscription. It is possible that the 'C' is merely decorative, though such an interpretation must remain tentative.

The translation of '*vici*' also needs some care. Over time the term *vicus* has been used loosely by archaeologists to define the often rather informal agglomeration of houses, shops, taverns and other structures outside Roman forts such as housesteads on Hadrian's Wall. According to Roman literary sources such as Terentius Varro, however (Lott 2004, 13), it can have a number of meanings: an agrarian village or district comprising a collection of farms, a collection of buildings in or adjacent to a town, or a single apartment building with a number of residents. In the ancient city of Rome itself the term tends to refer to a neighbourhood, not just the structures themselves but the community who resided within them. The *vici* possessed the equivalent of town

Fig.43 The Brough theatre inscription. (P. Halkon courtesy Hull and East Riding Museum: Hull Museums)

councils and office holders were elected by the local population. Graffiti from Pompeii include election slogans promising support for prospective office holders including aediles. We do not know whether this would have been the case in Roman Brough.

An *aedile* was a member of the town council responsible for public order and public buildings and amenities which implies that the settlement here was sufficiently large and of an appropriate status to possess these by the reign of the Emperor Antoninus Pius in the early AD 140s. Marcus Ulpius Januarius was probably the son or grandson of someone who was given Roman citizenship by the Emperor Trajan, as Ulpius was one of the Imperial family names.

So far neither the theatre itself nor any other public buildings such as a forum and basilica, which one might expect in a civitas capital, have been found. Wacher (1995) goes so far as to list reasons why Brough should not be considered as a typical town, arguing that factors such as the surprisingly early date for stone buildings in the Hadrianic to Antonine era (AD 120–180) suggests that these must have had a military function and that the settlement should also possess an organised grid-like street system like the other civitas capitals of Roman Britain. A geophysical survey carried out in Bozzes Field by S. Jallands (1989) whilst a student at Durham University, however, did locate what he interpreted as part of a regular pattern of streets and a large building, possibly serving a public function, such as a forum or basilica, though this has yet to be confirmed by excavation.

Unlike other Roman towns which have benefited from co-ordinated research programmes, the archaeological investigation prior to the modern expansion of Brough has been somewhat piecemeal and it is difficult to work out the precise layout of the settlement and how it functioned and developed. The foundations of stone buildings dating from the second century AD have been found in a number of places which, as we have seen, Wacher thought were unusual for a civil settlement of this date. During rescue excavations by ERAS in 1980 (Halkon 1980) at Welton Road, adjacent to the former annexe of the Flavian fort (SMR 12049), the stone footings of several long, narrow strip-like buildings were partially excavated, but there was insufficient time to record them properly. Few complete ground plans of the houses have been revealed, but some were decorated with painted wall-plaster and their occupants relatively well-off. Secure dating of many of these structures is problematic because of the circumstances of their excavation, but coins of the third century AD were found in a number of buildings in what is now Elloughton (Humber SMR 12507, 12049, 2943, 3481).

Most houses so far excavated were of timber or at least had timber superstructures though some had walls of stone and were roofed with ceramic tiles. A structure on Cave Road, however, which sealed a pit and occupation debris from the mid-second century AD, had stone walls of flat slabs and undressed limestone 0.8m thick which stood to seven courses high. The excavator suggests this was part of a range of outbuildings rather than for living and was utilised for a relatively short time in the first half of the 4th century AD. A narrow gulley running parallel to the building contained the burial of an infant (Evans and Steedman 2001, 77).

The largest area of Brough yet excavated immediately east of the defences, to the south of Welton Road, contained buildings, yards, surfaces and pits, four phases of a ditch-system, wells and a timber structure with a T-shaped 'corn drier' and other evidence for agricultural activity The building plots, probably laid out in the second century AD, running east-north-east from the east gate of the walled enclosure, were aligned along the road (Hunter-Mann *et al.* 2000) (SMR 16500).

The purpose of the walled enclosure is unclear and various explanations have been put forward including the idea that the walls were erected as an expression of civic pride (Esmonde-Cleary 2003). Alternatively the triple ditch and bank system to the east of the enclosure and the presence of bastions may lend support to the idea that the walled area had a military function of some kind, possibly a naval base (Wacher 1969; 1995) as there are precedents for such military installations within towns elsewhere, such as Corbridge (Burnham and Wacher 1990). Only large-scale new work will solve this puzzle, though sadly the rapid rate of development of the modern town may mean that some of the data is already lost. Later Roman Brough will be considered in the context of the end of the Roman period in Chapter 11.

MALTON AND NORTON

The military aspects of Malton and Norton have already been covered. As with Brough the main discoveries have been made through a combination of developer-funded excavation and antiquarian investigation and the evidence has recently been reviewed (Wilson 2003; 2006). Some of the earliest civilian settlement around the fort at Malton grew up near the gateway of the north-eastern side of the fort in the gap between the fort and the River Derwent, particularly in the area now known as Orchard Field constructed, as Hayton was, during the conquest period of Yorkshire (Fig. 44). By AD 79–108 some timber buildings had been built but it is difficult to tell whether these are military or civilian (Wilson 2006). During the period in which the northern frontiers of Hadrian's Wall and the Antonine Wall were being constructed the annexe of the fort was built over with a combination of timber and stone buildings with low stone walls to support a timber superstructure.

In the third century AD there was some new development, but the area of Orchard Field was also used for dumping waste. Excavations as a result of development at Sheepfoot Hill (Wilson 2006; Finney 1990) showed that buildings were also being constructed here. Excavations at the New Rugby Club site (Stephens and Ware 1995)

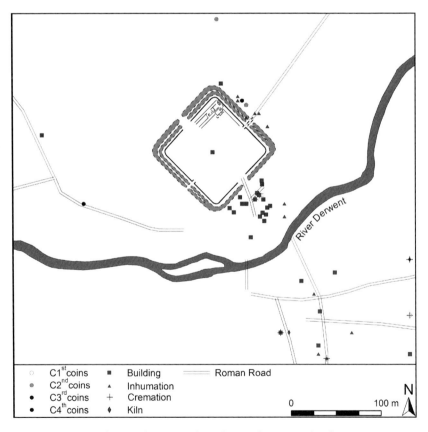

Fig.44 Roman Malton and Norton – based on Robinson and Wilson. (T. Sparrow)

showed that three limestone buildings had been erected dated to the second and third centuries AD.

At the beginning of the fourth century AD a major period of rebuilding commenced, which included the so-called 'Town house' (Mitchelson 1964; Wilson 2006; Wenham and Heywood 1997) decorated with a mosaic and painted wall plaster and further masonry buildings (Plates 28, 29, 30). A possible *mansio* and accompanying bath house were also erected at this time (Wilson 2006, 41). The front part of a larger-than-life copper-alloy foot (Plate 31) from a well-exercuted classical-style statue probably of an emperor, suggests the presence of important official or religious buildings.

All in all the Roman settlement originally thought to have been centred on the fort has now been shown to have been more extensive to the north of the River Derwent than the area mapped by Robinson (1978), with development along the Roman road at the New Rugby Club site and in Old Malton. At the junction between roads entering from the west and north near St Leonard's Lane, third and fourth-century stone buildings with painted wall plaster were built (Wilson 2006).

To the south of the River Derwent in what is now Norton, settlement spread along the Roman roads from the mid-second century onwards. This was largely confined to an area to the east of the present Langton Road and to the south of Commercial Street (Wilson 2003). The remains of buildings are recorded in twenty-four locations (Wilson 2003, 265); some of these being quite well appointed with *opus signinum* floors. A number of these started out as residences but were reused for industrial purposes. Norton became the centre for the manufacture of greyware pottery, with at least half a dozen kilns located around the fringes of the main settlement foci. The pottery production will be discussed in more detail in Chapter 9, but it is possible that the increase in development noted in the third century AD may be associated with this industry.

Perhaps the most intriguing find from Norton is a stone inscription (*RIB* 712), unique in Roman Britain, found in 1814 during the construction of a church. Now in the Yorkshire Museum, York, it reads:

FELICITER SIT
GENIO LOCI
SERVVLE UTERE
FELIX TABERN
AM AUREFI
CINAM

It has been variously translated; 'Good wishes to the Spirit of this Place. Prosper, young slave in your use of this goldsmith's shop' (Ramm 1978, 64) or 'Good luck to the Genius of this place. Young Slave, use to your good fortune this goldsmith's shop'

(Collingwood and Wright 1965, 239). With a cruder style of script than the Brough theatre inscription, it probably dates from the third or fourth century AD. It attests to the presence of slaves in Roman eastern Yorkshire, providing a reminder that it was possible for slaves to prosper. The fact that there was a goldsmith's shop here at all implies the presence of those with sufficient disposable income to purchase gold jewellery. Items of adornment such as gold earrings and finger rings which will be considered more fully in Chapter 10 have been found by metal detectorists in various East Yorkshire locations and recorded by the Portable Antiquities Scheme.

Most of the burials known from Roman Malton/Norton were located to the south of the Derwent and on the fringes of the main area of settlement, although there is evidence for burials outside the north-east, north-west and south-west gates of the fort north of the river. These included cremations and inhumations and will be discussed in Chapter 10.

HAYTON

The fort at Hayton was probably occupied until at least the first two decades of the second century AD. By that time the Roman road from Brough to York had been constructed along higher ground to the east of the Walling Fen tidal inlet. In the Iron Age the settlement pattern in the Hayton area had been focussed on the beck, but with the construction of the Roman road the landscape was realigned. The evidence from field walking, such as pottery and building material demonstrates that a settlement developed at each side of the road, extending for around 400m in a band about 80m wide to each side of it (Fig. 45) (Halkon 2008; Halkon et al. forthcoming).

A combination of geophysical survey and aerial photography shows that the roadside settlement was divided into narrow plots fronting onto the road, with several lanes running at right angles to the main road between the plots. The plots contained pits and wells and from the distribution of field-walked pottery it would appear that rubbish was dumped on middens at the back of the enclosures. Limited excavation and watching briefs prior to development uncovered the foundations of stone buildings of regular-sized masonry resembling the strip houses of the extramural settlements outside the forts along Hadrian's Wall.

All that survived of other buildings were foundations outlined by blocks of red clay of the type which underlies the natural gravel. Material recovered during field walking showed that some of the buildings had bath suites or at least under-floor heating systems. One such structure was what appeared to be a courtyard building aligned on the Roman road, visible in the parching of growing crops. It is possible that this may have been some kind of staging post along the Roman road. The discovery of two seals, one bearing an eagle, the other the stamp of the VI Legion within the settlement perhaps

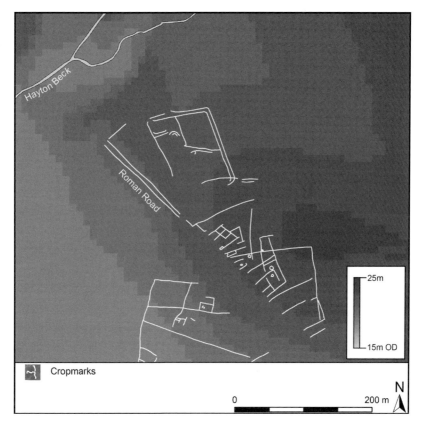

Fig.45 Roman roadside settlement at Hayton based on crop marks. Note the enclosures at the side of the Roman road.

supports this idea. Some of the buildings had glazed windows and mosaic floors, though the majority were probably much simpler and of timber construction.

Roofing material included both ceramic tiles of *imbrex* and *tegula* type and diamond-shaped tiles made from stone quarried in the vicinity of Leeds, known as Elland Flag, which would have overlapped on the roof resembling fish scales. The depth of archaeological layers observed during the digging of service trenches to the new farm buildings was surprising and it was clear that the roadside settlement underwent phases of rebuilding.

Analysis of the pottery found provided some information about the lifestyles of the people who lived there and the length of time that the settlement was occupied. Sherds of amphorae from what are now Spain and Portugal indicated that olive oil was used in cooking and possibly filled oil-lamps, however, although the latter are plentiful in larger towns such as York, they are yet to be found at Hayton. The settlement was supplied with samian tableware imported from southern and central Gaul, some of it decorated and orange earthen ware known by archaeologists as Ebor ware fired in the kilns of the IX and VI Legion based in York. Large food processing bowls or *mortaria* with their characteristic gritted insides and pouring spouts some stamped with the name of the potter or owner of the factory were also found. It is clear that whoever lived at Hayton roadside settlement had adopted a Roman-style cuisine typical of forts and urban centres. As time went on the pottery also included fineware beakers from the Nene Valley around Peterborough, which were probably used for drinking beer.

By the third century AD the bulk of the pottery on the site was grey earthenware produced in the Holme-on-Spalding Moor area which would have been used in the kitchen for a variety of purposes. The presence of large amounts of heavy-duty coarse pottery, the fabric of which contained crushed calcite known by archaeologists as Huntcliff type after the signal station on the North Yorkshire coast, shows that the settlement remained occupied in the late Roman period.

Other artefacts were generally speaking of a kind to be expected from such a Roman roadside settlement and were of higher status and more plentiful than those from Shiptonthorpe which will now be discussed.

SHIPTONTHORPE

Cropmark and palaeo-environmental evidence shows that there was much activity in the surrounding area. Soon after the road was built, probably in the earlier second century AD, it was flanked by a series of enclosures for around 800m (Fig. 46). Investigation shows that some of these were used for settlement, others for gardening and farming or contained cemeteries (Taylor 1995; Millett 2006). In one of them a single horseshoe-shaped building similar to Iron Age roundhouses was constructed which was replaced in the early third century AD by a large aisled hall, 8m x *c.* 21m, with a floor area of *c.* 168 m² (Plate 33b). Standing gable end on to the Roman road, and probably at least 6m high, this building would have certainly impressed those travelling along the road. It may have been roofed with heather (Millett 2006, 311).

The doorway was in the side of the building, dividing it into two portions, one being slightly larger and possibly more prestigious. In the other, furthest away from the road, was an oven. The distribution of finds shows that efforts were made to keep both the aisled hall and the street frontage clean with rubbish heaps or middens at the back.

Judging by the number of settlement enclosures found in the survey and excavation, about twenty family groups totalling around 480 people may have lived here (Millett 2006, 308). The large quantity of finds showed a variety of activities took place. Animal bones with butchery marks and iron blades showed that meat-processing had been

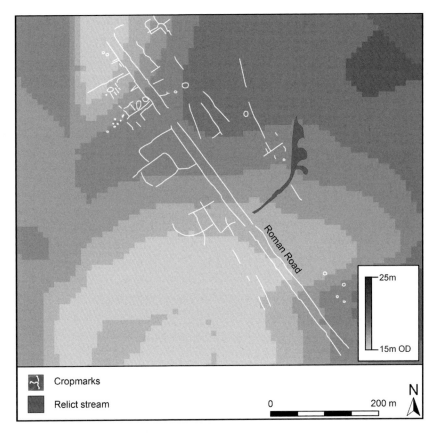

Cropmarks

Relict stream

25m

15m OD

0   200 m

N

Fig.46 Roman Shiptonthorpe taken from crop mark data. The plots of land laid out along the road contained houses, stock and a cemetery. (T. Sparrow)

undertaken. There was an unusual concentration of quern stones for grinding cereals into flour on a large scale (Gwilt 2006). An important group of finds associated with writing included two wooden writing-tablets. Although these were relatively common in Roman Britain, their presence here may imply bureaucratic control of surplus production (Fig. 47).

The writing tablets were found in the back-fill of a communal pond or water-hole dug adjacent to the enclosure in the first half the fourth century AD which may have refreshed stock kept at the settlement and horses and draft animals using the road. Access was provided by a ramp and a small stone trough was found. The damp anaerobic conditions in the first half of the fourth century AD within the pond preserved organic remains such as leather shoes, a wooden comb, two writing tablet fragments and seed and plant remains which were included in the backfill. The best explanation for the presence of some of the objects was deposition as part of ritual. The ritual and

Fig.47 Writing tablets from the waterhole at Shiptonthorpe. Made from Silver Fir, probably recycled from a wine barrel stave, they are of the wax recessed type. Length of largest tablet 88.5mm. (M. Park courtesy Hull and East Riding Museum: Hull Museums)

religious aspects of the waterhole will be discussed in Chapter 10. The settlement may have been a gathering point for produce and perhaps serviced traffic that passed along the Roman road. The general mixture of artefacts showed military, indigenous and overseas influences of a kind to be expected on a roadside site in this region.

STAMFORD BRIDGE

Although the existence of a fort and settlement here was postulated by Ramm (1978, 34), including a possible military oven, it was largely due to the work of Ian Lawton (1994; 1999) that the scale and significance of this site was recognised. A programme of field walking, geophysics and limited excavation showed that occupation began soon after the Roman conquest of the region, continuing until the fourth century AD. There is some evidence for an army presence, particularly around Reckondales (Lawton 1999, 10) as various military fittings have been discovered, though such finds are hardly surprising considering the type of traffic that would have travelled to and from the nearby legionary fortress at York. As at both Hayton and Shiptonthorpe, the focus of settlement was the main Roman road running between York and Brough, near the point where the road crossed a stream, in this case the River Derwent. The *agger* or embankment of this road as it approached the river crossing was identified during a watching brief by Northern Archaeological Associates (NAA) as part of the Etton Wold Water Treatment Works Nitrate Reduction Scheme (Evans and Atkinson 2009, 292). The roadside ditch contained pottery of second to third century date. A further road ran north-west-south-east across Brown Moor continuing through the centre of the present town with a short section joining this and the main road.

Aerial photography, geophysical survey and excavation have shown that the road attracted ribbon development consisting of rectangular plots between 12 and 50m wide, extending between 60 and 150m away from the road (Lawton 1999, 7) which is at its most dense close to the junction of the east-west and north-east to south-west roads before they converge to cross the river. Three main areas of roadside enclosures have been identified: to east of the River Derwent towards Reckondales, to the west at North Farm and at Moor Lane, further away from the road itself there is a cluster of enclosures around a trackway (Fig. 48) (Roe and Lawton 2009).

The excavation by NAA prior to the laying of a new water main showed that Roman activity extended for at least 260m (Parry 2005; Evans and Atkinson 2009). Some of the roadside plots contained residences, pits and wells and 'crop driers'. Some ceramic roof tile was found, though little relative to the size of the settlement (Lawton 1994, 9), however, a concentration of building debris found during excavation led to the partial excavation of a well-appointed house with bath suite, decorated with painted

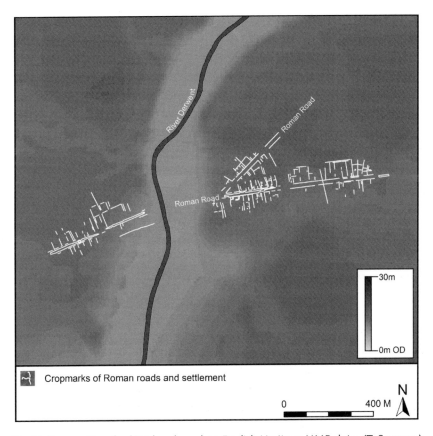

Fig.48 Roman Stamford Bridge, based on English Heritage NMP data. (T. Sparrow)

wall plaster (Lawton 2005). A rare find was an oil lamp, probably manufactured in York. Lamps are generally found on military and urban settings and this example may have been associated with a burial ritual as there were a number of human burials, both cremation and inhumation on this site. The lamp, samian pottery and Dressel 20 olive oil amphorae might be expected on a roadside settlement close to York.

RUDSTONE DALE

Finds of pottery coins and other items have been found for some time around South Cave but an excavation prior to the construction of the Ganstead to Asselby pipeline revealed a settlement similar to Shiptonthorpe which had developed along the Brough-on-Humber to York road (Daniel *et al.* in prep.). The road itself was revealed as a metalled surface. A trackway aligned east-west ran along the site at a right angle to the Roman road, flanked on either side by large drainage ditches. The land on either side was divided into plots, containing buildings of both timber and stone. Crop-driers and possible stock enclosures indicate agricultural activities on the settlement. The burials of seventeen adults, fifty-six neonate burials and five cremations were also excavated.

CONCLUSIONS

One of the aims presented above was to assess the contribution of the larger settlements of eastern Yorkshire to our understanding of the depth of absorption of 'Roman' culture within the region. It is clear that none of the larger Roman settlements in the territory of the Parisi resembled the large towns of southern England such as Verulamium or Wroxeter. Brough and Malton fit into the category of Roman 'Small Towns' (Burnham and Wacher 1990; Wilson 2006), though the status of Hayton and Shiptonthorpe is less secure. Malton, Brough and Hayton, and possibly Stamford Bridge, had military origins, and the army may have provided an initial economic impetus to their growth, which continued at Malton and possibly at Brough. Shiptonthorpe seems to have developed after the construction of the main Roman road between Brough and York. This road also changed the axis of activity at Hayton which had previously focussed along the stream. The construction of the Roman road and ensuing settlements provided market opportunities for the rural hinterland and all the larger settlements were situated at economically strategic locations; Malton and Stamford Bridge were at crossing points of the River Derwent, Hayton and Shiptonthorpe crossed streams and the recently discovered roadside settlement at Rudstone Walk was also associated with a watercourse.

All were in landscape settings allowing easy access along natural route ways to a range of resources such as the chalk uplands of the Yorkshire Wolds, lower heathland environments and riverside wetlands. The increased emphasis on environmental archaeology is enabling us to acquire a clearer picture of conditions within the settlements themselves. Malton/Norton developed the most intensive 'industrial zone', although pottery kilns have been recognised at both Brough and Stamford Bridge, though these were of small scale and short-lived by comparison and conversely a building with a mosaic floor noted amongst the pottery kilns of Norton. The large number of querns associated with an aisled building at Shiptonthorpe implies that this may have been a focus for the processing of crops (Millett 2006) and a millstone was also found at Stamford Bridge (Parry 2005).

The animal bone assemblages from the larger settlements can also shed light on their status. Greater emphasis on sheep rather than cattle is thought to reflect a 'native' rural rather than 'urban' or military emphasis where cattle bones predominate (Mainland 2006; King 2001), however, some caution is needed in areas of wool production. Diet will be discussed in more detail in Chapter 10. The study of Roman coins from settlements can also be used as a method of site characterisation (Reece 1987; Sitch 1998). The presence of early imperial silver coins amongst assemblages for example is usually taken to suggest military influence and there are clear differences between urban and rural sites in terms of the date, quantity, frequency and value of coins lost. Careful comparison across a range of sites has been carried out in East Yorkshire (Sitch 1998) and the pattern of coin loss from Brough equates with military or urban sites, whereas Shiptonthorpe is closer to rural settlements (Sitch 2006, 100).

At Malton and Brough, some of the inhabitants lived in substantial houses with stone walls or footings, glazed windows and a good standard of interior decoration. The varieties of pottery show the adoption of some aspects of 'Roman' cuisine, such as the use of mortaria and amphorae, and in the first two centuries of Roman rule, good-quality imported tablewares such as samian. Again pottery types have been used in settlement differentiation (Evans 2001; Willis 1996), urban and military sites using more fine wares, amphorae and mortaria than rural sites. The Hayton Roman roadside settlement is closer to the urban/military sites in its proportion of these types of pottery than Shiptonthorpe. The Hayton roadside settlement also had buildings with stone footings, ceramic and stone roof tiles, painted plaster and possibly mosaic floors. The houses at the Shiptonthorpe and Stamford Bridge roadside settlements seem to have been of slightly lower status, though recent research implies that substantial timber buildings would still require a substantial level of investment (Martins 2005).

Only at Brough is there any evidence for public buildings in the form of a theatre with a new stage dedicated by the kind of official one would expect to find in a town elsewhere in the Roman world. The Brough theatre inscription also provides a reminder that the adoption of writing has also been regarded as an indicator of the level of integration into the Roman world; tombstones and inscriptions from Malton and Norton, the Brough inscription itself, writing tablets and styli from Shiptonthorpe indicate some level of literacy. What is striking is the paucity of inscriptions as a whole from the region, which may partly be due to lack of suitable stone. The lack of objects such as pottery sherds inscribed with graffiti, usually personal names, has also been noted (Evans 2006(b), 137). Only the theatre inscription from Brough provides a clue as to the name of a settlement. It is important to remember, however, that this inscription itself is damaged in a key place and all we have left are the letters PETV, which has been presumed to be Petuaria.

Some reference has already been made to the speculation concerning the names of the larger settlements of Roman East Yorkshire (Creighton 1988; Hind 2007). The earliest reference to Petuaria is in Ptolemy's *Geographia* referred to above dating from AD 130 to 168. Most authorities agree that the *Decuaria* listed in *Ravenna Cosmography*, a manuscript compiled around AD 700, which survives as a thirteenth and two fourteenth century copies, is a scribal misunderstanding of Petuaria. Praetorio, listed in the *Antonine Itinerary*, is also thought to be a scribal error for Petuaria, however it could simply be derived from *praetorium* (Hind, 2007, 61), the standard Latin word for a headquarters building of a fortress. If that reasoning is adhered to, the route may back-track to York, or perhaps Brough had an important military function at the time of the compilation of the *Antonine Itinerary*, though this seems unlikely. The various attributions and possible meanings of the names of what are presumed to be the significant places of Roman east Yorkshire are tabulated below:

Table 4 The place names of Roman East Yorkshire

Ptolemy	Inscription	Antonine Itinerary	Ravenna Cosomography	Modern Place	Meaning
Petouaria	PETV(ARIA) RIB 707 (1)	Praetorio (2)	Decuaria	Brough (Rivet and Smith 1979; Millett 1989; Hind 2007; Creighton 1988) OR Scarborough or Filey (Creighton 1988) if 'Praetorio' OR York ?	(1) 'The fourth part' (Rivet and Smith 1979; Hind 2007) (2) 'The Praetor's tent'; Headquater's building (Hind 2007; Rivet and Smith 1979)
		Derventione		Malton (Ramm 1978) OR Stamford Bridge (Lawton 1997)	'At the oak-tree river' (Hind 2007)

Continued . . .

Ptolemy	Inscription	Antonine Itinerary	Ravenna Cosomography	Modern Place	Meaning
		Delgouicia	Devovicia Devouicia Denouicia	Millington (Rivet and Smith 1979) OR Wetwang (Rivet and Smith 1979) OR Malton (Creighton 1988) OR Shiptonthorpe (Lawton 1997) OR Hayton	'The thorn bush region' 'The oak-tree region' (if Dervovica) (Hind 2007) 'the town or settlement of the spear fighters' (Isaacs 2004)

The Iter (Journey) 1 of *Antonine Itinerary*, which runs from the northern frontier, provides measurements in Roman miles (*mille passuum* literally 1,000 paces), equivalent to 1,479m or 1,617yds, between the places listed:

> *Eburacum leug. VI*   – Eboracum the VI Legion Victrix , 17 miles (15.6 miles
> *Victrix m.p.XVII*   or 25.116km)
> *Derventione m.p. VII* – At Derventio, 7,000 paces (6.43 miles or 10.34km)
> *Delgouicia m.p. XIII* – At Delgouicia, 13,000 paces (11.94 miles or 19.21km)
> *Praetorio m.p. XX*   – At Praetorium, 25,000 paces (22.96 miles or 35.95km)

Various attempts have been made using this document as a guide to fixing the positions of the named settlements based on these (e.g. Creighton 1988) but as none of them are definite, little is to be gained from further speculation until there is more substantial evidence.

The archaeological evidence shows that three of the larger settlements of Roman East Yorkshire, Stamford Bridge, Hayton and Shiptonthorpe, relate to the road between York and Brough (Margary 2e) as does the recently discovered roadside settlement near South Cave. Similar settlements have yet to be found along the other roads, which may partly be due to lack of investigation, though there are hints of a focus of roadside activity near Goodmanham on the York to Malton road. Roman burials, coins and other artefacts were discovered during the construction of the railway (Kitson Clark 1935). Much Roman coarse pottery and some animal bone was found in the late 1990s by Mr C. Thompson, followed up by systematic field walking coordinated by the writer and Goodmanham residents (Halkon 2008) and there may well be a roadside settlement here though its extent remains unknown. The sheltered location, presence of springs and a beck would have made this site particularly attractive. Further to the north along the same road is Millington, which has, since the discovery of the possible temple site referred to in the first chapter, been regarded as one of the lost named settlements referred to in the Roman sources, Drake's 'Roman Station' of Delgovicia (Drake 1736; Henrey 1986; Ramm 1978). Field work (Halkon 2008) relocated Roman and possibly Iron Age activity, but this was clustered around the site of the possible temple and not along the nearest section of Roman road which runs over steeply undulating terrain to the east.

Locating larger Roman settlements in the Hull Valley and Holderness is much more problematic, partly due to the lack of fieldwork in these areas and the character of the soils which are not as conducive to showing cropmark as the Yorkshire Wolds and Vale of York. The number of sites found during the recent spate of pipeline construction across the region should also be borne in mind. A recent survey of the available evidence in Holderness (Hyland 2009) which will be discussed in more detail in the next chapter, together with antiquarian sources, however, shows clusters of activity in the form of cropmark data and artefacts around Leven, Swine, Hedon, Patrington and Kilnsea/ Easington, though insufficient fieldwork has been done to ascertain the extent of these potential Roman settlements. Roman material has been found in the major towns of modern East Yorkshire: Hornsea, Bridlington, Beverley and Driffield, but none of these locations has sufficient evidence to confirm their prominence in this period. Beverley, Patrington and Bridlington in East Yorkshire and Filey and Scarborough in North Yorkshire have been equated with the 'lost' Roman settlements of the *Antonine Itinerary* (Creighton 1988). It has been suggested that Scarborough and Bridlington, which by tradition have been associated with a larger Roman settlements, may equate with places referred to by Ptolemy (Ramm 1978), but this seems uncertain due to lack of evidence.

None of the larger settlements within Roman East Yorkshire referred to in this chapter could have existed in isolation; they were nodal points on communication systems, and would have had close relationships with the countryside surrounding them, which will be considered in the next chapter.

CHAPTER 8

THE IMPACT OF ROME – THE COUNTRYSIDE

SETTLEMENT AND LANDSCAPE

From the previous chapter it can be seen that the contrast between town and country in this part of Roman Britain was not as clear as it is today. Even the largest settlements of Brough and Malton would probably have had a 'village' feel to them and we know that along the roads out of these settlements were fields and enclosures relating to agriculture. There would have been a greater contrast between the countryside and Roman York, the only place in the wider region which would have been recognisable as a town to Mediterranean visitors. The popular perception is that the Roman countryside was full of villas, largely the country seats of retired soldiers or officials; many years of fieldwork and aerial photography, however, has demonstrated that most people either lived in discrete enclosures, some still containing roundhouses, or continued to occupy the 'ladder' settlements described earlier, which are at their most dense on the Yorkshire Wolds (Fig. 49). The characteristic shape of features appearing as cropmarks sites and their overall distribution provides a broad view of the settlement pattern of Roman eastern Yorkshire. It must be borne in mind, however, that cropmarks show better on well-drained sandy soils and soils over chalk and gravel than clay soils and where soil cover is eroded, so in Holderness in particular, where clay soils predominate, we cannot be absolutely certain that aerial photography can provide the whole picture of past settlement distribution. The dry summer of 2010 revealed a surprising number of new sites revealed as cropmarks, which are in the process of being mapped.

Without surface survey or excavation it can be difficult to work out the precise dating of sites visible as cropmarks, though large-scale field-walking surveys, such as that undertaken in the 20 x 30km Foulness Valley research area (Halkon and Millett 1999; Halkon 2008) can provide a broad chronology. The arrival of hard-fired, mass-produced, wheel-thrown pottery and ceramic building material in the Roman period makes activity within the landscape much more visible. Analysis of the pottery recovered can provide clues as to the date and status of the site on which it was found. Research has shown that hand-thrown clamp-fired pottery does not weather well on the surface of arable fields when compared to the robust kiln-fired Roman fabrics, so again caution is needed when interpreting the evidence. 'Investigator bias' must also be borne in mind when viewing distribution maps: generally speaking the more time spent in an area and the closer the resolution of the survey, the more sites will be found. With these caveats in mind a comparison of the distribution of sites detected through aerial and surface surveys with topographical factors shows that the type and form of rural settlement in Roman East Yorkshire, as in the Iron Age, related closely to the landscape. What follows is a brief survey of settlements across the region, highlighting this relationship. As they are by far in the majority, the first to be considered are those of the more humble kind and the highly 'Romanised' sites will be discussed in a separate section. Partly due to the detailed cropmark coverage and the greater emphasis placed

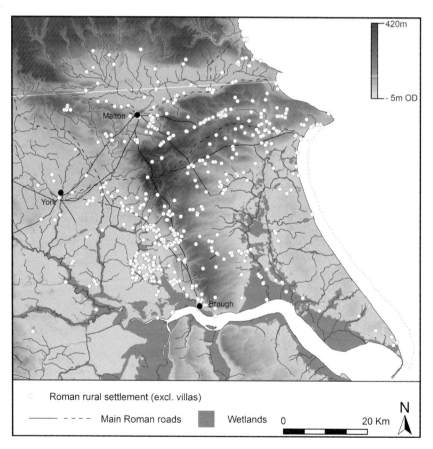

Fig.49 Roman rural settlements in eastern Yorkshire (excluding villas). (T. Sparrow)

on them, rural settlements on the Yorkshire Wolds will be considered after the lesser known and newly found sites in the East Yorkshire lowlands.

LOWLAND SETTLEMENTS

The Aeolian sand ridges and glacial gravel undulations of the Vale of York (Van De Noort, R. and Ellis, S. 1999), Foulness Valley (Halkon and Millett 1999; Halkon 2008), Hull Valley (Didsbury 1988; Van De Noort and Ellis 2000; Wilson *et al.* 2006; Coates 2010) and Holderness (Van De Noort and Ellis 1995; Hyland 2009), especially those close to water sources, were of particular significance. Clusters of settlements continued to develop upon this better drained, slightly elevated land as they had in the Iron Age and in such low-lying areas, enclosure ditches were important for drainage as well as settlement demarcation. Until the excavations at Lingcroft Farm, Naburn (Jones 1988), Roman activity in the Vale of York to the east of the city, at the western boundary of the territory of the Parisi, was little explored. Air photography by Addyman (1984) had picked up clusters of cropmarks and the densest of these, an extensive field system with farmsteads consisting of rectilinear enclosures and roundhouses which developed across a sand ridge, was chosen for further investigation. Significantly, of the five settlement foci excavated, only in Area D was there a clear sequence of features. Here two superimposed roundhouse ring gullies were cut through by a narrow slot and the enclosure slightly realigned and enlarged. The roundhouses were demolished, one possibly by fire and associated enclosure ditches filled in. In great contrast to the hand-thrown pottery of the Iron Age settlement, the new features contained sherds of amphora, mortaria, samian and Ebor ware, glass vessels and ceramic building material, evidence which showed that, according to the excavator, 'the people living in the area rapidly adopted the key elements of the Roman domestic repertoire' (Jones 1988, 168).

It is worth considering finds such as those from Lingcroft Farm more deeply; there is an assumption here of an indigenous population willingly taking on the trappings of a new lifestyle. The site, however, lay only 5km from the legionary fortress at York. Does this 'represent integration ...into the Roman economic system' of native populations (Jones 1988, 169) or could it be evidence for the take-over of local farms as part of the *territorium* or *prata legionis*, the land around a legionary fortress which lay under its direct control (Mason 1988)? The extent to which material culture alone can be used to assess the relationship between the Roman army and newly conquered areas is problematic, but common sense would suggest that the presence of the IX Legion, followed by VI Legion, from *c.* AD 71 to *c.* AD 409, would have had a considerable impact. A legion alone consisted of around 5,000–6,000 men without all the associated personnel and would have required large quantities of grain, meat, timber and other commodities.

There is also the question of the effect that the grants of land to soldiers, or cash lump sums which may have been used for the purchase of land on their retirement (Keppie 2000), might have had on the Parisi. In the territories of the Iceni and Trinovantes the brutal seizure of land by veterans from the Colonia of Colchester, encouraged by the legionaries, was one of the factors which provoked the revolt of Boudicca in AD 60 (Tacitus, *Annals*, 14:31). As we have seen, unlike their neighbours the Brigantes who rose in rebellion after a long period of collaboration, the Parisi have often been perceived as peaceful and accepting of Rome, though the discovery of the South Cave weapons cache demonstrates their capability to be otherwise. Unlike the South, which demilitarised relatively quickly, the army remained influential in the North and the archaeological and epigraphic evidence implies that northern peoples continued to be troublesome well into the second century AD. Ramm (1978) suggested that a series of square enclosures, particularly on the northern Wolds such as Brough Hill, Settrington, Langton and Crossgates, Seamer, represented attempts to 'Romanize' the native population by the 'plantation' of veteran's in farmsteads, though most would now disagree with this idea. On a number of sites in East Yorkshire, however, decorated samian, first to mid-second century coins, often silver denarii, copper-alloy fittings, sometimes enamelled and early brooch types have been found. Are all these finds 'trinkets' acquired in some kind of attempt to take on the trappings of a new way of life, or did these indeed belong to ex-soldiers? Without documentary evidence, this remains a matter of how the evidence is interpreted.

A combination of developer-funded projects, especially the construction of long-distance pipelines and detailed surveys both surface and aerial (Van de Noort and Ellis 1999; Whyman and Howard 2005; Kershaw and Horne forthcoming) are beginning to shed more light on Iron Age and Roman activity in the Vale of York as a whole. Recent plots comparing Roman finds against river systems (Whyman and Howard 2005, 27) demonstrate a close correlation. LiDAR (Light Detection and Ranging) has enabled the detailed reconstruction of the topography (Whyman and Howard 2005, 11) and when Roman site distributions are plotted, it is clear that the higher ground, particularly the Aeolian sand ridges, was favoured. Blank areas correspond to the flood plains of the rivers, particularly the Derwent and the wetter clay soils which developed over the former glacial Lake Humber. Close to a relict stream of the River Derwent near Sutton-on-Derwent, a Roman settlement was discovered by field walking and geophysical survey which may have related to a crossing point (Van de Noort and Ellis 1999). The finds from the site are an intriguing mixture: domestic pottery types typical of the third and fourth centuries AD, slag from blacksmithing, some ceramic building material and more surprisingly fine vessel glass and a gold earring (Plate 39).

The Vale of York surveys confirmed the results of fieldwork at Holme-on-Spalding Moor in the Foulness Valley (Halkon and Millett 1999; Halkon 2008) on its eastern edge, where aerial archaeology has revealed a complex web of enclosures and other features on the sand ridges close to the River Foulness. Their morphology suggests that many of them originated in the Iron Age and were later superimposed with rectilinear enclosures and possible buildings. Many of the densest palimpsests of features within the 8 x 8km Holme-on-Spalding Moor study area yielded Roman pottery on field walking, the best examples being at Skiff Lane and Throlam (Halkon and Millett 1999). The ridges of sand along the river itself at Bursea and Hasholme are also covered in Iron Age and Roman cropmark features. The longevity of these sites was confirmed by excavations at Hasholme Hall (Hicks and Wilson 1975; Halkon and Millett 1999) and Bursea House (Halkon and Millett 1999). Around both sites there was extensive evidence for furnace-based industrial activity with pottery and iron production which will be considered in more detail below. The acidity of the sandy soils was such that animal bone did not survive, but what palaeo-environmental evidence there was showed that the settlements were part of a mosaic of managed woodland, wetland and possibly a little arable, with grazing for cattle (Halkon and Millett 1999; Halkon 2008). The small amount of samian pottery and mortaria sherds showed at least a familiarity with the Roman world before the commencement of major pottery production in the later third-fourth centuries AD, endorsed by the discovery of a trumpet brooch and a few Roman coins associated with a large double-ditched rectilinear enclosure on a sand hill to the west of the Hasholme Hall site. Amongst the finds here was a small votive axe pierced for suspension. Axes such as this are thought to relate to Vulcan, the god of furnace-based industries, and similar finds will be considered in more detail in Chapter 10.

The construction of the Asselby to Gansted pipeline provided an opportunity to sample the flat landscapes of the Vale of York to the south-west of Holme-on-Spalding Moor, where little archaeological investigation had been carried out. At Howden Common and a few other places there was evidence for low-density activity in the later Iron Age and Roman period in the form of roundhouses, field ditches and the occasional inhumation demonstrating increased exploitation of a low-lying wetland environment by native subsistence farmers (Daniel *et al.* in prep.) coinciding with an amelioration in climate and marine regression at this period. Closer to the past and present course of the River Derwent, the densest activity along this stretch of the pipeline may have been associated with a possible villa at Thorpe Hall to the north of Howden (Daniel *et al.* in prep.).

The settlement excavated at Hawling Road, Market Weighton, prior to the construction of the Market Weighton bypass (Creighton 1999) compares closely in both methods of subsistence and lifestyle to the sites around Holme-on-Spalding Moor. There was no evidence for major industry here and it is likely that the settlement was primarily agricultural as palaeo-environmental evidence shows the landscape here was less wooded than the lower Foulness Valley (Creighton 1999). Analysis of pottery from field walking provided some evidence for settlement shift (Evans 1999, 190–191).

The Hawling Road site is at the northern end of a dense concentration of cropmarks immediately to east of the Walling Fen, extending almost to the Humber itself, along the sand and gravel ridge at the base of the Lias Bench, which forms the foothills of the Yorkshire Wolds. At South Cliffe (Halkon 2008), two of these sites were systematically field walked and there was an interesting contrast between the finds recovered. The most southerly site consisted of overlapping square enclosures and small ring ditches, possibly hayrick stands, to the east of a major boundary feature, probably of later Bronze Age/early Iron Age date, remained influential into the Roman period. A surprising amount of Iron Age pottery was found here and continuing Roman activity attested by samian pottery, Ebor oxidised wares from the legionary kilns at York, and Flavian period Lincolnshire greywares, but there were no later pottery types such as Crambeck or Huntcliff. During subsequent metal detecting a number of high-quality brooches of late first and second century date and other metal artefacts were found which complement the pottery well both in terms of date and status (Chris Fenn pers. comm.).

The dearth of later Roman material here was paralleled around a kilometre to the north-east, just west of Hotham Beck on well-drained sandy soil at 25m OD, where a series of intercutting field boundaries found during the construction of the Ganstead to Asselby pipeline may relate to a nearby settlement (Daniel *et al*. in prep.). A small assemblage of animal bone, a large quern or millstone and pottery dating from the late second to mid-fourth century AD were associated with these features, but there was no Huntcliff or Crambeck pottery present, suggesting that this settlement had also ended by the mid- to late fourth century AD. The remains at Hotham Beck were sealed by a layer of overburden and the site was not visible as a cropmark. It is possible, therefore, that the land close to the Lias Bench between the Wolds and the Vale of York may have been more extensively utilised in the Roman period than the cropmark data suggests. In contrast, a larger and denser palimpsest of features 2km to the north had very little evidence for early Roman activity with very little fine ware and much pottery from the later Roman period (Halkon 2008).

Further south along this complex of cropmarks, quarrying for sand and gravel at North Cave provided opportunities for further archaeological investigation. Following a few chance finds such as a Dragonesque brooch, ornamental knife handle and some coins (Loughlin and Miller 1979), a series of excavations was carried out prior to quarrying. In the 1970s Rodney Mackey investigated an Iron Age and Roman settlement consisting of a series of enclosures, some containing roundhouses, along a droveway, overlain by a further enclosure and a post-built rectangular structure. Much pottery was found showing that the site was occupied up to the late third or early fourth century, along with the rare evidence for bronze casting discussed earlier. Sporadic excavation between 1986 and 2008, largely carried out by the Humberside Archaeology Unit and its successor Humber Field Archaeology (Dent 1989; Brigham *et al*. 2008; Evans and

Atkinson 2009) complemented the findings of Mackey but covered a much larger area, revealing further droveways, fields, enclosures and houses, both round (some of which may have continued to be occupied into the Roman period) and rectangular in construction. A number of human burials, both cremations and inhumations, were found. Although Roman burial and religious matters will be dealt with later, it is worth highlighting one of the burials from North Cave excavated in 2002 (Evans and Atkinson 2009, 292; British Archaeology August 2002, Issue 66) for it encapsulates the character of these settlements. Without the Roman wheel-thrown jars at its head and feet and the wide-mouthed bowl at its back, this inhumation, with its crouched position, was almost identical to Iron Age Arras culture burials from any cemetery on the Yorkshire Wolds (Fig. 76). Roundhouses may have been replaced to some extent by rectangular structures, with some adoption of wheel-thrown greyware pottery, but the general impression is of relatively poor peasant communities of Iron Age local origin continuing much as they had before the Roman conquest.

There are similarities between human/landscape interaction in the lowlands of the Vale of York and Foulness Valley in the Roman period to those in the valley of the River Hull on the other side of the Yorkshire Wolds. A Roman road from Malton (Ramm 1978) on the Wolds dip-slope may have extended through Bishop Burton towards the Humber at Hessle Haven, where there may have been a portage or other form of access point to the estuary (Didsbury 1990) which has yet to be fully investigated. This road hugged higher ground in a very similar way to the Brough-Stamford Bridge road to the west of the Wolds.

Before the 1980s, little Roman material had been found between the Yorkshire Wolds and the River Hull in and around the Haltemprice district villages such as Hessle, partly due to the fact that many of these expanded before the need to carry out pre-development archaeological investigation was recognised and general lack of interest in these areas. Roman pottery is recorded from the garden of Alexander Lodge, Kirk Ella (Loughlin and Miller 1979, 29). Of particular note, however, is a small copper-alloy figurine wearing a heavy gown and the mask of an actor, probably the comedy/slave character of the Roman theatre found near Great Gutter Lane, Willerby, and now in the Hull and East Riding Museum. This is possibly the most overtly classical object yet found in the East Yorkshire region. Whilst the object itself is almost certainly genuine, its precise context is insecure, as the letter accompanying the find reports it as having been unearthed whilst gardening, together with what are described as Victorian toys. On the other hand it may be associated with a Roman road running eastwards from Brough and may be a souvenir from the theatre itself.

The glacio-fluvial sands and gravels between Beverley and Cottingham are conducive to showing cropmarks, particularly around Woodmansey (Didsbury 1989) and an opportunity to ground-prove these came during salvage excavation near

Park Grange Farm (Didsbury 1989, 25). Discoveries included cobble spreads and various ditches contained Iron Age and Roman pottery, including some samian and butchered animal bones. Close by, a relict spring seems to have become the focus of ritual activity. In the same cropmark complex, at Burn Park Farm, field walking located an extensive spread of Roman pottery associated with settlement and possible manuring for arable farming (Didsbury 1989). Once again the construction of a pipeline presented a further opportunity to investigate the landscape between Brough and Woodmansey (Dickson 2003) which confirmed exploitation of the slightly higher land for agriculture and some settlement throughout the Roman period.

In the Vale of York and the western margins of the Hull Valley, extensive evidence for Roman activity has been located, particularly on slightly raised land, with sites close to watercourses being particularly favoured. For many years, however, it was supposed that much of the lower Hull Valley around the City of Kingston upon Hull itself was devoid of Roman activity because it was under water and the few Roman finds handed in to Hull Museums were attributed to servicemen returning from overseas losing the ancient souvenirs picked up during their foreign postings in the First and Second World Wars (Didsbury 1990). In the series of excavations undertaken in the Old Town, the discovery of Roman pottery showed that buried Roman land surfaces may exist (Bartlett 1971), but it was not until 1984 that this suspicion was confirmed when the owner of a new house at Greylees Avenue, on the outskirts of the city just off Beverley High Road, not far from the west bank of the River Hull, recognised samian and other Roman pottery as he prepared his new garden. The occupant informed Hull Museums and the subsequent excavation yielded 4,000 Roman finds from the later first to fourth centuries AD, including building remains and ditches suggestive of land management, and a detailed survey of the lower Hull Valley followed (Didsbury 1988; 1989; 1990; Evans and Steedman 2000, 198). The importance of this work cannot be over-emphasised, for unlike other parts of the region such as the Yorkshire Wolds, where Roman finds could be expected and a tradition of fieldwork established, new ground was being broken in the face of much scepticism. Geographical investigation including a study of boreholes (Didsbury 1988; 1990) allowed the construction of subsurface contours demonstrating that fluctuations in sea level had taken place, covering the boulder clay deposited during the Ice Age with alluvium; what was once dry land flooded and then became dry land again. The distribution of sites and finds (Didsbury 1988, 32) showed that the -3.8m OD contour was crucial in demarcating the area dry enough to support settlement during the later Iron Age and early to middle Roman period, yet close enough to the river to facilitate its use for transport and allowing exploitation of the alluvial silts flanking the River Hull for pasture and other purposes.

Apart from the Greylees Avenue site, the most significant amount of Roman pottery was found at Haworth Hall, not far from the west bank of the River Hull. Much of this material had been buried during subsequent periods of flooding. One of the most fascinating Roman finds from Hull, and indeed one of the first to be documented (Sheppard 1912b; Kitson Clark 1935) was a complete later third to fourth century AD wheel-thrown greyware jar with two small loop handles, typical of the East Yorkshire pottery industries, recovered during the building of a laundry on Thoresby Street. There were marks on the pot made by the tunnels of rag worm, showing that at this time the area lay in the intertidal zone (Didsbury 1988, 32).

Didsbury's fieldwork alerted those responsible for planning and development to the possibility that further Roman material lay buried under alluvium deposited by late/ post Roman flooding, particularly in the northern part of the city and its outskirts and this was found to be the case at a number of locations on both banks of the River Hull. Excavation in the 1990s in the Sutton Fields industrial estate at Malmo Road, to the east of the River Hull, revealed drip-gullies from rectilinear buildings, postholes, pits and ditches and a 60m cobbled trackway (Evans and Steedman 1997, 124; 2000; 2001, 88). Further investigation was undertaken here in 2005 (Evans and Atkinson 2009, 289) with finds including ceramic building material, animal bone and pottery from the second and third centuries AD. The ceramic building material included tile from both roofs and central heating systems and a fragment from a stamped tile of the VI Legion. These finds are intriguing: is this a demonstration that people local to the area here had fully absorbed Roman lifestyles, or was the site in some way connected along the river system to the legionary fortress at York?

Further upstream at Gibraltar Farm, now under the Kingswood development, was a riverside settlement at least 60m in extent, occupied from the second half of the second century AD into the fourth century AD. Again traces of rectilinear buildings within a series of enclosures were found along with evidence that cattle had been butchered on site. Palaeo-environmental remains showed that the area had been meadow and pasture, so it seems likely that just as it had been in medieval and more recent times, the riverside was exploited for the raising of livestock, with settlements spaced around 0.8km and 1.2km, particularly on bends (Evans and Steadman 2000, 197). The range of pottery which included imported continental types provided evidence for trade and access arrangements had been made for shallow-draught boats (Evans and Steedman 2001, 88). Recent discoveries of Roman pottery and debris from the manufacture of glass bangles at Thearne, on the Woodmansey gravels to the west of the River Hull (Campbell 2008) confirm its use as part of a trading network.

The archaeological evidence demonstrates widespread activity along the River Hull in and around the present city throughout the Roman period. The small cluster of pottery on both banks at its present confluence with the River Humber (Didsbury 1988, fig. 2.3) may be from some kind of trading centre, which is to be expected at such a location and subsequently hidden or lost completely in the considerable changes associated with the growth of Hull as a leading port and city. The borehole data, however, did make it possible to present a reconstruction of the Humber shoreline around this point (Didsbury 1989, 23–24). A series of creeks fanned northwards, forming embayments, the most significant at the mouths of the main stream of the River Hull and the 'Old Fleet'. The Roman sites at Haworth Hall and Frog Hall are conveniently situated at either side of the River Hull and the Iron Age and early Roman settlement at Salthouse Road referred to above and a fourth century AD coin hoard from Sutton are on the west bank of the Lambwath stream. Close to these there was a small settlement at Bransholme. Activity on many of the sites so far excavated in the lower Hull Valley is punctuated by phases of marine transgression and regression (Metcalfe et al. 2000; Coates 2010). This probably follows the relationship between sea level and availability of land for exploitation observed at Adlingfleet near Goole, and further south at Littleborough-on-Trent (Riley, Buckland and Wade 1995) referred to earlier.

The relationship between settlement location and topography in Roman Holderness as in the lower Hull Valley is marked and this region too has been neglected by archaeologists. The combined distribution of coins, pottery, artefacts and settlements from aerial photography shows that the past and present streams and former meres were most favoured (Van de Noort and Ellis 1995; Hyland 2009). This is particularly noticeable in the south-east of Holderness between Kilnsea and Easington, between Patrington and Withernsea, at the southern entrance to Winestead Carrs and to the east of Hedon, as in all these locations Roman activity appears to have been placed to exploit former creeks or 'fleets' now reduced by medieval and modern drainage, but still visible on soil maps as 'fingers' of alluvium (Sheppard 1966, 3) or in some cases still flowing along managed courses. From south to north, the Easington, Winestead, Keyingham and Hedon fleets had valleys 1km wide in places and would have been flooded for part of the year. Access to these watercourses, which flowed south-westwards, was via the Humber estuary rather than into the North Sea and it is likely that some were navigable.

The sources of these streams which rose from higher ground to the east have largely been lost due to coastal erosion. As we saw in Chapter 2, it is estimated that between 2–4km of Holderness has been lost since the Roman period (De Boer 1996(a), 7). At Old Kilnsea, for example, one of around twenty lost settlements, the twelfth-century church described as standing on a hill, fell into the sea in 1824 (Sheppard 1912a). In the Roman period, however, such a location proved attractive, as the densest cluster of finds in South Holderness lies on each side of the Easington/Kilnsea Fleet. On a rise of glacial till surrounded by alluvium, ninety-five sherds of Roman pottery of the third to fourth century AD were found during systematic field walking on a site known as Kilnsea 8 (Head et al. 1995, 290). This assemblage included East Yorkshire wheel-thrown greywares, and Huntcliff and Crambeck fabrics so typical of later Roman East Yorkshire. Earlier finds which have eroded out of both the Humber and North Sea shores at Kilnsea include a bronze figurine of the god Mercury 11.4cm high (Poulson 1829, 13), bronze brooches, one of enamelled Dragonesque type, many bronze and silver coins, querns and much pottery (Clark 1935, 95; Loughlin and Miller 1979, 52). From the lighthouse Sheppard reported seeing the lines of ditches, presumably from enclosures, and a complete pot and headless skeleton were found in a peat bed near Kilnsea Beacon close to the present seashore (Clark 1935, 95). The narrow, reinforced and beautifully bleak Spurn peninsula one sees today makes it difficult to visualise the extensive arable farmland that must have spread over the area, only apparent today in the small amount of medieval rig and furrow still visible between Kilnsea and Easington. Even more land would have been available in the Roman era and the querns recorded provide evidence for at least the processing of cereal crops and perhaps their cultivation.

At Easington there are reports of sections across Roman features visible in the cliffs, some substantial at over 2m deep and 2m wide, their fills containing complete vessels, animal bones and oyster shells (Clark 1935, 78). Brooches including one of headstud type and coins ranging from a denarius of Hadrian to small bronze coins of Valentinian, have also been listed (Hyland 2009). These casual finds from the southern tip of Holderness provide a glimpse of considerable activity. Quantities of Roman pottery had been reported in 1967, when the first gas terminal was built, close to the sea to the north of the village and the material described makes it likely that the main focus of settlement has been lost (D. Evans pers.comm.). The construction of the Langeled Receiving Facilities between 2003 and 2004 (Richardson 2011) provided the first opportunity for large-scale excavation in the region and an insight into how a rural settlement changed from the Iron Age to Roman periods. A group of late Iron Age roundhouses was built to north-east of the junction of two trackways with radiocarbon dates of between 60 BC and AD 90. Sometime between AD 10 and AD 150, however, the houses were demolished and replaced by a square enclosure within a palisade. A 12m-diameter roundhouse and smaller ovate structure were built within the enclosure. Whilst the structure itself is of typical Iron Age form, other features in the same phase produced samian pottery and a mid-first to earlier second century AD headstud brooch. To the south of the trackway, part of a further enclosure contained a pit with 600 pottery sherds of the first century AD in its fill and fired clay. The bases of possible kilns may relate to the firing of handmade pottery, but within the fill of the structure was a silver denarius of Trajan dated AD 103–111 and a decorated bridle cheek piece of first to second century type. A pit at the junction of the two trackways contained the complete skeleton of a horse at least fourteen years old at death standing to just over 12 hands. It is just possible that the horse and bridle fragment are contemporary as the horse bone was dated between AD 70 and 240. An inhumation of an adult human and cremated human bone in a pit also fell in the same broad date range as the horse. Other finds included evidence for blacksmithing and fragments from several glass bangles.

At Scorborough Hill near Skeffling, the Iron Age settlement referred to in Chapter 5 excavated during the construction of the Asselby to Easington pipeline (Daniel *et al.*

in prep.; Rowland 2012; Wilson 2011, 349) continued into the Roman period with the construction of further ditched enclosures. The relatively large assemblage of Roman finds in the Roman phase included material imported into the area from south of the Humber. At nearby Welwick (Site J) a small late Iron Age and Roman settlement also received pottery from North Lincolnshire including rusticated wares, though half the pottery assemblage was in local handmade wares. A field system was appended to the enclosures in the second century AD. The appearance of large quantities of oyster shells at this location reveals a new component in the diet, as it would seem that the eating of large amounts of shellfish, so popular in the Roman period was avoided in the Iron Age. This and other aspects of food consumption will be considered further in Chapter 10.

In the southern tip of Holderness, we have seen evidence for considerable Roman settlement, especially on the edges of the Easington Fleet. It must be remembered, however, that recent finds along the shore of the North Sea here were not coastal in the Roman period and a great deal of material and in all probability key sites have been lost. There is a similar range of Roman finds along the valley between Patrington and Withernsea, though not as many, and insufficient as yet to support the various antiquarian claims that Patrington was the lost *Praetorio* of the *Antonine Itinerary* (Poulson 1841). The only find to suggest any importance is a gold coin of Gratian (AD 367–83) found 'in a bean field' at Winestead in 1828 (Clark 1935, 120) and a range of coins of lesser denomination has been reported at various locations. Querns were recovered from stone walls at Patrington (Clark 1935, 120) but their original findspots are unknown. The Paull to Easington pipeline revealed a few more sites around Patrington. Site 10 near Patrington Haven referred to in Chapter 5 was remodelled and Roman features included a large waterhole, trackway and enclosure system for stock management. In the second century the increase in field size here suggests that arable farming became more important. The pottery recovered included Holme-on-Spalding Moor and Dales ware pottery and the presence of Crambeck and Huntcliff fabrics shows continued activity until the end of the Roman period (Wilson 2011, 349, Rowland 2012).

Little excavation has been done at Withernsea, though a pit containing the sherds of a second to third century AD bowl was observed in a watching brief at Queen Street (Evans and Steedman 2000, 94). A Roman coin of Salonina, wife of Gallienus, AD 253–68, more querns, 'Roman urns' and a hoard of coins from the mid-third century washed out of the cliff have also been reported (Clark 1935, 140–41). Again it must be remembered that in the Roman period Withernsea was not at the seaside, the suffix '-sea' is derived from a word for lake as in Hornsea.

There are less Roman finds recorded in the block of land between the Winestead and Keyingham Fleets, but at Keyingham itself, in the mouth of the Fleet Valley, there are first and fourth-century coins, pottery finds and lead. Roman pottery has been found at Roos and at Halsham, the possible Roman barrow (Loughlin and Miller 1979, 53) or more likely reuse of a Bronze Age barrow for burial, will be discussed later. A Roman cemetery is recorded at Ken Hill, Keyingham, but was destroyed by gravel extraction in 1973 (Loughlin and Miller 1979, 55). Roman pottery has also been found in the cliffs at Tunstall. All these finds eroding from the soft Holderness cliffs provide a reminder that important information concerning Roman East Yorkshire is now beyond recovery.

The alluvium around the Hedon Fleet, the most northerly of the South Holderness watercourses, extends for only 6km. Overlooking this at Market Hill, Hedon, was a settlement of some kind deliberately situated on chalky till, excavated in 2004 (Evans and Atkinson 2009, 287). A ditch cut into gravelly subsoil contained Roman pottery of the second to third century AD and ceramic tile. Although its precise findspot is unknown, a hoard of third-century coins was found in the town in 1922 (Loughlin and Miller 1979, 54). A greater concentration of coins dating from the third and fourth century AD is recorded at Paull (Hyland, 2009, 184) and brooches found there are of earlier Trumpet and Headstud type. In contrast very little pottery has been picked up, even during systematic survey (Head *et al.* 1995), though a Roman pottery sherd was found buried by alluvium at a depth of 1.5m (Hyland 2009, 193) showing that here also Roman activity may still lie hidden. The finds that have been made are associated with a series of what would have been 'islands' providing drier locations for various activities and perhaps settlement.

North of Hedon, the landscape of Holderness changes slightly with long ridges of gravel corresponding with those to the west of the River Hull providing easier access across the Hull Valley wetlands. Partly because of the more freely draining gravel soils, sites are revealed as cropmarks which can be dated typologically to the Iron Age and Roman periods. Few of these have, however, been investigated on the ground and consequently finds remain sparse. The finds that have been made are concentrated in and around the present villages of south-west Holderness such as Preston, where third and fourth-century coins are recorded. Further north still, it is possible that a Roman road may have crossed into Holderness, somewhere in the parish of Swine, though there is little evidence to support Drake's projected route, which depends largely on the now discredited presumption that Beverley was Petuaria and Patrington was the Praetorio of the *Antonine Itinerary*. However, if the Roman road running from Brough is projected eastwards across the River Hull it is possible that it may have reached this location. The rolling boulder clay here, rising to between 12–27m OD, provides a suitable settlement location, though the village itself is only at 3m OD.

Seven hoards of Roman coins are reported in the parish of Swine (Leake 2012). One found in 1826 by a group of boys contained between 1,400 and 1,500 coins of fourth-century date. They are described as being placed on their edges (Kitson Clark 1935, 130; Poulson 1841, 215). In 1850 in a field near Castle Hill, a further hoard was found which included silver denarii of Trajan and Marcus Aurelius, and Domitian. Another found during ploughing near Abbey Garth was contained in a narrow-necked greyware jar consisting of 3,099 coins all of Constantine I, dating from the AD 320s and 330s (Humber SMR 1516). Another hoard found in 1940 comprised silver and copper-alloy coins ranging from the 30s BC to AD 183, associated with a samian sherd. A small hoard of seventeen copper-alloy Constantian coins were found between North and East Carr in 1987 (Didsbury 1990, 207). There are several other findspots of coins within the parish of Swine.

The reason for the discovery of so many coins here is not known, but it may relate to its position on a suitable crossing point across the Hull Valley wetlands. Cropmarks of linear features and enclosures have been recorded on the gravel rises around the village, which are probably of Iron Age and Roman date. As no detailed survey has been carried out here, the extent of settlement is not known but extensive pottery scatters, including samian, have been reported (S. Thompson pers. comm.; Loughlin and Miller 1979, 60). One of the coin hoards was found in 1826 near an enigmatic series of earthworks, now ploughed out, and described as a 'Roman camp' (Thompson 1824, 213–4). One can see why this was thought to be Roman, as at first glance the playing card shape of the earthworks does resemble the corner of a fort, however the double banks made up of five pairs of long banks separated by gaps, with a ditch between them, make this identification very unlikely. The large ovate mound with three smaller equally spaced mounds to the north may be a barrow cemetery.

Further to the north, the distribution of coins, pottery and cropmark sites shows that the Lambwath stream between Aldbrough near the coast and the eastern suburbs of the city of Hull continued to influence settlement location as it had in the lower Hull Valley. As we have seen, fieldwork prior to the construction of gas pipelines and storage facilities around Aldbrough has led to the discovery of Iron Age and Roman activity (Evans and Atkinson 2009). At Garton Road, Aldbrough, and at several places in the neighbouring East Garton parish, later Iron Age settlements with field systems continued in occupation and underwent some remodelling in the first and second centuries AD. On farmland to the north of Coldharbour Farm and to the north-west of Northfield House, samian pottery, mortaria, a flagon in an oxidised fabric with a white slip and greyware from North Lincolnshire kilns were excavated. Other finds included items of personal adornment: a copper-alloy disc, blue glass bead and part of a jet finger ring, and iron slag, hammer scale and burnt clay provided evidence for industrial activity on a domestic scale (Evans and Atkinson 2009, 261). The same caveats in interpreting site distributions in Holderness, as in the other lowland areas outlined above, must be borne in mind, for these finds lay buried under alluvium which enabled the preservation of charred vegetation including barley grain, oats and hazelnuts together with wood fragments.

Following the pattern elsewhere in Holderness, the distribution of Roman finds between Leven on the margins of the Hull Valley and Hornsea on the coast relates to watercourses, and again slightly raised land was favoured. The construction of the Leven to Brandesburton bypass provided an opportunity for survey and excavation across this landscape and settlements of the second and fourth centuries AD were identified (Evans and Steedman 1997). The ditches, pits and other features of the second-century settlement included both native style hand-thrown fabrics with some fine wares. Within the fourth-century enclosure there were features relating to buildings and the palaeo-ecological data shows that this was probably a mixed arable/pastoral farm (Hall and Huntley 2007); although only a single charred cereal grain was found, the weeds present provided evidence for disturbed ground, presumably cultivation and dung heaps, indicating the presence of livestock, which the bone evidence showed was mainly cattle. Some sheep or goats were also kept and there was at least one horse (Dobney *et al.* 1993). Once again the distribution of evidence for Roman activity in the countryside between Leven and Hornsea is focussed along watercourses, though the original courses of these have been largely lost in the creation of the Leven Canal but still detectable in the Carr Dike as it runs towards Hornsea Mere. Roman pottery dating from the second century has been found in Hornsea itself as well as fourth-century coins (Loughlin and Miller, 1979, 54).

In northern Holderness the landscape changes, especially towards the north and east, closer to the Yorkshire Wolds, with higher ground created by deposits of glacial gravel and sand. There are more cropmark sites here. Although the majority of these remain uninvestigated, they are likely to be of Iron Age and Roman date. Once again finds cluster around streams, such as the ancient watercourse of the Earl's Dike, although field walking by the Humber Wetlands Project along the North Holderness coast around the meres (Van de Noort and Ellis 1995) produced little in the way of evidence for Roman rural settlement apart from a few sherds of pottery. As elsewhere along the coast, finds distribution is also skewed by erosion, with artefacts being recovered from the beach casually and with metal detectors and antiquarians such as the Morfitts of Atwick and Thomas Boynton who farmed at Barmston. The hoard of first and second-century coins in a pot from Auburn recovered from a house as it fell into the sea referred to earlier (Kitson Clark 1935, 63) is especially intriguing as the age of this house is not clear. As well as coins, a small silver Trumpet brooch was found at Ulrome and a copper-alloy Headstud recorded at Barmston. Pottery including mortaria sherds is recorded in a number of places such as West Furze, once thought to be lake-village, but subsequently shown to be a Bronze Age timber trackway (Van de Noort and Ellis 1995).

A number of Roman finds have been made in the area of north Holderness closest to the east bank of the River Hull and the carr land which flanks it. At Gransmoor, the Granthams found Roman pottery close to the village, again on raised land on the wetland margins. A hoard of sixteen bronze and one silver coin excavated in 1897 whilst a drainage ditch was deepened at Copper Hall Farm, Skerne, was found on similar terrain. Accompanying the coins were two pieces of copper alloy which were interpreted as the handles of some form of organic container, possibly a purse or casket (Mortimer 1905, 352). At Copper

Hall and nearby Cleaves Farm, Skerne, Roman pottery and ditches were reported (Dent 1990, 105) though little Roman material was found in the vicinity during subsequent fieldwork by the Humber Wetlands team (Chapman *et al.* 2000). This may be due to masking by flood deposits which include marine diatoms (Dent 1990, 105). At Wansford, on low-lying land on the opposite side of the river from Skerne, a small later Iron Age and Roman site was excavated prior to the construction of a water treatment plant, which provided a reminder that sites may lie buried under alluvium.

In the north of the tribal territory detailed landscape analysis has been undertaken around West Heslerton in the Vale of Pickering (Powlesland 1988; 2003(a); Powlesland *et al.* 2006). Again there was a close relationship between activity and landscape morphology. Perhaps due to masking by alluvial and Aeolian deposits, little evidence for Roman period activity was found on the floor of the Vale itself, perhaps due to its wetness at certain times, especially in the fourth century AD. Some relief was provided by low ridges running across the Vale, but most Roman period activity was concentrated at around 30m OD, where linear settlements with their origins in the Iron Age developed to north and south of the wetlands. Geophysical survey shows that the linear settlement extended to 12km in length, comprising a droveway with flanking enclosures nucleating around every 250m. Judging from the number of frog bones found in their upper fills, some of the ditches excavated at Sherburn remained wet and were frequently re-cut (Powlesland 1988, 145). It is clear that the enclosures were used for a range of activities, including stock rearing, particularly cattle, and habitation which may account for their variation in shape and size. The overlapping and realignment of the enclosures provides evidence for constant remodelling of the settlement. One of the most remarkable Roman period discoveries at West Heslerton was the late Roman shrine and associated buildings which will be discussed in Chapters 10 and 11.

THE YORKSHIRE WOLDS AND FOOTHILLS

The cropmark coverage of the Yorkshire Wolds is dominated by linear enclosure complexes or ladder settlements (Stoertz 1997) which, as we have seen, developed in the mid- to late Iron Age. The significance of their landscape setting has been discussed already. Too few have been excavated to enable a full picture to be gained, but from the work done so far (Atha 2007) many of the strings of enclosures along droveways remained in use, some until the end of the Roman period and beyond. Remodelling and the addition of features have been noted on most of the examples excavated. Those that have been investigated offer a convenient opportunity to compare and contrast Roman rural activity in different parts of the Yorkshire Wolds. Towards the north-east escarpment, the Wharram Research project, combining aerial photography, geophysical surveying and field walking with excavation (Hayfield 1988; Atha 2007) has focussed on an area of high Wolds with deep valleys. On the eastern fringes of the Wolds, long-term research prior to the extraction of gravel at Garton-Wetwang Slacks has enabled examination of the transition of a settlement from the Iron Age to the Roman period (Dent 2010).

On the southern margins of the Wolds close to the Humber estuary, at Melton, a series of evaluations undertaken before improvements to the A63 (Bishop 1999; Fenton-Thomas 2011) have included investigation of linear enclosure settlements. Some of the ladder settlements between Sancton and Bishop Burton showed evidence of Roman activity (Ainsworth 2003; Halkon 2008).

In the Wharram area a number of complexes of linear enclosures have been identified from the air. A string of enclosures runs from Birdsall Brow to Wharram Crossroads and further to the north between the village of Wharram le Street and Duggleby (Stoertz 1997). No pottery was recovered from field walking along the Birdsall Brow 'ladder' which lacks a droveway and may be a linear arrangement of small fields for agricultural use rather than settlement if it continued in use during the Roman period, though the fragility of hand-thrown, clamp-fired pottery must be remembered. By contrast the other Wharram area ladder settlements yielded much pottery, particularly on the densest agglomerations of cropmark features at their ends (Hayfield 1988; Atha 2007). Some of the field walking assemblages were difficult to date precisely, due to the longevity of calcite-gritted wares, but at Wharram Grange and Wharram le Steet concentrations of material were identified as being derived from villas, which will be considered in the next section.

At Swaythorpe, near Kilham, in the Great Wold Valley, cropmarks reveal a series of ladder settlements and field systems. An excavation here uncovered several rectilinear timber structures and corn-drying ovens and other agricultural buildings, dating from the third and fourth centuries AD (Mackey 2001). Analysis of animal bones shows that there were more sheep than cattle here, more suited to a chalk grassland environment and that the bones of sheep feet may have been used for non-culinary purposes. Perhaps surprisingly for a settlement with only a single *tegula* (ceramic roof tile) on the whole site, one structure with a pit and series of post holes has been interpreted as a purpose-built latrine. Tile, if locally rare, could, however, be quite attractive for removal and reuse. The pottery assemblage was typical for similar sites in East Yorkshire and other finds include copper-alloy bangles and a jet finger ring.

One of the clearest examples of the changes in the landscape of East Yorkshire that took place in the first and second centuries AD has been identified at Garton-Wetwang Slack. The open settlement of roundhouses and large square barrow cemetery had already been overlain by a series of enclosures forming a nucleated settlement along a droveway before the Roman incursion. In the second century AD the ditches of this settlement were infilled, with deposits including casually disposed human remains. The replacement of roundhouses by rectilinear building and appearance of Roman coins and wheel-thrown pottery on the site indicate cultural change here (Dent 1983a).

The excavation of the ladder settlement at Melton (Bishop 1999) is also important in understanding the transition between Iron Age and Roman East Yorkshire. It is clear from excavation that not all the components of the apparently complex settlement revealed by the magnetometer survey were contemporary. The pre-Roman Iron Age enclosures which had contained roundhouses ceased to be used and a pair of enclosures added to the east of a new north-south linear feature containing rectangular buildings. At the same time, new types of wheel-thrown pottery from southern England or the near continent appeared, although hand-thrown jars in the 'native' tradition remained in use. There were a few sherds of samian pottery, a single piece of Dressel 20 amphora and mortaria, including an import from northern France (Bishop 1999). In Phase 3 additional enclosures were added, dated from the pottery which mainly comprised wheel-thrown greywares. The settlement had ceased to be occupied by the end of the first half of the second century AD. One of the most interesting aspects of the excavated animal bone assemblage is the switch between Phase 2, with 13 per cent (of a total of 195) cattle/large ungulate bones, 68 per cent sheep/goat and 19 per cent pig to 70 per cent cattle, 23 per cent sheep/goat and 7 per cent pig in Phase 3. The molluscan remains complemented this change well, with an increase in taxa associated with damp grassland, which would have been suitable for grazing cattle.

The ladder settlement excavated on the A63 Grade Separated Junction at Melton (Fenton-Thomas 2011) discussed in Chapter 5 continued to develop in the Roman period. The portion of the settlement to the north of the east-west trackway fell into disuse and woodland regenerated there. To the south a number of new enclosures were established; the complex nearest to the junction of what remained of the linear earthwork contained a number of buildings including a well-preserved crop drier or malting oven. There was evidence for both arable and pastoral farming. It is interesting to note that here too, unlike other settlements where sheep bones predominated, there was a higher proportion of cattle, especially younger beasts. A possible explanation for this is the proximity of the fort and growing town Brough with a higher demand for beef (Fenton-Thomas 2011, 381). Dietary preferences will be considered in more detail in Chapter 10.

At Arras, one of the longest of linear enclosure complexes on the southern Wolds, careful study of the cropmark plots shows the insertion of a cluster of smaller enclosures of slightly different form to the others on the droveway. Field walking resulted in the collection of a few sherds of Roman wheel-thrown greyware pottery here (Halkon 2008, 98) and Roman activity was confirmed by excavation during the construction of the BP TSEP pipeline. Near Arras Cottages (TSEP 328), both Iron Age and Romano-British pottery was found in the settlement ditches and a number of pits contained third-century AD pottery and a grave of the same date. Several later Roman burials and pits were found around 320m further to the north along the same linear settlement complex (TSEP 909) (Evans and Atkinson 2009, 289). It seems likely, therefore, that the route along which this settlement was laid out, which runs for well over 3km from the head of Sancton Dale down to the 'Market Weighton gap', probably joining a complex of linear enclosures on Goodmanham Wold (Stoertz 1997), remained significant.

There are a number of clusters of enclosures visible as cropmarks which may be farmsteads between Sancton Dale and the junction of the York and Malton Roman roads near North Newbald. One of these, to the north of Sancton, has been investigated by metal detecting and field walking (Fenn 2002). Activity here extended from the later Bronze Age to the end of the Roman period. The scatter of low value later Roman coins, greyware pottery and lack of good-quality metal finds suggests that this site was relatively poor. Melted lead and iron slag showed that some metal working had been undertaken here.

There are many other cropmark complexes yet to be investigated on the Wolds. Whoever was responsible, it is clear that transformation within the eastern Yorkshire countryside was beginning to take place, but penetration of Roman material culture in the form of first and second fineware pottery and coins seems to be restricted to a corridor along the roads themselves, particularly between Brough and York. It is not clear whether the spread of sites and finds further away from the road in the later third and fourth centuries AD is due to a growth in population or activity is simply more visible due to the greater availability and wider adoption of Roman coins and wheel-thrown East Yorkshire greyware pottery which became ubiquitous in the mid- to later Roman period. Excavation on a number of sites has shown that hand-thrown products were still used widely, and like most Iron Age pottery does not weather as well on the surface. In this case absence of evidence does not necessarily mean evidence for absence.

THE VILLAS

The survey of rural Roman East Yorkshire so far has deliberately focussed on the more numerous 'ordinary' settlements in which the majority of the population would have lived. Aerial photography, chance finds, field survey and excavation has, however, identified structures which have come to be known as villas.

According to the most authoritative Latin dictionary a *villa* is a 'rural dwelling with associated farm forming the headquarters of a farm or country estate, a large country residence' (Glare 1968–82, 2063), but there has been much debate amongst archaeologists and historians of Roman Britain concerning the characterisation of villas, often reflecting changes in intellectual fashion and differing perceptions of the effect of Rome on this province. There have been many definitions: 'the villas mostly represent the adoption of Roman standards in greater or lesser degree by natives of substance' (Richmond 1963, 109), or 'country residence designed to impress' (Potter 1997, 32) and distinguished from other Roman rural settlements as 'structures which reveal attempts to appear Roman' (Millett 1995, 68). It has also been argued that some may have been religious centres or tax-depots (Walters 2009). The term 'villa' has been used to cover a wide range of sites, from simple stone structures to grand estates, reminiscent of the great country houses of eighteenth-century England. More recently a move away from the preoccupation with description and classification of plans to analysis of villas in their social context has been advocated (Taylor 2007), following Smith (1997) who would argue that much can be learned about the societies that built them from a 'reading' of the changing plans of these buildings. Smith, preferring to substitute new terms for traditional nomenclature such as the replacement of 'pavilion' and porticus for the corridors and wings, suggested that some villas may belong to communities, rather than wealthy individuals. Others such as Millett argue that the term 'villa' itself is unhelpful and over-generalised. Although it is important to bear such recent reappraisals in mind, the term 'villa' will be used here for the sake of convenience, to distinguish them from lower-status farmsteads.

It is clear that there are structures within the countryside of Roman East Yorkshire that possessed one or more of the following: a rectilinear plan, ceramic or stone tiled roof, building in stone with architectural features, a bath house, solid floors sometimes embellished with mosaics, painted wall plaster and window glass. Most are associated with aisled barns, stock enclosures and corn driers and other components of an agricultural system (Fig. 50). Since the publication of *The Parisi* (Ramm 1978) the number of villas identified within what is thought to be their tribal territory has almost doubled to over thirty, representing one of the most northerly concentrations in Roman Britain (Taylor 2007, figs 4.9, 54). A smaller group of villas further north in the Tees Valley including Ingleby Barwick and Holme House may relate to the forts and associated settlement at Binchester and Piercebridge and the settlement at Sedgefield (Carne 2001; 2006). The distribution of villas is by no means random: within the Foulness Valley 20 x 30km survey (Halkon 2008, 195) all but two of the fourteen villas so far identified were on the best-quality agricultural land close to Roman roads providing easier access to markets. Nearly all were on or close to streams or springs (Plate 34). The traditional viewpoint that villas represent an expression of wealth generated from the production of agricultural surplus seems to be sustained by the material evidence.

Much of the debate concerning the origins of and ownership of villas focuses on the concept of continuity; the evolution from native farmstead into stone rectilinear buildings and associated structures, embellished with various 'Romanised' features. Brantingham and Rudston villas for example, amongst the most fully excavated and published so far in Parisi territory, both overlie Iron Age settlements. As we have seen in Chapter 6, the Brantingham late Iron Age settlement was of high status (Dent 1989). The concentration of Corieltauvian coins and a coin of Cunobelin, ruler of the south-eastern British kingdoms of the Catuvellauni and Trinovantes, and wheel-thrown Gallo-Belgic-style pottery and imported brooches confirm its widespread connections. By the second century AD, a rectilinear building with at least stone footings, a curved western end and entrance in the narrow eastern side had been constructed over the large in-filled Iron Age ditch. There is a passing resemblance between this and buildings 3 and 8 at Beadlam (Neal 1996) and Structure 3.2, Phase 2 at Shiptonthorpe (Millett, 2006 illus 4.14, 5), although the latter was constructed in timber rather than stone. By the fourth century, one of the largest villas of the North of England had been constructed on the site. Is this a case of the growing prosperity of a 'native' farmstead enabling its gradual evolution, or was this site taken over as the neighbouring town of Petuaria developed, its owners benefiting from the good soils and favourable location close to the Humber estuary, or was this indeed the country seat of a prosperous official from the nearby town?

Settlement around the Rudston site (Stead 1980) began in the late Iron Age, with a series of roundhouses related to a ditched droveway and enclosures, the gulley of one in mid-sequence contained parts of a shield binding (which could be Iron Age or Roman) and a sherd of a pre-Flavian flagon (Stead 1980, 35). The network of ditches, pits and other features was filled and levelled by the early third century AD with a time-lag before the construction of the villa buildings which were arranged around a square. The pottery report includes an unusual amount of figured samian pottery, mortaria and brooch types of the first half of the second century AD and there are also a few earlier Roman coins including a Republican denarius, and coins of Vespasian, Hadrian, Antoninus Pius, though the bulk of the coins date from the third and fourth centuries. The earlier Roman material may be associated with timber buildings. As at Brantingham, there is a clear break between the Iron Age settlement and construction of the villa itself (Bolton 2004).

Unlike Brantingham and Rudston, the earliest features at Langton were three almost square enclosures, one of which was interpreted by the original excavators as a Roman fortlet (Corder and Kirk 1932), largely due to the regularity of its 3m-wide and 2m-deep ditch, the figured samian, head-stud brooch and mint condition sestertius of Trajan. This idea was quickly dismissed by Richmond (1932) although Ramm (1978, 73) still advocated a military connection, suggesting that it may have belonged to a soldier who retired soon after the Roman take-over in the later first century AD. On re-examination of the pottery, a date of the mid-second century was proposed by Webster (1969). If it was a foundation by a retired soldier, there is a noticeable lack of oxidised white/orange flagons from the Legionary potteries at York which have been found at other sites such as Lingcroft Farm referred to earlier, the majority of the pottery from the early phase being hand-thrown calcite-gritted-style jars which also caused Ramm (1988, 84) to change his mind and suggest a native origin for the enclosure. The first stone structure was Building M, which was rectilinear with a curious apse-like projection on its short southern side, dated from coins to the late second or early third century AD.

The villa at Welton Wold, near Brough is one of the most extensively excavated in East Yorkshire (Mackey 1998) and had its origins in the Iron Age (Fig. 51). A small rectilinear enclosure possibly containing a roundhouse was positioned in the angle between two wide droveways, one running north before narrowing and curving towards the west which continued as the main axis for the site throughout its use, the other ran towards the east. Around 60m from the south-western corner of the enclosure was an Arras-style crouched inhumation with two pots. This enclosure seems to have continued for a little time after the eastern droveway fell out of use.

At the beginning of the second century AD, a more regular square enclosure c. 60 x 60m was dug respecting the western side of the remaining droveway ditch, resembling the slightly smaller Langton enclosures. At the back of the enclosure, a stone house was built with a rear corridor and two pairs of rooms at each side of a larger central room. A 30m-deep well was dug in the opposite corner of the enclosure to the house. The compound also contained several possible corn driers. A timber roundhouse was constructed to the north of the courtyard house, behind which were several crouched

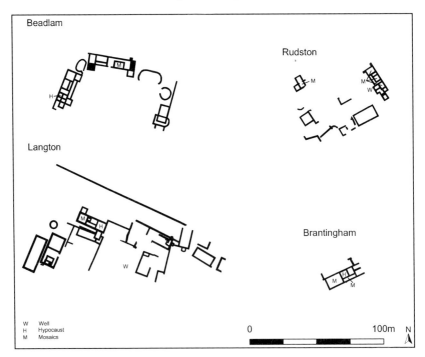

Fig.50 Villa plans in eastern Yorkshire. (T. Sparrow based on Neal 1996, Stead 1991, Corder 1932, Liversidge et al, 1973)

and flexed inhumations in shallow graves. These two related elements are of particular interest as they clearly follow continuing Iron Age traditions, yet the corridor house, the earliest so far recorded in the region, in something quite new. In the view of the excavator, the roundhouse was, along with some of the other timber structures, accommodation for a subservient workforce and the corridor house for the quarry owner or manager. One explanation for the sudden development of the whole complex was the exploitation of chalk, as there were substantial quarries at either end of the droveway. Chalk, was a vital ingredient for the manufacture of mortar which would have been needed for the construction of the new town at Brough. The Welton chalk quarries were also close enough to the Humber for transportation up the River Ouse to the Roman fortress at York. It is therefore somewhat ironic that it was the expansion of the quarries at Welton Wold to feed the modern cement works at Melton Bottom, which necessitated the excavation of the Roman site in the first place. Evidence for Roman chalk quarries has also been found near Roman Canterbury during modern quarrying (Wacher 2000, 93). At the same time further larger polygonal enclosures were dug, most of them respecting the droveway. The enclosures contained a range of timber structures including a five-posted granary, a large aisled barn and two smaller timber structures. A second stone building erected in a polygonal enclosure on the other side of the droveway 13m square with precise corners, beyond the opposite end of the droveway to the corridor house, has been interpreted as the site of a family mausoleum or shrine.

A further interpretation of the layout of the Welton site is that the enclosures along the droveway, which can be roughly divided into four groupings, each with a 'house' either of timber or stone, a crop drier and an aisled barn, formed separate units, each belonging to a family group within a community similar to those that may have inhabited late Iron Age ladder settlements, with one family within the settlement becoming more dominant. The idea of communal ownership has been used to explain the duplication and division within 'villa' structures themselves (Smith 1997).

At Burnby Lane, Hayton (Fig. 52) (Halkon and Millett 2003; Halkon *et al.* forthcoming) the Iron Age settlement also underwent a transformation in the second century AD. One of the enclosures showed a decline in activity, whilst the adjoining one had its boundary ditches re-cut and the roundhouse was replaced by a substantial rectilinear timber building. A new enclosure was cut and a large aisled timber building constructed inside it. Eventually the ditch at the northern boundary of this enclosure was filled in and a new ditch dug 5m to the south, and a stone-built bath house constructed over the backfilled earlier ditch and attached to the north-east corner of the rectilinear timber building.

The villa at Beadlam (Neal 1996) at the north-western extremity of Parisi territory also had some form of settlement in the later second century AD, consisting of a sub-circular enclosure, though this appears to be very different from the regular rectilinear enclosures discussed so far. Masonry buildings did not appear until the fourth century, which will be discussed below.

Although it was the first of its type to be constructed in the region found so far, the Welton corridor house received none of the embellishments of the other villas such as Langton, Rudston or Brantingham and was reconfigured in the mid-second century. The well was filled in and the excavator suggests that some form or ritual was involved, for rather bizarrely, at its bottom was a 2.1m-thick deposit of animal bone, mainly consisting of complete skeletons. At least sixty-eight animals had been thrown down the shaft before and during its infilling. The animals identified included fifteen puppies and dogs, twenty-eight kittens and cats, twenty sheep, a goat, two cows and two horses. The skeletons of twenty-two small wild species may have fallen into the well by accident. Although drowning of kittens is known to have been carried out on farms in living memory, the presence of sheep, cattle and horses seems strange. Ritual deposition of animals, which will be discussed in a later chapter, has been identified on a number of sites elsewhere, but it would seem that at Welton almost all the stock of a small farm had been slaughtered. If this is the case, the much greater proportion of sheep to cattle is worthy of note. The well fittings were also dismantled and thrown into the well. According to the excavator the infilling of the well and lack of embellishment marked the departure of the villa owner, even though the estate continued to develop.

In the later third century, deep ditches were excavated around the clusters of buildings, the roundhouse next to the stone corridor house had been removed and further aisled buildings erected associated with crop driers and sunken floored buildings. In this phase the site was at its most extensive and the animal bones show an increase in the ratio of cows to sheep, with cattle predominating. This compares well with the nearby site at Melton referred to above. The humans, both adult and infant, were disposed of in a casual manner and it has been suggested that these were slaves (Mackey 1998).

By the fourth century only the compound around the courtyard house remained in use, an interesting contrast to other villa sites which expanded at this time. There was a switch towards a greater proportion of barley rather than wheat, which had been predominant in the second century. More respect seems to have been shown to the dead, some of whom were buried in coffins still wearing their boots, detectable from the small iron studs from their soles, and the graves were arranged in an orderly way. The end of the Welton settlement will be considered in Chapter 11.

At Rudston (Stead 1980), stone buildings were constructed over the trenches and ditches of the timber phase and although some aspects reflected the old layout of the site, none were built before the third century and the line of former droveway was broken. It is clear that some of these were for storage or agricultural purposes, although several contained ovens. By the mid-third century, a corridor building was constructed

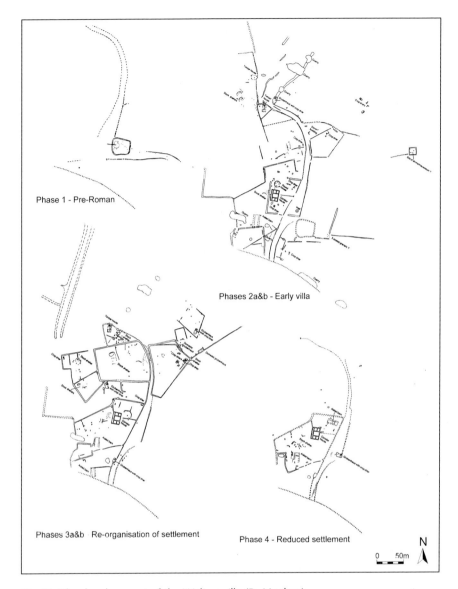

Fig.51 The development of the Welton villa (R. Mackey).

at the east side of a square facing west with a bath suite in the south range. The floor of the changing room of the bath suite was embellished with a mosaic of aquatic theme, of which only a quarter survive. In the centre there may have been the head of Oceanus or Neptune, surrounded by sea creatures including lobsters, dolphins and fish (Smith 2005). In mainly orange tesserae, it has a rather cartoon-like quality, looking rather crude when compared to the mosaics of the Mediterranean. The mosaic may well represent the Truimph of Neptune, a popular theme in Italy and North Africa, with examples in Britain at Cirencester and at Hemsworth, Dorset (Witts 2005, 125). The central room of the corridor house at Rudston has a geometric pattern on its floor.

It is the mosaic in the northern wing that has created the most controversy, the Venus mosaic (Plate 37). The central circle contains a rather pear-shaped depiction of a naked woman with flowing hair and a diadem, assumed from the mirror and golden apple she is holding, to be Venus. Next to her is a Triton holding a torch, the former possibly being a reference to the birth of Venus from the sea. The birds at each corner of the mosaic which may be doves, with apples or pomegranates, are also associated with this goddess.

Around the central panel are various animals, two of which bear inscriptions, TAURUS OMICIDA, 'the bull (called) man-slayer', and LEO F(L)AMMEFER, 'the fiery lion'. The lion has clearly been speared, with blood dripping from a wound, and above the bull is a crescent-shaped object. Between the bull, lion, a leopard and a deer are a naked man, a woman with a spear and a bearded man holding either a net or a rope, who are *bestiarii* or animal fighters in the amphitheatre. According to Sir Ian Richmond (1933, 5; 1968, 8) in the leaflet produced soon after its discovery, 'There is no need to dwell upon the badness of this work. It is a misapprehension which would ruin the reputation of a craftsman of today, and in a cultivated Roman environment, the effect would have been the same.'

Fig.52 The bath suite of the settlement at Burnby Lane, Hayton, under excavation. The hypocaust is clearly visible. (P. Halkon)

Opinions have moderated since, as according to Millett (1989, 191) 'the form of the figure betrays a native perception of beauty and the workmanship is rather crude but the design is classical in intent'. This interpretation neatly encapsulates the idea accepted by many archaeologists of Roman Britain today that most villas were occupied by native people emulating Roman tastes. There are, however, a few elements that connect the Venus mosaic with North Africa and although its execution may appear crude, according to Witts (2005, 148) 'it is one of the most iconographically sophisticated in the country'. The crescent on a stick above the bull has been identified as an ox-goad, the symbol of the *Venatores Telegeniorum*, a team of animal fighters from the African amphitheatres (Smith 2005, 13). The portrayal of Venus on this mosaic also has parallels in North Africa and may be associated with games held in honour of the goddess. The usual explanation for these similarities is that design pattern books were in circulation across the Empire, one arriving at Rudston in a similar way perhaps to carpet and wallpaper samplers today. There may, however, be an alternative explanation for the African connection. Archaeological evidence, such as casseroles designed to sit on braziers and other pottery vessel forms made by potters associated with Legio VI in York found in northern Britain (Swan 1992; Swan and Monaghan 1993) have been interpreted as demonstrating the presence of African troops with a distinctive ethnic cuisine. It is highly likely that Emperor Septimius Severus, born at Leptis Magna, modern Libya, who died in York in AD 211 had African troops with him (Swan 2002). Recent research on the Y chromosome of males in Yorkshire (King *et al.* 2007) and isotope analysis of the burial of a well-to-do Roman woman from Sycamore Terrace, York, dated to the fourth century AD (Leach *et al.* 2010) provides further evidence for African influence, and a reminder of the cosmopolitan character of Roman Britain and the possibility that the occupants of villas in East Yorkshire may not all have been native Britons adopting the Roman lifestyle.

Across the 'square' from Building I, around 70m to the north-west, excavation in 1971–72 uncovered a further building (Building 8) which included a large L-shaped room divided into three units. At its north-west end was a mosaic measuring 4.78m x 4.20m, named after its central circular panel, which contains the frontal view of a charioteer in a quadriga, a racing chariot pulled by four horses, brandishing a wreath in his right hand and the palm frond symbolising victory in his left (Plate 35). His costume shows that he is a member of the *russata factio*, or 'Red Club', one of the four chariot racing 'stables' of ancient Rome. At the corners of this mosaic are three of the four seasons, as Winter is damaged by a later pit. The quality of Spring, identified from the swallow on her shoulder (Fig. 53 and cover), is very high with subtleties of light and shade picked out in the different coloured stone. The fact that it is noticeably better than the others shows that more than one mosaicist was involved. Although this mosaic laid between AD 325–250 may be a century later than the Venus mosaic, there are some iconographic parallels between the two, particularly the bird and fruit motifs used on both mosaics. It is possible that Building 8 replaced Building 1 (Smith 2005, 26) and the theme continued in the new house. The leaping leopards either side of a crater, a form of metal container for mixing wine, between the two rooms which form the 'L' shape of Building 8 are reminiscent of the magnificent silver tigress from the early fifth-century Hoxne Treasure (Johns 2010) which provides a reminder of the wealth of the upper echelons of society elsewhere in Roman Britain. As well as possessing mosaic floors, Buildings 1 and 8 both had good-quality painted wall plaster in a range of colour schemes.

Rudston was one of a cluster of villas on the north-eastern Wolds. The most recent addition to this group was investigated at Thwing in the Great Wold Valley, 2004–2008 (Ferraby et al. 2009). It was located through the discovery of a scatter of pottery and other material around a ladder-type settlement visible as a cropmark, further elucidated by field walking and magnetometer survey. An excavation undertaken by Cambridge University 2004–07 revealed a similar sequence to other sites starting with a substantial Iron Age boundary, which was largely infilled before a series of enclosure ditches was dug cutting across it. These contained second-century midden deposits and were partially back-filled prior to the building of a stone house in the late second or early third century. The house developed into a winged-corridor form, not by extension but by reduction (Ferraby et al. 2008). The building was of good-quality chalk blocks, with internal walls decorated with painted plaster. The building was associated with mixed arable-pastoral farming and the occupants clearly fond of seafood, judging from the quantity of oyster and other shells in rubbish deposits. By the early fourth century the front of the building was demolished and an iron smelting furnace constructed inside one of the rooms.

Further to the south, a stone building was found in 1904 at Harpham, to the east of the Kilham road. On excavation the following year, several mosaic pavements were uncovered (Sheppard 1905) and a further example in 1950 during the re-excavation of the site (Mellor 1952). The largest of these depicted a 3m-square maze in dark blue/grey tesserae on a white ground with a floral motif of four petals in red, yellow and blue in the centre. This is one of five others in Roman Britain (Smith 2005) including Caerleon (Witts 2005) and was probably a reference to the labyrinth in which Theseus encountered the Minotaur. In execution it is very similar to the geometric or swastika mosaic from Rudston. The mosaic was laid in the first part of the fourth century, dated by a mint condition coin of Constantine (AD 305) under the floor. There was polychrome wall plaster, with a second coat present on some fragments. This villa was clearly extensive with rooms larger than those at Rudston and probably 'E' shaped with the wings connected by corridors (Ramm 1978, 98).

As Welton was in decline, Langton, like Rudston, saw an expansion of building activity in the fourth century including a small corridor house, albeit with a simpler plan than Rudston and a less lavish bath house (Fig. 54). Unfortunately ploughing has destroyed the mosaics, but the walls were decorated with painted plaster. One of the reasons given for the growth in prosperity by the excavator (Corder and Kirk 1932, 62) was the provision of cereal crops to the neighbouring town and fort of Malton. There are a number of substantial barn-like buildings, corn driers, a possible mill and in a small room which had a burnt floor were quantities of burnt wheat. Surprisingly, however, the finds report only lists two upper stones from beehive querns.

The sequence and date of expansion at Beadlam (Neal 1996) is similar to Rudston and Langton. Three ranges of buildings were constructed, leaving a roughly square open area in the centre. To the west was Building 2 which was of corridor type with two forward projecting rooms forming wings, with the corridor between them acting as a verandah. As at Rudston a bath suite was built at the south end of the range. Building 1 at the centre of the ranges of buildings was broadly similar in plan and may have been contemporary. Both buildings have mosaic floors, although only the mosaic in Room 2, Building 1, built over a hypocaust, remained intact. Windows were glazed and the painted wall plaster of good quality. The most remarkable find at Beadlam was the large and varied assemblage of late Roman glass vessels (Price and Cottam 1996). The eastern range of buildings seems to have been the 'working' rather than residential and included a possible circular mill broadly similar to the one at Langton and the large iron scythes and a range of quern types indicate the harvesting and processing of cereals was undertaken, though the scythe may equally have been used for cutting hay for fodder. Around 20km to the west of Beadlam in what is now Blansby Park, a villa developed at the southern end of a complex of prehistoric and Roman sites. Evidence was found for a large building, probably a bath house, with mosaic floors, a hypocaust and painted wall plaster and the usual range of pottery and other artefacts (Watts et al. 2003).

The villas at Beadlam and Langton are the best excavated of a group within a 20km radius of Malton and there were affinities between them, such as the similarity of the Beadlam mosaic to that excavated in the grounds of Hovingham Hall in 1745, which also had a bath suite. Part of the plan of this has recently been mapped by geophysical survey by the Landscape Research Centre (Powlesland pers. comm.). There were also villas at Oulston to the west of Hovingham, and Musley Park and Rowborough, to the south-west of Malton which all had mosaic floors (Ramm 1978). The growth of Malton may have been one of the reasons for the development of villas at Wharram Le Street and Wharram Grange, identified by field walking and magnetometry and sample excavation (Rahtz et al. 1986; Hayfield 1987; 1988).

Like Welton and Langton, the villas at Wharram Grange and Wharram Le Street buildings developed in a square enclosure, which were in turn added to and subdivided. There is a possibility, due to its close proximity to the source of the Gypsy Race at the head of the Great Wold Valley, that the Wharram Le Steet villa may have served a ritual/religious function, which may explain the regular and distinctive 50m square enclosure

Fig.53 The head of Spring from the Charioteer mosaic. Note the swallow on her shoulder. (M. Park courtesy Hull and East Riding Museum: Hull Museums)

at the core of the palimpsest of features revealed in the magnetometer survey, which contained buildings and will be discussed below. In contrast, the Wharram Grange villa was situated on a spur of the Wolds with panoramic views. It too was on a site that had been occupied in the Iron Age, off-set from the ladder settlement described above and the main square enclosure contained pottery dating from the first to the third century (Hayfield 1987; 1988). Like almost all the villas discussed so far, features such as stone-lined drains and a mosaic pavement were added in the fourth century. There was probably a villa at North Manor, in the village of Wharram Percy itself (Rahtz and Watts 2004).

It is not clear why these three sites prospered rather than the other five or six farmsteads around Wharram. Perhaps the villas were the equivalent to medieval manors, with a similar hierarchical relationship to the ladder-type village settlements as the two medieval manors at the medieval village Wharram Percy. There may be a broad parallel here with the villa that eventually developed at Langton which may have brought together earlier Roman farmsteads at Middle Farm and Langton Crossroads under a single ownership (Ramm 1988, 86). Field walking around Wharram has resulted in the discovery of small abraded pottery sherds, largely of the third and fourth centuries which have been interpreted as evidence for manuring as domestic middens were incorporated with spoil from the farmyards and spread on the land, another parallel with the use of night-soil in the medieval and post-medieval eras.

A similar grouping of villas to that round Malton can be seen around Brough-on-Humber, the most impressive of these being Brantingham (Stead *et al.*1973) the earlier phases of which have been outlined in previous chapters. Sadly quarrying has resulted in the destruction of a large portion of the building, but enough remains to show that it was extensive, the range partially uncovered in 1961 measuring 25 x 8m. The villa was originally discovered in 1941 (Slack 1951) during quarrying and two geometric mosaic pavements were uncovered. They were re-excavated and lifted in 1948, but one mysteriously disappeared overnight, though fortunately it had been photographed and detailed notes taken. A further figured mosaic was uncovered in 1961 in a large room 11.13 x 7.7m, much bigger than any of the other rooms excavated in East Yorkshire villas (Plate 36) (Liversidge *et al*. 1973, 90). At the centre of the mosaic was the bust of a female wearing a white tunic or dalmatic with a broad red stripe (a wide-sleeved loose gown). On her head is what has been interpreted as either a mural crown, or a feathered headdress, its identification based on whether the central figure is a *Tyche*, the personification of a city (in this case perhaps York, Brough, or the Parisi tribal area) or one of the nine muses of classical mythology, the other eight represented by the nimbed figures in niches along the top and bottom of the mosaic (Smith 2005). The half naked, robed reclining figures around the central figure may represent water nymphs or rivers. The Tyche mosaic was dated by coin and pottery evidence to the mid-fourth century AD. When it was discovered, a large amount of painted wall plaster was found which had collapsed onto the floor, which turned out to be a series of nimbed female heads, mirroring the design on the mosaic floor, which is very rare in Roman Britain. There are broad similarities with painted wall-plaster from the imperial palace at Trier in Germany (Liversidge 1973) and the Town House at Malton referred to in Chapter 7.

A metal detecting and field walking survey (Oliver 1995) showed Roman activity to be spread over several fields around the villa bulding itself, split by the Roman road running from Brough to the north-west. There are a number of other villas along this road, which probably relate to the town at Brough, but none of these, apart from Welton, have been excavated or published to the same extent or quality as those at Brantingham. Several are recorded from South Cave, as a piece of tessellated floor is recorded from the crossroads at the centre of the village (Kitson Clark 1935), and on the outskirts on Beverley Road

Fig.54 Corder's excavation at Langton villa (Malton Museum Trust).

part of the foundation of a stone building with a ceramic and stone-tiled roof, along with a range of pottery dating from the first to late fourth centuries AD (Loughlin and Miller 1979), was found during the construction of a bungalow and salvaged by the late Mrs M. and Mr D. Cutts. Other finds included the skeleton of a youth framed by ceramic tiles.

Further to the north, just to the south of the point where the Roman road forks, with one branch leading on to Malton and the other York at North Newbald, a pair of villas was excavated by Maurice Barley (Corder 1941; Loughlin and Miller 1979). The first of these fits in well with the pattern found on other villa sites, with some activity in the second century AD represented by a few sherds of samian pottery, with the main activity between AD 220 and the end of the fourth century. With stone walls, roof tiles, a hypocaust and tesserae in one of the widest colour ranges of any villas in the region, it is a shame that we do not know more of its plan. The most significant finds were parts of a frilled votive lantern or lamp-chimney, which is very rare in Roman Britain (Corder 1941, 23; Lowther 1976). Further excavation was undertaken here by Mr D. Brooks in 1973. It is possible that these villas may relate to the newly discovered roadside settlement at Rudstone Dale discussed in the previous chapter.

An outlier of the Brough group was found at Bishop Burton in 1715 referred to in Chapter 1. The discovery was described by Thomas Gent (1733, 77): '... as a countryman plowing in Bishop Burton field his Plow happened to go deeper than usual, grated on some harder matter ... he uncovered ... and found a curious Pavement of red, white and blue Stones; each about an Inch Square'.

Another mosaic was noted close by from a concentration of *tesserae* on the surface. For many years the site of the villa was lost, but was relocated by a local archaeologist/ metal detectorist to the west of the present village (Williamson 1997). The building was clearly associated with the Roman road running north-east from Brough, visible as a cropmark. To the north-west and roughly parallel to the road were a series of overlapping enclosures. A gridded field survey recovered much material from which it was possible to make some inferences. Like a number of sites described above, there were sherds of plain and decorated samian, Ebor ware and amphora sherds, which all dated from the second century AD, according well with the coins, which included those of Trajan, Hadrian and Antoninus Pius. The finds also included a number of copper-alloy harness and belt fittings, which could well be military and probably dated from the same time. The most unusual find was a small copper-alloy mount in the form of a bust wearing a Greek-style helmet which is almost certainly the goddess Minerva. The coin list shows a gap until the mid-third century AD, with the majority dating from the fourth, contemporary with the pottery found on the surface. Although it is difficult to be certain from surface material alone, the ceramic tile which included *tubuli* for intra-wall heating, floor supports and tesserae all suggest that there was a villa-type building here from the later third to the end of the fourth century AD.

Around 3km to the south there is a broadly similar complex of enclosures which may also relate to the Roman road on high ground near Monckton Walk (Ainsworth 2003; Halkon 2008). This was not the only similarity with the Bishop Burton site, as metal detecting and field walking here resulted in the recovery of a similar assemblage of Roman pottery and small finds from the later first and mid-second century AD. These included a denarius of Domitian (AD 81–96) with a peak of coins in the late third and early fourth century, again extending to the late fourth, corresponding with the calcite-gritted Huntcliff jars and Crambeck mortaria typical of late Roman pottery assemblages. Unlike the Bishop Burton site, however, there is no evidence for a stone house with any of the fixtures and fittings associated with villas. The explanation for this may be the relatively exposed position of the site and lack of easily accessible water.

At Burnby lane, Hayton (Easthaugh *et al.* forthcoming; Halkon and Millett 2003), the earlier timber buildings referred to above were replaced in stone, with a series of structures, incorporating an enlarged bath house, aligned east-west extending across most of the area excavated. A further building contained an oven. The buildings all seem to respect a track running east-west, a precursor to Burnby Lane. The ditches contained pottery dating to the third and fourth centuries. A further building on a slightly different alignment housed a stone corn drier or malting oven. After it fell out of use, a dog and piglets were buried in the northern flue. A cow and sheep were buried in a pit close by. There were also a number of infant burials around the buildings, in a similar arrangement to those around the large aisled building at Shiptonthorpe which will be considered further in Chapter 10. The timber-lined well remained in use into the late fourth century. The back-fill of the well contained rubbish deposits including animal burials, building material, painted wall-plaster and window glass which showed that nearby buildings had been well appointed. The most remarkable finds were two pieces of worked wood; one may be part of a chair leg or bedpost, decorated with a pyramid-shaped finial, the other part of a panelled door decorated with marquetry and triangles and lozenges of bone.

There were several other structures with tiled roofs and hypocausts within the 3 x 3km Hayton study area and these may form a cluster associated with the Roman roadside settlement, similar to Malton and Brough. Just outside the Hayton 3 x 3km study area near the Cocoa beck, Brian Hawe, then a part-time Archaeology student at Hull University, noticed pottery and ceramic building material on a gravel rise to the south of Pocklington. *Tesserae* were picked up during the potato harvest and subsequent field walking was organised, covering 2.21ha. A total of 1,153 Roman pottery sherds and around 9,000 pieces of stone and ceramic roof tile and box flue and hypocaust tile were also recovered during a programme of field work directed by the author of this book. Further *tesserae* and painted wall plaster were collected in clear concentrations, in and around the rectangular outline of a stone building, confirmed by a fluxgate gradiometer survey revealing the outline of a winged corridor building with a series of rooms, aligned north-south, facing eastwards. It was very similar in plan to Building 2 at Beadlam and lay at the western boundary of a rectilinear enclosure *c.* 100 x 50m. Several concentrations of samian and Ebor ware found during field walking coincide with a ladder-type geophysical anomaly and a vague linear feature visible in aerial photographs. The 237 Huntcliff and 634 greywares sherds, showed that the site continued to be occupied into the third and fourth century.

By field walking, geophysics and aerial photography, it was possible to identify what may be a villa of winged corridor type associated with fields and enclosures near Ousethorpe. It would seem that this was based on a pre-existing Iron Age settlement, though without excavation it is not possible to be certain about this. Ousethorpe provides a good example of the close relationship between villas, soils and watercourses outlined above and judging from analysis of the surface finds and cropmarks, the settlement seems to follows a similar sequence of development as those discussed above.

SUMMARY

Although there were many elements of continuity within the Iron Age and Roman countryside, there were some key changes, the clearest innovation being the appearance of 'villa' buildings with central heating systems, bath suites and tiled roofs with ancillary buildings relating to agriculture. The 30m-deep well at Rudston with its complex winding gear and bucket system and the deep wells at Welton and Langton demonstrate engineering skills hitherto unseen in this region.

Some of the villas may have belonged to people or communities of native Iron Age stock, as many are placed within or near pre-existing settlements. The villas associated with ladder settlements at Wharram may have been equivalent to the manor houses of the medieval settlements and a similar pattern has been noted in the ladder settlement which runs along the 30m contour between Heslerton and Sherburn (pers.comm. Dominic Powlesland) and elsewhere. In some cases, as at Rudston, however, there are clear gaps in occupation between Iron Age and Roman phases of activity. There is sufficient evidence to suggest that not all villa buildings can be explained as expressions of the adoption of Roman culture by local elites. Some of the iconography on the mosaics in particular displays familiarity with 'classical' culture beyond a random selection from a pattern book. Scientific analysis has shown that not all who inhabited Roman Yorkshire were born here, and some of the villa inhabitants may indeed have been retired soldiers or people from the wider Empire, perhaps even with African connections. It has already been noted that there are a number of square enclosures associated with fields, usually close to Roman roads upon which decorated samian, oxidised pottery generally from the Legionary kilns at York, late first to mid-second century coins and military-style harness and belt fittings dating from the later first and second centuries AD have been found. Do these represent 'buying in' to Roman culture by Iron Age people, settlement of retired soldiers in the landscape, or the presence of troops at some sites? Although further excavation is needed to prove this, it is possible that these items were the belongings taken to a new country home by soldiers on their retirement. Copper-alloy shield bindings were found in the lower fills of ditch RB at Rudston, although this could be late Iron Age in date (Stead, 1980, 35).

Later in the period, the villas at Rudston (fig. 66 no. 47, 102) and Beadlam (fig. 32 no. 20, 47) both produced highly decorated prick spurs with zoomorphic projections of a type largely found in military contexts on the northern frontiers of Britain, with a scatter in eastern England, closely paralleled in Gaul (Leahy 1996; Dixon and Southern 1997, 59) which will be considered in Chapter 10. Amongst the iron items found at Beadlam are a number of weapons, including a *ballista* bolt, several arrowheads and what may be an arrowhead or a small socketed spearhead and a larger socketed lance head. Some of these were amongst a hoard of scrap iron found in Building 1, Room 6 (Neal 1996) best explained as items collected from the site ready for removal elsewhere at the end of the life of the villa. It is unlikely that these can all have been used for hunting, particularly the *ballista* bolts, and a military origin seems more likely. The evidence from these two sites points to a military connection of some kind. What have been described as '*ballista* balls' of flint are recorded at Langton (Corder and Kirk 1932, 75), though these may be natural nodules.

The majority of villas are situated on or close to the best available agricultural land, which is to be expected if they were an expression of farming success. Food and farming will be considered more fully in Chapter 10. There is evidence for both pastoral and arable agriculture. There are scythes from Welton (Fig. 55) and Beadlam, although these would have been suitable for either hay or cereal harvest and corn driers or malting ovens at all excavated sites.

Although an indication of the processing rather than the cultivation of crops, querns provide information about the agricultural economy. Surprisingly only two upper stones from beehive querns were recorded at Langton, compared to twenty-six from Rudston and nine from Beadlam, which may have been due to the presence of the round structure interpreted as a mill house. Reference has already been made to cereal remains from Welton and Langton. The palaeo-environmental evidence recovered from the well at Rudston (Buckland 1980; Grieg 1980; Dalby 1980) indicated mixed farming in a landscape largely cleared of woodland with weeds associated with chalk grassland and disturbance. Crops, apart from wheat and barley, included brassicas. Opium poppy seeds identified in the well at Rudston are known from other sites in Roman Britain and were used for medicinal purposes and to decorate and flavour bread. The well deposits also contained a large quantity of moss in the later period as the well fell out of use,

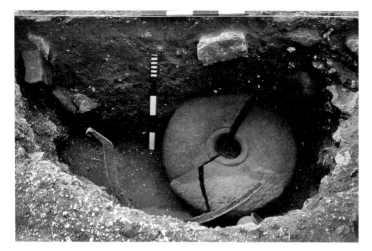

Fig.55 A scythe blade and millstone in a pit at Welton Wold. (R. Mackey)

which was possibly the equivalent of the sponges used as toilet paper elsewhere in Roman Britain.

The most detailed published bone report is also from Rudston (Chaplin and Barnetson 1980) and shows interesting changes. In the early phase, animals were killed and processed on site with selection of specific joints of meat, especially legs of sheep and use of most parts of cattle, suggesting on-site slaughter and butchery. In the later phase, beef (the favoured meat in both phases), lamb or mutton and pork were brought in as dressed carcases and the animals were not killed and processed near the villa building itself. Pigs were eaten before reaching maturity contrasting with horses, which were only consumed after they had served their useful purpose. There was little evidence for the consumption of fish or game. Shellfish, especially oysters were a favourite food on most villa sites and diet will be considered further in Chapter 10.

There are clear contrasts in rural settlement across the territory of the Parisi. Although this may be partly due to lack of fieldwork, Holderness and the lower Hull Valley lack the opulent houses of the Yorkshire Wolds and fringes. None of the recent pipeline trenches across Holderness have located villas. The only Hull Valley site so far identified as a 'villa' was discovered at Risby near Rowley, on the lower slopes of the south-eastern wolds (Didsbury 1988, 26). The discovery of sherds from two Aylesford-type wheel-thrown cordoned vessels like those from Brantigham and Arram, along with Flavian samian pottery and other fine wares, and a copper-alloy openwork military fitting, provide evidence for early Roman activity akin to that found on early Roman rural sites elsewhere. The concentration of roof tile, later Roman pottery and quern fragments may indicate development into a villa following the pattern elsewhere.

CHAPTER 9

CRAFTS AND INDUSTRY

THE LANDSCAPE BACKGROUND

As we have seen in the previous chapter, agriculture was the predominant activity in Roman eastern Yorkshire, which can only be understood within its landscape setting. Not everywhere was suitable for arable farming, however, and in marginal areas, natural resources provided raw materials for the development of a number of industries. Palaeo-environmental investigation in the Foulness Valley, for example, shows that the conditions which enabled the growth of the Iron Age iron industry continued into the Roman period (Halkon and Millett 1999). Considerable woodland remained as fuel for the development of another high temperature, fire-based industry: pottery production. Clay was plentiful in alluvial form along the river valleys and in glacial tills. In the Vale of York glacio-lacustrine clays deposited by Ice Age Lake Humber lay beneath the ridges of sand (Furness and King 1978). Around Crambe in the north of the region, there were outcrops of Oxford clay, which fires to a white fabric under the right conditions (Evans 1989). The Roman pottery industries will be discussed more fully in the next section.

The river valleys, as they had done in the Iron Age, continued as a vital means of communication and the concentration of lead pigs around the Humber tidal inlet near Brough referred to earlier shows that this network was exploited soon after the Roman arrival in the region. By the beginning of the second century AD roads also provided a means of transportation, especially those running between the major centres and in places, particularly at stream crossings, they attracted settlement, providing market opportunities. At Hayton, the realignment of activity along the main road between York and Brough has already been noted. By the third century AD it is clear that villa location was also influenced by the roads which provided a means of access to markets for their produce in the larger settlements. A new infrastructure was therefore established in East Yorkshire contributing to the development of a 'Romanised' economy. The following sections present a brief survey of the main crafts and industries within the territory of the Parisi.

THE POTTERY INDUSTRIES

Wheel-thrown pottery was a relatively late introduction in eastern Yorkshire compared with the South East of Britain. We have already seen that Gallo-Belgic-style cordoned vessels from the territory of the Corieltauvi, to the south of the Humber, have been found at various places along the lower reaches of the Foulness and Hull valleys. Excavation has shown, however, that locally produced hand-thrown jars in 'native' style with calcite inclusions in their fabric, continued in use throughout the Roman period on many sites (Swan 2002). In the four phases of occupation defined at Welton, for example, between a quarter and a half of all the pottery from the site was of this type (Mackey 1998). Knapton ware, common at many locations in the region in the earlier Roman period, is a variant of this vessel type, named after its probable production site 11km north of Malton (Corder and Kirk 1932). There is little difference between Knapton ware and the straight-sided jars of the Arras culture, apart from their slightly flaring everted rims. These vessels are completely different from the fine, wheel-thrown pottery decorated with stamps known as 'Parisian ware' once thought to have been made in this region (Corder 1958) but subsequently recognised as a Lincolnshire and South Yorkshire product (Elsdon 1982). Some of this contrast may be purely functional as Knapton ware was generally used for cooking and storage and decorated Parisian ware was clearly meant for display as drinking vessels or at the table in a similar way to samian and other Roman pottery types. The proportion of fine tablewares and the other typically 'Roman' styles of vessels, such as mortaria, heavy, wide rimmed bowls with grits incorporated in the internal base for grinding and amphorae, large storage vessels for olive oil, fish sauce, has been used as a method of site characterisation and differentiation (Evans 2001). In the earlier phases of the Roman era in East Yorkshire, the wheel-thrown pottery supply was dominated by vessels from North Lincolnshire and South Yorkshire production centres, and indeed pottery found in the ditch in which the South Cave weapons cache was deposited included North Lincolnshire wares.

The Roman army needed large quantities of pottery to supply their basic needs for transport, storage, food preparation and consumption. Most forts had their own pottery workshops or *figlinae* and a number of these have been identified in northern England (Swan 2002) the most significant for this region being at Rossington Bridge near Doncaster (Buckland *et al.* 2001) and York (Monaghan 1997). Apart from the native-style wares, the first fully 'Romanised' pottery to be manufactured in the territory of the Parisi was at Brough. This consisted of mortaria and colour-coated beakers amongst other types (Darling *et al.* 2000) and was presumably made to supply the garrison there. It has been argued that this short-lived industry, operating sometime in the first quarter of the second century AD was made by potters with origins in the Upper Rhine/Danube frontier, from the provinces of Raetia (Switzerland) or Pannonia (Austria, Hungary and northern Balkan states), as it is so similar to contemporary wares from forts in these regions (Swan 2002). This pottery also provides a reminder of the ethnic diversity of the Roman army in Britain. Possible Pannonian connections, such as the Holme-on-Spalding Moor head pot have already been mentioned in Chapter 6.

By the second century, products of the kilns of the *Legio VI Victrix* which replaced *Legio IX Hispania* at York, including ring-necked flagons and bowls in orange oxidised fabric, arrived at a number of sites, especially the larger settlements such as Brough and Hayton along with samian pottery from Gaul.

By the third century AD a number of pottery industries developed in eastern Yorkshire: at Lockington in the Hull Valley, Holme-on-Spalding Moor in the Foulness Valley, on the fringes of Malton, first at Norton in the *vicus* of the fort itself and then at Crambeck, around 7km away (figs 56, 57, 58). Various explanations have been given for the growth of these industries. The increasing demand for kiln-fired, wheel-thrown vessels may

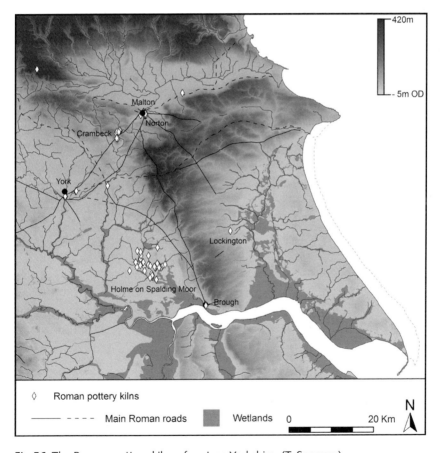

Fig.56 The Roman pottery kilns of eastern Yorkshire. (T. Sparrow)

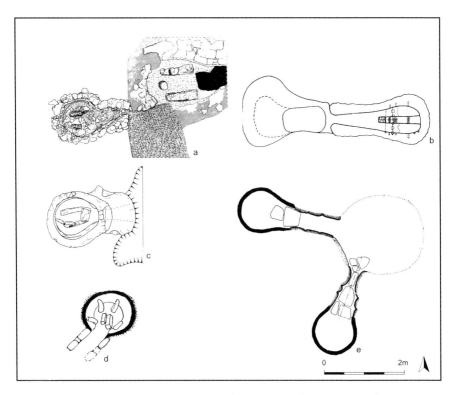

Fig.57 A comparison of the pottery kilns of eastern Yorkshire. a) Bursea b) Lockington c) Hasholme d) Norton e) Crambeck. (P. Halkon after James, Lloyd, Wilson, Hayes and Whitley)

have been due to the expansion of the larger settlements in the region including York, which became capital of the newly created province of *Britannia Inferior* at the end of the second century. The introduction of lower value copper-alloy coinage may have also been significant as it enabled wider participation in a money economy than the relatively high value silver coinage of earlier times. Another stimulus may have been the fact that the East Yorkshire industries were closer to the forts and *vici* of the northern frontier and transport was therefore cheaper and more convenient. The relationship between rivers and pottery industries has been noted by Swan (1984) all over Roman Britain, for example in the Nene Valley (Taylor 1996). That the River Foulness was navigable at least as far as Welham Bridge in the late Roman/early medieval period is apparent from the remarkable discovery in 2004 of pieces of a logboat, which was subsequently radiocarbon dated to AD 350–560 (Allen 2007; Dean 2005).

Expansion of the citizenship and the retirement of soldiers into the rural hinterland may also have contributed to increasing demand for Roman-style pottery. A further suggestion is that the Holme-on-Spalding Moor pottery industries and the

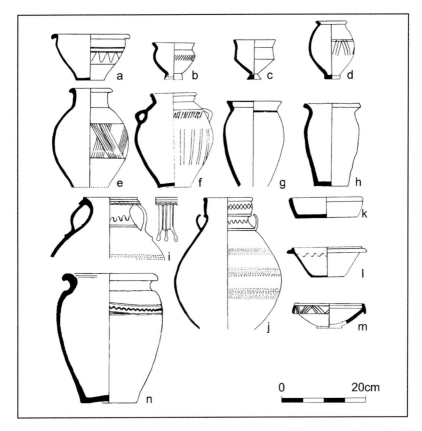

Fig.58 Romano-British pottery forms from eastern Yorkshire. a) wide-mouthed bowl, b) and c) carinated bowls from Hasholme, d) small jar from Throlam, e) flagon from Hasholme, f) two-handled jar from Throlam, g) Dales-type jar from Hasholme, h) Knapton type jar, i) and j) decorated large flagons from Hasholme, k) bowl, l) flanged bowl from Crambeck, m) Crambeck Painted Parchment bowl, n) Huntcliff-type jar. (P. Halkon after Swan 2002, Hicks and Wilson 1975)

Black-burnished production sites around Poole Harbour in Dorset and the Kent marshes developed due to population pressure in the countryside in the third century forcing peasants to live on land unsuitable for agriculture and turning to potting as a survival strategy (Monaghan 1997).

There are various ideas concerning the identity of the potters of these new industries. At Rossington Bridge, not far from the borders of Parisian territory in South Yorkshire, the use of slaves has been proposed (Buckland *et al.* 2001(b)). In contrast it has been suggested that some potteries may have been initiated by soldiers retiring into the countryside setting up businesses (Swan 2002). Similarities in the pottery between areas may be explained by mobile potters, as certain traits have been recognised in vessels at Malton which closely resemble those around Verulamium (St Alban's, Herts.). Both kilns and pottery in the eastern Yorkshire region show signs of influence from Lincolnshire (Swan 1984; Swan 2002), possibly a historical development of the earlier contacts already referred to. It has been argued from the pottery assemblage at the Shiptonthorpe roadside settlement, that 'its inhabitants were an intrusive group originating in Lincolnshire' (Evans 2001, 29). This could, however, be explained more simply as a result of trade with Lincolnshire, especially in the period before the Holme-on-Spalding Moor industries became the major producer in the region.

One of the aims of the first phase of the Foulness Valley fieldwork around Holme-on-Spalding Moor was to attempt to establish the relationship between potting and farming, but the results were inconclusive (Halkon and Millett 1999) and apart from the fingerprints left on kiln furniture and the pots themselves (Corder 1930(a)), we are no nearer to finding out the identity of eastern Yorkshire potters, for unlike the Nene Valley or South Yorkshire production centres, where potters left their names on the vessels themselves, the potters of East Yorkshire remain anonymous. As pottery production is such a key element of Roman East Yorkshire, the next section will briefly outline each of the main centres.

Norton

Like the industries in York and the short-lived Brough production centre, the main potteries at Norton (Hayes and Whitley 1950) were established in the *vicus* of the Malton fort and date from third century AD, though it is possible that there was some earlier production (Robinson 1978; Swan 1984). In all around twenty kilns have been discovered, the major concentration during the excavation of a watermain trench for the Model Farm Estate on Howe Road. A further kiln was discovered and excavated during the extension to Norton Primary School in March 2012 (Stephens *et al.* 2012).

In certain characteristics, such as the shape of the kiln bars and the length of the flues, the Norton kilns resembled those from Lincolnshire and were of two main forms: those with almost circular firing chambers with banana shaped supports and flues made from limestone blocks, and deeper, barrel-shaped examples. The fabric of the pottery was generally dark grey and hard fired and the forms included bowls and dishes, jars and flagons, some imitating the Black Burnished 2 (BB2) types from the Thames estuary and decorated with wavy lines diagonals and occasionally lattice patterns. Most remarkable were the jars depicting smith's tools (Fig. 68), wheels and faces, which will be discussed in the section on religion and ritual.

Holme-on-Spalding Moor

Although the first mention of this industry was in 1853, when 'urns' were presented to the Yorkshire Philosophical Society in York (YPSAR 1853; Halkon and Millett 1999) the pottery was so ubiquitous that an enquiry about Roman finds from a touring antiquary provoked the following reply from an agricultural worker cleaning out a ditch near Throlam: 'When we sees owt we knows nowt aboot, we just call it Roman and throws it in tiv drean ageaan' (Smith 1923, 17).

Eventually, as outlined in Chapter 1, kilns and a very large waster-dump known as Pot Hill (Fig. 4) were excavated at Throlam and for many years the wheel-thrown hard grey pottery recognised on sites across eastern Yorkshire became known as Throlam ware (Corder and Sheppard 1930). The fabric of the pottery was generally hard and blue-grey and the main vessel forms included bowls with an external flange below the rim and two-handled jars and flagons.

In 1971–72 ERAS excavated three kilns at Hasholme Hall (Fig 57c and 59) (Hicks and Wilson 1975) on a sand hill close to the River Foulness. The site had been previously occupied by an iron-producing Iron Age settlement, which continued to be occupied into the Roman period. Much pottery was recovered in a variety of forms, including two-handled jars, some decorated with criss-cross lattice patterns, large flagons with strap handles at the shoulder with 'pie-crust'-type finger-impressed decoration on the rims reminiscent of the tazza produced in the York legionary kilns. Wide-mouthed bowls with a wavy line round the girth, shallow dishes and sharply carinated cups with small feet resembling metal drinking vessels were also made here.

The most distinctive vessels were wheel-thrown jars with a triangular-sectioned rim and a lid seat in a grey-brown gritted fabric, sometimes with crushed slag inclusions. There is some debate as to whether this form is a development of late Iron Age lid-seated jars or a version of a jar with origins in *Gallia Narbonenis* (Swan 1992; 2002), perhaps another expression of ethnic identity in Roman eastern Yorkshire. Whatever their origin, they may have inspired the so-called Dales ware hand-thrown shell-gritted cooking jars common on many sites, and are therefore known as Dales type vessels. This jar type was not found in the Throlam excavation and there were other subtle differences which show that the Hasholme pottery was slightly earlier. The Hasholme vessels were also decorated with a wider range of motifs, especially roulette patterning.

The three kilns excavated at Hasholme were slightly different; the one associated with Dales-type pottery had a longer flue. They were all made of clay but the best preserved example still contained internal supports comprising two parallel fired clay uprights with a slab across the top (Fig. 59). Another kiln was associated with banana-shaped removable bars on which pottery rested, which along with the form of the kilns themselves, resembled those from Linwood and Swanpool in Lincolnshire (Halkon 2002; Swan 1984). This again demonstrates cross-Humber connections, although the similarities in pottery and presence of Lincolnshire greyware on sites in the Humber zone of East Yorkshire may be due to chronology and trade rather than movement of people (Evans 2006(a), 140).

191

Fig.59 Kiln 2 from Hasholme Hall. Note the in situ supports for the pottery. (J. Wilson)

Fig.60 Pottery from Holme-on-Spalding Moor. (M. Park courtesy Hull and East Riding Museum: Hull Museums)

Pottery production has been known at Bursea House, around 1km to the west of Hasholme, for many years and in 1983–84 excavation was carried out on a grassy bank at the edge of the farmyard, which located two pottery kilns and large quantities of wasters (Halkon and Millett 1999). The site had been occupied by an Iron Age settlement with Dragonby type pottery. The two kilns (Fig. 57a) were rather different in form, the earlier being constructed out of clay blocks with two parallel internal supports and the later very similar to Kiln 2 as Hasholme. The firing chamber of the larger, earlier kiln comprised clay blocks and its inner flue contained the carbonised remains of a bundle of alder, willow and poplar (Cartwright 1999), probably the product of managed woodland. Environmental information shows that there was some cultivation around Bursea (Huntley 1999) but the bulk of the evidence reveals a landscape dominated by wooded wetland close to the Foulness, with settlement clustered on the sandy ridges. The clay kiln roofing material contained the imprints of wetland vegetation (Halkon and Millett 1999) and shore weed (*Litorella uniflora*) was found at Bursea during environmental analysis (Palmer 1999).

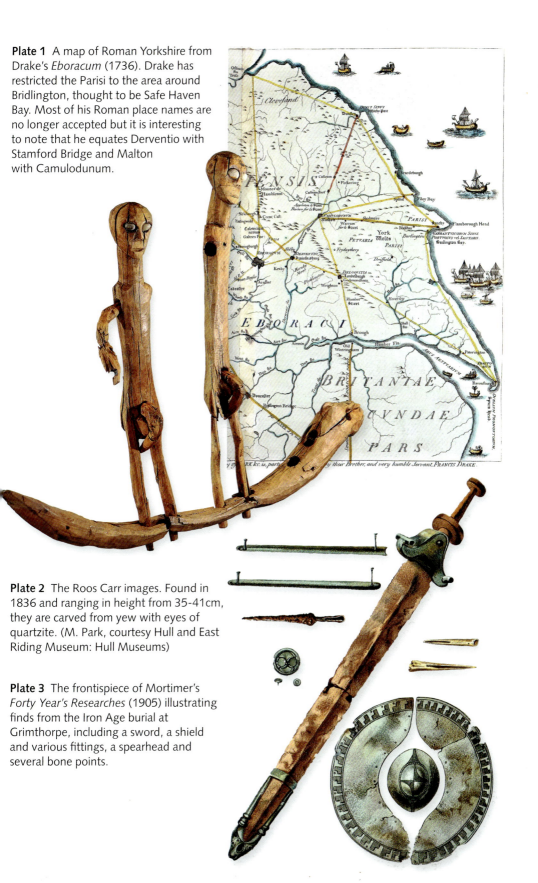

Plate 1 A map of Roman Yorkshire from Drake's *Eboracum* (1736). Drake has restricted the Parisi to the area around Bridlington, thought to be Safe Haven Bay. Most of his Roman place names are no longer accepted but it is interesting to note that he equates Derventio with Stamford Bridge and Malton with Camulodunum.

Plate 2 The Roos Carr images. Found in 1836 and ranging in height from 35-41cm, they are carved from yew with eyes of quartzite. (M. Park, courtesy Hull and East Riding Museum: Hull Museums)

Plate 3 The frontispiece of Mortimer's *Forty Year's Researches* (1905) illustrating finds from the Iron Age burial at Grimthorpe, including a sword, a shield and various fittings, a spearhead and several bone points.

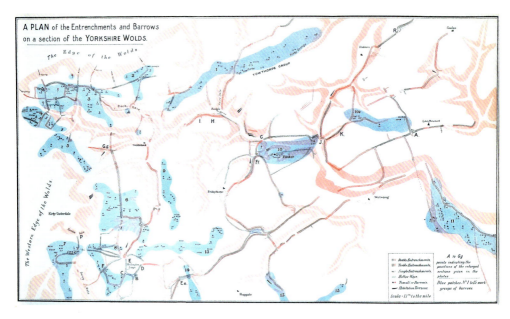

Plate 4 Mortimer's (1905) map of the entrenchments around Fimber. Many of these are now only visible as crop marks.

Plate 5 Huggate Dykes from the air (P. Halkon 2010)

Plate 6 Simplified soil map of eastern Yorkshire based on National Soil Research Institute mapping. Note the marine alluvium of the Walling Fen deposited in the Mesolithic/Neolithic transition and the early Iron Age, when sea levels reached their Holocene maximum. Marine alluvium in the Hull Valley was deposited at a similar time. The freely draining soils over chalk and limestone provide the best farmland. (T. Sparrow and P. Halkon)

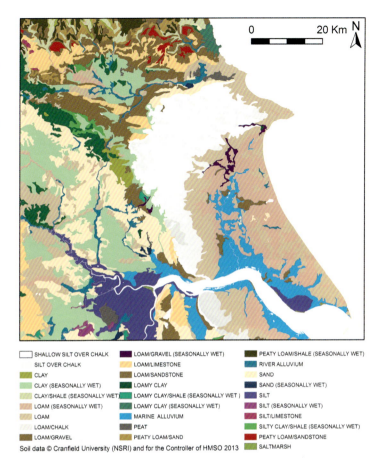

SHALLOW SILT OVER CHALK	LOAM/GRAVEL (SEASONALLY WET)	PEATY LOAM/SHALE (SEASONALLY WET)
SILT OVER CHALK	LOAM/LIMESTONE	RIVER ALLUVIUM
CLAY	LOAM/SANDSTONE	SAND
CLAY (SEASONALLY WET)	LOAMY CLAY	SAND (SEASONALLY WET)
CLAY/SHALE (SEASONALLY WET)	LOAMY CLAY/SHALE (SEASONALLY WET)	SILT
LOAM (SEASONALLY WET)	LOAMY CLAY (SEASONALLY WET)	SILT (SEASONALLY WET)
LOAM	MARINE ALLUVIUM	SILT/LIMESTONE
LOAM/CHALK	PEAT	SILTY CLAY/SHALE (SEASONALLY WET)
LOAM/GRAVEL	PEATY LOAM/SAND	PEATY LOAM/SANDSTONE
		SALTMARSH

Soil data © Cranfield University (NSRI) and for the Controller of HMSO 2013

Plate 7 Section across the irrigation pond at Hasholme showing the dramatic change of environments through time. Note the clear difference between the peat and preserved wood of the Bronze Age and the Iron Age grey estuarine clay above. (P. Halkon)

Plate 12 Kirkburn chariot burial, 1987. The dark rectangular stain over the torso of the skeleton is the remains of one of the earliest mail tunics in Europe. (P. Halkon)

Plate 13 Plan of the Wetwang village chariot burial, 2001. Note the different arrangements of the wheels within the grave. (Trustees of the British Museum)

Plate 14 Finds from the 'King's Barrow', Arras. Top to bottom: iron tyre, bit, nave band, linch pin and rings, and terrets (scale 10cm). (M. Park: courtesy Yorkshire Museum, York)

Plate 15 Items from the 'Queen's Barrow', Arras. Glass beads, copper-alloy disc with a central sandstone setting surrounded by pieces of coral (diameter 50mm) and a copper-alloy pin. (M. Park: courtesy Yorkshire Museum, York)

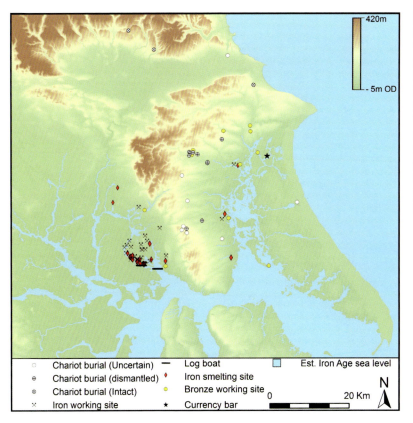

Plate 16 Middle Iron Age eastern Yorkshire. Note the effect of the high sea level in the Hull and Foulness valleys. The North Sea coastline has been extended to the approximate Iron Age position. (T. Sparrow, P. Halkon)

○	Chariot burial (Uncertain)	—	Log boat	☐	Est. Iron Age sea level
⊕	Chariot burial (dismantled)	♦	Iron smelting site		
⊗	Chariot burial (Intact)	○	Bronze working site		
✕	Iron working site	★	Currency bar		

420m

5m OD

N

0   20 Km

Plate 17 The Iron Age slag heap at Moore's Farm, Welham Bridge. One of the largest yet discovered in Iron Age Britain, it contained over 5 tonnes of iron slag. (P. Halkon)

Plate 18 The Hasholme logboat. Made from an 800-year-old oak felled 321-277 BC, it sank in a tidal estuarine inlet. (P. Halkon)

Plate 19 The Kirkburn sword. Its hilt is made of thirty-seven pieces of iron, bronze and horn, and is decorated with red glass. The scabbard is decorated with La Tène-style scroll pattern. (Length of sword 70cm.) (Trustees of the British Museum)

Plate 20 The anthropomorphic hilt of the short sword from North Grimston found in 1902. (Total length of sword 70cm.) (M. Park courtesy Hull and East Riding Museum: Hull Museums)

Plate 21a&b a) *below* South Cave weapons cache under excavation. (York Archaeological Trust) b) *right* Detail of sword with copper-alloy cast openwork panels, enamel inlay and a whale ivory hilt guard and pommel. (East Riding of Yorkshire Council)

Plate 22 Part of the hoard of Corieltauvian gold staters from Walkington (20mm diameter). (M. Park courtesy Hull and East Riding Museum: Hull Museums)

Plate 23 Excavation in 1988 of the late Iron Age/early Roman settlement at Redcliff, North Ferriby. (P. Halkon)

Plate 24 Crop mark of Hayton Roman fort, July 1996. Note the annexe ditch and Iron Age enclosures in the grass field to the right. (P. Halkon)

Plate 25 Reconstruction of a cavalryman of the *ala Gallorum Picentiana* by Peter Connelly. (Malton Museum Trust)

Plate 26 Military equipment from Malton: bone sword pommel, grip, guard and copper-alloy chape, copper-alloy scale and iron mail armour. These are illustrated in the reconstruction of the cavalryman. (M. Park courtesy Malton Museum Trust)

Plate 27 Military strap fittings from Malton. (Width of belt 3.5cm.) Some of these can be seen on the horse harness in the reconstruction. The third from the right is a late Roman 'propeller' mount. (M. Park courtesy Malton Museum Trust)

Plate 28 Decorated ceramic chimney pot/ finial from Malton (height 45cm). (M. Park courtesy Malton Museum Trust)

Plate 29 Decorated limestone winged victory caryatid from Malton (height c.1m). (M. Park courtesy Malton Museum Trust)

Plate 30 The so-called 'goddess' painted wall plaster from Malton. (M. Park courtesy Malton Museum Trust)

Plate 31 A larger than life copper-alloy right foot from a large Roman statue found at Malton. (M. Park courtesy Malton Museum Trust)

Plate 32 A selection of jewellery and personal items from Malton. Top down: glass bangles, glass beads, complete glass bangle with twisted copper-alloy bangle inside, bell, toilet set, jet necklace, late Roman bone comb (length 8.5cm) bone pins. (M. Park courtesy Malton Museum Trust)

Plate 33 a) Excavating the Roman aisled hall at Shiptonthorpe. (P. Halkon) b) Reconstruction of the Shiptonthorpe hall. (M. Faulkner) c) Roman calf-skin shoe with hobnailed sole from the waterhole (length: 240/250mm). d) Double-sided comb in boxwood from the waterhole (length: 65mm). (M. Park courtesy Hull and East Riding Museum: Hull Museums)

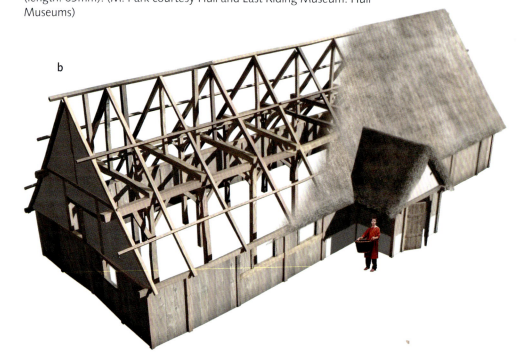

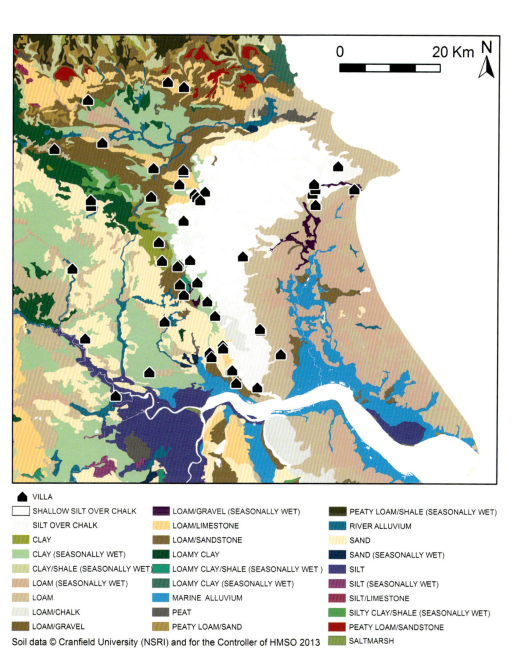

VILLA

☐ SHALLOW SILT OVER CHALK	◼ LOAM/GRAVEL (SEASONALLY WET)	◼ PEATY LOAM/SHALE (SEASONALLY WET)
SILT OVER CHALK	LOAM/LIMESTONE	RIVER ALLUVIUM
CLAY	LOAM/SANDSTONE	SAND
CLAY (SEASONALLY WET)	LOAMY CLAY	SAND (SEASONALLY WET)
CLAY/SHALE (SEASONALLY WET)	LOAMY CLAY/SHALE (SEASONALLY WET)	SILT
LOAM (SEASONALLY WET)	LOAMY CLAY (SEASONALLY WET)	SILT (SEASONALLY WET)
LOAM	MARINE ALLUVIUM	SILT/LIMESTONE
LOAM/CHALK	PEAT	SILTY CLAY/SHALE (SEASONALLY WET)
LOAM/GRAVEL	PEATY LOAM/SAND	PEATY LOAM/SANDSTONE
Soil data © Cranfield University (NSRI) and for the Controller of HMSO 2013		SALTMARSH

Plate 34 The Roman villas of eastern Yorkshire against the soils. By far the majority are situated on the better drained more fertile soils over chalk and limestone, close to sources of water such as the spring line of the western Wolds escarpment and in the Great Wold Valley. (T. Sparrow and P. Halkon)

Plate 35 The 'charioteer' mosaic from Rudston (central panel 2.1m square). (M. Park courtesy Hull and East Riding Museum: Hull Museums)

Plate 36 The Tyche mosaic at Brantingham (5.10 x 9.70m). (Painting by David S. Neal and reproduced here with his kind permission)

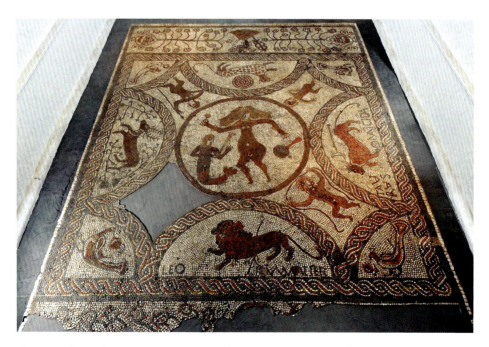

Plate 37 The Rudston Venus mosaic (panel 4.67 x 3.20m). (M. Park courtesy Hull and East Riding Museum: Hull Museums)

Plate 38 Brooches from East Yorkshire: Top (L-R): Copper-alloy Colchester derivative headstud, Cottam, AD 100-200, 63mm; Copper-alloy Aucissa/P-shaped hybrid, Newbald, AD 43-100, 42mm; Dragonesque, Brough, AD 50-150, 48mm; Copper-alloy and enamel fantail, Kilham, AD 150-200, 68mm. Middle (L-R): Copper-alloy T-shaped North Ferriby AD 75-200, 95mm; Penannular, Faxfleet AD 50-150, 46mm. Bottom (L-R): Trumpet, Wetwang, AD 40-200, 60mm; Dolphin, Hayton, AD 70-150, 42mm; 'Hod Hill', Rudston Villa AD 43-100, 57mm; Enamelled copper-alloy Umbonate disc, Newbald, AD 100-200, 23mm. (M. Park courtesy Hull and East Riding Museum: Hull Museums).

Plate 39 Gold earrings: Sutton-on-Derwent, with green glass setting AD 150-300, 25mm; drop earring, Barmby Moor, AD 100–300, 47.8mm; hoop earring AD 200–400, 26.1mm. (M. Park courtesy Hull and East Riding Museum: Hull Museums)

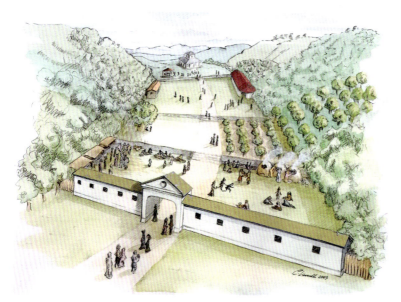

Plate 40
Reconstruction of the shrine complex at West Heslerton (C. Venables). (Courtesy D. Powlesland)

Plate 41 A member of late Roman army re-enactors – Comitatus – at Sewerby, 2012. They are based on a unit that may have served in Roman eastern Yorkshire. (P. Halkon)

Plate 42 Part of a cupboard door from the well at Hayton inlaid with marquetry consisting of bone and different woods (width 67mm). (Durham University)

Plate 43 The Goodmanham plane which has an elephant ivory stock (330mm). (Bill Marsden, courtesy K. Steedman, HFA)

In September 1996 a kiln was excavated at Skiff Lane, Holme-on-Spalding Moor (Evans and Steedman 2001) by Humber Field Archaeology and ERAS. This was one of a cluster of kiln sites in the Tollingham/Throlam area of the present parish. The kiln base was well preserved and very similar to the kilns from Bursea House, being built from clay blocks with two internal parallel supports which originally carried bars radiating from the centre. Similar bars had been found at Bursea. At the mouth of the kiln which faced east was a stoke pit filled with masses of pottery and ash. The forms of vessels were similar to those from Throlam (Corder 1930(a)), the majority being loop-handled, narrow-mouthed jars, wide-mouthed bowls and flanged bowls and dishes, varying in colour from dark grey to buff.

There were subtle differences between the pottery from the excavated sites in terms of form and decoration (Fig. 60) suggesting the presence of different potters. Research (Halkon 1987; 1999; 2002) has shown that the Throlam pottery was one of the latest in the Holme area and may represent a consolidation of the industry here. A combination of commercial and environmental reasons may have caused this concentration, as rising water levels in the late Roman period probably made production in the southern Foulness Valley around Bursea and Hasholme difficult.

Systematic field survey located thirty-four kiln sites within an 8 x 8km area centred on the present village (Halkon 1983; Halkon and Millett 1999; Halkon 2002). Products of the Holme kilns are to be found on many Roman sites in the territory of the Parisi, including the town of Brough, the roadside settlements of Hayton and Shiptonthorpe and all the villas including Langton, which is surprising as it is much closer to the Norton and Crambeck production centres. Holme products reached York, but in relatively small quantities (Monaghan 1997) and even the northern frontier, as vessels have been found in the forts and *vici* along Hadrian's Wall. The Holme production centre was eventually eclipsed by the Crambeck potteries in the later fourth century AD, its products having been identified throughout north-west as well as north-east England, the most likely explanation for this sudden expansion being some form of military contract (Evans 1989, 80).

Lockington

The only pottery kiln site so far identified in the Hull Valley was at Lockington near Beverley (Fig. 57b), excavated in 1958 (Lloyd 1968). It was situated on a slight sandy rise close to a beck and dug into the natural clay beneath. Although it was roughly the same size as the kilns from Holme, it had a single central support running parallel to the kiln walls. The impressions of sticks preserved in the baked clay of the kiln walls and on top of the central support may indicate some kind of former for a temporary floor. Although this kiln produced roughly the same repertoire as the Holme kilns, with 36 per cent dishes, 29 per cent jars, 22 per cent wide-mouthed bowls and 13 per cent flagons (Lloyd 1968, 31) the forms were subtly different. This industry seems to have been small and short lived and may have operated from *c.* AD 150–250, though the presence of both samian pottery and Huntcliff types shows that there was activity here from the early to late Roman periods.

Stamford Bridge

In 1998 excavation at Moor Lane, Stamford Bridge, produced evidence for greyware pottery production from the mid-second into the fourth century AD. Although no kilns were located, 49kg of sherds were recovered, many of them wasters, along with clay plates bearing the impressions of vegetation and hand and finger prints, similar to those from Hasholme and Bursea (Lawton 2009). The vessel forms also resembled those from Hasholme, and included Dales-type jars, though the deep wide-mouthed bowls and narrow-necked flagons were absent from the Moor Lane assemblage.

Crambeck

This industry is named after a stream, the Crambe Beek, at Castle Howard, and the village of Crambe not far from Malton, and was first investigated in 1923 with excavation following in 1926–27 (Corder 1928) although there are accounts of earlier finds of Roman pottery. Further work was undertaken at various times up until the 1980s, which showed that this was an industry of considerable extent. The kilns (Fig. 57e) themselves were of roughly the same shape as those from Norton and Holme, but incorporated limestone walling in their structure, a trait which may have been derived from the Norton. The inclusion of stone in the fabric of the kilns enabled greater longevity of use. There is some dispute about the commencement of production and its origins (Swan 2002; Evans 1989) but it probably began in the later decades of the third century AD, continuing until the later fourth to early fifth century. The clay sources have already been mentioned and the fabrics produced included hard, dark grey reduced wares with a characteristic soapy feel, white vessels, usually known as parchment ware and some red ware. There were many similarities in the greyware forms with those produced at Holme-on-Spalding Moor, particularly the two-handled jars, wide-mouthed bowls and flanged dishes. Parchment ware was almost exclusively used for mortaria and bowls, which were often embellished with orange-red slipped decoration.

The success of the Crambeck potteries and their ubiquity in later Roman contexts in the frontier zone and later forts and settlements across the North of England has been mentioned above. It has also been proposed that the location of the Crambeck potteries was also an advantage, benefiting from the proximity of the York to Malton major road and social constraints which seem to have operated in the third century, between East Yorkshire and the rest of the northern region (Evans 1989, 80).

Contrasting but contemporary with parchment ware, which appears around AD 340, were hand-built calcite gritted vesicular jars and bowls with very characteristic heavy hooked rims and a lid-seat groove, which may have been finished on a wheel.

First recognised in the signal stations of the north-east Yorkshire coast, this became known as Huntcliff pottery (Hull 1932; Wilson 1989) and is common in pottery assemblages across the north, replacing the Dales ware jars as the main vessel for storage. Crambeck and Huntcliff products are the latest mass-produced pottery found on many sites in East Yorkshire.

CERAMIC BUILDING MATERIAL

The various types of Roman tile are fundamental to our understanding of Roman building techniques. Buildings were roofed by large flat ceramic tiles with flanges on their sides called *tegulae*, with half-cylindrical *imbrices* arching over the flanges to hold them together. The gap at the gable end of the roof was sometimes filled with a roughly triangular *antefix*. Buildings roofed like this contrasted greatly with the thatched roundhouses of the Iron Age. The other main ceramic building materials were the components of heating systems or hypocausts: *bessalii*, plain square tiles stacked as *pilae*, allowing the passage of hot air and sufficient space to allow maintenance, larger bipedalii mortared to the top of the *pilae* to support the floor in the case of built rather than channelled hypocausts and intra-wall flue tiles or *tubuli*.

The biggest consumers of ceramic building materials within the wider eastern Yorkshire region were the legionary fortress and *Colonia* of York and tiles stamped with LEG IX HISP have been found there. When *Legio VI Victrix* replaced *Legio IX Hispana* sometime around AD 109, tile production was continued with tiles stamped in various ways including LEG VI VIC. The significance of small numbers of stamped tiles away from the legionary fortress has been mentioned in Chapter 8. Stamped tiles of *Legio IX* at Malton may represent a connection between the garrison there and the legionary headquarters at York, but examples in the countryside are more difficult to explain and have usually been dismissed as 'ballast' or simply the result of random deposition. Stamped tiles of *Legio VI* have been found at a number of sites along the Hull Valley including Leven and at a number of locations in and around the city of Hull. To the west of the territory of the Parisi stamped military tile was found at Dalton Parlours villa (Wrathmell and Nicholson 1990). It has been argued that these may represent some kind of territorial marker associated with the legion, perhaps demarcating its *territorium* or *prata* (Mason 1998).

All the villa sites in East Yorkshire and the Roman roadside settlement at Hayton used ceramic building materials and tile has been found at various sites along the Hull Valley in and around the modern city of Hull at Malmo Road, Foredyke, Kingswood, Greylees Avenue and Haworth Hall, referred to in Chapter 8. At Beck View Road, Beverley, fifty-one pieces of tile, mainly tegulae, were found in a pit. The fresh condition of these and the presence of wasters may indicate that they were manufactured here (Tibbles 2000). Further evidence of this activity may have been removed as large-scale medieval tile works developed here exploiting the same clay resource. It is therefore logical to presume that the ceramic building material in the Hull Valley and its environs were made in the locality, rather than being transported large distances by cart. So far no evidence for the production of Roman ceramic building material as an adjunct to the pottery industry has been found in the Foulness Valley, despite the existence of extensive brickworks in later times.

MOSAICS

Mosaics consisted of *tesserae* cut from locally available stone and ceramic material. The most common colours used in eastern Yorkshire were black, white, brick-red, yellow and grey. The most common size used was 15mm square for finer work, with 20–35mm tesserae being used elsewhere (Monkman 2003). Generally the borders were set directly into a fine, carefully levelled mortar, and in some cases guidelines painted or simply scratched onto the surface have been found. Central roundels and more detailed sections were probably created using an indirect method, laid face down on some kind of backing and brought onto site as a prefabricated section. The mosaics of the villas, particularly Rudston, have already been discussed. Certain similarities between them led to the idea that there was a workshop of mosaicists based in Brough known as the 'Petuarian school' (Ramm 1978). This is now no longer believed and resemblances in the design are more likely to be due to the familiarity of the workmen with stock patterns used throughout the Roman world which they took around with them (Smith 2005). Neal and Cosh (2002, 23) have, however, argued on the strength of similarities between them, that there might have been a wider 'Northern Group' of mosaics. Apart from the finished floors themselves, the only evidence for manufacture in this region were the piles of tesserae sorted according to colour found arranged along the wall of Building 3 during the early excavations (Stead 1980).

STONE

As we have seen, the solid geology of East Yorkshire largely comprises chalk, with limestone rocks of the Lias and Jurassic along the edge of the western escarpment (Buckland 1988; Gaunt and Buckland 2002). Excavation of a number of Roman buildings at Hayton and elsewhere in East Yorkshire has shown that blocks of chalk, not commonly considered robust enough, were used. The Norman church at Nunburnholme which includes chalk in its construction provides a testament to its durability. Chalk was used as a building material in early modern times in the villages of the northern Wolds. If laid flat and not used in exposed locations such as corners or quoins, chalk can be a reasonable construction material, its durability being partially dependent on the bed from which it was extracted. It has been suggested that it is necessary to allow chalk to 'harden-off' before use (Brewster 1972). In Holderness, where the chalk lies deeply buried under glacial drift deposits, erratics of various types, particularly cobbles, were available.

Chalk was not usually favoured for inscriptions and tombstones as harder limestone, sandstone and grits were more suitable, however the fragmentary relief of Fortuna from the well of the Rudston villa was carved from chalk (Philips 1980). This may partially explain the small number of stone coffins, altars and inscriptions compared with other regions of Roman Britain. Where stone buildings have been found, they tend to be relatively close to sources of stone, particularly the Jurassic rocks on the western and northern escarpments of the Yorkshire Wolds and the Howardian Hills.

Some stone, however, travelled considerable distances, over 30km in the case of the Hayton Roman roadside settlement, where pieces of diamond-shaped pennant roof tile were frequent finds. Sometimes known as Elland Flag after quarries in the Leeds area, this easily split rock comes from the Coal Measures and has been identified at Wharram, Harpham and Rudston (Buckland 1988, 251; Gaunt and Buckland 2002) and on the Pocklington area and Langton villas. It is not clear whether the tiles were transported by road or water, though the latter would have been cheaper (Buckland 1988); whatever method was used, the cost implication may have been an expression of status. Excavated evidence from places such as Dalton Parlours in West Yorkshire (Wrathmell and Nicholson 1990), shows that stone flag roof tiles were favoured from the third century AD.

Building stones identified by Richard Myerscough on the site of the possible temple at Millington included Coal Measures flagstone, Lower Jurassic limestone from the North Yorkshire Moors, and sandstone from the Pennines near Leeds. Stone from the Lias Bench on the western fringes of the Yorkshire Wolds and some Lower Magnesian Limestone from the Tadcaster area (Buckland 1988; Gaunt and Buckland 2002) are also evident.

Querns have already been mentioned in the context of agriculture; however, they also provide useful information about the trade networks operating at the time. The most detailed study carried out so far has been at Shiptonthorpe where forty-five quern fragments were recovered (Gwilt 2006). The absence of Iron Age-style saddle and beehive querns supports the other dating evidence for the foundation of the site as a Roman roadside settlement, for all the querns were of flat rotary type, characteristic of the Roman period. The majority were of non-calcareous fine and medium-grained sandstones which may have derived from local Jurassic strata (Gwilt 2006). There were a number manufactured from non-calcareous Pennine gritstones and calcareous gritstones from the Filey area of North Yorkshire. Calcareous gritstone querns probably from the same source were present at a number of other sites in Parisian territory including Hayton Fort, Welton villa, Faxfleet, Elmswell and Brough (Gwilt 2006). From further afield were pieces of rotary lava quernstones imported from the Mayen area of the German Rhineland which are also known as Niedermendig querns (Gwilt 2006).

Research by the Yorkshire Quern Survey has shown that the beehive querns of eastern Yorkshire were distinctive in form, with smaller bun-shaped top stones in the Iron Age tradition, contrasting with those discovered elsewhere in the Yorkshire region (Cruse forthcoming).

JET

One of the best known products of Roman eastern Yorkshire is jet, the black fossilised remains of *Araucaria araucana*, the monkey puzzle, which is most plentiful on the north-east coast around Whitby, where it erodes out of the cliffs from Jurassic deposits. It may have been drift-mined in the Roman period as it was in the nineteenth century (Allason-Jones 2002). Jet has also been found further south along the beaches of the Holderness coast and inland on the Jurassic/Lower Lias Bench around North Cliffe. Jet has been utilised for the manufacture of jewellery since the Bronze Age, and fine necklaces and collars comprising hundreds of beads have been found in prehistoric burial mounds. In the Roman period York became a major centre for jet working, where it was made into items such as hair pins, beads, bangles and pendants, which can be found all over Roman Britain. Jet jewellery became particularly fashionable from the second to fourth centuries AD and it is interesting to note that similar tastes developed across the North Sea in the Rhineland at the same time, to the extent that some form of direct communication between these regions has been suggested (Allason-Jones 2002).

METALS

Iron

The necessary raw materials for the production of iron were still available in the Roman period as they were in the Iron Age. Around Holme-on-Spalding Moor iron slag was found with Roman pottery and smelting took place on three of the pottery kiln sites. The appearance of tap slag rather than slag blocks demonstrates a change in the technology of the smelting process, with slag flowing out of the furnace rather than forming in a pit inside its base. The pottery from both of the excavated kiln sites at Hasholme Hall (Hicks and Wilson 1975) and Bursea House contained crushed slag or ore which demonstrate pottery and iron production continuing together and indeed it has been

Fig.61 The iron anvil from Hasholme. The narrow end would have been placed into a wooden block or bench. (M. Park courtesy Hull and East Riding Museum: Hull Museums)

suggested that 'there was a technology transfer, with knowledge from iron furnace technology being adapted to potting' (Millett 1999, 226). At Hasholme Hall (Hicks and Wilson 1975), a small furnace was excavated and an iron anvil was discovered during the excavations of the early 1970s (Manning 1975), designed to be set into a block of wood or work bench and is paralleled on the European continent as well as elsewhere in Roman-Britain (Fig. 61).

Iron production at Elmswell, at the head waters of the River Hull (Congreve 1938), has already been referred to and probably continued through the Roman period and into the Anglian era, as smithing slag was spread across the site. Smithing slag has been found at a number of other locations in the territory of the Parisi. On the Roman roadside settlement at Shiptonthorpe (Allason-Jones *et al.* 2006) for example, smithing slag and an unstratified small hammer suitable for fine metal working was found. At the Hayton Roman roadside settlement geophysical survey and smithing slag on the surface of the field indicated a probable smithing hearth. On both these roadside settlements a blacksmith's shop would have served the needs of both passing traffic and the local communities for activities including construction. At Shiptonthorpe, for example, 94 per cent of the 864 iron small finds recovered during the excavation of a plot of land containing a sequence of timber buildings were nails (Millett 2006). Similarly around 80 per cent of the 2,703 iron small finds on a settlement site at Burnby Lane, Hayton, (Halkon *et al.* 2000 and forthcoming; Halkon and Millett 2003) were nails of a type associated with timber building construction (Snetterton-Lewis 2006). At Rudston villa there is also good evidence for a resident blacksmith.

The iron finds from the Shiptonthorpe roadside settlement included several styli corresponding with the wooden writing tablet fragments found in the waterhole (Allason-Jones *et al.* 2006). There were seven knives (Allason-Jones *et al.* 2006) including the larger part of the blade of a heavy knife or cleaver of the type associated with Roman-style butchery techniques which involved chopping through the bone rather than the Iron Age technique of disarticulation at the joints by cutting the sinew (Seetah 2004). Cleaver butchery is also apparent on the cattle bones from the Roman fort at Hayton. Previously regarded as crude (Monk 1978), it is now considered to be a sophisticated technique designed to aid the rapid preparation of meat for a hungry garrison. The more frequent use of iron for commonplace tasks is also a distinguishing feature between Roman and Iron Age, reflecting changes in lifestyle between the two eras.

At Langton villa (Corder and Kirk 1932) 50 per cent of the twenty-eight iron items listed are nails; other objects included fittings, a ladle-bowl, and a key. At Rudston villa (Stead 1980) iron finds included a stylus, keys, a spit and a flesh hook. Iron was used in engineering such as the bucket hoops, bars, pivot plates, chains and handle frames which made up the lifting gear for the 30m-deep well (Pacitto 1980).

The two major deposits of iron objects from Beadlam Roman Villa referred to in the previous chapter (Neal 1996) consisted of Hoard 1 containing thirty-seven objects including a pick, saws, chisels and axe-heads, hinges and other fittings probably gathered up as scrap. Hoard 2 was broadly similar to Hoard 1, though the presence of weapons including spearheads, ballista bolt-heads, arrows and a possible throwing axe is surprising. The quantity of weapons found here strongly suggests a military connection.

Iron agricultural tools are relatively uncommon on Roman sites in East Yorkshire and include a scythe blade and spade-irons from Welton, a reaping hook from Brantingham (Liversidge *et al.*1973). Woodworking tools have been found on a number of sites, the best preserved being a complete woodworking plane from Goodmanham. The plane has an iron sole with capped iron rivets for attaching it to the stock made unusually from elephant ivory. This remarkable tool probably belonged to a master carpenter (Long *et al.* 2002) (Plate 45).

At Thwing a small Roman iron smelting furnace was built into the floor of one of the rooms of the villa-type house, possibly after its abandonment (Martin Millett pers. comm.; Ferraby *et al.* 2008). Only one smelt was undertaken in the furnace, probably using bog ore from the narrow band of wetland around the nearby Gypsey Race.

Copper alloy

Copper in its various alloys remained important in the Roman period as it had been in the Iron Age, for the production of utilitarian items and for personal adornment, particularly for brooches which will be discussed in the next chapter. Brooches become so common and of such standardised types that they can almost be regarded as mass-produced products. The usual method of manufacture for most copper-alloy objects was the lost-wax process. A wax model of the object was made and a clay mould formed around it. Molten metal was poured into the mould vaporising the wax. After cooling, the mould was broken open and the object polished and finished off. Evidence for the working of copper-alloys has been found in Roman contexts at a number of sites in East Yorkshire including Elmswell, Harpham, Langton and Rudston (Bayley 2002).

Lead

The cluster of stamped pigs of lead around the Humber estuary has been noted in Chapter 7 (Fig. 41). In contrast to the Iron Age, lead was widely used in building, generally where water needed to be contained or excluded. Fragments of lead are common metal detector finds on many Roman sites and objects include small items such as weights and repairs for ceramic vessels. Larger lead items are known from a number of sites including a lead coffin found near Tollingham, Holme-on-Spalding Moor, which was used as an ornamental trough outside the vicarage and subsequently stolen (Halkon and Millett 1999).

Lead was used in alloying, particularly with copper alloys for such things as votive figurines and with tin for making pewter vessels. Moulds for casting pewter vessels were found at Langton villa (Goodhall 1972).

GLASS

The majority of glass in Roman East Yorkshire comes from higher status sites such as the forts, larger settlements and villas and was used for vessels, windows and jewellery. The two basic methods of manufacture were casting or blowing (Allen 1998). In the wider Yorkshire region, evidence for glass manufacture, which tends to be ephemeral compared to other high-temperature industries, has been found at Castleford and at York (Price 2002). There is some dispute as to the age of the glass waste from Bursea House, Holme-on-Spalding Moor, where the high-temperature industries of potting and iron production were also undertaken in the Roman period (Halkon 1983; Price 2002). Certainly part of a melted glass bangle was found there. Glass bangles of various types occur in the East Yorkshire region and rare evidence for their manufacture has been found at Thearne, close to the River Hull, near Beverley (Campbell 2008). This consisted of many pieces of broken glass vessels which were ready for recycling and many fragments of bangles, some melted and bearing tool marks, and small twisted glass cords usually in dark blue and white, which were inserted into the lighter green glass body of the bangle as a decorative effect. The Thearne material is some of the best evidence for the production of glass bangles and beads in Roman Britain.

TEXTILE PRODUCTION

The ubiquity of spindle whorls in ceramic, stone and occasionally lead, suggests that spinning was carried out in many households, most likely by women, and according to one estimate it would have taken five hand spinners to keep one weaver going (Fig. 62) (Wild 2002, 57). The warp weighted upright loom was largely abandoned in favour of the horizontal loomby the end of the second century AD (Wild 2002, 11). Most clothes would probably be made in the home; however, more intensive production can be inferred from references to British woollen products across the Empire. The emperor Diocletian's Edict on Maximum Prices (Lewis and Reinhold 1966, 464–472) refers to a *Birrus Britannicus*, a waterproof and windproof hooded cloak, priced at 6,000 denarii, which we can calculate would have taken a shepherd, who would no doubt have had benefited from its properties, around 300 days to earn and a top lawyer a mere six days! The same document also mentions a *Tapete Britannicum*, a heavy woollen rug at 4,000–5,000 denarii (Bennett 2001, 42). It is quite possible therefore, that wool and

Fig 62 Textile equipment from Roman Malton. Back: Chalk loom weight from an upright loom, weaving combs (length *c.* 15cm), bone triangles for tablet weaving and replicas with woollen thread, spindle whorls in chalk and samian pottery, bone needles and a bone object of unknown function, perhaps a shuttle. (M. Park courtesy Malton Museum Trust)

cloth production formed an important part of the Roman economy of eastern Yorkshire, as it did in the medieval period, though this is very difficult to be certain. Further aspects of dress will be discussed in Chapter 10.

SALT

Before the modern era and the advent of refrigeration, the main methods of preserving food, especially meat and fish was drying, salting and smoking. Salt was therefore a most important commodity. There were two main ways of producing salt: mining or evaporation of salt-water. Reference was made to briquetage from the Iron Age settlement of Faxfleet Site A (Sitch 1989) and at Preston Road, Hull (Evans and Steedman 2000, 196) in Chapter 5, and the process was continued into the Roman period. As one would expect the distribution of briquetage and other ceramic material associated with salt production is distributed in the wetlands of the lower Hull Valley and around the Walling Fen (pers. comm. L. Wastling). Further evidence for salt production was found at Snake Hall near Hotham during the construction of the Asselby to Easington pipeline (Daniel *et al*. in preparation).

SUMMARY

It is clear from the above that there was substantial industrial activity undertaken in Roman eastern Yorkshire and partly because of its robusticity when compared to other materials, the bulk of this relates to pottery production. Pottery from this region was traded all over northern Britain, but the fact that it is distinguishable from the products of other kilns suggests the development of regional traits (Evans 1988). There is evidence for the production of iron and other metals and one of the most significant sites in Roman Britain for the manufacture of glass bangles so far discovered. Jet is one of the best-known products of the region, and was popular particularly in the later Roman period.

It is more difficult to assess the amount of trade in organic products such as leather, cloth and wool and we have to rely on associated items such as loom weights and spindle whorls and a few surviving fragments, for information about textile production. Analysis of the animal bone also implies that wool production formed an important part of the region's economy.

CHAPTER 10

THE INDIVIDUAL IN ROMAN EASTERN YORKSHIRE

INTRODUCTION

The aim of this chapter is to shed some light on the life of ordinary people in the territory of the Parisi through examination of the archaeological evidence and to assess the extent to which it is possible to determine whether the distinctiveness of this region in the Iron Age expressed through such aspects as religion and ritual, burial, dress and diet was maintained in the Roman period. Without documentary material, it is very difficult to work out how the Parisi viewed themselves or whether they possessed any kind of group identity.

We know a few of the names of the people living here from inscriptions on stone, but the majority of these are in contexts associated with the military and therefore unrepresentative of the population as a whole. In Malton Museum there is a tombstone bearing the well-known Roman name Aurelius, found in a garden on Langton Road (*RIB* 715; Wenham 1974, 47). We have already encountered Marcus Ulpius Januarius

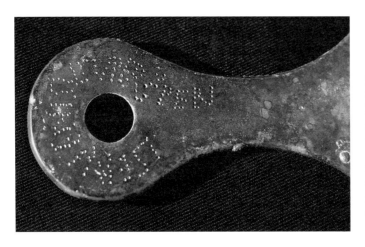

Fig.63 Close up of a patera handle from Malton bearing the punched name Lucius Servenius Super (diameter of end of handle 5cm). (M. Park courtesy Malton Museum Trust)

who dedicated the theatre inscription in the *vicus* at Brough and Candidus, Prefect of the *Ala Picentiana* and trooper Aurelius Macrinus, whose names appear in inscriptions found at Malton. Another soldier had his name, Lucius Servenius Super, punched on the handle of his patera, a small saucepan (Fig. 63). The name Candidus was also scratched into a tile built into the hypocaust of the small bath suite at Burnby Lane Hayton (Halkon and Millett 2003; Halkon *et al.*forthcoming), though it is almost certain that these are different people. The tombstones and religious dedications such as these suggest permanent commemoration was important, but what can we learn of the beliefs which inspired these artefacts?

RELIGION

Unlike the generally sceptical or agnostic population of Britain today, it is probable that religious belief and superstition was closely integrated into the lives of people in the Roman period, although in the absence of written material in Parisi territory we can only deduce this through interpretation of material evidence and comparison with other areas of Roman Britain. Apart from the large number of burials, anomalous for Iron Age Britain, our evidence for ritual and religion in Iron Age East Yorkshire is slight (Dyer 2001), but seems to follow trends in Britain and Europe. Possible evidence for the well-known head cult can be seen in some of the chalk figurines referred to previously (Fig. 33), clustered on the Yorkshire Wolds, as a number of these may have had their heads deliberately removed (Stead 1988). It has been argued that the short sword with the anthropomorphic hilt from North Grimston (Plate 20) was used in human sacrifice (Green 2001) though this association is difficult to prove.

The stuctured depsition of 'special' objects (Hill 1995) animals and indeed human body parts in pits and ditches around Iron Age settlements has been referred to in Chapter 5, although others are more sceptical, viewing much of this material as merely rubbish (Morris 2010). The deliberate disposal of precious items including weapons in watery places, such as bogs, streams and lakes throughout prehistory has been more widely accepted, and some of the most famous items of metalwork from Iron Age Britain have been found in such contexts. The highly decorated shield from the River Witham near Lincoln (Stead 1996) is a good example of this activity. Although such fine specimens of Iron Age art are yet to be found in the watery places of eastern Yorkshire, the late Bronze Age Leven swords and the Roos Carr wooden images do, however, show that such finds are possible. We will return to the subject of structured deposition in the Roman period later in this chapter.

When the Roman army arrived in the region they brought with them a new set of deities and belief systems. Religion in Roman Britain was varied and multi-ethnic, the core being based on the familiar, but renamed Greek gods of Mount Olympus, which were often conflated with 'native' deities. Evidence for religion in the territory of the Parisi includes fragments of sculpture, several with inscriptions and small figurines, generally in copper alloy, depicting deities and their attributes. Some of these may have been placed in a *lararium* or household shrine, others carried about the person.

At the top of the hierarchy of Roman deities were Jupiter, Juno and Minerva, the so-called 'Capitoline Triad', named after the temple on the Capitol Hill in Rome. However, dedications to these gods are rare in East Yorkshire. Every January, like their counterparts throughout the Roman world, the garrisons of Malton, Brough-on-Humber and Hayton would have held a ceremony involving the sacrifice of an ox in honour of the Roman state before the parade ground altars, which were usually dedicated by the unit commander to *Iuppiter Optimo Maximo*, to Jupiter Best and Greatest (Henig 1995, 89). The eastern Yorkshire examples have yet to be found. A copper-alloy figurine from Hayton fort (FT080 Halkon *et al.*forthcoming) has a passing resemblance in pose and attire to a life-size stone statue of Juno Regina from the museum at Chesters on Hadrian's Wall, which by coincidence is also headless and armless (Coulston and Phillips, 1988, 44).There is a copper-alloy head of Minerva from Wetwang (PAS SWYOR-7FOD33) which may have been purely decorative as there is a socket in its base.

Evidence for another Olympian god in the form of the base of a stone altar was found at Malton in 1835, somewhere between Commercial Street and the River Derwent, inscribed:

DEO MAR (ti)
RIGAE
SCIRVS DIC
SAC (rum) V (otum) S (olvit) L (ibens) M (erito). (*RIB* 711)

'To the god Mars Riga, Scirus consecrated this sacred (altar). He willingly and deservedly fulfilled his vow.'

Mars was the god of war and Riga has been variously interpreted as 'king' in a Celtic language, or the name of an unknown, perhaps local god. It has been argued that 'DIC' may be an abbreviation of Decurion, which is either the commander of thirty cavalry or an official on a Roman town council.

Several figurines of Mars have been found in the territory of the Parisi including an example from the Yapham area (Andrews-Wilson 2008) recorded through the Portable Antiquities Scheme. Although it is rather battered and worn, missing feet and a left arm, he wears a Corinthian-style helmet with a tall crest, a cuirass and flaring tunic. His right arm is held high and part of the spear shaft can still be seen in his hand. As might be expected, there is a concentration of such figurines and dedications in the northern, more militarised parts of Roman Britain (Henig 1995, 77). It is possible that the stone relief of Victoria (Victory) (Fig. 64) found at Bolton, near York (Halkon 1992), was probably dedicated by a serving or retired soldier. This sculpture shows Victory with a palm frond over her shoulder, placing a wreath on an altar. It is likely that there was an inscription at the base which is now lost. The rather crude execution of this piece is reminiscent of the grave stone of Lucius Duccius Rufinus, Signifer of the Ninth Legion (*RIB* 673) from York, who himself may have marched through the territory of the Parisi.

Fig.64 The altar of Victory from Bolton (height 30cm). (A. Arnott)

A further dedication to a personification was the lower part of a relief of Fortuna (Fortune) carved in chalk, found in the well at Rudston villa. It shows the right leg with flowing robes and the bottom of a wing, with Fortuna's attribute, a spoked wheel, to the rear (Phillips, 1980, 129). As Fortuna is a deity appealing as much to civilians as to the military (Henig, 1995,77), the sculptures do little to shed light on the identity of the person responsible for the dedication, other than their familiarity with Roman culture and belief systems.

A small votive figurine of Apollo, another member of the Olympian hierarchy who was associated with the sun, the arts, healing and prophecy was found on the Roman roadside settlement at Hayton in 2009 (Fig.

Fig.65 Figurine of Apollo the lyre player from the Roman roadside settlement at Hayton (height 6cm). (M. Park)

65) (Halkon *et al.* forthcoming). Cast in leaded bronze, he is depicted naked, leaning nonchalantly on a lyre on a stand, holding a rather oversized plectrum in his right hand. Though a little crude, some care has been taken to add detail such as chest hairs and pony tail. This figurine is one of a cluster in and around the Roman roadside settlement. Elsewhere in Roman Britain both Apollo and Mars are often conflated with 'native' deities. Mars, as befits the month which was named after him, was also associated with fertility (Henig 1995, 51).

Venus is depicted on the mosaic from Rudston, which has been discussed in some detail in Chapter 8. Although at first glance the depiction of the goddess of love and beauty amongst *bestiarii*, the beast-fighters of the Roman amphitheatre, would appear incongruous, she was also the patroness of the amphitheatre (Neal and Cosh 2002, 355). The rather badly drawn bust above the friendly-looking leopard has variously been interpreted as Mercury or Bacchus. At first glance he seems to be wearing the winged hat of the messenger of the gods with the caduceus – a staff entwined with winged serpents. However, if the foliage at either side of him are bunches of grapes on a vine, and the vessels at each side of his head *canthari*, or large vessels for storing wine, and the staff the *thyrsus*, made of twisted vine, the figure may be Bacchus, god of wine (Neal and Cosh 2002, 355). It is interesting to note that the birds on the 'Charioteer' mosaic, like those on the Venus mosaic, may be attributes of that goddess and that the leaping leopards and *cantharus* in the small lobby between the 'Charioteer' and a large damaged mosaic can be best explained as attributes of Bacchus, a suitable deity for the entry to the major room of the house, where its owner would have entertained. It has also been argued that vines, fruit and birds, especially peacocks, which can be found on mosaics and sculpture all over the Roman world, particularly in the catacombs in Rome, are hidden symbols of Christianity (Henig, 1995, 123). It could even be possible, though perhaps stretching the evidence, that the commissioner of the Rudston mosaics was a Christian. Whatever the deities depicted at Rudston, the Venus mosaic should no longer be seen as a poorly executed mismatch of random figures chosen by an uneducated native aspiring to be Roman, but by someone fully integrated into Roman religion and culture.

The most commonly found votive copper-alloy figurines from Roman Britain are associated with Mercury (Woodward 1992; Green 1994, 33) and either represent the god himself, or his main attendants, a sheep or goat and a cockerel. There is a cockerel

Fig.66 Votive figures of a sheep/goat (height 3cm) and chicken which were associated with the cult of Mercury. (S. Stratton)

from the Driffield area (Morris 2010) and a cockerel and goat from the Roman roadside settlement at Hayton (Fig. 66). A figure of Mercury is also engraved in an intaglio from a finger ring found at the fort at Hayton, now in Hull Museum.

In Malton, a battered limestone statue thought to be of Mercury holds the purse and *caduceus* associated with this deity (Tufi, 1983, 9). Another rather enigmatic stone sculpture from the region is built into the south-west buttress of the north aisle of the church at Kirby Underdale. Its original archaeological context is by no means secure, however, as it was discovered in the rectory garden in 1916. It has been suggested that it is a representation of Mercury (Tufi 1983, no.19, Plate 4). The figure is clearly male with an emphasised penis. He wears a cap, which has been variously interpreted as horned or winged, the latter being an attribute of Mercury, and he carries a roughly circular object interpreted as a bag or purse. In his other hand he holds what is thought to be a wand, the *caduceus* of Mercury. Due to its worn condition and crudity in execution of the sculpture, it is very difficult to be certain about the identity of this figure, however with its triangular tip it looks more like a spear point than a winged staff and the projection from the top of his head the crest of a helmet, rather than the winged cap of Mercury. At the waist is a narrow linear zone which may be a belt. If all this evidence is put together, the figure may represent Mars, or a conflation of the war god with a native deity with similar attributes. Although both his shield and spear are missing, the copper-alloy figurine of Mars Ultor from Dragonby, North Lincolnshire (Alcock 1996, 265, figs 11.5, 2) bears some resemblance in pose and demeanour to the Kirby Underdale sculpture.

The copper-alloy votive sheep/goat from a villa site in the Millington area may well relate to the possible circular temple and associated structures discussed in Chapter 1. Placed at the junction of a number of valleys and close to springs, the circular structure is associated with several rectilinear buildings with hypocausts and mosaics, which may have formed a rural sanctuary similar to those at West Hill, Uley (Gloucestershire), Nettleton Scrubb (Wiltshire) and Springhead in Kent (Penn 1962; Rodwell 1980, 217). The Millington site is smaller in scale and there seems to be no equivalent small town here, despite large-scale geophysical survey between the temple site and the Roman road (Halkon *et al.* 2007). Circular temples are not common in Roman Britain and may derive from pre-conquest structures of which Hayling Island and Frilford are the best-known examples. There is, however, some resemblance in both the form of the complex and its landscape setting, with examples from Gaul, where circular temples are also to be found (Horne and King 1980).

Like Millington, a late Roman stone building dated from coin evidence to around AD 340 excavated at West Heslerton (Powlesland 2003(b), 288) interpreted as a shrine or small temple, is associated with a dry valley which leads down to a spring. This stone rectilinear structure with curved short sides, flanked by what may be ancillary buildings,

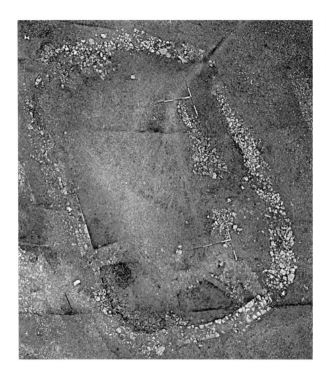

Fig.67 The foundations of the possible shrine from West Heslerton. (D. Powlesland)

blocks the entrance to this valley. There is evidence that large numbers of people may have visited this site on a seasonal basis. Large quantities of animal bones, oyster shells, and some bread ovens associated with a large rectangular structure suggest some form of mass catering for pilgrims. The replacement of the pathways and surfaces associated with the structures, shows that the complex was used for a considerable time (Fig. 67, Plate 40). The finds collected during field walking from a series of enclosures revealed by geophysical survey to the west of the Millington temple site may represent similar activity.

The most noticeable concentration of votive and religious objects in eastern Yorkshire is associated with Vulcan, god of blacksmiths and other craftsmen. The son of Jupiter and Juno, husband of Spring Goddess Maia and Venus, his smithy was reputed to be underneath Mount Etna in Sicily. He is generally depicted with a withered leg, caused alternatively by his being hurled from Olympus by Jupiter in a rage or by Juno due to his ugliness. He is shown as bearded, wearing a brimmed hat and a tunic, his right shoulder exposed to enable free use of his hammer (Henig 1997, 128).

The pots decorated with blacksmith's tools from the kilns at Norton and Malton (Fig. 68) have been referred to in Chapter 8 and a complete vessel with a bearded face and smith's tongs and a sherd with an applied bearded face were found in the Shiptonthorpe roadside settlement (Halkon 1992; 2006).

Fig.68 Part of a pottery vessel decorated with smith's tools from Norton (height 15cm). (M. Park courtesy Malton Museum Trust)

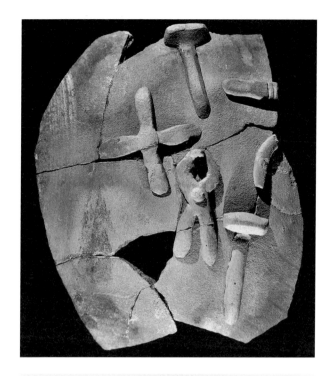

Fig.69 Miniature anvil in copper alloy from Brough. It was probably worn as an amulet (width 36mm). (M. Park courtesy Hull and East Riding Museum: Hull Museums)

A further smith's tool pot sherd was discovered at Bielby (Didsbury 1984), on a Roman site where some iron smelting had also taken place. A miniature anvil (Fig. 69) found just outside the gateway of the walled enclosure at Brough, now in the Hull and East Riding Museum, and miniature axes and a hammer discovered by metal detectorists at the Hayton roadside settlement (Stratton 2005; Halkon 2008; Halkon *et al.* forthcoming) together with concentration of smith-tool and Vulcan pots, strongly suggests that there was a regional cult associated with the smith god in this region, appropriate in an area with the furnace-based industries of iron smelting and potting.

Apart from the Millington and West Heslerton temple sites, other evidence for formal religious worship is rare in Parisi territory. In the Yorkshire Museum, York, there is a small altar which was found south of Dunnington Common, a few miles to the east of York (Tufi, 1983, 21). Despite its weathered condition it is possible to see an axe, a knife and a *guttus* (a spouted vessel), all items associated with religious ceremony. Similar altars can be seen elsewhere in Roman Britain and beyond. Fragments of stone altars were found at Bramble Hill, Elmswell, during fieldwork by the Granthams, associated with robbed walls and stone floors (Dent 1988). Three of these were pieces of a relief depicting three human figures, possibly from a religious frieze, the others were from altars. One of the fragments of a sandstone altar had a circular dished hollow or focus carved in the top, presumably to take libations, offerings of sacrificial blood, wine or other substances which were sometimes burnt. Another fragment, in different fossiliferous sandstone, bore an inscription, illegible apart from the letters D I I O. This may be a version of DEO – 'to the god' which is seen on altar inscriptions at York (*RIB* 645), Wallsend (*RIB* 1303), Carrawburgh (*RIB* 1522, 1528) and Newcastle-on-Tyne (*RIB* 1321) on Hadrian's Wall, and Castlesteads, Cumberland (*RIB* 1991), all military installations. It has been argued that the deity may be Rigisamus (most kingly), a deity found at West Coker, Somerset, and identified here with Mars (*RIB* 187) (Dent 1988, 95). Might there not be a parallel with the Malton altar dedicated to Mars Riga referred to above?

Reference has already been made to the importance of the Elmswell area in the Iron Age. Here were the springs which fed the River Hull, a highly significant place within the landscape of Parisi territory. The Granthams reported finding many Roman coins around here and the fine decorated copper-alloy plaque described earlier may also have been an offering. All the evidence implies strongly the presence of a shrine here, and its location compares well with the Millington and West Heslerton religious complexes. Although the altars and inscription are highly Roman in character, the location at the mouth of the Great Slack close to springs is redolent of an Iron Age past; the Elmswell plaque (Congreve 1938) with its combination of repoussé rosettes in late Iron Age style and classical running scroll of vine leaves in enamel neatly symbolises the mixture of 'Celtic' and Roman artistic elements which are reflected in the religion of the region.

Elmswell's location close to water, in this case the source of the River Hull, follows a strand running through the religion and ritual of Roman East Yorkshire, suggestive of continuity from the Iron Age. This is perhaps best illustrated at the Shiptonthorpe roadside settlement discussed in Chapter 7, where a waterhole near the junction of the main York to Brough road and a side road heading towards the present village of Holme-on-Spalding Moor became the focus for animal burials and other objects (Millett 2006). At the waterhole, animals including pigs, cattle and calves were deposited during the infilling and after it had been levelled and fenced off. Some items from the earlier phase had been carefully placed, for example two very similar dog skulls were found on

Fig.70 The waterhole at Shiptonthorpe which became a focus for ritual activity by the later Roman period. (P. Halkon)

opposite sides of the feature. As all were buried after the waterhole had ceased to be used as a water source, they may be seen as offerings associated with the closure of the feature (Fig. 70).

It is interesting to note that the deliberate deposition of either portions of or complete animals has been identified at many sites across the region, including the settlement at Burnby Lane, Hayton (Halkon and Millett 2003; Jacques forthcoming). It has become customary to regard such animal burials as displaying continuity with an Iron Age past (Grant 1991; Fulford 2001), however recent detailed examination of the bones may suggest at least some of them indicate 'Roman'-style sacrifice and feasting (Jacques forthcoming). As in the case of the Shiptonthorpe waterhole, at Hayton, animal skulls, in this case cattle, were deliberately placed in the top fill of a timber-lined well and a nearby pit contained the partial remains of two dogs and the incomplete skeleton of a pig.

As well as animal remains, pollen analysis of the infill of the Shiptonthorpe waterhole revealed the presence of holly and mistletoe (Millett 2006, 314), plants with strong ritual association even today. The ancient Roman writer Pliny the Elder (*Natural History* XVI, 251) reports that 'the Druids hold nothing more sacred than mistletoe'. The stomach of 'Lindow Man' found in a Cheshire peat bog and possibly the victim of ritual killing, was found to contain mistletoe pollen (Stead *et al.*1986, 167).

Tacitus (*Annals* XIV, 29–37) describes graphically the crushing of the Druids on Anglesey and Suetonius (*Life of Claudius* XXV, 5) tells us that the 'cruel and inhuman' religion of the Druids was utterly abolished in Gaul. The main threat to the Roman state from the Druids was perhaps largely political, however, at least in early Roman Britain (Henig 1995, 206). Such evidence as the Shiptonthorpe mistletoe reminds us that aspects of the old religion probably continued into the later Roman period. The writing tablets found in the waterhole may have been deposited in order to communicate a vow to the gods, in a similar way to the so-called 'cursive' tablets from the sacred springs at Bath or the temple at Uley (Tomlin 2002) and therefore clearly 'Roman' in inspiration and written in Latin.

BURIAL

One of the best ways of understanding the lives of individuals in the territory of the Parisi is by the study of the dead. As we have seen in Chapter 4, the examination of burials and skeletal remains can provide clues concerning the age at death, health, diet, pathology, status and profession and studies of isotopes surviving within bones are also beginning to shed light on movement of peoples across the Roman Empire. As the dead do not bury themselves, the way in which they are disposed of tells us about customs associated with death in living populations.

According to Table X of the *Lex Duodecim Tabularum* (Laws of the Twelve Tables) (Johnson *et al.* 2003, 12) laid down in Rome in around 450 BC: 'A dead person may not be buried or burned in the city'. Archaeologists studying the Roman period have tended to apply this across the Empire and therefore any burials found within a settlement have been regarded as unusual. The evidence from eastern Yorkshire, however, shows that burial did occur within settlements, particularly those in the countryside. The Twelve Tables also show that even then both cremation and inhumation were undertaken concurrently. In the late Iron Age, particularly in south-eastern Britain, closer to Gallo-Roman influence, cremation was the favoured method of the disposal of the dead. Until relatively recently, it was presumed that in the north, inhumation continued to be the normal practice, however, as we have seen, late Iron Age cremations under small round barrows in the large ladder settlement near Rillington show that there was some variation (Powlesland 2003). In general, cremation was the most common practice in the earlier Roman period, largely replaced by inhumation as the main method in the later third and fourth centuries AD.

One of the problems of studying the burials in eastern Yorkshire is that they are few in number when compared with those of the Iron Age: around 450 Roman period burials of which 14 per cent were cremations, the rest inhumations (Law 2004), compared with several thousand Iron Age examples. Whereas Iron Age cemeteries are visible as distinctive cropmarks, Roman period burials are not as easily distinguishable from the air, the vast majority having been discovered accidentally during development in and around areas of Roman settlement, for example the recent pipeline trenches cut across eastern Yorkshire. As yet no large cemeteries such as those at Poundbury, Dorset (Farwell and Molleson 1993), or Lankhills (Booth 2010) have been excavated in East Yorkshire, the largest number of burials being found at Malton and Norton and at Hayton.

At Malton around fifty burials, comprising thirty-eight inhumations (Robinson 1978; Law 2004) and around a dozen cremations have been recovered, though many of these have not been scientifically investigated. There are clusters outside the east entrance and south-western corner of the fort, others on the slopes running towards the River Derwent. At Norton two main concentrations of burials have been located. During building work in 1966–67 at The Ridings, at least thirty-three burials dating from the second century to fourth centuries AD were recovered in what may be a walled cemetery (Robinson 1978, 39, no. 355). There were at least seven cremations, some contained in pots, the remainder were inhumations with a range of finds including crossbow brooches. The cemetery probably extended behind No. 98, Langton Road, as up to six cremations and thirty inhumations with bracelets and other trinkets, and pottery of third-century date were found there.

A glance at the distribution of burials in eastern Yorkshire shows that many are positioned along the Roman roads, close to settlements which would appear to be in line with Roman burial law (Fig. 71). One only has to consider Rome itself, Pompeii or northern Roman cities such as Köln in Germany, to observe that there was competition for burial plots close to the road and town gates, with families displaying their wealth in rich tomb monuments. At Shiptonthorpe, however, phosphate analysis, geophysical survey and excavation showed that a plot within the roadside settlement became a cemetery (Taylor 1995, 47–49; Millett 2006, 24). A copper-alloy mount in the form of a lion's head (Allason Jones 2006 *et al.*, no 88, 227) is likely to have been attached to a casket containing cremated remains. There is a similar mount from Hayton.

The discovery of most burials on roadside settlements in the territory of the Parisi has been haphazard, however housing development close to the main Brough-York road at Town Street, Hayton, led to careful excavation of a cemetery of some forty-one inhumations and several cremations in which there was a clear sequence. The earliest were the Iron Age inhumations of a female aged twenty-five to twenty-nine and an older child. Both were flexed and positioned in a north-south alignment, which are typical Iron Age traits. The child was buried with a short iron knife with a handle and two iron objects. These burials were contemporary with features including roundhouse gullies (Stephens 2004).

Two cremations, both in greyware pots, one surrounded by a small sub-circular cut, demonstrate the adoption of a new burial rite in the earlier Roman period and were

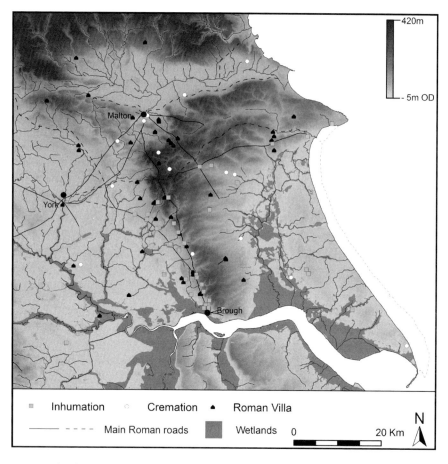

Fig.71 The distribution of burials in Roman eastern Yorkshire. (T. Sparrow)

associated with the settlement along the road. In the later Roman period thirty-nine inhumations were found in four clear groups. Most of the graves were aligned south-west-north-east, perpendicular to the road, parallel to a boundary ditch, though four were at right angles to this arrangement, two of which were buried face down, rather than on their backs. One of these had a chicken carcass on its right hand. Prone burial becomes more common in the later Roman period and has been regarded as a pagan trait in contrast to the Christian position of supine, extended burial (Watts 1998, 46). A full range of age groups was represented, however on average women died younger than the men, which may relate to hazards of childbirth. Males with an average height of 1.70m (5ft 7in) were taller than females 1.55 (5ft 1in) which compares well with the much larger population of the Trentholme Drive cemetery in York where males were 1.70m (5ft 7in) and women 1.55m (5ft 1in) (Wenham 1968; Ottaway 2004, 126).

So far no large Roman cemetery has been located at Brough and indeed few burials have been found compared to Malton and Norton. Wacher's 1958 excavation only recovered four infant burials (Wacher 1969, 233). The majority of burials are, as elsewhere, situated along the main Roman roads, particularly the equivalent to Welton Road which runs roughly east-west and Cave Road, which leads northwards. To the north of Welton road, burials were found during the construction of the Grange Park housing estate (Humber SMR 3481), though not recorded thoroughly, and to the south during the York Archaeological Trust excavations off Welton Road (Hunter-Mann *et al.* 2000). Here, as at Norton and Hayton, the first Roman period burials were two cremations. The condition of the bone did not allow any indication of age or sex to be recognised. One of these was in a pottery vessel dating from the third century AD. The only complete inhumation from the site was a male aged between thirty and forty, who had bad teeth, having lost a few before death, many of the remainder being worn. He had also broken his right fibula, though it had healed well. Other pathology included evidence for leg sores apparent as pitted striations on the surface of the bone.

Also on Welton Road, skeletons were found during the construction of a bungalow and garage in September 2006 (Holst 2007). One was supine and extended; the other prone. Two other burials were too disturbed for their burial posture to be determined. From the better-preserved inhumations it was possible to identify one mature or elderly male with osteoarthritis, degenerative joint disease, inflammation of the shins, fractured ribs and a fractured collar bone. The pronounced muscle attachments showed that he had undertaken a lifetime of hard physical work. He had a small benign tumour and had a blood clot which had become bony. The younger man may have limped slightly, as he had congenital anomalies of the spine. Both had iron deficiency anaemia in childhood, and the bones of a child from the same group also bore witness to physical stress caused by poor diet. The relative position of the burials and shared congenital traits showed that this was possibly a family group. They had no grave goods and the burials were dated from pottery sherds in the fill of the graves.

Perhaps the most interesting and enigmatic burial from Roman East Yorkshire was found in 1936 under thin limestone slabs close to the Roman road to the north of Brough (Corder and Richmond 1938). This adult male had been placed in a wooden coffin, though only the large nails survived. The burial was accompanied by unusual grave goods consisting of iron hoops, about 12cm in diameter, which would have held together the wooden staves of a small bucket. The bucket was decorated by a small bronze human bust around 1cm across shoulders. Iron sceptres, one deliberately bent, topped with bronze-helmeted heads were buried in the grave too (Fig. 72). According to Corder, similar sceptres have been found at Willingham Fen in East Anglia. It is possible that this man may have been some kind of priest. He is reported as being 1.75m (5ft 9in) in height, which is somewhat taller than average for the time, however, the

Fig.72 Copper-alloy heads from the 'Priest's' burial near Brough. The male head from a bucket mount with spiked hair and a moustache is 'Celtic' in appearance (height 19.05mm), the copper-alloy helmeted head (30mm) which decorated one of a pair of iron sceptres is more classical in style. (M. Park courtesy Hull and East Riding Museum: Hull Museums)

assertions of Sir Arthur Keith, who examined the skeleton, that he 'had a big head' with 'jaws degenerate' and therefore belonged to the 'squire class' (in Corder and Richmond 1938, 74) cannot be taken seriously today.

Apart from the larger settlements, clusters of burials have been found at Millington (10+), Goodmanham (20), Blealands Nook, between Wetwang and Fimber (16). The Blealands Nook cemetery, associated with a ladder-type complex of enclosures and droveways was first recognised after the discovery of an adult skeleton at the railway crossing in 1868 and further burials were excavated by Mortimer (1905, 194–200) 1873–74. It began in the Iron Age, with the standard flexed and crouched Arras-style burials (Dent 1983(b)) but also contained some cremations, though these are not described in much detail. The Millington burials are described as being very like those at Blealands Nook (Mortimer, 1905, 170–171) in typical Iron Age posture, yet a complete wheel-thrown Roman pottery vessel was found there.

Had it not been for the inclusion of wheel-thrown greyware vessels dating from the late second century to third century AD, a burial on the fringes of a settlement at Newport Road quarry, North Cave (Evans and Atkinson 2009, 292) could well have been mistaken for one of the Arras culture due to its crouched position (Fig. 76).

The Goodmanham burials were found during the excavation of a railway cutting (Kitson Clark 1935, 123) not far from the Roman road, however the presence of spearhead and beads suggests that some of the burials may have been Anglian in date. More recently eleven adult burials were found associated with a settlement consisting of enclosures and timber buildings (TSEP 907). The majority of these were buried supine and extended in contrast to the flexed Iron Age inhumations from the same site (Evans and Atkinson 2009, 284).

There is an intriguing reference to Roman burials found during the construction of the mausoleum to the Constable family at Halsham, Holderness, to the east of the church in what is reported as a tumulus. Several urns were discovered containing 'a great number of copper coins' which were taken to Burton Constable Hall. At the same time considerable numbers of skeletons were found with urns placed at their heads. An elderly inhabitant also reported the finding of a key of brass (Poulson 1841, 387).

Excavations on the Burnby Lane settlement at Hayton (see Chapter 8) provided the opportunity to examine the full range of burial practices in the Iron Age and Roman periods.

The flexed Iron Age burial of a female with a copper-alloy toe ring, interred within the corner of an enclosure, has been discussed above. In the earlier Roman phase three cremation burials were found: a female in her mid-twenties buried with a child aged two to four years, both contained in one pot, an adult in a vessel which had been disturbed, scattering the cremated bone, and a vessel containing the remains of a woman in her mid-twenties, with a child aged between six and eight years (Langston and Gowland forthcoming). In the fourth century AD, perhaps after the bath house had fallen out of use, a rectangular grave aligned almost north-south contained an extended and supine male in his mid-twenties. Even at this relatively young age, he showed some evidence of minor arthritic changes which may have caused some backache. His burial position is worthy of comment as his left arm was placed over his lower ribs with his right arm held upwards with the hand under his chin (Halkon *et al.* 2000; Halkon and Millett 2003; Easthaugh *et al.* forthcoming; Langston and Gowland forthcoming).

In the rural hinterland of Parisi territory, both settlements and burials appear to have remained largely 'Iron Age' in tradition, however, the occurrence of stone or lead coffins indicates a difference in social status or perhaps cultural identity. Raw materials may also have been a factor and where stone was freely available stone coffins may not have been as expensive (Phillpott, 1991, 53). Unfortunately most of these burials were antiquarian finds and no scientific record was made of the skeletons within them and the coffins lost, as they made convenient troughs for livestock or plants. Such was the fate of the three stone coffins found at Raskelf, near Easingwold (Kitson Clark 1935, 121), and a lead coffin from Tollingham, Holme-on-Spalding Moor, which was stolen from the vicarage garden (*Yorkshire Evening News*, 4 January 1899; Halkon and Millett 1999, 5).

The Raskelf coffins are also of some interest as they were found with stone foundations at Spring House Farm, hinting at a further possible ritual association with water.

Unique amongst the stone coffins within this region, now lost, was an example from East Ness near Hovingham. Discovered during ploughing in 1616 and therefore one of the first Roman antiquities recognised in the region, it was drawn in 1665 by Sir William Dugdale who fortunately recorded the inscription on its side which read:

TITIA PINTA VIXIT ANN(os) XXXVIII
ET VAL(erio) ADIVTORI VIXIT ANN(os) XX
ET VARIALO VIXIT ANN(os) XV VAL(erius)
VINDICIANUS CONIVGI ET FILI(i)s
F(aciendum) C(uravit)

'To Titia Pinta (who) lived 38 years
and Valerius Adjutor (who) lived 20 years
and Varialus (who) lived 15 years, Valerius
Vindicianus had (this) set up to his wife and sons'
(*RIB* 720, Collingwood and Wright 1965, 241; Kitson Clark 1935, 79).

One cannot help but feel sorry for Valerius Vindicianus and wonder what tragedy took away his family. These people may have been associated with the villa found at Hovingham Hall discussed in Chapter 8. A further stone coffin was excavated in 1983 after being struck by the plough at Bishop Wilton (Yorkshire Post, 10.11.1983). Measuring 2.29m in length and 0.76m wide, weighing over 2.5 metric tons, the coffin was made from stone from North Yorkshire and its owner may be associated with several villas located within the Bishop Wilton area.

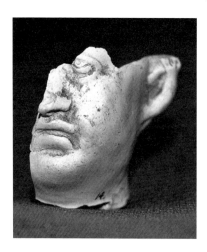

Certain traits brought in from the wider Roman Empire can be seen in the religious and burial practises of eastern Yorkshire. Part of the face of a middle-age man with large ears in white pipe-clay, perhaps from the Allier district of central Gaul, was found at Brough (Corder and Romans 1936, 37, fig. 8 no. 14).

Fig.73 Part of the face of a pipe-clay figurine perhaps from the Allier district of central Gaul, found at Brough. (Corder and Romans 1936, 37, fig. 8 no. 14) (Caroline Rhodes, Hull & East Riding Museum, Hull Museums)

It was discovered amongst stones in the base of the Period II clay rampart and therefore probably dates from the later part of the late first to mid-second century AD. It resembles the figures of diners and reciters such as those from a grave at Colchester (Henig pers. comm.; Toynbee 1964, 419, pl. xcvi), the closest parallels being in France, and therefore represents further evidence of continental contact (Fig. 73).

At Heslington (Wellbeloved 1881, 8), Malton (Corder 1948, 177) and Pollington (near Goole) (Wright 1950) 'gypsum burials' in which an attempt was made to preserve the remains of the deceased by encasing them in plaster were found. The best known burials of this type in the wider region have been found at York. Gypsum burial probably originates from the Rhineland or North Africa and may be associated with Christianity, with its belief in bodily resurrection (Philpott 1991, 93; Carver 2006, 101). A possible source of gypsum was identified during field walking to the south of Church Hill, Holme-on-Spalding Moor. A further Mediterranean element in the burial process were so-called lachrymatory bottles, which were once believed to hold the tears of mourners at funerals and were placed with the deceased. These small containers are now thought to have contained unguents and perfumes or perhaps cosmetics and were usually made from glass (Allen 1998, 27). Examples have been found made in glass at Market Weighton (Fig. 74) (Hull and East Riding Museum) and at Malton and Norton.

One element of Roman burial which has caught attention is the frequent discovery of infant burials on Roman sites and the possibility that deliberate infanticide was common practice and has been noted in sites across Roman Britain. In the fort at Malton, thirty-two infant burials were excavated dating from the period between AD 296 and 367 (Corder 1930(b), 67). Many of the infants appear to have died soon after birth (Smith and Kahila 1992). At Shiptonthorpe fifteen infants, all full term, were excavated (Langston 2006, 252), however the burial of many of these had been careful, particularly around the large

Fig.74 So-called lachrymatory bottles from Market Weighton. They probably contained perfumes for deposition with the dead (*c.* 50mm in height). (M. Park courtesy Hull and East Riding Museum: Hull Museums)

aisled building. At Burnby Lane, Hayton, where between thirty-three and thirty-eight infant burials were excavated, a similar pattern was observed, with the majority of the infants in the sample dying at or soon after birth. Examination of one infant who lived to around nine months to a year, showed that it may have suffered from infantile scurvy or rickets, which when found in infants suggest prematurity. The discovery of the remains of two children in the cremations described above aged two to four and six to eight years, shows that not all children on this site died at birth and although infanticide was a possibility, there were many other possible causes of death. (Langston and Gowland forthcoming)

Amongst the thirty-two infant burials at Malton, found in the cemetery outside the north-east gate of the fort, one has attracted much attention, as it was buried with a small bear carved from jet. A plain bracelet in copper-alloy, a jet bead and a denarius of Caracalla (AD 215–218) were also included in the grave (Fig. 75) (Corder 1948, 173–4). Recent research has shown that the Malton jet bear is not unique, but one of a cluster in eastern England and Germany, which are to be interpreted as a protective guardian for dead children (Crummy 2010, 60). Such careful burials seem to run counter to the idea of infanticide and a seemingly casual attitude to the disposal of bodies found at Welton Wold (Mackey 1998, 29). This difference may be due to the status of the dead and other socio-economic factors.

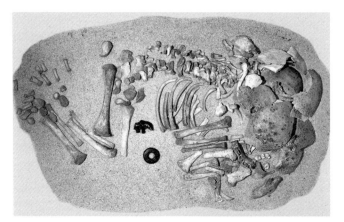

Fig.75 Infant burial with a jet bear from Malton. (M. Park courtesy Malton Museum Trust)

Fig.76 Burial from Newport Road quarry, North Cave. An adult male aged twenty to thirty. He had little evidence of arthritic disorders but relatively poor dental health (Boylston 2002). (Humber Field Archaeology (Photo: Tony Hatfield))

DRESS

Burials can also provide clues concerning costume in Roman eastern Yorkshire as dress accessories and jewellery have been found in graves throughout the region. The textiles seldom survive and sculptures, wall paintings and mosaics provide depictions of what people wore. Of the 450 or so Roman burials from the territory of the Parisi, relatively few contain items of personal adornment have been excavated to a standard which makes it possible to tell whether or not an item was worn by the deceased at the time of burial, or was simply placed into the grave. Items in a range of materials include brooches and bangles, which will be discussed in more detail below, beads, pins for hair and dress as well as cosmetic equipment (Laws 2004). Widespread metal detecting has resulted in the discovery of hundreds of brooches and other dress accessories, the majority of which are casual losses, but their careful recording through the Portable Antiquities Scheme has enabled patterns of distribution to emerge (Plate 38 and Fig. 77) (Norman 2010).

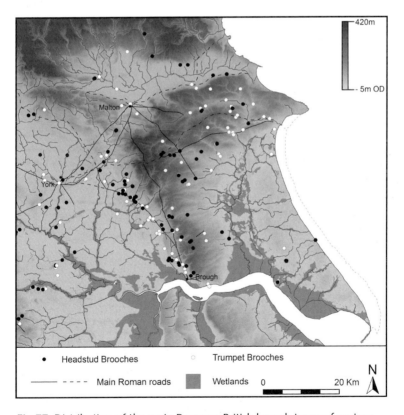

Fig.77 Distribution of the main Romano-British brooch types of eastern Yorkshire. (Based on Norman 2010) (T. Sparrow)

For many years brooches have been used in Roman archaeology as a means of dating, as clear typologies can be constructed; more recently researchers have become interested in what they can tell us about the costume, status and regional identity of their wearers. There were two main types: bow brooches or *fibulae* with a curved upper component and plate brooches with a flat upper component, both forms having a hinged pin, usually of the same metal as the upper part, similar to a modern safety pin. A third type was the penannular brooch where the cloth of a garment was trapped by a pin against the main body of the brooch. This type of brooch appears in the Iron Age and continues in use throughout the post-Roman era.

The larger brooches were generally worn by men on the right shoulder to fasten a heavy cloak of which there were various types (Croom 2002). Pairs of brooches with loops on the end, joined by a chain, are thought to have been worn by women to fasten a tubular dress at the shoulders (Allason-Jones 2005). New types of brooch were already entering Britain in the late Iron Age, such as the Nauheim and Colchester types. As we have seen, a number of these brooch types were found at Redcliff, North Ferriby. Others may have been linked with the army, such as Aucissa and 'knee' types (Swift 2011, 212). Trumpet brooches, so called because of their shape, appear in the mid-first century and are common in second-century civilian and military contexts, along with the so-called head-stud type, the latter often having loops for a chain and therefore are more likely to have been worn by females. Plate brooches were often in the form of an animal, an object or geometric shape and usually enamelled. A type of plate brooch with a particularly northern distribution is the dragonesque brooch, made in the form of an s-shaped beast often showing 'Celtic' influence, in its decorative motifs. Penannular brooches which also had Iron Age antecedents were also more favoured in the north (Swift 2003).

Brooches do not have a uniform distribution across East Yorkshire. First and early second centuries AD examples such as the Aucissa and Hod Hill types are concentrated in a corridor along the Roman roads, particularly between Brough and Barmby Moor and on the foothills of the Wolds, whereas trumpet and head-stud forms are more evenly distributed across the region. There are, however, more brooches on better-quality soils on the Yorkshire Wolds foothills and higher and drier parts of Vale of York and Holderness (Norman 2010, 64).

Wider regional preferences can also be detected in brooch types, as a comparison of brooches from the Portable Antiquities Scheme from the counties of Essex, North Lincolnshire, East and North Yorkshire showed. Essex was dominated by Colchester types, in North Lincolnshire Hod Hill and Dolphin types were favoured and head-stud and trumpet brooches were the most common type in East and North Yorkshire (Norman 2010, 70). It is interesting to note that the greatest difference in preference is between Essex and North Yorkshire. The explanation for these differences is by no means clear; however on a superficial level they would seem to reflect tribal identities.

Of the other items of personal adornment, certain objects are regarded as 'Roman', including earrings, which have been attributed to females associated with the military and urban dwellers. It has, however, been pointed out that some may have belonged to provincial males (Swift 2011, 211). A number of gold examples have been found in the East Yorkshire region and recorded through the Portable Antiquities Scheme including an earring from the Market Weighton area (Andrews-Wilson 2009) of a type more common in Britain and plainer than some continental counterparts (Allason-Jones 1989, 8–9). A single gold earring, with a gold box setting containing a green glass setting, was discovered during excavation at Sutton-on-Derwent, close to the river itself mentioned in Chapter 8 (Chapman *et al.*1999, 186) (Plate 39).

Reference has been made in Chapter 9 to the manufacture of glass bangles, which have been found at a number of locations across the region, though few are complete, like the example found by Rod Mackey close to Beverley Westwood (Dennett 2004, 4). In East Yorkshire it is noticeable that the twisted cords of glass encapsulated within the D-shaped section of the main body of the bangle were mainly blue and white and are the bangles themselves mainly of Kilbride Jones's Type 2, a common variety north of the River Humber (Price 1988; Evans 2007). They are of varying sizes and could have been worn as anklets, armlets and bracelets, or tie up hair. Glass beads are also quite common, particularly those in blue glass.

The presence of hair pins of bone and copper alloy registered with the Portable Antiquities Scheme and housed in museums, and combs found on a number of sites demonstrate that people took care over their personal appearance and may have followed fashion. Portraits of the imperial family influenced the hairstyles of women, particularly Julia Domna, wife of Septimius Severus, and the difference in hairstyles between generations can be seen on the well-preserved tombstone of Julia Velva in the Yorkshire Museum, York (Tufi 1983, no 42, 27). In East Yorkshire wall-paintings such as the so-called 'goddess' from Malton and figures on the villa mosaics, provide some clues as to the appearance of people in this region, though these cannot be taken as representative of the population as a whole. The widespread use of coinage in the third and fourth centuries AD may have provided some models. There is a very striking difference between portraits of emperors after Constantine I and their predecessors which became influenced by the eastern Roman Empire. It is not certain whether such changes were reflected amongst the ordinary population of the Parisi.

A well-preserved double-sided comb of boxwood of type known across the Roman world was found in the waterhole at Shiptonthorpe (Allason-Jones *et al.* 2006, 238) (Plate 33d). With carefully cut teeth which were wider on one side than the other, it also provides a reminder that headlice would have been endemic. Bone combs are also recorded from Malton, Beadlam and Langton. Other evidence for Roman-style grooming is also present in the region as pieces from so-called 'toilet' sets have been found

(Plate 32). These usually included tweezers for removing unwanted hair, nail cleaners and *ligulae*, probes with a tongue-shaped spatula-like end used for dispensing cosmetics or medicine. Toilet items are relatively few in number with a distribution largely restricted to the Roman road corridor to the west of the Yorkshire Wolds, with small concentrations at Hayton and Shiptonthorpe, and in and around the more opulent villas such as Rudston. An outlier in the form of a hanger for a toilet set decorated with blue enamel was found on a settlement close to the tidal estuarine creek system at Hasholme (Leahy 2011).

Another fashion introduction into Britain was new types of shoes, particularly those with iron hobnails in the soles. Hobnails are sometimes found with burials showing that the deceased was shod and where soil conditions allow, complete examples have survived, the largest number yet found in Roman Britain at Vindolanda. In East Yorkshire some of the best preserved were discovered in the waterhole at Shiptonthorpe, all in adult sizes (UK size 7 and 7½, and above) made from cattle skin and goatskin (van Driel-Murray 2006). All showed evidence for wear, some hard. The footwear recovered from Shiptonthorpe resembles that from larger military or urban complexes dates to before AD 200. The Shiptonthorpe shoes were probably deliberately deposited, as shoes, usually the left, are well known in watery contexts from prehistoric times onwards throughout northern Europe (Plate 33c) (van Driel-Murray 1999).

DIET

Certain aspects of the agricultural economy have been discussed in Chapter 8. The key purpose of agriculture in the Roman period as it is now was the production of food. Roman recipe books such as that attributed to by Apicius, probably compiled sometime in the later Roman period based on earlier texts (Edwards 1984; Cool 2006), survive and there are accounts of banquets, such as the famous Trimalchio's feast described in the *Satyricon* of Petronius (Sullivan 2011, 51–92) which has had such an impact on modern perceptions of Roman life. Such accounts are largely applicable to the Mediterranean world. The Vindolanda writing tablets provide lists of ingredients, quantities and prices and some clues as to what was eaten on the northern frontier of Britain (Bowman and Thomas 1984). The absence of documentary sources for this region makes us reliant on evidence that can be gleaned from examination of animal bones, seed and plant remains, pottery and utensils.

So far pottery has been considered in the context of trade, industry and dating; over the last few decades, more attention has been paid to its function and what it can tell us about the people who used it. Mortaria and amphorae have been referred to in previous chapters, but their everyday purpose has not been discussed in detail so far. Mortaria, heavy bowls with broad rims, a pouring spout and grits of stone, slag, or crushed ceramic fired into the inside base of the vessel, were used for crushing herbs and spices and mixing purees or dough, or similar foodstuffs. It has usually been suggested that their presence on a site implies that the people using them had a relatively sophisticated cuisine which involved a degree of careful preparation and by inference the inhabitants enjoyed eating in Roman style as there was no real equivalent in Iron Age Britain. It has, however, been argued that once adopted they were used for other purposes including cheese making and it has also been noted that there are far more mortaria of different types in Roman Britain than in Italy (Cool 2006, 43).

Amphorae, which have been referred to in earlier chapters, were used for the storage and importation of commodities such as wine, olive oil and fish sauce. Marked with a potter's stamp and occasionally an inscription describing their contents, they were categorised by Henrich Dressel who numbered each form, one of the best known being the large globular Dressel 20 olive oil amphorae from the Iberian Peninsula. Their presence on sites implies that people were using oil for frying food or mixing with salads. Oil was also used to fuel oil lamps, which themselves are rare in Roman East Yorkshire. Some caution is needed as the presence of amphorae in small numbers does not necessarily mean the wholesale adoption of Roman lifestyles as they also made handy vessels for the storage of other commodities.

Pottery assemblages from over a hundred scatters of material recovered during field walking in an 8 x 8km block of land around Holme-on-Spalding Moor (Halkon 1987; Halkon and Millett 1999) contained a very small number of mortaria sherds in comparison with the large quantities of greyware jars and wide-mouthed bowls produced in the region, the settlement excavated at Hawling Road, Market Weighton (Evans 1999, 195), being a good example. It has been noted that jars especially have the marks of sooting on their outer surfaces. This is presumed to be caused by flames or embers during the cooking (Cool 2006, 36). All the eastern Yorkshire potteries outlined in Chapter 9 were dominated by jars following the pattern observed elsewhere in rural Roman Britain (Cool 2006, 191). There is also a clear difference, between the quantities of fine tablewares such as samian to be found on forts and the larger settlements such as Brough, Malton and Hayton and rural settlements, observed in detail on sites investigated in the Foulness Valley (Halkon 2008; Willis forthcoming), suggesting conservatism in cooking and eating habits and strong continuity from the Iron Age. This contrast can be observed in pottery assemblages across the wider region. It has been argued that the coarse pottery of the north owed more to Iron Age antecedents than Roman forts and *vici* and remained regionally distinctive (Evans 1988). Although some vessel and kiln types may have had their origins in North Lincolnshire, the potters of East Yorkshire developed their own styles. In terms of what the use of pottery tells us about diet, at rural sites like Hawling Road, Market Weighton, people probably continued to eat in much the same way as they had done in the Iron Age. In the roadside settlements of Shiptonthorpe and Hayton, however, there was greater take up of tablewares and a wider variety of food enjoyed.

As we have seen in Chapter 4, the isotopes from the bones of the Iron Age dead at Wetwang showed no evidence for the consumption of seafood and indeed the eating of fish may have been taboo (Dobney and Ervynck 2007). In some late Iron Age sites in southern Britain there is, however, a significant increase in oyster consumption (Hill and Willis 2010, 15), matching the increase in demand for wine from the Mediterranean exemplified by the amphorae at Hengistbury Head and the Welwyn types burials. In eastern Yorkshire, the taste in seafood was probably a Roman introduction and oyster shells are a common find on many Roman sites within the region. Oyster farming was also brought in during the Roman period and British oysters became a highly favoured export to Rome itself (Yonge 1960). On the settlement at Burnby Lane, Hayton, there was extensive evidence for oyster consumption and careful analysis shows that they were brought live onto the site, probably from the Humber estuary rather than the sea coast itself (Light forthcoming). There was also some evidence for the consumption of mussels and a few shells of *Helix aspersa*, the edible snail, which was also a Roman introduction (Evans 1972). Large quantities of shellfish were also consumed at Langton 'villa'.

Animal and plant husbandry has been discussed in Chapter 8, but the different proportions of animal bones found in excavation, pollen and macro-plant remains can reveal much information about food consumption. The careful analysis of animal bone assemblages is relatively new and so it is not possible to precisely determine what was eaten on some sites. The presence of acidic soil conditions such as those encountered at Bursea, Holme-on-Spalding Moor, also affects the survival of bone, making analysis impossible.

We have seen that in the Arras period, portions of pork were placed in the graves of the upper echelons of society; the poorest were buried with a portion of leg of mutton or lamb and a single pot. It is interesting to note that pork was also favoured by Roman legionaries with less being consumed by auxiliaries (Stallibrass and Thomas 2008, 5). Much beef was also eaten by the army and in towns, in greater proportion to sheep than on surrounding settlements. The presence of more sheep is thought to be a 'native' trait (King 1984) but the possibility that in certain areas this difference was due to wool production rather than dietary preference, must be borne in mind. The majority of animal bones from the fort at Malton were of cattle and there were many bones of male pigs and evidence for 'Romanised' cleaver butchery techniques (Sewpaul forthcoming) which have also been observed at Hayton Fort (Seetah 2005 and pers. comm.) where holes in the scapula of cattle for the insertion of suspension hooks may also indicate curing of joints of meat (Dobney 2001, 41).

The animal bone assemblage from Brough provides comparative material. At Welton Road (Hamshaw *et al.* 2000) the meat diet was clearly based on the consumption of beef, with much smaller quantities of mutton and pork. The evidence showed that primary butchery took place on the site, although some of the larger joints of meat may have been consumed, and the bones deposited, elsewhere. The pattern of butchery and the way the carcass was reduced closely resembles both early and late Roman urban assemblages (Maltby1989; Dobney *et al.* 1996). As at Hayton Fort, bones had been chopped using a heavy knife or cleaver, a trait also seen on the Roman roadside settlement at Shiptonthorpe (Mainland 2006). There appears to be a subtle difference between the bone assemblage at Welton Road and that from Cave Road where sheep were more common (Sewpaul forthcoming). Amongst the Cave Road, Brough assemblage, there was evidence for 'improvement' of stock through cross-breeding and the introduction of new breeds. At Shiptonthorpe, sheep bones were dominant in all phases, with cattle more common than pig or horse. The number of young animals suggested that they were bred there and butchery of whole animals took place on site. Horses and cattle were relatively old at death and sheep and pigs young. Evidence that whole sheep were spit roasted has been found in the form of burnt skeletons at Welton Road, Brough (Hamshaw-Thomas and Jaques 2000), Burnby Lane, Hayton (Halkon *et al.* 2000; Halkon and Millett 2003; Jacques forthcoming), Goodmanham (Hall *et al.* 2000) Rudston (Chaplin and Barnetson 1980) and North Cave (Hall *et al.* 2004(a), 2004(b)) and the possibility that these may have had a religious or ritual association have been discussed above.

Chickens and other fowl were also kept, presumably for eggs as well as meat and there is an unusually large number of chicken bones from Langton villa (Sewpaul forthcoming). The small size of bird bones compared with larger mammals means that they may be underrepresented. At Shiptonthorpe, little use was made of wild mammals and birds or fish (Mainland 2006) a trait that has been noted elsewhere in Roman Britain (Cool 2006).

Analysis of plant macro and pollen remains show wheat including spelt, emmer, bread wheats, barley, rye and oats were consumed in various ways and other fruit and vegetables included leeks, cabbages, onions, watercress, blackberry or raspberry hazel and walnut were also exploited (Hall and Huntley 2007). In terms of flavouring it is likely that wild plants were exploited but coriander is known from North Cave (Allison *et al.* 1997) and the Leven Bypass (Hall and Huntley 2007, 90).

Many of the grains found during the sieving of deposits from Roman settlements in the region are charred as a result of drying or malting in specially constructed ovens, possibly another Roman period introduction, excavated on a number of rural sites including Welton (Mackey 1998), North Cave (Dent 1989) and Swaythorpe (Mackey 2001). The dangers of drinking water were already known and recorded by the Roman writer Pliny, who recommended boiling (Cool 2006, 141). A safer alternative to straight water were alcoholic beverages and most households within the region would have drunk ale (un-hopped beer) instead. The repertoire of most of the eastern Yorkshire pottery industries included beakers and small bowls for drinking, some third and fourth-century AD vessel forms in hard-fired burnished greyware such as those made at Hasholme and Throlam (Corder 1930(a); Halkon and Millett 1999; Halkon 2002) resembled the pewter and silver vessels from more prestigious sites. Fine ware colour-coated beakers from Gaul and Germany and their successors produced in the Nene Valley, are present in varying quantities on all of the larger settlements within Parisi territory, though we know from applied slogans on pottery vessels elsewhere (Cool 2006, 147) that wine was drunk in these as well as beer.

In the later first and earlier second century AD pottery flagons, generally in white or orange oxidised fabrics, are probably associated with the serving of wine rather than beer. There are very few wine amphorae in the region, however vessels of Gauloise types from the wine-producing areas of central and southern Gaul are known from Welton Road, Brough (Darling *et al.* 2000). The writing tablets from the waterhole at Shiptonthorpe were made from the staves of sliver fir wine barrels from southern and central Europe, though we do not know the history of the barrels themselves (Allason-Jones *et al.* 2006, 238). Other copper-alloy items including jugs handles and other parts of vessels may be associated with the serving of wine and the preparation of infused or spiced drinks. An escutcheon in the form of a bearded head, possibly Silenus, appropriate on such a vessel, was found on the Burnby Lane settlement at Hayton (Halkon *et al.* 2000; Halkon and Millett 2003; Spradley-Kurowski *et al.* forthcoming). Glass vessels for serving and drinking from are known from all the larger

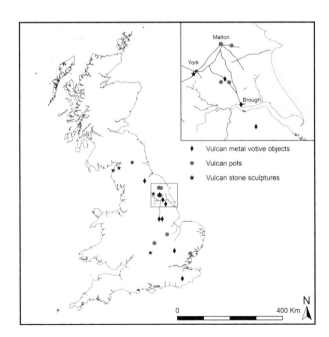

Fig.78 The distribution of items associated with Vulcan in Roman Britain. (T. Sparrow)

settlements but the most spectacular is the large quantity of high-quality glass vessels, largely relating to drinking, from the villa at Beadlam (Price and Cottam 1996), one of the largest assemblages north of the Humber.

So far foodstuffs and their containers have been considered. Although it is likely that much eating was done with fingers, seven spoons, from Barmby Moor, Catton, Thwing, Sherburn (Ryedale) and Yapham, are however recorded in the Portable Antiquities Scheme database. Small spoons of this type were a Roman introduction (Mould 2011, 163) and those from the region include the 'rat's' tail type, so called due to its long tapering handle, and ones with hinged handles that could be folded and carried around more easily. Iron knife blades are fairly common discoveries on the larger Roman sites within the region, mainly from excavations; however, the Portable Antiquities Scheme database only records Roman knife blades from North Ferriby and Market Weighton, a disparity which might be explained by the fact that many detectorists adjust their machines to discriminate against iron.

SUMMARY

The aim of this chapter was to explore the everyday lives of the people in the region of the Parisi during the Roman period and to gauge the extent of assimilation of 'Roman' material culture. It is clear that much new was introduced in terms of religious belief, new technology in the form of wheel-thrown kiln-fired pottery, new foodstuffs and ways of consuming them. On the surface it would appear that the people of eastern Yorkshire were opened up to a wider world. However, there were strong elements of continuity with the Iron Age past particularly in more remote rural areas away from the larger settlements and Roman road corridors. Although certain items were adopted, such as greyware pottery, it accrued a regional identity. In terms of religion, although Vulcan was venerated all over the Empire and there is a thin spread of metal votive objects, stone sculptures and pots across Roman Britain (Webster 1989), the concentration of pots and other items in Parisi territory probably harks back to a strong tradition of Iron Age metalworking, appropriate in a region where furnace-based industries played an important part in the Roman economy (Fig. 78). Although Type 2 glass bangles and trumpet brooches are common elsewhere in the province, there is a clear concentration of these items of personal adornment within eastern Yorkshire, perhaps expressions of a sense of regional identity. In many ways the following comment applied to the small finds assemblage from the roadside settlement of Shiptonthorpe provides an apt summary of Roman period material culture for much of this region: 'There is a strong sense of Roman meeting native, either as individuals from different ethnic groups or as an indication of the process of assimilation.' (Allason-Jones 2006, 220).

CHAPTER 11

FROM THE PARISI TO DEIRA

In Chapter 8 we saw that by the later third and into the fourth century AD, the countryside of the territory of the Parisi appeared prosperous. Well-to-do 'villa' buildings such as Rudston and Brantingham were at their peak, decorated with mosaics and wall paintings, following the trends seen elsewhere in Roman Britain. The large number and distribution of coin finds in both the third and fourth centuries shows that East Yorkshire was embedded into some form of monetary system in a similar way to the rest of the province, with peaks in the period of the Gallic Empire between AD 260–273 and 330–348 (Sitch 1998, 41) though the largest concentrations remained along the Roman roads (Fig. 79).

The widespread use and loss of coins coincides with the expansion of the pottery industries of eastern Yorkshire which were firmly established by the later third century and wheel-thrown, greyware vessels became ubiquitous within the region and reached the northern frontier. Judging by the most extensive fieldwork projects in the Foulness and Hull valleys and areas further north in the Vale of Pickering and Wharram, even the humblest rural settlements in East Yorkshire seem to have had access to these ceramics. The markets for these industries included the larger settlements, and Malton/Norton may have gained some of its prosperity as a result of the pottery industry based there. In both Brough and Malton substantial houses with stone walls and the usual decorative features (Wilson 2003) were being constructed well into the fourth century, although the lack of large-scale investigation of the former make it difficult to define any coherent plan.

By the later Roman period extensive defences had been constructed at Brough, which are open to various interpretations (Fig. 80). It has been argued that here and at other towns in Roman Britain such walls were built as an expression of civic pride (Esmonde-Cleary 2003). A counter argument is that the walled area had some kind of military purpose (Wacher 1969), possibly a naval base, at some time in the period AD 200–270. At a later date, the defences were refurbished and large stone towers or bastions added, protruding from the line of the wall allowing enfilading fire along the defences and may have provided a platform for catapults. The walled enclosure was heavily protected to the east with three sets of banks and ditches, although the extent of the fortifications in

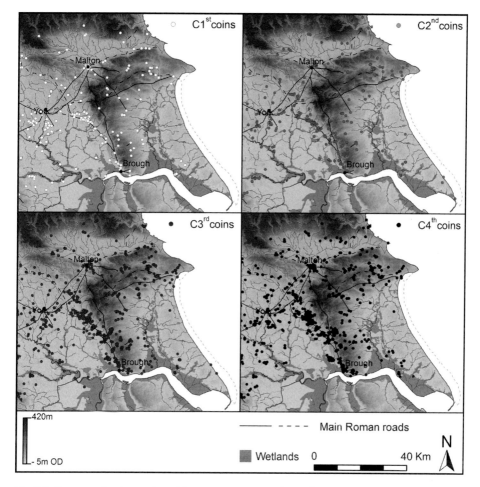

Fig.79 Roman coins by century. The concentrations along the Roman roads are obvious. (T. Sparrow)

other sectors remains unclear. The southern and western portions were protected by the river Humber and estuarine inlet.

The circuit of these defences only encloses 5ha, too small for a small town but similar in size to the larger forts of the Saxon shore such as Richborough (Bidwell and Hodgson 2009, 180). There is some resemblance between the walled enclosure at Brough and those at Caistor and Horncastle in Lincolnshire (Leahy 2007, 27). Horncastle possesses similar bastions and staggered lengths of wall as Brough (Bidwell and Hodgson 2009, 163) and was constructed in the late third or early fourth century at the midpoint between Lincoln and a possible fort at Skegness (Leahy 2007, 26). Caistor, built around the same time with thick walls and bastions, lay just over half way

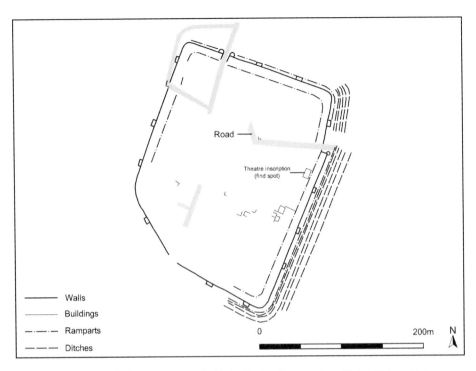

Road

Theatre inscription
(find spot)

——— Walls

——— Buildings

—·—·— Ramparts

——— Ditches

0   200m   N

Fig.80 Top: The walled area at Brough. Note the bastions and multiple ditches (T. Sparrow after Corder). Bottom: Corder (in trench) shows off Tower 1, excavated in 1934 (Hull and East Riding Museum: Hull Museums)

between Horncastle and the Humber estuary and between them would have protected the north-east approaches to Lincoln itself.

The identification of a peak of coin losses from Brough of the usurper emperors Carausius and Allectus (AD 286–296) (Sitch 1998), supports Wacher's idea that the walled enclosure may have been a base from where the British fleet, with which Carausius and Allectus (Casey 1994) have been associated, controlled the Humber estuary. As the Sixth Legion remained at York throughout the period of Roman rule, the Humber basin and its tributaries, particularly the Ouse, were surely of strategic importance. The deaths there of the Emperor Septimius Severus in AD 211 and Constantius Chlorus who had recently been promoted to Augustus, followed by the acclamation of his son Constantine I as his successor in AD 306 (Hartley *et al.* 2006), confirm its importance. York was probably the seat of the governor of *Britannia Inferior* (Bidwell 2006). It is therefore highly likely that the walled enclosure of Brough formed part of the network of coastal fortifications elsewhere in Roman Britain (Whitwell 1988) with a chain of almost equidistant defences running along the North Sea coast. This consisted of a series of small forts, each consisting of an enclosure 50m square, with curtain walls, slightly curved at the corners with four projecting towers. In the centre was a 15m square central tower which may have been up to 21m high. They would have made excellent vantage points from which to spot the ships of barbarian raiders and send out warning signals; they may also have been built to provide protection for nearby inhabitants in times of danger (Ottaway 2000; Wilson 1991). Similar structures are shown in sculptures which depict a large flaming torch at the top of the tower (Ottaway 2001, 14). Only the 'signal stations' at Huntcliff, Goldsborough, Scarborough and Filey, all in what is now North Yorkshire, have been excavated (Ottaway 2001; Bidwell and Hodgson 2009, 172). At Ravenscar, an inscription, the latest known from Roman Britain (*RIB* 721), discovered during the digging of the foundations of Raven Hall, reads:

IVSTINIANVS P(rae)P (ositus) VINDICIANVS MASBIER TVRR(e)M CASTRVM FECIT A SO (l)

It has been translated as:

'Justinianus the commander; Vindicianus magister, built this tower and fortification from its foundations.'

There is some debate about the identity and role of the people named (Collingwood and Wright 1965, 242), but it has been suggested that Justinianus was a general who according to the Roman writer Zosimus was present in Britain in 407. *Masbier* is a corruption of *magister*, a late Roman military position. The coin evidence implies that the signal stations were constructed in the AD 380s during the reign of Magnus Maximus, or else during the restoration of the northern frontier by *Comes* (Count) Theodosius in the 360s (Breeze and Hodgson 2009, 174). There may have been a signal station under the abbey at Whitby (Bell 1999) and at what may have been the northern extremity of Parisi territory, the signal station at Scarborough (Collingwood 1931) in the grounds of the medieval castle. Goldsborough is probably the best preserved being further away from the cliff. Excavations carried out on the signal station at the Carr Naze, Filey, in 1993–94 following those of 1923, rescued valuable information as only a narrow central band remained as the rest had fallen into the sea or had been quarried away (Fig. 81). Coin evidence showed that some form of activity continued on the site into the fifth century AD as coins, dating from AD 395 and 402, of Theodosius I and his sons Arcadius and Honorius were found there.

It seems almost certain that this defensive chain continued southwards along the Holderness coast and at either side of the Humber estuary; however the effects of erosion make this hypothesis very difficult to prove. Flamborough Head and Spurn Point would have made ideal locations and both have modern lighthouses. A candidate for some kind of coastal fortification is Aldbrough, a place name almost certainly derived from (e)ald (Old) burgh (fortification) (Mills 2003, 7) although 'Alde's fortified place' has also been suggested (Watts *et al.* 2004, 6). There is an antiquarian reference to a castle there (Thompson 1824, 76) which may account for the name, but 'quantities' of Roman material including coins, pottery and other finds have eroded from the cliffs (Kitson Clark 1935, 61; Loughlin and Miller 1979, 49) and are still being reported at the time of writing (PAS and Philip Harrison pers.comm.). Although much land had

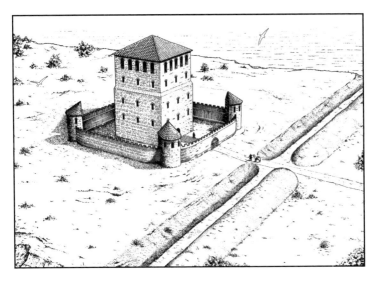

Fig.81
Reconstruction of a signal station from Filey. (York Archaeological Trust)

already been lost to the sea, the network of beacons which once signalled impending invasions best known from the threat of the Spanish Armada in 1588 (Nicholson 1887), may provide some clues as to the location of a Roman system of signalling, as beacons were sited at Flamborough Head and there is a Beacon Hill to the south of Aldbrough itself. Trenching around the Beacon at Flamborough, however, failed to find any Roman material apart from a foot-ring from a samian bowl, which is unlikely to be associated with a signal station (Kitson Clark 1935, 84). Fieldwork at other inland sites, such as Church Hill, Holme-on-Spalding Moor, where there was a beacon in 1588 (Nicholson 1887, 38) and much evidence for later Roman activity in the vicinity and High Hunsley (Nicholson 1887, 41), which remains unexplored, may prove worthwhile, endorsing the possibility of a network of inland signal stations.

What of the troops associated with the signal stations and other military installations? The later Roman period saw considerable changes in the role, organisation and equipment of the army (Plate 41). It has been presumed that a unit, the *numerus supervenientium Petuariesium*, were related to the network of coastal defences operating in late Roman East Yorkshire and may have been a mounted rapid deployment unit whose main role was to intercept the increasing number of raiders along the coast. Listed in the *Notitia Dignitatum* (*Occ.* XL, 31) a late Roman document relating to military deployment, as being based at Derventio, and under the overall command of the *Dux Britanniarum*, their name has been interpreted in a number of different ways. A *numerus* comprised between 2–300 troops and *Petuariesium* implies that they served for some time or were raised at Brough (Wacher 1969; Jarrett 1994, 71). *Supervenientium* has been variously translated as 'anticipators' (Morris 1973, 16), those who arrive unexpectedly or 'surprise attackers', or merely reinforcements (Tomlin 1969, 74–5). As we have seen, the location of Derventio is also problematic as it need not necessarily be Malton as is often presumed. If *Supervenientium* is interpreted as relating to the navy, relocation to Papcastle in Cumbria, another Derventio (Creighton 1988, 390), would seem more logical than Malton, as the former has suitable evidence for later fourth-century activity and is much nearer the sea, though this has been dismissed by other authorities (Jarratt 1994, 71). The naval attribution is by no means certain and if Stamford Bridge is Derventio (Lawton 1994), it may suggest the movement of the unit nearer to York, thus providing greater protection along the Roman road at the approaches to the city. Although Ramm (1978, 30) has proposed that there was a fort at Stamford Bridge, its location remains elusive. During recent research, however, a number of military fittings associated with horse-harness, fragments of mail armour, copper-alloy studs and buckles have been found in the roadside settlement at Reckondales (Lawton 1999, 10) and it could be that soldiers were billeted within the settlement rather than in a separate military installation. Certainly no large-scale fortifications of the variety one would associate with a late Roman military base have yet been found.

The *Equites Dalmatarum*, a light cavalry unit, were, according to the *Notitia Dignitatum*, stationed at *Praesidio*, which various authorites have placed in East or North Yorkshire (Thompson Watkin 1884, 258; Collins, 2012, 46). *Praesidium* simply means defence or enclosure in Latin, so a fort occupied in the late Roman period would be a likely candidate for this location. Although some items could have been used by both soldiers and civilians, the decorated spurs from the Rudston and Beadlam villas referred to in Chapter 8 strongly resemble those worn by cavalry (Dixon and Southern 1997, 59). A further example was found during excavations at the Filey signal station (Cool 2000, 124, illus. 29, 123) and it is tempting to suppose that it once belonged to cavalryman stationed there. Several spurs of the same type are recorded from Hayton (Halkon *et al.* forthcoming), an entirely appropriate context for such finds, which could have been casually lost by troops on the way to Eboracum, or represent soldiers living amongst civilian populations. Similar spurs have been found at Catterick (Wilson 2002, 45) (Fig. 82).

Other items possibly worn by the military include crossbow brooches, a modern term relating to their shape. A good depiction of the way these brooches were worn can be seen on an ivory diptych from Monza in Italy (Johns 1996, 166), showing Stilicho, the military ruler of the western Empire, and his son. The brooch, pin upwards, fastens a cloak high on the right shoulder. Such brooches may have also been worn by civilian officials (Swift 2011, 212). There are three crossbow brooches associated with burials from the cemetery excavated at The Ridings, Malton mentioned in Chapter 10 (Robinson,

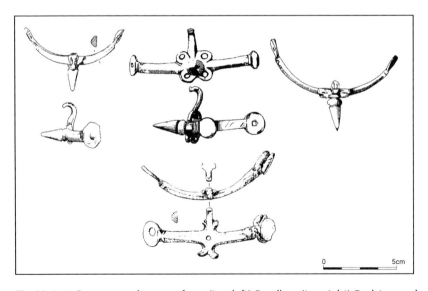

Fig.82 Late Roman cavalry spurs from (top left) Beadlam (top right) Rudston and (bottom) Filey. (P. Halkon after Neal 1996; Stead 1980; Ottaway 2001)

1978, 39) (Fig. 83) and a cluster in the Hayton/Pocklington area found by detectorists (Stratton 2005; Halkon *et al.* forthcoming; Norman 2010). Found close to Roman roads and probably derived from cemeteries, the brooches complement the pattern observed elsewhere and may also indicate the presence of soldiers amongst civilian populations (Swift 2011, 212). Crossbow brooches are often found in association with belt fittings, some with zoomorphic and chip-carved ornamentation, which were once thought to indicate the presence of Germanic mercenaries and other irregular troops (Hawkes and Dunning 1961). These are now regarded as part of the standard equipment of the late Roman army (Bishop 2011, 131) and a number have been found in the territory of the Parisi at Cottam and intriguingly near the coast at Bempton. Further examples have been recorded at Buttercrambe (McIntosh 2008) between Stamford Bridge and Malton and Castle Howard (Crump 2007). There are far fewer of this type of belt fitting than across the Humber in North Lincolnshire, where they are thought to represent local or tribal militia, following a pattern observed elsewhere in late Roman Britain (Leahy 2007, 31; Laycock 2009).

The items of military equipment including spear and ballista bolt-heads and a throwing axe from the Beadlam villa (Neal 1996, 38) have already been referred to and together with the spur make it very likely that either troops or perhaps a veteran were associated with the site. A throwing axe was also recorded amongst the finds in the final phase of the Welton villa, a site which may have ended in violent destruction in the early fifth century (Mackey 1998, 29 and forthcoming). In a sunken floored building, a crop-drier was excavated containing the burnt skeleton of a woman (Fig. 85), who according to the excavator was:

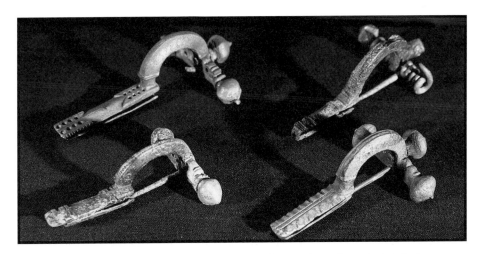

Fig.83 Crossbow brooches from Malton (length of largest brooch 9cm). (M. Park courtesy Malton Museum Trust)

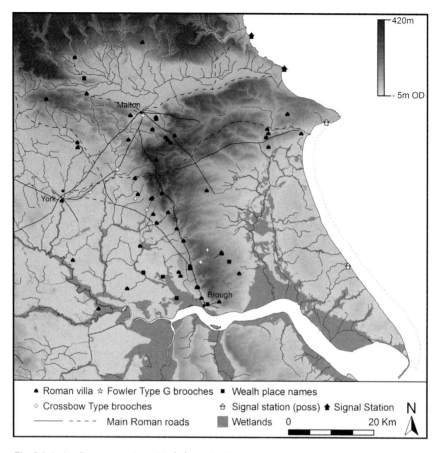

Fig.84 Later Roman eastern Yorkshire. (T. Sparrow)

working in the stoke pit when she met her end. A complete cooking pot, found in the corner of the oven above the flue, may well have contained her next meal. The timber and thatched, sunken-floored building attached to this drier was burned down, collapsing over the crop-drier, thus preserving the whole structure. Had this been an accidental fire, she would hardly have ended up in this position, but would have made some attempt to climb out. She may have been killed or rendered unconscious and pushed into the flue before the building came down. Only the top of her skull and one lower arm bone were found at a higher level in the fill, which suggests that the rest of her may have been scavenged by dogs or wild animals from the burnt-out ruins. A nearby aisled barn and the corridor house were also destroyed by fire. Someone did return to the site to bury fire-damaged goods in three pits.

Perhaps this destruction was at the hands of raiders as the site lies close to the River Humber. The excavator would argue that the pits containing fire-damaged goods may represent a ritual act marking an abrupt end to all activity on the site, which remained vacant until medieval rig and furrow was laid out over it, with no reference to any of the Roman boundaries. These pits may correspond with examples from the latest phase of the Roman city of Silchester where pits containing items such as a dog, stone pillar with Ogham script and a number of vessels, were thought to 'signal the intention never to return to the site' (Clarke and Fulford 2000; Fulford 2001, 180).

A tradition of burial associated with kilns and similar structures has, however, been identified in eastern Yorkshire, and believed to be as a 'British' trait surviving into the fifth century (Faull 1977). Cist burials were cut into the Crambeck pottery kilns, North Yorkshire (Fig. 86) (Corder 1928; Loveluck 1999; 2003). A burial from Town Street, Hayton (Stephens 2004), described as anomalous due to its alignment and arrangement, cut into a fourth-century 'kiln' or possibly a corn drier, may also represent this rite. Given the presence of a possible cult associated with Vulcan in the region discussed in Chapter 10, such a method of burial would seem entirely appropriate.

Fig.85 The leg bones of a woman in the flue of a crop-drier or malting oven at Welton. Was this an atrocity indicating a violent end to the villa? (R. Mackey)

Fig.86 The cist burial cut into a pottery kiln at Crambeck. (Malton Museum)

Other evidence for destruction within the wider region was discovered on the signal station at Goldsborough on the North Yorkshire coast referred to above and it is worth quoting a section of the report in full:

Close to the socket stone was a human skull... In the south-east corner we made discoveries which can only be described as sensational. A short thick-set man had fallen across the smouldering fire of an open hearth, probably after having been stabbed in the back. His skeleton lay face downwards … another skeleton, that of a taller man, lay also face downwards near the feet of the first. Beneath him was the skeleton of a large and powerful dog, its head against the man's throat, its paws across his shoulders – surely the grim record of a thrilling drama, perhaps the dog of one of the defenders, the man an intruder.

Silver coins of Eugenius amd Honorius were found near the feet of the second skeleton (Hornsby and Laverick 1932, 210–11).

The signal station at Huntcliff also seems to have met a violent end as the remains of fourteen people were found in the well including women and children with evidence of trauma on their skulls (Hornsby and Stanton 1912). It has been presumed that barbarian raiders were responsible for these attacks. We are told that Nectaridus, the 'Count of the Sea Coast', had been killed and Fullofades, *Dux Britanniarum* was surprised and cut off by 'predatory bands' (Ammianus Marcellinus, *Res Gestae*, 27, 8 (Rolfe 1952, 50)). Historical accounts report intensive raids in AD 367, the so-called *barbarica conspiratione*, in which the northern tribes (Picts, Attacoti and the Scotti) raided extensively (Ammianus Marcellinus *Res Gestae*, 27, 8 (Rolfe 1952, 51)) at the same time as the Saxons and Franks were attacking the coast of northern Gaul. There is some dispute about the extent of the damage. It is possible that the signal stations were built after this event, during the reconstruction of the province under Count Theodosius.

Distinguishing accidental fire from deliberate action is difficult and apart from Welton and two of the signal stations, the archaeological evidence elsewhere suggests that the end of Roman rule in the territory of the Parisi was one of gradual decline rather than wholesale destruction. It has been proposed that Brough was a 'failed' civitas capital (Wacher 1975, 397), the transfer of the *numerus supervenientium Petuariesium* being one of the explanations for its demise. Inside the walled enclosure, at both side of what is now Bozzes's lane, buildings and hearths were excavated associated with Huntcliff pottery and Crambeck painted parchment wares (Wacher 1969, 69). Re-dating of Crambeck pottery, with some types appearing as late as the AD 370s (Swan 2002, 73), may mean occupation at Brough continued longer than previously thought. There are, however, lower numbers of Valentinianic period coins (AD 364–78) recorded here, nineteen coins out of 211 examined, in marked contrast to the sample of coins from the roadside settlements of Shiptonthorpe (900 out of 1,111 coins) and Hayton (656 out of 1864). There are no Theodosian coins (AD 378–402) listed for Brough, compared with eighty-two out of 1,111 for Shiptonthorpe and forty-seven out of 1,864 for Hayton (Sitch 1998, 43). This suggests that the two roadside settlements were still the foci for considerable activity by comparison with Brough. Systematic field walking at Hayton supported the coin evidence in showing the continuation of the roadside settlement, as Huntcliff and Crambeck pottery (Halkon 2008, 115 and 126) have been found across the whole of the 360 x 120m area surveyed. At Shiptonthorpe, excavation demonstrated continued activity and remodelling of the site in the late fourth century AD and beyond, with the implication that the Roman road itself remained an important line of communication (Millett 2006, 307). Further to the west at Stamford Bridge the pottery assemblage contains much fewer later types than the other roadside settlements although the coins show continued activity in the Reckondales area with coins of Theodosian coins (Lawton 1999, 9).

Amongst the explanations for the decline of Brough was the effect of natural factors. These have included the silting up of its harbour (Wacher 1969, 26–27), the movement of the navigable channel of the River Humber towards the Lincolnshire shore, an alteration in currents (Whitwell 1988, 51) and marine flooding (Ramm 1978, 124; Radley and Simms 1970, 1–16; Eagles 1979, 190–93). Caution is, however, needed in the identification of flood deposits as excavations at a number of locations in York have failed to find any evidence for the Roman period flooding once thought to have been a contributory factor in the decline of the Roman city (Hall 1978, 32). A large-scale flooding event around AD 370 was also thought to have caused the end of the Holme-on-Spalding Moor pottery industry (Eagles 1979, 197), however the presence of Crambeck parchment wares and Huntcliff products on a number of kiln sites shows that they continued in production after this date and were in decline due to economic rather than environmental factors. Some later Roman flood deposits have, however, been observed in the wider region outside the Foulness Valley at Littleborough (Riley *et al*. 1995) and Adlingfleet (Fenwick *et al*. 1998) by the River Trent and in the Hull Valley. Much more work is needed if flooding and its effects are to be fully understood.

At Malton it is clear from the archaeological evidence that civilian occupation continued around its defended core in the late fourth and into the fifth century AD (Wilson 2006, 255). Over the two last decades, the traditional image of galleys of departing soldiers being summoned back to Rome in AD 410 can no longer be sustained as an explanation for the end of Roman Britain. It has been argued convincingly that the passage by the Roman historian Zosimus (*Historia Nova* VI, 11) in which the Emperor Honorius was supposed to have instructed the British cities to look after their own defences actually refers to events in Italy surrounding the sack of Rome by Alaric, with Bruttium, a north Italian town, having been confused with Britannia (Esmonde Cleary 1990, 117). Some troops had already been withdrawn from Britain by Magnus Maximus in AD 383 (Zosimus *Historia Nova* IV, 35, 2–6 in Ireland 1996, 155) but according to Gildas returned in triumph (*De Excidio Britanniae*, 16–17, in Ireland 1996, 160), although this source must be treated with extreme caution. In AD 409 further troops left Britain with the usurper Constantine III (Zosimus ibid. VI 2–5 in Ireland 1996, 162). It is not clear how many troops were taken abroad, but it is unlikely that frontier bases in the North or on the coast were left devoid of garrisons. The near contemporary sources tell us that by this time the Britons themselves had rebelled against Roman rule (Zosimus ibid. VI, 5, 2–3, in Ireland 1996, 165). It is therefore possible that at Malton, as at other locations in the North of England such as the forts and civilian settlements at Binchester in County Durham (Ferris 2011) and Birdoswald on Hadrian's Wall (Willmott 2001), soldiers remained, forming into what have been called 'war bands' (Casey 1993; Collins 2012 and forthcoming).

Outside the larger settlements of eastern Yorkshire, pottery from field walking on the villas around Pocklington, supported by excavation on the settlement at Burnby Lane, Hayton, demonstrates continued activity into the late fourth century at least. It is likely, though, as the excavations at Brantingham (Liversidge *et al*. 1973) have shown that architectural features, such as mosaics, were no longer being repaired and were indeed being cut through by rubbish pits. There is some debate concerning the oven which was constructed against the west wall of the main room of the house on the Tyche mosaic itself. It is not clear whether this represents continued settlement on a much reduced scale or the oven structure was a lime-kiln associated with later demolition and stone robbing (Stead 1973, 87). Later excavation (Dent 1989) and metal-detected coins showed continued activity around the site into the later fourth century and beyond (Whitwell 1988, 64). At Thwing the 'pavilion' rooms of the corridor house had been demolished by the early fourth century AD and a small iron-smelting furnace was built within the main room of the building (Ferraby *et al.* 2009, 8).

A small coin of Valentinian found amongst a deposit of pottery dumped in the well at Rudston implies that it fell out of use in the 360s (Stead 1980, 30) and was subsequently filled with building debris. A coin of Gratian dating from AD 367–78 shows that there was continued activity of some kind after that date. The well at Langton was filled with very similar building material dated from the pottery to the last few decades of the fourth century AD (Corder and Kirk 1932, 52). It is clear however that people continued to live there, from the Huntcliff and Crambeck pottery and coins, which include issues of Valentinian I, Gratian (AD 368–75), Valentinian II (AD 392), Theodosius I (AD 390–95) and Honorius (AD 393–5), albeit without luxuries such as heated bath houses. Although it remains unexcavated, the presence of Huntcliff and Crambeck pottery with coins of Valentinian and Theodosius at the Bishop Burton Villa demonstrates continued activity (Williamson 1997). At Beadlam too there is a relatively high number of Valentinianic (AD 364–78) and Theodosian (AD 388–402) issues (Barclay 1996, 64) and again much Crambeck and Huntcliff pottery, some of this associated with buildings that continued in use. A disarticulated but relatively complete skeleton of a woman in her twenties was found amongst demolition debris in Building 1, either from a grave cut into the demolition debris or laid on the floor and then covered with the material from the collapsed building (Mays and Strongman 1996, 115). This was one of a number of late graves located within the building and it would seem that parts of the farm were functioning although the house itself had been abandoned. The scenario at Beadlam is similar to villa sites elsewhere and the following explanation has been provided:

> ...although such placing (of graves) may be a way of keeping burials to the margin of the new settlements and using marginal land, it is possible that the old villa buildings may have been identified as a foci of native families anxious to retain links with their ancestors. (Neal and Wilson 1996, 45).

The stone buildings at Burnby Lane, Hayton, were dismantled and debris including a decorated panel from a cupboard door (Plate 42) dumped in the timber-lined well, which may once have served the bath house (Halkon and Millett 2003; Halkon *et al.* forthcoming). The evidence presents a picture of decline and abandonment rather than destruction at the hands of barbarians as was once thought.

In Chapter 8 we saw that the majority of the rural population of the Parisi lived outside 'villas' either in the ladder settlements on the Wolds or clustered groups of enclosures in lowland areas. Excavation of a ladder settlement at Goodmanham near Market Weighton during the construction of the Teesside-Saltend Ethylene pipeline presents a picture of the end of Roman east Yorkshire. The woodworking plane with an elephant ivory stock referred to in Chapter 9 may have been brought here from a prosperous location elsewhere, as nothing else on the site matched it in status (Plate 43). Evidence for small-scale metalworking was also found involving the recycling of bronze and iron objects, which may account for the fragmentary remains of an elaborately decorated copper-alloy lock-plate from a large chest also found there. As Steedman (Long *et al.* 2002, 19) writes: 'The plane, therefore, may have reached this location through salvage or scavenging from a wealthier site in the neighbourhood, which had been abandoned, perhaps at the very end of the Roman period, or into the sub-Roman period'.

The circumstances surrounding the disposal of the Hayton panel and Goodmanham plane provide a picture of a changing world; the people who lived here remain shadowy, but were still active in the East Yorkshire landscape at this time. The end of large-scale pottery production and coin supply make it difficult to provide accurate dating evidence. We have seen from excavation at Welton, that the proportion of wheel-thrown, kiln-fired pottery decreased compared to less robust locally made clamp-fired fabrics, which are more difficult to date and do not survive as well on the surface of a ploughed field. Cultivation on many rural sites has also destroyed the upper layers vital to our understanding of the end of the Roman era. Excavation at Elmswell provides some evidence for settlement continuity (Congreve 1938) in contrast to the ladder settlement at Sherburn at the edge of the Vale of Pickering referred to in Chapter 8, where constant recutting of enclosure ditches was undertaken and along with environmental evidence, including many frog bones in the upper ditch fills, demonstrates that there was a problem with rising groundwater, due to increasing rainfall, to the extent that the population relocated to the better drained ground above sometime in the early fifth century AD (Powlesland 1988, 145–6; 2003(b), 288). Although the ladder settlement fell out of use, attention was still focussed on the late Roman shrine at West Heslerton discussed in the previous chapter, well into the fifth century AD. The reason why the people of the Sherburn ladder settlement remained in their increasingly wet surroundings for so long may have been due to unknown late Roman tenurial arrangements which remained in place until the collapse of Roman authority allowed movement onto better land (Powlesland 2003(b), 288). A further reason may have been the establishment of a new settlement and associated cemetery founded close by which displayed a completely different cultural identity: one of the most extensive Anglo-Saxon landscapes yet to be excavated in England (Powlesland 2003(b), 288).

The arrival of these people, whether they came as a result of mass migration from northern Germany and southern Denmark, or had been brought in as mercenaries to support a threatened province of the Roman Empire, is a matter for discussion elsewhere (Härke 2011). It is, however, noticeable that some of the earliest Anglo-Saxon evidence anywhere in Britain is to be found around the Humber estuary (Loveluck 1999 and 2003; Leahy 2007) and DNA and other forms of scientific investigation have shown that a substantial number of those buried in Anglo-Saxon cemeteries were indeed migrants. Stable isotope analysis of skeletons at West Heslerton revealed that up to 17 per cent of the skeletons sampled among the first generation of the people buried in the cemetery were immigrants from Scandinavia or eastern continental Europe, with considerable movement of people from elsewhere in Britain (Härke 2011, 6). The early Anglo-Saxon incomers would have stood out in terms of costume from the existing population, their womenfolk wearing ornate cruciform brooches with a horse-like animal head at the foot, festoons of brightly coloured beads and sleeves fastened at the wrists with 'hook and eye'-type decorated clasps. These dress fasteners, along with distinctly decorated cremation pots, closely resemble those from northern Germany and southern Scandinavia, supporting the recent scientific data. Although clearly a foundation myth, there may be an element of fact in the account of Bede (Sherley-Price 1972, 51), concerning the origins of the Anglo-Saxon peoples, who states that those who occupied the North and East of England were from 'Angulus' the district of Angeln, between northern Germany and southern Denmark listed as *Anglii* by Tactitus (*Germania* 40, Birley 1999, 58).

The precise relationship between the Anglian newcomers and the sub-Roman inhabitants of the region is ambiguous. The archaeological and linguistic evidence is scanty and sometimes difficult to interpret, however, it is possible to tease out information concerning this pivotal period of the region's past. The positioning of the large and early Anglo-Saxon cremation cemetery at Sancton (Timby 1993) was probably not coincidental, as it was established at the southern end of Sancton Dale, an important route between the Wolds and the wetlands of the Foulness Valley and the Humber basin. The Iron Age square barrow cemetery at Arras was at its northern end, with the Neolithic Market Weighton Wold Long barrow and Bronze Age round barrow cemetery nearby (Halkon and Woodhouse 2009). The placement of this cemetery may represent a statement of ownership, entitlement or control at a significant position in the landscape. Anglo-Saxon burials have also been excavated in Bronze Age barrows on a number of sites (Mortimer 1905) and Iron Age cemeteries themselves, for example, at Garton Station (Stead 1991).

The continuation of various British traits into the sub-Roman period has, however, been recognised for some time, particularly in burials. Inhumations in stone-lined cists within the region have already been referred to and certain items of dress, particularly Fowler Type G penannular brooches (Fowler 1963; Dickinson 1982, 53) more usually found in 'Celtic' areas, have been recognised at a number of locations in East and North Yorkshire. One example, now in the Hull and East Riding Museum, was found in the Driffield group of barrows opened during the construction of the Driffield to Market Weighton railway and investigated by Mortimer (1905, 282, fig. 825) though he did not recognise it for what it was, probably because its pin was missing. A very similar brooch was found in a cemetery at Londesborough (Dickinson 1982, 63, figs 5, 17). Are these items expressions of identity by women of native British origin? What is most interesting is that both of these were found in cemeteries which were otherwise mainly Anglian in character, as by the end of the fifth century AD large cemeteries of urned cremations had been replaced by inhumation and it is likely that by this time populations were beginning to merge. Groups of inhumations in crouched or 'anomalous' postures, such as one at Nunburnholme, buried with arms turned up behind the head, which coincide with finds of penannular brooches clustered around Market Weighton, Fimber, Hornsea, Staxton and Driffield (Faull 1977, 53–54) may also represent British survival within otherwise Anglian communities, perhaps through intermarriage.

It is noticeable that all the larger settlements along the main Roman road between Brough and York eventually nucleated around churches offset from the roadside settlements, forming the present villages of Shiptonthorpe, Hayton and Stamford Bridge, though further investigation is needed to date this transition. The late Roman cemetery at Hayton did, however, contain one Anglian inhumation burial (Stephens 2004) and the discovery of a late Roman 'Coptic' bowl of a type known from Anglo-Saxon burials elsewhere may indicate the presence of a cemetery at Shiptonthorpe (Millett 2006, 308).

Place names provide further clues concerning the relationship between sub-Romano-British and Anglo-Saxon populations as the first element of the place names Walling Fen, Wholsea (Watts *et al.* 2004, 646) and possibly Welton, are derived from 'Wealh' or 'foreigner', a name by which the Anglo-Saxons knew the native British population – hence Wales – and it has been noted that these settlements tend to be marginal to better agricultural land associated with more overtly Anglo-Saxon settlement names (Faull 1977, 18). The name of the kingdom which eventually developed to coincide with the territory of the Parisi was Deira. In a passage dated to the beginning of the reign of King Alfrid of Northumbria (AD 685) Bede states that there was a monastery '*In-Derawuda*', which has been translated as 'in the wood of the Deiri', most probably Beverley (Sherley-Price 1972, 271). As '*deri*' (the plural of derwen) means 'oak trees' in modern Welsh (Meurig-Evans and Thomas 1963, 168) and *wudu* is the Old English for wood, it is most probable that both Germanic and Brythonic languages were spoken in the region at this time and syncretised to provide the place name (Loveluck 1999, 233), in effect the equivalent of a bi-lingual signpost. Bernicia which merged with Deira to form the great Anglo-Saxon kingdom of Northumbria also had a name derived from Celtic languages. This and the presence of a number of obviously Celtic names mentioned by Bede and other sources implies that a form of Celtic language continued to be spoken in the region, which runs counter to recent suggestions, drawn principally from genetic evidence, that the peoples of eastern England were speaking Germanic languages before the Roman conquest (Oppenheimer 2007, 364).

The most famous mention of this new kingdom is in what Bede tells us is a traditional story explaining the mission of Pope Gregory the Great to convert the pagan Anglo-Saxons. When he saw a group of fair-haired boys ready for sale in the market place in Rome, Gregory asked who they were. 'They are called Angles,' was the reply. Gregory responded with a punning comment about their angelic faces. When he asked which province they were from, he was told 'Deira'. 'Good,' said Gregory, 'they shall indeed be rescued from de ira, the wrath of God' (Sherley-Price 1972, 100).

Although the story of the Anglo-Saxon kingdom of Deira and its flourishing as part of the Kingdom of Northumbria is told elsewhere (e.g. Geake and Kenny 2000; Hawkes and Mills 1999), it is significant that the region retained a discrete identity, which may partly have been the result of geographical factors. The distribution of square barrow cemeteries, chariot burials and chalk figurines distinguishes eastern Yorkshire from the rest of Iron Age Britain. Despite the fact that many of the developments within the region in the Roman period match those elsewhere in the province, subtle factors, such as a preference for certain types of brooches, querns and pottery and the concentration of arefacts related to Vulcan, make it distinctive. The rich farmland of the region made it relatively prosperous with more villas than the rest of northern Roman Britain, and its link to the European continent though the Humber estuary provided a conduit for exchange and innovation.

BIBLIOGRAPHY

Abbreviations

CIL   *Corpus Inscriptionum Latinarum* – Corpus of Latin Inscriptions (see Nesselhauf 1936
        and 1974 below)
RIB   Roman Inscriptions of Britain (see Collingwood and Wright 1965 below)

Classical sources

Ammianus Marcellinus – *Res Gestae* (see Rolfe 1952 below)
Bede – *A History of the English Church and People* (see Sherley-Price 1972 below)
Caesar – *Gallic Wars* (see Handford 1976 below)
Gildas – *De Excidio Britanniae* (see Ireland 1996 below)
Notitia Dignitatum (see Fairley 1894 below)
Pliny the Elder – *Natural History* (see Healey 1991 below)
Ptolemy – *Geographia* (see Stückelberger and Graßhoff 2006 below)
Strabo – *The Geography* (see Ireland 1996 below)
Suetonius – *The Twelve Caesars* (see Graves 1986 below)
Tacitus – *Agricola and Germany* (see Birley 1999 below)
Tacitus – *The Annals of Imperial Rome* (see Grant 1996 below)
Tacitus – *The Histories* (see Wellesley 2007 below)

Addyman, P.V. 1984 York in its archaeological setting. In P.V. Addyman and V.E. Black (eds)
    Archaeological Papers from York presented to M.W. Barley. York: York Archaeological
    Trust, 7–21.
Ainsworth, G. 2003 *How did the surrounding landscapes influence the development of ladder
    complexes on the southern Yorkshire Wolds*. Unpublished BA Dissertation, Faculty of Arts,
    University of Hull.
Albone, J. 2002 *Land off Spa Hill, Kirton in Lindsey*. North Lincolnshire Archaeological Project
    Services.
Alcock, J.P. 1996 Figurines of Mars from Dragonby. In J. May *Dragonby. Report on excavations
    at an Iron Age and Romano-British settlement in North Lincolnshire*. Oxford: Oxbow Books,
    264–267.
Aldhouse-Green, M. 2004 *An Archaeology of Images. Iconology and cosmology in Iron Age and
    Roman Europe*. London: Routledge/Taylor Francis.

Allason-Jones, L. 2005 *Women in Roman Britain*. York: Council for British Archaeology.

Allason-Jones. L. 1989 *Ear-rings in Roman Britain*. Oxford: British Archaeological Reports British Series **201**.

Allason-Jones, L. 2002 *The jet industry and allied trades in Roman Britain*. In P. Wilson and J. Price (eds) Craft and Industry in Roman Yorkshire and the North. Oxford: Oxbow Books, 125–133.

Allason-Jones, L., van Driel-Murray, C., Gwilt, A., Emeleus, C. M., Hill, P., Jones, J.M., Pilling, K. A., Snetterton-Lewis, V., and Huntley, J. 2006 The small finds. In M. Millett (ed.) *Shiptonthorpe, East Yorkshire. Archaeological Studies of a Romano-British roadside settlement*. Yorkshire Archaeological Report **5**. Leeds: Roman Antiquities Section Yorkshire Archaeological Society and East Riding Archaeological Society, 220–249.

Allen, D. 1998 *Roman glass in Britain*. Princes Risborough: Shire Publications.

Allen, S. 2007 *An Early Medieval Logboat from Welhambridge, East Riding of Yorkshire*. (ERYMS 2004.19). Report on the Conservation of a logboat for East Riding of Yorkshire Museums Service. York: Archaeological Trust Conservation Laboratories.

Allen S. and Dean G. 2005 Wooden Artefacts (including logboat and trackway. In G. Dean (ed.) *A614 Welham Bridge to Spaldington. An assessment report on an archaeological watching brief and excavation*. York: York Archaeological Trust, 90–92.

Allison, E., Carrott, J., Hall, A., Kenward, H., Large, F., McKenna B. and Robertson, A. 1997 Publication draft: *Plant and invertebrate remains from Iron Age and Romano-British deposits at North Cave, East Yorkshire*. York: Reports from the Environmental Archaeology Unit, York 97/37

Andrews-Wilson, L. 2008 YORYM-CA4661 a roman figurine Webpage available at: http://finds.org.uk/database/artefacts/record/id/214850.

Andrews-Wilson, L 2009 YORYM-7CB0A7 a roman ear ring Webpage available at: http://finds.org.uk/database/artefacts/record/id/279488.

Anthoons, G. 2007. The origins of the Arras Culture: migration or elite networks? in R. Karl and J. Leskovar (eds), *Interpretierte Eisenzeiten* **2**. Fallstudien, Methoden, Theorie. Tagungsbeiträge der 2. Linzer Gespräche zur interpretativen Eisenzeitarchäologie. Studien zur Kulturgeschichte von Oberösterreich, Folge 19. Linz: Oberösterreichisches Landesmuseum, 141–151.

Anthoons, G. 2010 It's a small world... Closer contacts in the early third century BC. In M. Sterry, A. Tullett and N. Ray (eds) In Search of the Iron Age. *Proceedings of the Iron Age Research Student Seminar 2008*. Leicester: Leicester Archaeological Monograph 18, 127–43.

Anthoons, G. 2011 *Contacts between the Arras Culture and the Continent*. PhD Thesis, University of Bangor.

Armit, I. 2001 Warfare, violence and slavery in prehistory and protohistory. The Prehistoric Society and the University of Sheffield Archaeology Society, February 2–3, 2001, Sheffield. In *Past* – the newsletter of the Prehistoric Society **37**. http://www.ucl.ac.uk/prehistoric/past/past37.html#Warfare

Armstrong, P. 1981 Lecture summaries. *ERAS News* **10**. East Riding Archaeological Society.

Atha, M. 2007 *Late Iron Age Regionality and early Roman trajectories (100BC-200AD): A landscape perspective from East Yorkshire*. PhD Thesis, University of York.

Baillie, M.G.L. 1995 *A slice through time*. London: Routledge.

Barclay, C. 1996 The coins. In Neal, D.S. 1996 *Excavations on the Roman Villa at Beadlam, Yorkshire*. Leeds: Yorkshire Archaeological Report **2**, 63–69.

Barclay, C. 2000 Beverley area (Iron Age coin finds). Treasure Annual Report 1998–1999. London: Department for Culture, Media and Sport.

Barclay, C. 2004 Beverley, East Yorkshire (addenda): 18 Iron Age gold staters (2003 T281). Treasure Annual Report 2003. London: Department for Culture, Media and Sport, Cultural Property Unit.

Bartlett, J. 1967 A Roman pig of lead from Broomfleet, East Yorkshire. *Derbyshire Archaeological Journal* **87**, 167–8.

Bartlett, J. 1968 A pig of lead and other finds from Broomfleet, East Yorkshire. Hull: *Kingston upon Hull City Museums Bulletin* **1**, 2–6.

Barlett, J. 1971 *The medieval walls of Hull. Kingston upon Hull Museums Bulletin* Vol. 3–4.

Barrett, J. 1994 *Fragments from Antiquity*. Blackwell. Oxford.

Bayley, J. 2002 Non ferrous metalworking in Roman Yorkshire. In P. Wilson and J. Price (eds) *Craft and Industry in Roman Yorkshire and the North*. Oxford: Oxbow Books, 101–109.

Bayley, J. and Butcher, S. 2004 *Roman brooches in Britain: a technological and typological study based on the Richborough collection*. London: Society of Antiquaries Research Report Committee.

Bell, T.W. 1999 A Roman Signal Station at Whitby. *Archaeological Journal* **155** (for 1998), 303–13.

Bennett, J. 2001 *Towns in Roman Britain*. Princes Riseborough: Shire Archaeology.

Bennett, P. 2001 Roundhouses in the landscape: recent construction work at Castell Henllys, Pembrokeshire. Newsletter No. **21** Spring 2001 Council for British Archaeology Wales. http://www.britarch.ac.uk/cbawales/Newsletters/newsletter21/newsletter21.html#henllys

Beresford, M.W. and Hurst, J.G. 1990 *Wharram Percy: Deserted Medieval Village*. London: B.T. Batsford.

Bersu, G, 1940 Excavations at Little Woodbury, Wiltshire (1938–39). *Proceedings of the Prehistoric Society* **6**, 30–111.

Bidwell, P. 2006 Constantius and Constantine at York. In E. Hartley, J. Hawkes, M. Henig, and F. Mee *Constantine the Great: York's Roman emperor*. York: York Museums and Art Gallery Trust.

Bidwell, P. and Hodgson, N. 2009 *The Roman army in Northern England*. Newcastle upon Tyne: Arbeia Society.

Birley, A.R. (Trans.) 1999 *Tacitus: Agricola and Germany*. Oxford: Oxford University Press.

Bishop, M. 1999 An Iron Age and Romano-British ladder settlement at Melton, East Yorkshire. *Yorkshire Archaeological Journal* **71**, 23–63.

Bishop, M. 2011 Weaponry and military equipment. In L. Allason-Jones (ed.) *Artefacts in Roman Britain. Their purpose and use*. Cambridge: Cambridge University Press, 114–133.

Blackford, J.J. and Chambers, F.M. 1999 Harold's Bog, East Bilsdale Moor. In D.R. Bridgland, B.P Horton and J.B. Innes (eds) *Quaternary of North-East England. Field Guide*. Durham: Quaternary Research Association, 113–130.

Blundell, A. and Barber K. 2005 A 2800-year palaeoclimatic record from Tore Hill Moss, Strathspey, Scotland: the need for a multi-proxy approach to peat-based climate reconstructions. *Quaternary Science Reviews* 1261–1277.

Bolton, D. 2004 *New perspectives on Romano-British Landscapes: settlement change and dislocation within the territory of the Parisi*. Unpublished MA Thesis, Department of History, University of Hull.

Booth, P. 2010 *The late Roman cemetery at Lankhills, Winchester: excavations 2000–2005*. Oxford: Oxford Archaeology Monograph 10.

Boutwood, Y. 1998 Prehistoric linear boundaries in Lincolnshire and its margins. In R. Bewley (ed.) *Lincolnshire's archaeology from the air*. Lincoln: Occasional papers in *Lincolnshire History and Archaeology* **11**, 29–47.

Bowman, A.K. and Thomas, J.D. 1984 *Vindolanda: The Latin writing-tablets*. Gloucester and London: A. Sutton.

Boyle, A. 2004 Riding into history, *British Archaeology* **76**, 22–7.

Boylston, A. 2002 *North Cave (NCE 2001) Report on the human skeletal remains*. Sheffield: Dept of Science, University of Sheffield.

Bradley, R. 1984 *The social foundations of British Prehistory*. Longman: London.

Bradley, R. 1990 *The passage of arms – an archaeological analysis of Prehistoric hoards and votive deposit*. Cambridge: Cambridge University Press.

Bradley, R. 1994 Introduction. In R. Bradley, R. Entwhistle and F. Raymond, *Prehistoric land divisions in Salisbury Plain*. London: English Heritage.

Braithwaite, G. 1984 Romano-British Face Pots and Head Pots, *Britannia* **15**, 99–131.

Braund, D. 1996 *Ruling Roman Britain*. Routledge: London.

Brayshay, B. and Dinnin M. 1999 Integrated palaeoecological evidence for biodiversity at the floodplain-forest margin. *Journal of Biogeography* **26**, 115–131.

Breeze, D.J. and Dobson B. 1985 Roman military deployment in north England. *Britannia* **16**, 1–19.

Brew, D.S., Holt, T., Pye, K. and Newsham, R. 2000 Holocene sedimentary evolution and palaeocoastlines of the Fenland embayment, eastern England. In *Holocene Land-Ocean Interaction and Environmental Change around the North Sea*. Geological Society Special Publication 166, 253–257.

Brewster, T.C.M. 1957 Excavations at Newham's Pit, Staxton, 1947–8 *Yorkshire Archaeological Journal* **39**, 193–223.

Brewster, T.C.M. 1963 *The excavation of Staple Howe*. Scarborough: East Riding Archaeological Research Trust.

Brewster, T.C.M. 1971 The Garton Slack chariot burial, East Yorkshire. *Antiquity* **45**, 289–92.

Brewster, T.C.M. 1972 The excavation of Weaverthorpe Manor 1960. *Yorkshire Archaeological Journal* **44**, 114–33.

Brewster, T.C.M. 1980 *The excavation of Garton and Wetwang Slack*. East Riding Archaeological Research Commitee Exacavation Report 2. London: National Monuments Record.

Bridgford, S. 1997 The first weapons devised only for war. *British Archaeology* **22**, 7.

Brigham, T. Buglass, J. and Steedman, K. 2008 *A desk-based resource assessment of aggregate-producing landscapes in the East Riding of Yorkshire*. English Heritage Project No.4828. Humber Archaeology Report 261. Hull: Humber Field Archaeology.

Brigham, T. and Jobling D. 2011 Rapid Coastal Zone Assessment Yorkshire and Lincolnshire. Bempton to Donna Nook. English Heritage Project No. 3729. Hull: Humber Archaeology Report 235, Humber Field Archaeology.

Brown, F., Howard-Davis, C., Brennand, M., Boyle, A., Evans, T., O'Connor, S., Spence, A., Heawood, R. and Lupton, A. 2007 *The Archaeology of the A1 (M) Darrington to Dishforth DBFO Road Scheme*, Lancaster: Oxford Archaeology North.

Brunaux, J.P. and Rapin, A. 1988 *Gournay II: Boucliers et Lances, Dépôts et Trophées*. Paris: Revue Archéologique de Picardie, Special Éditions Errance.

Bryant, S. 1997 The Iron Age. In J. Glazebrook (ed.) *Research and Archaeology. A Framework for the Eastern counties*. East Anglian Archaeology Occasional Paper 3. Norwich: Scole Archaeological Committee, 23–31.

Buckland, P.C. 1979 T*horne Moors: a palaeoecological study of a Bronze Age site. A contribution to the history of the British Insect fauna*. Birmingham: University of Birmingham Department of Geography Occasional Paper 8.

Buckland, P.C. 1980 Insect remains from the well. In I.M. Stead *Rudston Roman Villa*. Leeds: Yorkshire Archaeological Society, 162–8.

Buckland, P.C. 1982 The Malton burnt grain: a cautionary tale. *Yorkshire Archaeological Journal* **54**, 53–61.

Buckland, P.C. 1986 *Roman South Yorkshire: a Source Book*. Sheffield: Dept of Archaeology and Prehistory University of Sheffield.

Buckland, P.C. 1988 The stones of York. Building materials in Yorkshire. In J. Price and P.R. Wilson, with C.S. Briggs and S.J. Hardman (eds) *Recent Research in Roman Yorkshire*. Oxford: British Archaeological Reports British Series **193**, 237–87.

Buckland, P.C., Parker-Pearson, M., Wigley, A. and Girling, M.A. 2001 'Is there anybody out there? A reconsideration of the environmental evidence from the Breiddin Hillfort, Powys, Wales'. *Antiquaries Journal* **81**, 51–76.

Buckland, P.C., Hartley, K.F. and Rigby V. 2006 The Roman pottery kilns at Rossington Bridge excavations 1956–1961. *Journal of Roman pottery studies* **9**. Oxford: Oxbow Books for The Study Group for Roman Pottery.

Burn, A.R. 1969 *The Romans in Britain – An anthology of inscriptions*. Columbia: University of South Carolina Press.

Burnham, B.C. and Wacher, J. 1990 *The 'Small Towns' of Roman Britain*. London: Batsford.

Burton, J. 1745 *Extracts of a letter from Mr. Thomas Knowlton to Mr. Mark Catesby concerning the situation of the ancient town of Delgovicia*. Hull: J.W. Leng.

Burton, J. 1753 A Dissertation on the situation of the Roman station of Delgovitia in Yorkshire. *The Philosophical Transactions of the Royal Society of London* **44**. (1683–1775), 541–556.

Burton, J. and Drake, F. 1747 A Dissertation on the situation of the Roman station of Delgovitia in Yorkshire. *The Philosophical Transactions of the Royal Society of London* **44**. London. 541–552, appendix, 553–556.

Caffell, A. and Holst, M. 2011 Osteological analysis. In C. Fenton Thomas (ed.) *Where Sky and Yorkshire and Water Meet: The Story of the Melton Landscape from Prehistory to the Present*. York: On-Site Archaeology Monograph 2, 323–331.

Cameron, K. 1961 *English Place Names*. London: Batsford.

Campbell, R. 2008 Manufacturing evidence of Romano-British glass bangles from Thearne, near Beverley, East Yorkshire, *Roman Antiquities Section Bulletin* **24**. Leeds: Roman Antiquities Section, Yorkshire Archaeological Society, 12–17.

Carr, M. 2005 *A weapons cache from South Cave in its landscape*. Certificate in Archaeology project, University of Hull.

Carne, P. 2001 A Roman villa and settlement at Ingleby Barwick, Teeside. *Roman Antiquities Section Bulletin* **18**. Leeds: Yorkshire Archaeological Society, 12–16.

Carne, P. 2006 *A Roman villa and settlement at Ingleby Barwick, Stockton-on-Tees: revised assessment report and updated project design*. Durham: Archaeological Services, Durham University.

Carter, A. 1995 *Howardian hills mapping project: a report for the National Mapping Programme*. Swindon: Air photography unit, Royal Commission on the Historical Monuments of England (pdf version 2011).

Carter, S. and Hunter, F. 2003a An Iron Age chariot burial from Scotland. *Antiquity* **77** (297), 531–5.

Carter, S. and Hunter, F. 2003b The Newbridge chariot. *Current Archaeology* **178**, 413–5.

Cartwright, C. 1999 Charcoal identification. In P. Halkon, and M. Millett (eds) *Rural Settlement and industry: Studies in the Iron Age and Roman archaeology of lowland East Yorkshire*. Leeds: Yorkshire Archaeological Report **4**, Yorkshire Archaeological Society, 126.

Carver, M. 2006 *The Cross Goes North: Processes of Conversion in Northern Europe, AD 300–1300*. Woodbridge: Boydell.

Casey, P.J. 1993 The end of garrisons on Hadrian's Wall: an historico-environmental model. In D. Clark, M. Roxan, and J. Wilkes (eds) *The Later Roman Empire Today*. London: University College of London, 69–80.

Casey, P.J. 1994 *Carausius and Allectus: The British usurpers*. London: Batsford.

Catt, J.A. 1990. Geology and Relief. In S. Ellis and D. Crowther *Humber Perspectives*. Hull: Hull University Press, 13–28.

Chadwick, A. 1999 Digging ditches but missing riches? Ways into the Iron Age and Romano-British cropmark landscapes of the north Midlands. In B. Bevan, (ed.) *Northern Exposure: interpretative devolution and the Iron Age in Britain*. Leicester: Leicester Archaeology Monograph **4**. Leicester, 149–172.

Chandler, J. 1993 *John Leland's Itinerary. Travels in Tudor England*. Stroud: Sutton Publishing.

Chaplin, R.E. and Barnetson, L.P. 1980 Animal bones. In I.M. Stead *Rudston Roman Villa*. Leeds: Yorkshire Archaeological Society, 149–162.

Chapman, H., Fenwick, H., Head, R., Fletcher, W. and Lillie, M. 1999 The archaeological survey of the Rivers Aire, Ouse, Wharfe and Derwent. In Van de Noort, R. and Ellis, S. (eds) *Wetland heritage of the Vale of York*. Humber Wetlands Project. Hull: University of Hull, 141–204.

Chapman, H., Fletcher, W., Fenwick, H., Lillie, M., Thomas, G. and Head, R. 2000 The archaeological survey of the Hull Valley. Van de Noort, R. and Ellis, S. (eds) 2000 *Wetland heritage of the Hull Valley*. Humber Wetlands Project. Hull: University of Hull, 105–175.

Challis, A.J. and Harding D.W. 1975 *Later Prehistory from the Trent to the Tyne*. Oxford: British Archaeological Reports **20**.

Childe, V.G.1940 *The prehistoric cultures of the British Isles*. London and Edinburgh: W. and R. Chambers.

Clark, G. 1954. *Excavations at Star Carr: an early Mesolithic site at Seamer near Scarborough, Yorkshire*. Cambridge: Cambridge University Press.

Clarke, A. and Fulford, M. 2000 Silchester and the end of Roman Towns. *Current Archaeology* **161**, 176–180.

Clarke, D. 1998 *Roman Brough*. Certificate in Archaeology Project, Department of History, University of Hull.

Coates, R.J. 2007 Work at Burshill Carrs. *ERAS News* **68**, 7–9.

Coates, R.J. 2010 Archaeological and environmental evidence of human utilisation and landscape change in the river Hull Valley. MA Dissertation, University of Hull.

Congreve, A.L. 1938 *A Roman and Saxon site at Elmswell, East Yorkshire, 1937*. Hull: Hull Museums Publications 198.

Coles, A. 2010 *Palaeogeographical and relative sea-level changes at Hotham Carrs, East Yorkshire: reconstruction of a Holocene landscape in the inner Humber estuary*. Unpublished BSc Dissertation, Department of Geography, University of Durham.

Coles, B. 1996 Roos Carr re-assembled. In S. Aldhouse-Green (ed.) *Art, ritual and death in prehistory*. Cardiff: National Museums and Galleries of Wales.

Collard, M., Darvill, T. and Watts, M. 2006. Ironworking in the Bronze Age? Evidence from a 10th century BC settlement at Hartshill Copse, Upper Bucklebury, West Berkshire. *Proceedings of the Prehistoric Society* **72**, 367–421.

Collingwood, R.G. 1931 The Roman Signal Station. In A. Rowntree (ed.) *The History of Scarborough*. Letchworth: Temple Press, 42–50.

Collingwood, R.G. and R.P. Wright 1965 *The Roman Inscriptions of Britain 1: Inscriptions on Stone*. Oxford: Clarendon.

Collins, R. 2012 *Hadrian's Wall and the End of Empire: The Roman Frontier in the 4th and 5th Centuries*. London: Routledge.

Collins, R. (forthcoming) Soldiers to Warriors: Renegotiating the Roman Frontier in the Fifth Century,' in F. Hunter and K. Painter (eds) *Late Roman silver and the end of the empire: the Traprain Treasure in context*. Proceedings of a conference held in Edinburgh, 9–10 May 2009. Edinburgh: Society of Antiquaries of Scotland.

Collis, J. 1994 Reconstructing Iron Age societies. In K. Kristiansen and J. Jensen (eds) *Europe in the First Millennium BC*. Sheffield: Sheffield Academic Press, 31–39.

Collis, J. 2003 *Celts: Origins and Re-inventions: Origins, Myths and Inventions*. Stroud: Tempus Publishing.

Collis, J. 2004 Weapons with warriors. Letters. *Current Archaeology* **192**, 573.

Congreve, A.L. 1938 *A Roman and Saxon site at Elmswell, East Yorkshire, 1937*. Hull: Hull Museums Publications 198.

Conneller, C. and Schadla-Hall, T. 2003. Beyond Star Carr: The Vale of Pickering in the 10th Millennium BP. *Proceedings of the Prehistoric Society* **69**, 85–105.

Cool, H. 2000 The Roman finds In P. Ottaway, Excavations on the site of the Roman signal station at Carr Naze, Filey, 1993–94. *Archaeological Journal* **157**, 122–131.

Cool, H. 2006 *Eating and Drinking in Roman Britain*. Cambridge: Cambridge University Press.

Corder, P. 1928 *The Roman pottery kiln at Crambeck, Castle Howard*. York: Roman Malton and District Report **1**.

Corder, P. 1930(a) The Roman pottery kiln at Throlam, Holme-on-Spalding Moor, East Yorkshire. *Transactions of the East Riding Antiquarian Society* **25**, 1934 (Reprint of Corder 1930).

Corder, P. 1930(b) The defences of Roman Malton. Leeds: Roman Malton and District Report 2.

Corder, P. 1934 *Excavations at the Roman fort at Brough-on-Humber*. Hull: Hull University Local History Committee by arrangement with the East Riding Antiquarian Society.

Corder, P. 1940 *Excavations at Elmswell, East Yorkshire 1938*. Hull: Hull University College Local History Committee by arrangement with Hull Museum.

Corder, P. 1941 *A Roman site at North Newbald, East Yorkshire*. Leeds: Proceedings of the Leeds Philosophical and Literary Society, Literary and History Section, 5 (4), 231–38.

Corder, P. 1948 Miscellaneous Small objects from the Roman Fort at Malton. *Antiquaries Journal* **28**, 173–177.

Corder, P. 1958 Parisian Ware. *Yorkshire Archaeological Journal* **39**, 48–52.

Corder, P. and Davies Pryce, T. 1938 Belgic and other early pottery found at North Ferriby, Yorkshire. *Antiquaries Journal* **18**, 262–77.

Corder, P. and Kirk J.L. 1932 A *Roman Villa at Langton, near Malton E. Yorkshire.* Leeds: Roman Malton and District Report 4. Leeds: Yorkshire Archaeological Society.

Corder, P. and Richmond, I.A. 1938 A Romano-British interment with bucket and sceptres from Brough, East Yorkshire. *Antiquaries Journal* **18**, 67–74.

Corder, P. and Richmond, I.A. 1942 Petuaria. *Journal of the British Archaeological Association* **3**, series 7, 1–30.

Corder, P. and Romans, T. 1935 *Excavations at the Roman Town at Brough-on-Humber, East Yorkshire 1934.* Hull: University Local History Committee by arrangement with the East Riding Antiquarian Society.

Corder, P. and Romans, T. 1936 *Excavations at the Roman Town at Brough East Yorkshire 1935.* Hull: East Riding Antiquarian Society by arrangement with the Hull University Local History Committee.

Corder, P. and Romans, T. 1937 *Excavations at the Roman Town at Brough, East Yorkshire 1936.* Hull: The Hull Museum Committee by arrangement with Hull University College Local History Committee.

Corder, P. and Romans, T. 1938 *Excavations at the Roman Town at Brough-Petuaria.* Reprinted from The East Riding Antiquarian Society Transactions by arrangement with Hull University Local History Committee.

Corder, P. and Sheppard T. 1930 *The Roman pottery kilns at Throlam East Yorkshire.* Hull: Hull Museums Publications 170.

Corder, P., Wright, C.W. and Wright, E.V. 1939 The pre-Roman settlement of the Parisi at North Ferriby. *The Naturalist* **1**, 237–43.

Cortis, W. 1857 Paper read at a meeting held in Filey Town Hall, 12 November 1857 http://www.fileybrigg.com/resources/DrCortis.pdf.

Coulston, J.C.N. and Phillips, E. 1988 *Corpus Signorum Imperii Romani, Great Britain I,6, Hadrian's Wall west of the River North Tyne, and Carlisle.* London: British Academy.

Cowgill, J., Godfrey, E. and Mcdonnell, G. 2003 *Evidence for iron production – the slags from TSEP site 238* (incorporating comments on TSEP sites 222 and 908) – unpublished report.

Creighton, J. 1988 The place names of East Yorkshire in the Roman Period. In J. Price and P.R. Wilson, with C.S. Briggs and S.J. Hardman (eds) *Recent Research in Roman Yorkshire.* Oxford: British Archaeological Reports British Series **193**, 387–406.

Creighton, J. 1999 (ed.) Excavations at Hawling Road. In P. Halkon and M. Millett, Rural Settlement and industry: Studies in the Iron Age and Roman archaeology of lowland East Yorkshire. Leeds: Yorkshire Archaeological Report **4**, Yorkshire Archaeological Society, 168–221.

Creighton, J. 2000 *Coins and Power in Late Iron Britain.* Cambridge: Cambridge University Press.

Crew, P. 1991. The Experimental Production of Prehistoric Bar Iron. *Journal of the Historical Metallurgy Society* **25** (1) 21–36.

Crew, P., 2013, Twenty five years of bloomery experiments: perspectives and prospects, in Dungworth, D. and Doonan, R. (eds) *Accidental and Experimental Archaeometallurgy. Proceedings of the 2010 Conference.* London: Historical Metallurgy Society.

Croom, A. 2002 *Roman Clothing and Fashion.* Stroud: Tempus Publishing.

Crowfoot, E. 1991 The textiles. In I.M. Stead *Iron Age Cemeteries in East Yorkshire. Excavations at Burton Fleming, Rudston, Garton-on-the-Wolds, and Kirkburn*. London: English Heritage Archaeological Report 22 London: English Heritage, 119–25.

Crowther, D.R. 1987 Sediments and Archaeology of the Humber foreshore. In S. Ellis (ed.) *East Yorkshire a Field Guide*. Cambridge: Quaternary Research Association, 99–105.

Crowther, D.R. and Didsbury, P. 1988 Redcliff and the Humber. In J. Price and P.R. Wilson, with C.S. Briggs and S.J. Hardman (eds) *Recent Research in Roman Yorkshire*. Oxford: British Archaeological Reports British Series **193**, 3–21.

Crowther, D.R., Willis, S. and Creighton, J. 1990 The topography and archaeology of Redcliff. In S. Ellis and D.R. Crowther (eds) *Humber Perspectives*. Hull: Hull University Press, 172–182.

Crummy, N. 2010 Bears and Coins: The Iconography of Protection in Late Roman Infant Burials. *Britannia* **41**, 37–93.

Crump, B. 2007 YORYM-4F4C23 A ROMAN buckle http://finds.org.uk/database/artefacts/record/id/19616.

Cruse, J. forthcoming *Yorkshire Quern Survey – Current Work in East Yorkshire*.

Cunliffe, B. 2003 *Danebury Hillfort*. Stroud: Tempus Publishing.

Cunliffe, B. 2005 *Iron Age communities in Britain*. London and New York: Routledge (fourth edition).

Curnock, N. 1938 *The Journal of the Reverend John Wesley*. Standard edition 6. London: Epworth Press.

Dalby, M. 1980 Moss remains from the well. In I.M. Stead *Rudston Roman Villa*. Leeds: Yorkshire Archaeological Society, 168.

Daniel, P., Casswell, C. and Moore, R. (in preparation) *Perspectives on ancient East Yorkshire: the Archaeology of the Ganstead to Asselby pipeline*.

Dark, K. and Dark, P. 1997 *The Landscape of Roman Britain*. Stroud: Sutton Publishing.

Darling, M.J. 2000 The Roman pottery. In K. Hunter-Mann (*et al.*) Excavations on a Roman Extra-Mural Site at Brough-on-Humber, East Riding of Yorkshire, UK. *Internet Archaeology* **9**. http://intarch.ac.uk/journal/issue9/brough_index.html.

Davies R.W. 1976 'Singulares' and Roman Britain *Britannia* **7**, 134–144.

Davis, J.B. and Thurnham, J. 1865 *Crania Britannica* **2**. London: Taylor and Francis.

Dean, G. 2005 *A614 Welham Bridge to Spaldington. An assessment report on an archaeological watching brief and excavation*. York: York Archaeological Trust.

De Boer, G. 1964 Spurn Head its history and evolution. *Transactions of the Institute of British Geographers* **34**, 71–89.

De Boer, G. 1996 (a) The coastal erosion of Holderness. In S. Neave and S. Ellis, (eds) *An historical atlas of East Yorkshire*. Hull: The University of Hull Press, 6–7.

De Boer, G. 1996 (b) The history of Spurn point. In S. Neave and S. Ellis (eds) *An historical atlas of East Yorkshire*. Hull: The University of Hull Press, 8–10.

Dennett, K. 2004 *ERAS News* **58** East Riding Archaeological Society, 4.

Dent, J.S. 1982 Cemeteries and settlement patterns of the Iron Age on the Yorkshire Wolds. *Proceedings of the Prehistoric Society* **48**, 437–457.

Dent, J.S. 1983(a) A summary of the excavations carried out in Garton Slack and Wetwang Slack, 1964–80, *East Riding Archaeologist* **7**, 1–14.

Dent, J.S. 1983(b) The impact of Roman rule on native society in the territory of the Parisi in *Britannia* **14**, 35–44.

Dent, J.S. 1985 Three chariot burials from Wetwang, Yorkshire. *Antiquity* **59**, 85–92.

Dent, J.S. 1988. Roman religious remains from Elmswell. In J. Price, P.R Wilson, C.S. Briggs, S.J. Hardman (eds) *Recent research in Roman Yorkshire: Studies in honour of Mary Kitson Clark (Mrs Derwas Chitty)*. Oxford: Britsh Archaeological Reports **193**, 89–97.

Dent, J.S. 1989 Settlements at North Cave and Brantingham. In P. Halkon (ed.) *New Light on the Parisi. Recent discoveries in Iron Age and Roman East Yorkshire*. ERAS University of Hull. Hull, 26–32.

Dent, J.S. 1990 The upper Hull Valley: archaeology under threat. In S. Ellis and D.R. Crowther (ed.) *Humber perspectives: a region through the ages*. Hull: Hull University Press, 102–8.

Dent, J.S. 1995 *Aspects of Iron Age Settlement in East Yorkshire*. PhD Thesis, University of Sheffield.

Dent, J.S. 1998 The Yorkshire Wolds in Late Prehistory. The emergence of an Iron Age Society. In P. Halkon (ed.) *Further Light on the Parisi. Recent research in Iron Age and Roman East Yorkshire*. Hull: ERAS, University of Hull, ERART, 4–14.

Dent, J.S. 2010 *The Iron Age in East Yorkshire*. Oxford: British Archaeological Reports British Series **508**. John and Erica Hedges.

Dickinson, T.M. 1982 Fowler's Type G penannular brooches reconsidered. *Medieval Archaeology* **26**, 41–68.

Dickson, A. 2003 Transco West Hull reinforcement gas pipeline. Summary of Romano-British discoveries. *Bulletin Roman Antiquities Section* **19**. Leeds: Yorkshire Archaeological Society, 18–20.

Didsbury, P. 1984 A Grey-ware Cult Shard from Bielby *Britannia* **15**, 239.

Didsbury, P. 1988 Evidence for Romano-British settlement in Hull and the Lower Hull Valley. In J. Price and P.R. Wilson, with C.S. Briggs and S.J. Hardman (eds) *Recent Research in Roman Yorkshire*. Oxford: British Archaeological Reports British Series **193**, 21–35.

Didsbury, P. 1989 Recent discoveries in Hull and district. In P. Halkon (ed.) *New Light on the Parisi. Recent discoveries in Iron Age and Roman East Yorkshire*. ERAS University of Hull. Hull, 23–26.

Didsbury, P. 1990 Exploitation of the alluvium in the Lower Hull Valley. In S. Ellis and D. Crowther (eds) *Humber Perspectives*. Hull: Hull University Press, 199–213.

Didsbury, P. 2003 *An assessment of the pottery from an excavation at South Cave* (RSC 2002). Unpublished assessment report.

Didsbury, P. and Vince A. 2011 First Millennium BC pottery. In C. Fenton Thomas (ed.) *Where Sky and Yorkshire and Water Meet: The Story of the Melton Landscape from Prehistory to the Present*. York: On-Site Archaeology Monograph 2, 184–196.

Dixon, K. and Southern, P. 1997 *The Roman Cavalry*. London: Batsford.

Dobney, K. 2001 A place at the table: the role of vertebrate zooarchaeology within a Roman research agenda. In S. James, and M. Millett (eds), *Britons and Romans: advancing an archaeological agenda*. York: Council for British Archaeology Research Reports 125, 36–46.

Dobney, K., Hall, A., Kenward, H. and Milles, A. 1993 *An assessment of environmental samples and bone from excavations on the route of the Leven-Brandesburton by-pass* (site code LEV92). York: Report to Humberside Archaeology Unit.

Dobney, K., Jaques, S.D. and Irving, B.G. 1996 Of Butchers and Breeds, Report on vertebrate remains from various sites in the City of Lincoln. Lincoln: *Lincoln Archaeological Studies* **5**.

Dobney, K. and Ervynck A. 2007 To fish or not to fish? Evidence for the possible avoidance of fish consumption during the Iron Age around the North Sea. Haselgrove C. and T. Moore *The later Iron Age in Britain and beyond*. Oxford: Oxbow books.

Drake, F. 1736 *Eboracum: or the History and Antiquities of the City of York from its Original to the Present Times*. London: printed by William Bowyer for the author.

Drake, F. 1747 An appendix to the foregoing paper. A dissertation on the situation of the ancient Roman station of Delgovitia in Yorkshire by Dr John Burton. *Philosophical Transactions* **44**, 553–5.

Dyer, C.T. 2001 *Aspects of ritual and religion in the landscape of Iron Age and Roman East Yorkshire*.Unpublished MA Dissertation, University of Hull.

Eagles, B. 1979 *The Anglo-Saxon Settlement of Humberside*. Oxford: British Archaeological Reports British Series **68**.

Easthaugh, E. Halkon P., Millett M. Woodhouse H. with contributions by Barclay, C. Brickstock, R., Clogg, P., Stratton, S, and Worrell S. forthcoming The Burnby Lane Site. In P. Halkon, M. Millett, H. Woodhouse (eds) forthcoming *Hayton, the archaeology of an Iron Age and Roman landscape in East Yorkshire*. Yorkshire Archaeological Report, Yorkshire Archaeological Society.

Edwards, J. 1984 *The Roman cookery of Apicius*, translated and adapted for the modern kitchen. London: Rider.

Elgee, F. and Elgee, H. 1933 *The Archaeology of Yorkshire*. London: Methuen.

Ellis, S. 1996 Physiography. In S. Neave and S, Ellis (eds) *An historical atlas of East Yorkshire*. Hull: University Press, 2–3.

Ellis, S. and Newsome, D. 1991 Chalkland Soil Formation and Erosion on the Yorkshire Wolds. *Geoderma* **48**, 159–72.

Elsdon, S.M. 1982 *Parisian ware: a study of stamped wares of the Roman period in Lincolnshire, Humberside and South Yorkshire*. Highworth: Vorda Research series.

Elsdon, S.M. 1989 *Later Prehistoric Pottery in England and Wales*. Aylesbury: Shire Archaeology.

Elsdon, S.M. 1996 Iron Age Pottery. In J. May *Dragonby, Report on Excavations at an Iron Age and Romano-British Settlement in North Lincolnshire*. Oxford: Oxbow Monograph 61, 317–512.

Esmonde-Cleary, S. 1990 *The Ending of Roman Britain*. London: Batsford.

Esmonde-Cleary, S. 2003 *Civil defences in the west under the high empire. The Archaeology of Roman Towns*. Studies in honour of John S Wacher. Oxbow Books. Oxford, 73–85.

Evans, D.H. 2006 Celtic art revealed. The South Cave weapons hoard. In J. May (ed.) *Current Archaeology* **203**, 572–577.

Evans, D.H. and Atkinson, R. 2009 Recent archaeological work in the East Riding. *East Riding Archaeologist* **12**, 249–389.

Evans, D.H. and Steedman, K. 1997 Recent Archaeological work in the East Riding. *East Riding Archaeologist* **9**, 116–171.

Evans, D.H. and Steedman, K. 2000 Archaeology in the modern city of Kingston upon Hull and recent research at Kingswood. In R. Van de Noort, and S. Ellis (eds) *Wetland heritage of the Hull Valley: Humber Wetlands Project*. Hull: University of Hull, 193–216.

Evans, D.H. and Steedman, K. 2001 Recent Archaeological work in the East Riding. *East Riding Archaeologist* **10**, 116–171.

Evans, G. 2007 *The distribution of Romano-British glass bangles in Yorkshire and Lincolnshire with a comparative look at size manufacture and decoration*. Unpublished BA Dissertation, University of Hull.

Evans, J.G. 1972. *Land Snails in Archaeology*. London and New York: Seminar Press.

Evans, J. 1988 All Yorkshire is divided into three parts: social aspects of later pottery distributions in Yorkshire. In J. Price and P. R. Wilson, with C. S. Briggs and S. J. Hardman (eds) *Recent Research in Roman Yorkshire*. Oxford: British Archaeological Reports British Series 193, 323–337.

Evans, J. 1989 Crambeck; the Development of a Major Northern Pottery Industry. In P.R. Wilson (ed.) *Crambeck Roman Pottery Industry*. Leeds: Roman Antiquities Section, Yorkshire Archaeological Society, 43–91.

Evans, J. 1999 The settlement shift: an introduction to the fieldwalked pottery. In P. Halkon and M. Millett, *Rural Settlement and industry: Studies in the Iron Age and Roman archaeology of lowland East Yorkshire*. Leeds: Yorkshire Archaeological Report **4**, Yorkshire Archaeological Society, 190–191.

Evans, J. 2001 Material approaches to the identification of different Romano-British site types. In S. James, M. Millett, and J. Thorniley-Walker (eds) 2001 *Britons and Romans: advancing an archaeological agenda*. York: CBA Research Report 125, 26–35.

Evans, J. 2006(a) The Roman pottery. In M. Millett, (ed.) 2006 *Shiptonthorpe, East Yorkshire. Archaeological Studies of a Romano-British roadside settlement*. Yorkshire Archaeological Report **5**. Leeds: Roman Antiquities Section Yorkshire Archaeological Society and East Riding Archaeological Society, 126–202.

Evans, J. 2006(b) Graffiti. In M. Millett (ed.) 2006 *Shiptonthorpe, East Yorkshire. Archaeological Studies of a Romano-British roadside settlement*. Yorkshire Archaeological Report **5**. Leeds: Roman Antiquities Section Yorkshire Archaeological Society and East Riding Archaeological Society, 137.

Falileyev, A. 2007 *Dictionary of Continental Celtic Place-Names*. Aberystwyth: CMCS Publications.

Fairburn, W.A. 2009 Landforms and the geological evolution of the Vale of York during the Late Devensian. *Proceedings of the Yorkshire Geological Society* **57**, 145–154.

Fairley, W. 1894 *Notitia Dignitatum or Register of Dignitaries, in Translations and Reprints from Original Sources of European History*, Vol. VI: 4. Philadelphia: University of Pennsylvania Press.

Farwell, D.E. and Molleson, T. 1993 *Excavations at Poundbury 1966–80 – Vol.2: The cemeteries*. Dorchester: Dorset Natural History and Archaeological Society.

Faulkner, N. 2006 'Suddenly there was a face staring back at me'. Excavating a Roman parade helmet. *Current Archaeology* **202**, 543–547.

Faull, M. 1977 British survival in Anglo-Saxon Northumbria. In L. Laing (ed.) *Studies in Celtic survival*. Oxford: British Archaeological Reports, 1–55.

Fenn, C. 2002 *The study of an ancient rural settlement site at Sancton Hill Farm*. Certificate in Archaeology project, University of Hull.

Fenton-Thomas, C. 2003 *Late prehistoric and early historic landscapes on the Yorkshire Chalk*. Oxford: British Archaeological Reports British Series **350**.

Fenton-Thomas, C. 2011 *Where Sky and Yorkshire and Water Meet: The Story of the Melton Landscape from Prehistory to the Present*. York: On-Site Archaeology Monograph 2.

Fenwick, H., Chapman, H., Head, R., and Lillie, M. 1998 The archaeological survey of the lower Trent valley and Winterton Beck. In R. Van de Noort and S. Ellis *Wetland Heritage of the Ancholme and Lower Trent Valley*. Humber Wetlands Project. Hull: University of Hull and English Heritage, 143–197.

Ferraby, R., Johnson, P. and Millett, M. 2008 Fieldwork and excavations near Thwing, East Yorks 2007. *Roman Antiquities Section Bulletin* **24**. Leeds: Roman Antiquities Section, Yorkshire Archaeological Society, 1–4.

Ferraby, R., Johnson, P. and Millett, M. 2009 Fieldwork and excavations near Thwing, East Yorks. 2008. *Roman Antiquities Section Bulletin* **25**. Leeds: Roman Antiquities Section, Yorkshire Archaeological Society, 3–10.

Ferris, I. 2011 Vinovia. *The Buried Roman City of Binchester in Northern England*. Stroud: Amberley Publishing.

Finney, A. 1990 Sheepfoot Hill, Malton. *Roman Antiquities Section Bulletin* **8**. Leeds: Roman Antiquities Section, Yorkshire Archaeological Society, 12–13.

Fitzpatrick, A.P. 2007 The Fire, the Feast and the Funeral: Late Iron Age Mortuary Practices in South-Eastern England. In V. Kruta and G. Leman-Delerive (eds) *Feux des morts, foyers des vivants – Les rites et symboles du feu dans les tombes de l'Age du fer et de l'époque romaine*. Lille: Revue de Nord, Hors série, 11, 123–45.

Fitzpatrick, A.P. 2011 *The Amesbury Archer and the Boscombe Bowmen – Bell Beaker burials at Boscombe Down, Amesbury, Wiltshire*. Salisbury: Wessex Archaeology.

Fowler, E. 1963 Celtic metalwork of the fifth and sixth centuries AD: a reappraisal. *Archaeological Journal* **120**, 98–160.

Fowler, P. 1984 From wildscape to landscape: enclosure in prehistoric Britain. In Mercer, R. (ed.) *Farming practices in British Prehistory*. Edinburgh: University Press, 9–54.

Fraser, J. and Brigham, T. 2009 A Romano-British and Medieval haven at Brough. *East Riding Archaeologist* **12**, 115–127.

Fulford, M. 2001 Links with the past: pervasive 'ritual' behaviour in Roman Britain. *Britannia* **32**, 119–218.

Furness, R.R. and King, S.J. 1978 *Soils in North Yorkshire IV* Sheet SE63/73 (Selby), Harpenden: Soil Survey Record 56.

Galliou, P. 1981 Three East Gaulish brooches found in Britain. *Britannia* **12**, 288–290.

Gaimster, D., McCarthy, S. and Nurse, B. (eds) 2007 *Making History: Antiquaries in Britain 1707–2007*. London: Royal Academy of Arts.

Garrow, D., Gosden, C., Hill, J.D. and Bronk Ramsey, C. 2009 Dating Celtic art: a major radiocarbon dating programme of Iron Age and early Roman metalwork. *Archaeological Journal* **166**, 79–123.

Gaunt, G.D. and Buckland, P.C. 2002 Sources of building materials in Roman York. In P. Wilson and J. Price (eds) *Craft and Industry in Roman Yorkshire and the North*. Oxford: Oxbow Books, 133–145.

Gaunt, G.D. and Buckland, P.C. 2003 The geological background to Yorkshire's archaeology. In T. Manby, S. Moorhouse and P. Ottaway (eds) 2003 *The Archaeology of Yorkshire: An Assessment at the beginning of the 21st Century*. Leeds: Yorkshire Archaeological Society with English Heritage, CBA, 17–30.

Gaunt, G.D. and Tooley, M.J. 1974 Evidence for sea-level changes in the Humber estuary and adjacent area. *Bulletin of the Geological Survey of Great Britain* **48**, 25–42.

Geake, H. and Kenny J. (eds) *Early Deira: archaeological studies of the East Riding in the fourth to ninth centuries AD*. Oxford: Oxbow Books.

Gent, T. 1733 *The ancient and modern history of the loyal town of Rippon*. York: The Printing Office.

Giles, M. 2000 *'Open weave – close knit' Archaeologies of identity in the later prehistoric landscape of East Yorkshire*. PhD Thesis, University of Sheffield.

Giles, M. 2006 Collecting the Past, Constructing Identity: The Antiquarian John Mortimer and the Driffield Museum of Antiquities and Geological Specimens. *Antiquaries Journal* **86**, 279–316.

Giles, M. 2007(a) Refiguring rights: later Bronze Age and early Iron Age landscapes of East Yorkshire. In C. Haselgrove, C. and R. Pope (eds) *The Earlier Iron Age in Britain and the near Continent*. Oxford: Oxbow Books, 103–118.

Giles, M. 2007(b) Good fences make good neighbours? Exploring the ladder enclosures of Late Iron Age East Yorkshire. In C. Haselgrove and T. Moore (eds) *The later Iron Age in Britain and Beyond*. Oxford: Oxbow Books, 235–249.

Giles, M. 2008 Seeing red: the aesthetics of martial objects in the British and Irish Iron Age. In D. Garrow, C. Gosden and J.D. Hill (eds) *Rethinking Celtic Art*. Oxford: Oxbow Books, 59–77.

Glare, P.G.W. (ed.) 1962–82 *Oxford Latin Dictionary*. Oxford: Oxford University Press.

Goodhall, I.H. 1972 Industrial evidence from the villa at Langton, East Yorkshire. *Yorkshire Archaeological Journal* **44**, 32–37.

Gough, R. 1789 *Britannia: or, A chorographical description of the flourishing kingdoms of England, Scotland, and Ireland*. Translated from the edition published by the author in 1607. Enlarged by the latest discoveries by Richard Gough. 3, London: J. Nichols.

Grant, A. 1991 Animal husbandry. In. B. Cunliffe and C. Poole (eds) *Danebury: an Iron Age Hillfort in Hampshire. 5. The Excavations 1979–1988: the Finds*. London: Council for British Archaeology Research Report 73, 447–487.

Grant, M. 1996 *Tacitus – The Annals of Imperial Rome* (Translation). London: Penguin Books.

Grantham, C and Grantham, E. 1965 An earthwork and Anglian cemetery at Garton-on-the-Wolds, East Yorkshire. *Yorkshire Archaeological Journal* **41**, 355–360.

Graves, R. 1986 *Suetonius – The Twelve Caesars* (Translation) London: Penguin Books.

Green, M. 1993 *Celtic myths*. London: British Museum Press.

Green, M. 1994 *The gods of Roman Britain*. Princes Risborough: Shire Publications.

Green, M. 2001 *Dying for the Gods: Human Sacrifice in Iron Age and Roman Europe*. Stroud: Tempus Publishing.

Greenwell, W. 1906 Early Iron Age burials in Yorkshire. *Archaeologia* **60**, 251–324.

Greenwell, W. and Rolleston, G. 1877 *British Barrows*. Oxford: Clarendon Press.

Grieg, J.R.A. 1980 Seeds from the well. In I.M. Stead *Rudston Roman Villa*. Leeds: Yorkshire Archaeological Society 169.

Gwilt, A. 2006 The Querns. In M. Millett, *Shiptonthorpe: archaeological studies of a Roman roadside settlement*. Leeds: Yorkshire Archaeological Report **5**, 206–219.

Halkon, P. 1980 Excavations at Brough 1980. *ERAS News* **8**. East Riding Archaeological Society, 1–3.

Halkon, P. 1983 Investigations into the Romano-British Landscape around Holme-on-Spalding Moor, East Yorkshire. *East Riding Archaeologist* **7**, 15–24.

Halkon, P. 1987 *Aspects of the Romano-British Landscape around Holme-on-Spalding Moor, East Yorkshire*. M.A. Thesis, Department of Archaeology, University of Durham.

Halkon, P. (ed.) 1989(a) *New Light on the Parisi. Recent discoveries in Iron Age and Roman East Yorkshire*. Hull: ERAS, ERART Department of History, University of Hull.

Halkon, P. 1989(b) The Holme Project. *Current Archaeology* **115**, 258–61.

Halkon, P. 1990 *Huggate Dykes*. In T. Manby (ed.) East Yorkshire: Prehistoric Society Meeting Sept 1990, Prehistoric Society, 51.

Halkon, P. 1992 Romano-British Facepots from Holme-on-Spalding Moor and Shiptonthorpe, East Yorkshire. *Britannia* **23**, 222–8.

Halkon, P. 1993 From elephants to Hypocausts – more fieldwork in the south-eastern Vale of York. *CBA Forum. Annual Newsletter of CBA Yorkshire*, 12–14.

Halkon, P. 1997(a) A log boat from South Carr Farm, Newport. In D.H. Evans (ed.) An East Riding Miscellany. *East Riding Archaeologist* **9**. Hull: East Riding Archaeological Society, 7–10.

Halkon, P. 1997(b) Fieldwork on early iron working sites in East Yorkshire. *Historical Metallurgy* **31**(1), 12–16.

Halkon, P. 1998 (ed.) *Further Light on the Parisi – Recent Research in Iron Age and Roman East Yorkshire*. Hull: East Riding Archaeological Society, University of Hull Department of History, East Riding Archaeological Research Trust.

Halkon, P. 1999 The Holme Project. R. Van De Noort and S. Ellis (eds) *The wetland heritage of the Vale of York*. Hull: Humber Wetlands Project, University of Hull and English Heritage, 133–138.

Halkon, P. 2002 The Roman pottery Industry at Holme-on-Spalding Moor, East Yorkshire. In P. Wilson and J. Price (eds) *Craft and Industry in Roman Yorkshire and the North*. Oxford: Oxbow Books, 21–33.

Halkon, P. 2003 Researching an ancient landscape: the Foulness Valley, East Yorkshire. In T. Manby, S. Moorhouse and P. Ottaway (eds) *The Archaeology of Yorkshire: An assessment at the beginning of the 21st century*. Leeds: Yorkshire Archaeological Society with English Heritage, CBA, 261–275.

Halkon, P. 2006 Face pots from Shiptonthorpe. In M. Millett, *Shiptonthorpe: archaeological studies of a Roman roadside settlement*. Leeds: Yorkshire Archaeological Report **5**, 29–35.

Halkon, P. 2007 Valley of the First Iron Masters. In P.Y. Milcent (ed.) *L'économie du fer protohistorique: de la production à la consommation du métal*. Actes colloque AFEAF Toulouse (Association Française pour l'Etude de l'Age du Fer). Bordeaux: Aquitania Supplément 14/2, 151–163.

Halkon, P. 2008 *Archaeology and environment in a changing East Yorkshire landscape: the Foulness Valley c. 800 BC to c. AD 400*. BAR British Series 472. Oxford: Archaeopress.

Halkon, P. 2012 Iron landscape and power in Iron Age East Yorkshire. *Archaeological Journal* **168**, 134–168.

Halkon, P., Chapman, H., Fenwick H., Taylor, J. and Woodhouse, H. 2003 The rediscovery of the Roman temple at Millington, East Yorkshire. *ARA – The Bulletin of the Association for Roman Archaeology* **5**, 8–9.

Halkon, P. and Innes, J. 2005 Settlement and Economy in a Changing Prehistoric Lowland Landscape – An East Yorkshire (UK) Case Study. *European Journal of Archaeology* **8** (3), 225–259.

Halkon, P., Middleton, R. with Barclay C. and Laverack, T. 2006 Roman coins from Shiptonthorpe in their landscape. In M. Millett, *Shiptonthorpe: archaeological studies of a Roman roadside settlement*. Leeds: Yorkshire Archaeological Report **5**.

Halkon, P. and Millett, M. 1996 Fieldwork and excavation at Hayton, East Yorkshire, 1995 *Universities of Durham and Newcastle upon Tyne Archaeological Reports* **19**, 62–68.

Halkon, P. and Millett, M. 1999 *Rural Settlement and industry: Studies in the Iron Age and Roman archaeology of lowland East Yorkshire*. Leeds: Yorkshire Archaeological Report **4** Yorkshire Archaeological Society.

Halkon, P. and Millett, M. 2003 East Riding: An Iron Age and Roman landscape revealed. *Current Archaeology* **187**, 303–309.

Halkon, P., Millett, M. and Taylor, J. 1999 Excavations at Hayton 1998. *Bulletin Roman Antiquities Section* **16**. Leeds: Yorkshire Archaeological Society, 36.

Halkon, P., Millett M., Easthaugh E., Taylor J. and Freeman, P. 2000 *The landscape archaeology of Hayton*. Hull: University of Hull.

Halkon, P., Millett, M. Taylor J. 2006 Survey. In M. Millett (ed) *Shiptonthorpe: archaeological studies of a Roman roadside settlement*. Leeds: Yorkshire Archaeological Report **5**.

Halkon, P. and Innes, J., Long, A., Shennan, I., Manby, T., Gaunt, G., Heath, A., Wagner, P., Schofield, J., Schreve, D., and Roe, D. 2009. Change and continuity within the Prehistoric landscape of the Foulness Valley, East Yorkshire. *East Riding Archaeologist* **12**, 1–66.

Halkon, P., Millett, M. Woodhouse, H. (eds) forthcoming *Hayton, the archaeology of an Iron Age and Roman landscape in East Yorkshire*. Yorkshire Archaeological Report, Yorkshire Archaeological Society.

Halkon, P. and Woodhouse, H. 2010 Market Weighton Wold Excavation September 2009. Interim Report. *ERAS News* (March 2010). Hull: East Riding Archaeological Society.

Hall, A., Rowland, S., Jaques, D. and Carrott, J. 2000 *Evaluation of biological remains from excavations north-east of Goodmanham (site code: TSEP 907)*. Reports from the Environmental Archaeology Unit, York 2000/73.

Hall, A., Jaques, D., Kenward, H., Carrott, J. and Johnson, K. *et al.* 2004(a) *Assessment of biological remains from excavations at Newport Road Quarry, North Cave, East Riding of Yorkshire: Phase 3 (site code: NCE2001)*. York: Palaeoecology Research Services 33.

Hall, A., Jaques D., Kenward, H., Carrott, J., Johnson, K. and Gardner S. 2004(b) *Assessment of biological remains from excavations at Newport Road Quarry, North Cave, East Riding of Yorkshire: Phase 4 (site code: NCE2002)*. York: Palaeoecology Research Services 52.

Hall, A.R. and Huntley, J.P. 2007 *A review of the evidence for macrofossil plant remains from archaeological deposits in Northern England*. Environmental Studies Report. Research Department Report 87. London: English Heritage.

Hall, R. 1978 The topography of Anglo-Scandinavian York. *Viking Age York and the North*. London: CBA Research Report 27.

Hamshaw-Thomas, J. and Jaques, D. 2000 The Environmental Evidence. In K. Hunter-Mann Excavations on a Roman Extra-Mural Site at Brough-on-Humber, East Riding of Yorkshire, UK. *Internet Archaeology* **9**. http://intarch.ac.uk/journal/issue9/brough_index.html.

Handford, S.A. 1976 *Caesar: the Conquest of Gaul* (translation). Harmondsworth: Penguin Classics.

Hanson, F. 2006 *Development of Roman Brough: from fort to a civitas capital?* BA Dissertation, Univeristy of Hull, Department of History.

Hanson, W.S. and Campbell, D.B. 1986 The Brigantes: from clientage to conquest. *Britannia* **17**, 73–91.

Harding, A. 2000 *European Societies in the Bronze Age*. Cambridge: Cambridge World Archaeology.

Harding, D.W. 1973 Round and Rectangular: Iron Age Houses, British and Foreign. In C. Hawkes and S. Hawkes *Greeks, Celts and Romans, Studies in Venture and Resistance*. London: Archaeology into History, 1.

Harding, D.W. 2004 *The Iron Age in Northern Britain: Celts and Romans, Natives and Invaders*. Abingdon and New York: Routledge.

Harding, D.W. 2007 *The Archaeology of Celtic Art*. Abingdon and New York: Routledge.

Härke, H. 1990 'Warrior Graves'? The background of the Anglo-Saxon weapon burial. *Past and Present* **126** 22–43.

Härke, H. 2011 Anglo-Saxon immigration and ethnogenesis. *Medieval Archaeology* **55**, 1–28.

Harrison, S. 2011 *J.R. Mortimer*. Pickering: Blackthorn Press.

Hartley, B.R. 1988 Plus ça change...or reflections on the Roman forts of Yorkshire. J. Price, P.R. Wilson, C.S. Briggs, S.J. Hardman (eds) *Recent research in Roman Yorkshire: Studies in honour of Mary Kitson Clark (Mrs Derwas Chitty)*. Oxford: Britsh Archaeological Reports **193**, 153–161.

Hartley, E., Hawkes, J., Henig, M. and Mee, F. 2006 *Constantine the Great: York's Roman emperor*. York: York Museums and Art Gallery Trust.

Haselgrove, C.C. 1982 Indigenous settlement patterns in the Tyne-Tees lowlands. In P. Clack and S. Haselgrove (eds) *Rural settlement in the Roman north*. Durham: CBA 3 Occasional Papers, 57–101.

Haselgrove, C.C. 1984 The Later Pre-Roman Iron Age between the Humber and the Tyne. In P.R. Wilson, R.F.J. Jones and D.M. Evans (eds) *Settlement and Society in the Roman North*. Bradford: School of Archaeological Sciences University of Bradford and Roman Antiquities Section, Yorkshire Archaeological Society, 9–26.

Haselgrove, C. 1990 Stanwick. *Current Archaeology* **119**, 380–384.

Haselgrove, C., Fitts, R. and Turnbull, P. 1991 Stanwick, North Yorkshire, part 1: recent research and previous archaeological investigations *Archaeological Journal* **147**, 1–15.

Hawkes, C.F.C. 1960 The ABC of the British Iron Age. In S.S. Frere, *Problems of the Iron Age in Southern Britain*. London: Institute of Archaeology Occasional Papers 11. Reprinted 1977, 1–16.

Hawkes, C.F.C. 1963 Foreword. In Brewster, T.C.M. 1963 *The excavation of Staple Howe*. Scarborough: East Riding Archaeological Research Trust.

Hawkes, G. and Browning, J. 2004 The animal bone. In V. Rigby (ed.) Pots in Pits. The British Museum Yorkshire settlements project 1988–92. *East Riding Archaeologist* **11**, 68–81.

Hawkes, J. and Mills, S. 1999 *Northumbria's Golden Age*. Stroud: Sutton Publishing.

Hawkes, S.C.and G.C. Dunning 1961 Soldiers and Settlers in Britain, Fourth to Fifth Century. *Medieval Archaeology* **5**, 3–70.

Hayes, R.H. and Whitley, E.1950 *The Roman Pottery at Norton, East Yorkshire*. Roman Malton and District Report 7. Leeds: Roman Antiquities Committee of the Yorkshire Archaeological Society.

Hayfield, C. 1987 *An archaeological survey of the parish of Wharram Percy, East Yorkshire: 1, The evolution of the Roman landscape*. Oxford: British Archaeological Reports British Series **172**.

Hayfield, C. 1988 The origins of the Roman landscape around Wharram Percy, East Yorkshire. *Recent research in Roman Yorkshire: Studies in honour of Mary Kitson Clark (Mrs Derwas Chitty)*. Oxford: Britsh Archaeological Reports **193**, 99–123.

Head R., Fenwick, H. Van de Noort, R., Dinnin, M. and Lillie, M. 1995 The survey of Southern Holderness. In: R. Van de Noort and S. Ellis (eds) *Wetland Heritage of Holderness*. Hull: Humber Wetlands Project, University of Hull and English Heritage, 241–3.

Healy J. 1991 *Pliny the Elder – Natural History* (translation). London: Penguin Books.

Heath, A. and Wagner, P. 2009 Coleopteran evidence from the Foulness Valley. In P. Halkon, *et al.*Change and continuity within the Prehistoric landscape of the Foulness Valley, East Yorkshire. *East Riding Archaeologist* **12**, 36–38.

Henrey, B. 1986 *No ordinary gardener: Knowlton's Life and Letters 1726–1781*. London: British Museum (Natural History).

Henig, M. 1995 *Religion in Roman Britain*. London: Batsford.

Henig, M. 1997 *Art in Roman Britain*. London: Batsford.

Hicks, J.D. and Wilson, J. 1975 The Romano-British Kilns at Hasholme. *East Riding Archaeologist* **2**, 49–70.

Hill, J.D. 1995 *Ritual and rubbish in the Iron Age of Wessex*. Oxford: British Archaeological Reports British Series **242**.

Hill, J.D. 1996 Hillforts and the Iron Age of Wessex. In T. Champion, and J.R. Collis (eds) *The Iron Age in Britain and Ireland: Recent Trends*. Sheffield: J.R. Collis Publications, 95–116.

Hill, J.D. 2002 Wetwang Chariot Burial. *Current Archaeology* **178** (15), 410–2.

Hill, J.D. and Willis, S. 2010 The Late Bronze Age and Pre-Roman Iron Age c. 1250 BC to AD50. *Maritime and Marine Historic.Environment Research Framework – Resource Assessment*. English Heritage. (Unpublished report).

Hind, J.G.F. 2007 Route in Roman Britain: from the frontier to the Humber. *Yorkshire Archaeological Journal* **79**, 55–63.

Hinderwell, T. 1798 *The History and antiquities of Scarborough, and the vicinity*. Scarborough: Printed by William Blanchard, for E. Bayley, successor to J. Schofield.

Hodson, R. 1964 Cultural Grouping within the British Pre-Roman Iron Age. *Proceedings Prehistoric Society* **30**, 99–110.

Holland, P. 1610 *Britain or a chorographical description of the most flourishing kingdoms of England, Scotland and Ireland...written first in Latin by William Camden*. London: George Bishop and John Norton.

Holdridge, L. 1987. The beetle remains. In M. Millett, S. McGrail (eds) The archaeology of the Hasholme Logboat. *Archaeological Journal* **144**, 88–89.

Holst, M. 2007 *Osteological Analysis. Land North of 25 and 27 Welton Road, Brough, East Yorkshire*. York: Report 1807.

Horne, P. and Kershaw, A. (eds) 2002 *The Vale of York National Mapping project*. London: English Heritage.

Horne, P. and King, A.C. 1980 Romano-Celtic temples in continental Europe: a gazetteer of those with known plans. In W. Rodwell (ed.) *Temples, churches and religion in Roman Britain*. Oxford: British Archaeological Reports British Series **77** (ii), 369–557.

Horne, P. and Lawton, I. 1998 Buttercrambe Moor Roman Camp, North Yorkshire. *Britannia* **29**, 327–329.

Hornsby, W. and Stanton, R. 1912 The Roman Fort at Huntcliff near Saltburn, *Journal of Roman Studies* **2**, 215–232.

Hornsby, W. and Laverick, J.D. 1932 The Roman Signal Station at Goldsborough near Whitby. *Archaeological Journal* **89**, 203–219.

Horsley, T.J. 2007 Malton Roman Fort, Malton, North Yorkshire. Report on Geophysical Surveys, July-August 2007. Bradford: University of Bradford. Dept of Archaeological Sciences.

Horsley, J. 1732 Britannia Romana, or the Roman Antiquities of Britain. London: John Osborn and Thomas Longman.

Horton, B.P., Innes, J.B., Plater, A. J., Tooley, M.J. and Wright, M.R. 1999 Post-glacial evolution and relative sea-level changes in Hartlepool Bay and the Tees estuary. In D.R. Bridgland, B.P. Horton and J.B. Innes (eds) *The Quaternary of North-east England Field Guide*. London: Quaternary Research Association.

Houghton, J.T., Black, S. and Ephraums, J.J. 1990 *Climate, the IPCC Scientific Assessment. Intergovernmental Panel of Climate Change*. Cambridge: Cambridge University Press.

Howarth, N. 2008 *Cartimandua: Queen of the Brigantes*. Stroud: The History Press.

Hull, M.R. 1932 The pottery from the Roman signal stations on the Yorkshire coast. *Archaeological Journal* **89**, 220–53.

Huntley, J. 1999 The plant remains. In P. Halkon and M. Millett (eds) *Rural Settlement and industry: Studies in the Iron Age and Roman Archaeology of lowland East Yorkshire*. Leeds: Yorkshire Archaeological Report **4**, Yorkshire Archaeological Society, 81.

Hunter-Mann, K., Darling, M.J., Cool, H.E.M. 2000 Excavations on a Roman Extra-Mural Site at Brough-on-Humber, East Riding of Yorkshire, UK. *Internet Archaeology* **9**. http://intarch.ac.uk/journal/issue9/brough_index.html.

Hyland, L. 2009 The Roman Archaeological Evidence of Holderness. *Yorkshire Archaeological Journal* **81**, 179–197.

Innes, J.B. and Blackford, J.J. 2003 Yorkshire's Palaeoenvironmental resource. In T. Manby, S. Moorhouse and P. Ottaway, (eds) 2003 *The Archaeology of Yorkshire An Assessment at the Beginning of the 21st Century*. Leeds: Yorkshire Archaeological Society with English Heritage, CBA, 25–31.

Ireland, S. 1996 *Roman Britain: A sourcebook*. London and New York: Routledge.

Isaac, G. R. 2004 *Place-Names in Ptolemy's Geographia. An electronic data base with etymological analysis of the Celtic name-elements*. CD CMCS Aberystwyth University.

Jackson, C. 1870 *The diary of Abraham de la Pryme the Yorkshire antiquary*. Durham: Publications of the Surtees Society **54**.

Jackson, K. 1948 On Some Romano-British Place-Names. *Journal of Roman Studies* **38** (1 and 2), 54–58.

Jacques, A. and Rossignol, P. 2001 La ferme indigène d'Arras Les Bonnettes (Pas-de-Calais). In J. Collis (ed.), *Society and Iron Age in Europe*, Actes du XVIIIe colloque de l'AFEAF Winchester, 1994. Sheffield, 246–261.

Jacques, D. Vertebrate remains from excavations at Burnby Lane, Hayton. In P. Halkon, M. Millett, H. Woodhouse (eds) forthcoming *Hayton, the archaeology of an Iron Age and Roman landscape in East Yorkshire*. Yorkshire Archaeological Report, Yorkshire Archaeological Society.

Jallands, S. *Roman Brough-on-the-Humber: a re-evaluation*. Unpublished dissertation, Department of Archaeology, University of Durham.

James, S. and Rigby, V. 1997 *Britain and the Celtic Iron Age*. London: British Museum Press.

James, S. 1999 *The Atlantic Celts: Ancient People Modern Invention?* London: British Museum Press.

James, S. 2007 A bloodless past: the pacification of Early Iron Age Britain. In C.C. Haselgrove and R.E. Pope (eds) *The Earlier Iron Age in Britain and the Near Continent*. Oxford: Oxbow Books, 160–173.

Jarman, M., Fagg, A. and Higgs, E.S. 1968 Animal bones. In I.M. Stead, An Iron Age hillfort at Grimthorpe, Yorkshire. *Proceedings of the Prehistoric Society* **34**, 148–190.

Jarrett, M.G. 1994 Non-legionary Troops in Roman Britain: Part One, The Units. *Britannia* **25**, 35–77.

Jay, M., Fuller, B.T., Richards, M.P., Knüsel, C.J. and King, S.S. 2008 Iron Age breastfeeding practices in Britain: isotopic evidence from Wetwang, East Yorkshire. *American Journal of Physical Anthropology* **136** (3), 327–337.

Jay, M., Haselgrove, C. Hamilton, D. Hill, J.D. and Dent J. 2012 Chariots and context: new radiocarbon dates from Wetwang and the chronology of Iron Age burials and brooches in East Yorkshire. *Oxford Journal of Archaeology* **31** (May 2012, Issue 2), 161–189.

Jay, M. and Richards, M.P. 2007 British Iron Age Diet: Stable Isotopes and Other Evidence *Proceedings of the Prehistoric Society* **73**, 171–193.

Jobey, G. 1962 An Iron Age homestead at West Brandon, Durham. *Archaeologia Aeliana* 4th series, **40**, 1–34.

Johns, C. 2010 *The Hoxne Late Roman Treasure: Gold Jewellery and Silver Plate*. London: The British Museum Press.

Johns, C. 1996 *The jewellery of Roman Britain: Celtic and classical traditions*. London: Routledge.

Johnson, A.C., Coleman-Norton, P.R., Bourne, F.C. 2003 Ancient Roman statutes: a translation with introduction, commentary, glossary and index. New Jersey: The Lawbook Exchange.

Johnson, S. 1978 Excavations at Hayton Roman fort, 1975. *Britannia* **9**, 57–115.

Jones, R. 1988 The hinterland of Roman York. In J. Price and P.R. Wilson, with C.S. Briggs and S.J. Hardman (eds) *Recent Research in Roman Yorkshire*. Oxford: British Archaeological Reports British Series **193**,161–170.

Jope, M. 1995 A gold finger-ring found at Arras, gone missing long since. In B. Raftery, V. Megaw and V. Rigby (eds) *Sites and sights of the Iron Age. Essays on fieldwork and museum research presented to Ian Mathieson Stead*. Oxbow Monographs in Archaeology **56**. Oxford: Oxbow Books, 111–17.

Jordan, D. 1987 The investigation of the minerogenic deposit. In M. Millett and S. McGrail, The Archaeology of the Hasholme Logboat. *Archaeological Journal* **144**, 90–97.

Jordan, M. 2005 *Vehicle Redistribution and Storage Facility, North Killingholme, N. Lincs*. Lincoln: Lindsey Archaeological Services.

Karl, R. 2003 Iron Age chariots and medieval texts: a step too far in 'breaking down boundaries'? *e-Keltoi: Journal of Interdisciplinary Celtic Studies* **5**: *Warfare*. Center for Celtic Studies, University of Wisconsin-Milwaukee.

Kent, P. 1980 British Regional Geology: eastern England from the Tees to the Wash. London: Her Majesty's Stationary Office.

Keppie, L.J.F. 2000 *Legions and veterans: Roman army papers 1971* Franz Steiner Verlag, 228–229.

Kershaw, A. 2001 Vale of York National Mapping Programme Project Review. York: English Heritage.

Kershaw, A. and Horne, P. (eds) (forthcoming) *'A perfect flat …' Understanding the archaeology of the Vale of York*. English Heritage.

King, A.C. 1984 Animal bones and the dietary identity of military and civilian groups in Roman Britain, Germany and Gaul. In T.F.C. Blagg and A.C. King (eds) *Military and Civilian in Roman Britain*. Oxford: British Archaeological Reports British Series **136**, 187–217.

King, A.C. 2001 The Romanization of diet in the Western Empire: comparative archaeozoological studies.In S. Keay and N. Terrenato (eds) *Italy and the West: Comparative Issues in Romanization*. Oxford: Oxbow Books, 210–22.

King, J., Tiffin, D., Drakes, D., Smith, K. and Weatherhead, K. 2006 *Water use in agriculture: Establishing a baseline*. SID 5 DEFRA Research Project Final Report WU 0102.

King, S.J. and Bradley, R.I. 1987 *Soils of the Market Weighton District*. Harpenden: Soil Survey of England and Wales.

King, S. 2010 *What makes war? Assessing Iron Age warfare through mortuary behaviour and osteological patterns of violence*. PhD Thesis School of Life Sciences, Division of Archaeological, Geographical and Environmental Sciences, University of Bradford.

King, T.E., Parkin, E.J., Swinfield, G., Cruciani, F., Scozzari, R. Rosa, A., Lim, S., Xue, Y., Tyler-Smith C. and Jobling, M.A. 2007 Africans in Yorkshire? The deepest-rooting clade of the Y phylogeny within an English genealogy. *European Journal of Human Genetics* **15**, 288–293.

Kinnes, I. and Longworth, I. 1985 *Catalogue of the excavated prehistoric and Romano-British material in the Greenwell Collection*. London: British Museum Publications.

Kirby, J.R. 2001 Regional Late Quaternary marine and perimarine record. In M.D. Bateman, P.C. Buckland, C.D. Frederick and N.J. Whitehouse (eds) *The Quaternary of East Yorkshire and North Lincolnshire*. London. Quaternary Research Association, 25–34.

Kitson Clark, M. 1935 *A Gazetteer of Roman Remains in East Yorkshire*. Roman Malton and District Report 5. Leeds: Roman Antiquities Committee of the Yorkshire Archaeological Society.

Koch J.T. 2007 *An Atlas for Celtic Studies: Archaeology and Names in Ancient Europe and Early Medieval Ireland, Britain and Brittany*. Oxford: Oxbow Books.

Langston, J. 2006 The human skeletal remains. In M. Millett (ed) *Shiptonthorpe: archaeological studies of a Roman roadside settlement*. Leeds: Yorkshire Archaeological Report **5**, 251–257.

Langston, J. and Gowland, R. (forthcoming) The human skeletal material. In Halkon, P., Millett, M. Woodhouse, H. (eds) forthcoming *Hayton, the archaeology of an Iron Age and Roman landscape in East Yorkshire*. Yorkshire Archaeological Report, Yorkshire Archaeological Society.

Lamb, H. 1988 *Weather, Climate and Human affairs*. London and New York: Routledge.

Law, J. 2004 *Roman burials in the territory of the Parisi*. Unpublished BA Dissertation, Department of History, University of Hull.

Lawton, I.G. 1994 Derventio. A Roman settlement at North Farm, Stamford Bridge. *CBA Forum. Annual Newsletter of CBA Yorkshire*, 8–13.

Lawton, I.G. 1997 The Roman roads around Stamford Bridge recent work. *CBA Forum. Annual Newsletter of CBA Yorkshire*, 23–29.

Lawton, I.G. 1999 Derventio. A Roman Stamford Bridge update. *CBA Forum. Annual Newsletter of CBA Yorkshire*, 7–11.

Lawton, I.G. 2000 Buttercrambe Temporary Roman Camp, Stamford Bridge. *Bulletin Roman Antiquities Section* **17**. Leeds: Yorkshire Archaeological Society, 4–11.

Lawton, I.G. 2005 A Roman Heated Building at Derventio, Stamford Bridge. *Bulletin Roman Antiquities Section* **21**. Leeds: Yorkshire Archaeological Society, 14–16.

Lawton, I.G. 2009 Appendix 1. Evidence for greyware production in the vicinity. In A. Roe, and I.G. Lawton *A Romano-British landscape at Moor Lane, Stamford Brige. East Riding Archaeologist* **12**, 70–87.

Laycock, S. 2009 *Warlords: The struggle for power in post-Roman Britain*. Stroud: The History Press.

Leach, S., Eckardt, H., Chenery, C., Muldner, G. and Lewis, M. 2010 A Lady of York: migration, ethnicity and identity in Roman Britain. *Antiquity* **84** (323), 131–145.

Leahy, K. 1993 The Anglo-Saxon settlement of Lindsey. In A. Vince (ed.) *Pre-Viking Lindsey*. Lincoln: Lincoln Archaeological Studies 1, 29–44.

Leahy, K. 1996. Three Roman Rivet Spurs from Lincolnshire. *Antiquaries Journal* **76**, 237–240.

Leahy, K. 2007 *The Anglo-Saxon Kingdom of Lindsey*. Stroud: Tempus Publishing.

Leahy, K, 2011 FAKL-B04E22 a roman toilet article Webpage available at:http://finds.org.uk/database/artefacts/record/id/451128

Leake, R. 2012 *A survey of the archaeology of the area of Swine Parish, East Yorkshire*. Unpublished dissertation, Department of History, University of Hull.

Legge, A.J. 1991 Animal bones. In Stead, I.M., *Iron Age Cemeteries in East Yorkshire. Excavations at Burton Fleming, Rudston, Garton-on-the-Wolds, and Kirkburn*. English Heritage Archaeological Report **22** London: English Heritage, 140–7.

Lemon, R. 1856 *Calendar of State Papers, Domestic Series, Edward VI, Mary Elizabeth 1547–1580*. London: Longman, Brown, Green, Longmans, and Roberts.

Lewis, N. and Reinhold, M. 1966 *Roman civilization. Sourcebook II: The Empire*. New York: Harper Torchbooks.

Light, J. (forthcoming) Analysis of the marine shell. In P Halkon, M. Millett, H. Woodhouse (eds) forthcoming *Hayton, the archaeology of an Iron Age and Roman landscape in East Yorkshire*. Yorkshire Archaeological Report, Yorkshire Archaeological Society.

Lillie, M. and Gearey, B. 1999 The palaeo-environmental survey of the Humber estuary, incorporating an investigation of the nature of warp deposition in the southern part of the Vale of York. In R. Van de Noort and S. Ellis (eds) *Wetland heritage of the Vale of York*. Hull: Humber Wetlands Project. University of Hull, 79–108.

Lister, M. 1681–2 On Roman Urns and other Antiquities near York. In C. Hutton, G. Shaw and R. Pearson *The Philosophical Transactions of the Royal Society of London, from Their Commencement, in 1665, to the Year 1800: 1672–1683* (Abridged) 1809. London: printed by and for C. and R. Baldwin, New Bridge Street, Blackfriars, 518–20.

Liversidge, J., Stead, I.M. and Smith, D.J. 1973 Brantingham Roman Villa: Discoveries in 1962. *Britannia* **4**, 84–106.

Lloyd, G.D. 1968 A Roman Pottery Kiln in the Parish of Lockington. *East Riding Archaeologist* **1** (1), 28–38.

Long, A.J., Innes, J.B., Kirby, J.R., Lloyd, J.M., Rutherford, M.M., Shennan, I. and Tooley, M.J. 1998 Holocene sea-level change and coastal evolution in the Humber estuary, eastern England: an assessment of rapid coastal change. *The Holocene* **8**, 229–247.

Long, D.A., Steedman, K. and Vere-Stevens, L. 2002 The Goodmanham Plane. *Tools and Trades Journal* **13**, 9–20.

Lott, J.B. 2004 *The Neighborhoods of Augustan Rome*. Cambridge: Cambridge University Press.

Loughlin, N. and Miller, K.R. 1979 *A survey of Archaeological sites in Humberside*. Hull: Humberside Libraries and Amenities, Humberside Joint Archaeological Committee.

Loveluck, C. 1999 Archaeological expressions of the transition from the late Roman to early Anglo-Saxon period in lowland East Yorkshire. In P. Halkon and M. Millett (eds) *Rural Settlement and industry: Studies in the Iron Age and Roman Archaeology of lowland East Yorkshire*. Yorkshire Archaeological Report **4**. Leeds: Yorkshire Archaeological Society, 228–236.

Loveluck, C. 2003 The Archaeology of Post-Roman Yorkshire, AD 400–700: overview and future directions for research. In T. Manby, S. Moorhouse, and P. Ottaway (eds) 2003 T*he Archaeology of Yorkshire An Assessment at the Beginning of the 21st Century Yorkshire*. Leeds: Yorkshire Archaeological Society with English Heritage, CBA Yorkshire, 125–151.

Lowther, A.W.G. 1976 Romano-British chimney-pots and finials, *Antiquaries Journal* **56**, 35–48.

Lukis, W.C. 1887 *The family memoirs of the Rev. William Stukeley and the antiquarian correspondence* **3**. Surtees Society 80, 380.

Mackey, R. 1998 The Welton villa-a view of social and economic change during the Roman period in East Yorkshire. In P. Halkon (ed.) *Further Light on the Parisi-Recent Research in Iron Age and Roman East Yorkshire*. Hull: East Riding Archaeological Society, University of Hull Department of History, East Riding Archaeological Research Trust, 23–35.

Mackey, R. 2001 An investigation of Romano-British enclosures at Swaythorpe Farm, Kilham. *East Riding Archaeologist* **10**, 29–41.

Mackey, R. 2005 Chariot burials and reconstruction. *Prehistory Research Section Bulletin* **42**. Leeds: Yorkshire Archaeological Society, 26–28.

Mackey, R. forthcoming. Welton and other eastern Yorkshire villas – evidence for change in the 4th century and beyond. In R.M. Friendship, D.E. Taylor (eds) *From villa to village*. Upper Nene Archaeological Society, Fascicule 7.

Macklin, M.G., Taylor, M.P. Hudson-Edwards, K.A. and Howard A.J. 2000 Holocene environmental change in the Yorkshire Ouse basin and its influence on river dynamics and sediment fluxes to the coastal zone. In I. Shennan and J.E. Andrews (eds) *Holocene Land-Ocean Interaction and Environmental Change around the North Sea*. Geological Society Special Publication **166**, 87–97.

Macklin, M.G., Johnstone, E. and Lewin, J. 2005 Pervasive and long-term forcing of Holocene river instability and flooding in Great Britain by centennial-scale climate change. *The Holocene* **15**, 937–943.

Mainland, I. 2006 The mammal and bird bone. In M. Millett *Shiptonthorpe, East Yorkshire. Archaeological Studies of a Romano-British roadside settlement*. Yorkshire Archaeological Report **5**. Leeds: Roman Antiquities Section Yorkshire Archaeological Society and East Riding Archaeological Society, 258–280.

Maltby, M. 1989 Urban rural variations in the butchering of cattle in Romano-British Hampshire. In D. Serjeantson and T. Waldron (eds) *Diet and Crafts in Towns*. Oxford: British Archaeological Reports British Series **199**, 75–106.

Manby, T.G. 1980 *Bronze Age settlement in eastern Yorkshire. Settlement and society in the British Later Bronze Age*. Oxford: British Archaeological Reports British Series **83**, 307–370.

Manby, T.G. 1990 Paddock Hill, Thwing. In T.G. Manby (ed.) Eastern Yorkshire. Prehistoric Society excursion conference papers Scarborough. East Riding Archaeological Research Trust, 21.

Manby, T.G. 2007 Continuity of monument traditions into the Late Bronze age? Henges to ring-forts, and shrines. In C. Burgess, P. Topping and F. Lynch (eds) B*eyond Stonehenge. Essays on the Bronze Age in honour of Colin Burgess*. Oxford: Oxbow Books, 403–424.

Manby, T.G., Moorhouse, S., and Ottaway, P. (eds) 2003(a) *The Archaeology of Yorkshire, An Assessment at the Beginning of the 21st Century*. Leeds: Yorkshire Archaeological Society with English Heritage, CBA.

Manby, T.G., King, A. and Vyner, B. 2003(b) The Neolithic and Bronze Age: a time of early agriculture. In T.G. Manby, S.Moorhouse and P. Ottaway, (eds) *The Archaeology of Yorkshire An Assessment at the Beginning of the 21st Century*. Leeds: Yorkshire Archaeological Society with English Heritage, CBA, 35–114.

Manning, W.H. 1975 An iron anvil from Hasholme, Yorkshire. In J.D. Hicks and J. Wilson (eds) *The Romano-British Kilns at Hasholme. East Riding Archaeologist* 2, 67–69.

Marchant, D. and Halkon, P. 2008 *Heavy metal in the Iron Age: The South Cave weapons cache and other treasures*. Beverley: East Riding of Yorkshire Council.

Margary, I.D. 1967 *The Roman roads of Britain*. London: Baker.

Marion, S. 2007 Les IVe et IIIe siècles avant notre ère en Ile de France. In C. Mennessier-Jouannet, A-M. Adam and P.Y. Milcent (eds) *La Gaule dans son contexte européen aux IVe et IIIe s. avant notre ère, Actes du XXVIIe colloque de l'AFEAF à Clermont-Ferrand en 2003* (Monographies d'Archéologie Méditerranéenne). Lattes: Association pour le Développement de l'Archéologie en Languedoc-Roussillon.

Marion, S. 2009 Des objets dans les tombes: éléments d'interprétations des assemblages funéraires du IIIe siècle dans les sépultures des environs de Paris. Revue Archéologique de Picardie 3/4 225–236.

Marsden A. 2003 A Roman military diploma fragment from mid-Norfolk. *The East of England region Portable Antiquities Scheme Newsletter* 1, 8–9.

Martin, L. 2003 *Mount Airy Farm, South Cave, East Yorkshire. Report on the Geophysical Survey, August – September 2003*. London: Centre for Archaeology, English Heritage Reports 103/2003.

Martins, C.B. 2005 *Becoming consumers: Looking beyond wealth as an explanation of villa variability: Perspectives from the East of England*. British Archaeological Reports British Series **403**, Oxford: Archaeopress.

Mason, D.J.P. 1988 'Prata Legionis' in Britain. *Britannia* **19**, 163–190.

Mattingly D. 2006 *An Imperial Possession: Britain in the Roman Empire, 54 BC-AD 409* London: Allen Lane.

Maule Cole, E. 1899 On the Roman roads in the East Riding. *Transactions of the East Riding Antiquarian Society* 7, 37–46.

May, T. 1922 *Roman Forts at Templeborough*. Rotherham: H. Garnett and Co.

Mays, S.A. and Strongman, S.R. The Human burials. In Neal, D.S. 1996 *Excavations on the Roman Villa at Beadlam, Yorkshire*. Leeds: Yorkshire Archaeological Report 2, 114.

McCarthy, M. 1985 Roman Carlisle. *ERAS News*, East Riding Archaeological Society February 1985, 19–21.

McInnes, I.J. 1968 The excavation of a Bronze Age cemetery at Catfoss, East Yorkshire. *East Riding Archaeologist* 1, 2–10.

McIntosh, F. 2008 LVPL-91B063 A Roman strap end Webpage available at:http://finds.org.uk/database/artefacts/record/id/212611 [Accessed: 17 May 2012 8:46:04 PM].

Mellor, E. 1952 The Harpham Villa. *Yorkshire Archaeological Journal* **38** (149), 117–8.

Metcalfe, S.E., Ellis, S., Horton, B.P., Innes, J.B., Mcarthur, J., Mitlehner, A., Parkes, A., Pethick, J.S, Rees, J., Ridgway, J., Rutherford M.M., Shennan, I. and Tooley M.J. 2000 The

Holocene evolution of the Humber Estuary: reconstructing change in a dynamic environment. In I. Shennan and J.E. Andrews (eds) *Holocene land-ocean interaction and environmental change around the North Sea*. London: The Geological Society, 97–118.

Meurig-Evans H. and Thomas W.O. 1963 *Y geiriadur mawr: the complete Welsh-English, English-Welsh dictionary*. Aberystwyth: Llandybie.

Miles, D. 2005 *The Tribes of Britain. Who are we? Where do we come from?* London: Phoenix.

Millett, M. 1989 *The Romanization of Britain: an essay in archaeological interpretation*. Cambridge: Cambridge University Press.

Millett, M. 1990 Iron Age and Roman settlement in the southern vale of York: some problems in perspective. In S. Ellis and D. Crowther (eds) *Humber Perspectives*. Hull: Hull University Press, 347–357.

Millett, M.1995. *English Heritage Book of Roman Britain*. London: Batsford.

Millett, M. (ed.) 2006 *Shiptonthorpe, East Yorkshire. Archaeological Studies of a Romano-British roadside settlement*. Yorkshire Archaeological Report **5**. Leeds: Roman Antiquities Section Yorkshire Archaeological Society and East Riding Archaeological Society.

Millett, M. and McGrail, S. 1987 The Archaeology of the Hasholme logboat, *Archaeological Journal* **144**, 69–155.

Mills, A.D. 2003 *A Dictionary of British Place-Names*. Oxford: Oxford University Press, 7.

Mitchelson, N. 1964 Roman Malton: the civilian settlement. Excavations in Orchard Field, 1949–1952. *Yorkshire Archaeological Journal* **41**, 209–61.

Monaghan, J. 1997 Roman pottery from York. Archaeology of York 16/8 York: CBA YAT.

Monk, J. 1978 The animal bone. In S. Johnson Excavations at Hayton Roman fort, 1975. *Britannia* **9**, 99–103.

Monkman, R. 2003 *Romano-British mosaics in the Humber region. A social statement?* Unpublished Dissertation, University of Hull Faculty of Arts.

Montgomery, J. 2010 Passports from the past: Investigating human dispersals using strontium isotope analysis of tooth enamel. *Annals of Human Biology* **37**(3), 325–346.

Moore, T. 2012 Detribalizing the later prehistoric past: Concepts of tribes in Iron Age and Roman studies. Time and empire in the Roman world. *Journal of Social Archaeology* June 1, 2012, **12**, 145–166.

Morris, J. 2010 Introduction: Integrating social and Environmental Archaeologies. In J. Morris and M. Maltby (eds) *Integrating Social and Environmental Archaeologies; Reconsidering Deposition*. Oxford: British Archaeological Reports International Series 2077, 1–4.

Morris, J. 1973 *The age of Arthur: a history of the British Isles from 350 to 650*. London: Charles Scribner's Sons

Morris, M.C.F. 1907 *Nunburnholme, its History and Antiquities*. York: John Sampson, London: Henry Frowde, Amen Corner.

Morris, R. 2010 YORYM-9913F6 a Roman figurine Webpage available at: http://finds.org.uk/database/artefacts/record/id/387772

Mortimer, C. forthcoming Metal-working debris from Pit Complex 2.1. In P. Halkon, M. Millett, H. Woodhouse (eds) *Hayton, the archaeology of an Iron Age and Roman landscape in East Yorkshire*. Yorkshire Archaeological Report, Yorkshire Archaeological Society.

Mortimer, J.R. 1905 *Forty years researches in the British and Saxon Burial Mounds of East Yorkshire. Including Romano-British discoveries and a description of the ancient entrenchments on a section of the Yorkshire Wolds*. London: A. Brown and Sons Ltd.

Mould, Q. 2011 Domestic life. In L. Allason-Jones *Artefacts in Roman Britain*. Cambridge: Cambridge University Press, 153–180.

Neal, D.S. 1989 The Stanwick Villa, Northants: an interim report on the excavations of 1984–88. *Britannia* **20**, 149–68.

Neal, D.S. 1996 *Excavations on the Roman Villa at Beadlam, Yorkshire*. Leeds: Yorkshire Archaeological Report **2**.

Neal, D.S. and Cosh, S.R. 2002 *Roman Mosaics of Britain: Northern Britain, incorporating the Midlands and East Anglia*. Bournemouth: Illuminata, for Society of Antiquaries of London.

Neal, D.S. and Wilson P.R. 1996 General discussion. In Neal, D.S. *Excavations on the Roman Villa at Beadlam, Yorkshire*. Leeds: Yorkshire Archaeological Report **2**, 40–45.

Nesselhauf, H. 1936 and 1974 *Corpus Inscriptionum Latinarum (CIL) Diplomata militaria. Post Th. Mommsen* (Supplementum Edidit. 1955 and 2001). Berlin: Berlin-Brandenburgische Akademie der Wissenschaften.

Nicholson, J. 1887 *Beacons of East Yorkshire*. Hull: A. Brown.

Niblett, R. 2004 The native elite and their funerary practices from the First Century BC to Nero. In M. Todd (ed.) *A Companion to Roman Britain*. Oxford: Historical Association/Blackwell Publishing, 30–41.

Norman, M. 2010 *An investigation into the distribution of Romano-British brooches in East Yorkshire*. BA Dissertation, Department of History University of Hull.

OA North (Oxford Archaeology North) 2011 Excavations on the Easington to Paull Natural Gas Pipeline Holderness. In *Humber Archaeology Partnership Newsletter* Autumn 2011. Hull: Humberside Archaeology Partnership, 8–10.

O'Brien, C. and Elliott, L. 2005 *Chapel Garth, Arram. East Riding of Yorkshire. Plant macrofossil assessment on behalf of the East Riding Archaeological Society*. Durham: Archaeological Services University of Durham Report 1378.

O'Connor, B. 2007 Llyn Fawr metalwork in Britain: a review. In C. Haselgrove and R. Pope (eds) *The earlier Iron Age in Britain and the near continent*. Oxford: Oxbow Books, 64–79.

O'Connor, S. 2008 The swords. In D. Marchant and P. Halkon *Heavy metal in the Iron Age: The South Cave weapons cache and other treasures*. Beverley: East Riding of Yorkshire Council.

O'Connor, S., Ali, E., Al-Sabah, S., Anwar, D., Bergström, E., Brown, K.A., Buckberry, J, Buckley, S., Collins, M., Denton, J., Dorling, K.M., Dowle, A., Duffey, P., Edwards, H.G.M., Faria, E.C., Gardner, P., Gledhill, A., Heaton, K., Heron, C., Janaway, R., Keely, B.J., King, D., Masinton, A., Penkman, K., Petzold, A., Pickering, M.D., Rumsby, M., Schutkowski, H., Shackleton, K.A. Thomas, J., Thomas-Oates, J., Usai, M.R., Wilson, A.S. and O'Connor, T. 2011 Exceptional preservation of a   prehistoric human brain from Heslington, Yorkshire, UK. *Journal of Archaeological Science* **38**, Issue 7, 1641–1654.

Oliver, G. 1829 *The history and the antiquities of the town and Minster of Beverley, in the county of York, from the most early period*. Hull: M. Turner.

Oliver, K. 1995 *The Archaeology of the Brantingham area*. A Level Project. Wilberforce College, Hull.

Oppenheimer, S. 2007 *The origins of the British – a genetic detective story*. London: Robinson.

Osgood, R. 2005 The dead of Tormarton – Middle Bronze Age combat victims? In M. Parker Pearson and I.J.N. Thorpe (eds) *Warfare, Violence and Slavery in Prehistory*: Proceedings of a Prehistoric Society conference at Sheffield University. Oxford: British Archaeological Reports S1374.

Oswald, A. 1991. *A Doorway on the Past: round-house entrance orientation and its significance in Iron Age Britain*. Unpublished BA Dissertation, University of Cambridge.

Oswald, A. 2011 *Prehistoric Linear Boundary Earthworks. Introductions to Heritage Assets*, London: English Heritage.

Oswald, A. and Pearson T. 2001 *An Iron Age promontory fort at Raulston Scar, North Yorkshire*. English Heritage sites investigation report A1/11/2001.

Ottaway, P. 2000 Excavations on the site of the Roman signal station at Carr Naze, Filey, 1993–94. *Archaeological Journal* **157**, 79–199.

Ottaway, P. 2001 *Romans on the Yorkshire Coast*. York: York Archaeological Trust Publication.

Ottaway, P. 2003 The archaeology of the Roman period in the Yorkshire Region; a rapid resource assessment. In T. Manby, S. Moorhouse, and P. Ottaway (eds) *The Archaeology of Yorkshire An Assessment at the Beginning of the 21st Century*. Leeds: Yorkshire Archaeological Society with English Heritage, CBA, 125–149.

Ottaway, P. 2004 *Roman York*. Stroud: Tempus Publishing.

Pacitto, A.L. 1980 Iron objects from the well. In I.M. Stead *Rudston Roman Villa*. Leeds: Yorkshire Archaeological Society, 110–116.

Pacitto, A.L 2004 English Heritage excavations at Scarborough Castle, 1978. In Pots in Pits. The British Museum Yorkshire settlements project 1988–92. *East Riding Archaeologist* **11**, 217–223.

Palmer, C. 1999 The charred botanical remains. In P. Halkon and M. Millett (ed.) *Rural Settlement and industry: Studies in the Iron Age and Roman Archaeology of lowland East Yorkshire*. Leeds: Yorkshire Archaeological Report **4**, Yorkshire Archaeological Society, 131–141.

Palmer, R 1984 Danebury. *An Iron Age Hillfort in Hampshire. An aerial photographic interpretation of its environs*. London: Royal Commission on Historical Monuments (England), Supplementary Series, 6.

Parfitt, K. and Green M. 1987 A Chalk Figurine from Upper Deal, Kent. *Britannia* **18**, 295–298.

Parfitt, K. 1995 *Iron Age burials from Mill Hill, Deal*. London: British Museum Press.

Parker-Pearson, M. and Sydes, R.E. 1997 The Iron Age enclosure and prehistoric landscape of Sutton Common, South Yorkshire. *Proceeding of the Prehistoric Society* **63**, 221–59.

Parker Pearson, M., Chamberlain, A., Collins, M., Cox, C. Craig, G. Craig, O. Hiller, J., Marshall, P. Mulville, J. and Smith, H. 2007 Further evidence for mummification in Bronze Age Britain. *Antiquity* **81**, 312 September, http://antiquity.ac.uk/projgall/parker/index.html

Parry, J. 2005 *A Bronze Age burnt mound and a Romano-British settlement site at Stamford Bridge, East Yorkshire*. Publication Report NAA 07/122. Barnard Castle: Northern Archaeological Associates.

Penn, W.S. 1962 Springhead: Temples II and V *Archaeologia Cantiana* **77**, 110–32.

Phillips E.J. 1980 Sculptures and architectural fragments. In I.M. Stead *Rudston Roman Villa*. Leeds: Yorkshire Archaeological Society.

Philpott, R. 1991 *Burial practices in Roman Britain: a survey of grave treatment and furnishing, 43–410 AD*. Oxford: Tempus Reparatum.

Pogrebova, M. 2003 The emergence of chariots and riding in the South Caucasus. *Oxford Journal of Archaeology* **22**, 397–409.

Pope, R.E. 2007 Ritual and the roundhouse: a critique of recent ideas on domestic space in later British prehistory. In C.C. Haselgrove and R.E. Pope (eds) *The Earlier Iron Age in Britain and the near Continent*. Oxford: Oxbow, 204–228.

Potter, T.W. 1997 *Roman Britain*, 2nd edition. London: The British Museum Press.

Poulson, G. 1829 *Beverlac: or, The antiquities and history of the town of Beverley, in the county of York...* Beverley: G. Scaum.

Poulson, G. 1841 *The History and Antiquities of the Seigniory of Holderness, in the East Riding of the County of York*. Hull: Thomas Topping, Bowlalley lane and London: W Pickering.

Powell, A., Northover, P., Cameron E., O'Connor, S. and Doherty A. (forthcoming) A hoard of Iron Age weapons from South Cave, East Yorkshire. *Britannia*.

Powlesland, D. 1988 Approaches to the excavation and interpretation of the Romano-British landscape in the Vale of Pickering. In Price, J. and Wilson, P.R. (eds) *Recent Research in Roman Yorkshire*. BAR British Series **193**, 139–150.

Powlesland, D. 2003 (a) *Twenty five years of archaeological research on the sands and gravels of Heslerton*. The Landscape Research Centre, English Heritage.

Powlesland, D. 2003 (b) The Heslerton Parish Project: 20 years of research in the Vale of Pickering. In T. Manby, S. Moorhouse and P. Ottaway (eds) 2003 *The Archaeology of Yorkshire An Assessment at the Beginning of the 21st Century*. Leeds: Yorkshire Archaeological Society with English Heritage, CBA, 275–293.

Powlesland, D., Lyall, J., Hopkinson, G., Donoghue, D. Beck, M., Harte, A., Stott, D. 2006 Beneath the sand: remote sensing, archaeology, aggregates and sustainability: a case study from Heslerton, the Vale of Pickering, North Yorkshire, UK. *Archaeological Prospection* **299**, 291–299.

Powlesland, D. 2011 *Excavations at Boltby Scar Hillfort 2011 An Interim Report*. Yedingham: The Landscape Research Centre.

Price, J. 1988 Romano-British glass bangles from East Yorkshire. In J. Price, and P.R Wilson (eds) *Recent Research in Roman Yorkshire*. Oxford: British Archaeological Report. British Series **193**, 339–66.

Price, J. 2002 Broken bottle and quartz sand: Glass production in Roman Yorkshire. In P. Wilson and J. Price (eds) *Craft and Industry in Roman Yorkshire and the North*. Oxford: Oxbow Books, 81–95.

Price, J and Cottam, S. 1996 The glass. In D.S. Neal (ed) *Excavations on the Roman Villa at Beadlam, Yorkshire*. Leeds: Yorkshire Archaeological Report **2**, 93–108.

Priest, V., Clay, P. and Hill, J.D. 2003 Iron Age gold from Leicestershire. *Current Archaeology* **188**, 358–362.

Proctor, W. 1855 Report of the proceedings of the Yorkshire Antiquarian Club in the excavation of barrows from the year 1849. *Proceedings Yorkshire Philosophical Society*, 175–89.

Pryor, F. 1999 *Farmers in Prehistoric Britain*. Stroud: Tempus Publishing.

Pughe, W.O. 1832 *Dictionary of the Welsh Language: explained in English*. Denbigh: Thomas Gee.

Rackham, O. 1980. *Ancient woodland in history, vegetation and uses in England*. London: Edward Arnold.

Radley, J.R. (ed.) 1967 Yorkshire Archaeological Register 1967 *Yorkshire Archaeological Journal* **42**, 109–118.

Radley, J. and Simms, C. 1970 *Yorkshire Flooding: Some effects on man and nature.* York: William Sessions.

Rahtz, P.A. 1988 From Roman to Saxon at Wharram Percy. In J. Price, P.R Wilson, C.S. Briggs, S.J. Hardman (eds) *Recent research in Roman Yorkshire: Studies in honour of Mary Kitson Clark (Mrs Derwas Chitty)*. Oxford: Britsh Archaeological Reports **193**, 123–139.

Rahtz, P.A., Hayfield, C. and Bateman, J. 1986 *Two Roman villas at Wharram Le Street, York*. York: University of York Archaeological Publications **2**.

Rahtz, P.A. and Watts, L. 2004 *Wharram: The North Manor Area and North-West Enclosure*. York: University of York Department of Archaeology.

Ramm, H.G. 1978 *The Parisi*. London: Duckworth.

Ramm, H.G. 1988 Aspects of the Roman countryside in East Yorkshire. In J. Price, P.R. Wilson, C.S. Briggs, S.J. Hardman (eds) *Recent research in Roman Yorkshire: Studies in honour of Mary Kitson Clark (Mrs Derwas Chitty)*. Oxford: Britsh Archaeological Reports **193**, 81–89.

Ramm, H.G. 1990 The Millington Roman temple and the Haynes map. *Bulletin of the Roman Antiquities Section* **7**. Leeds: Yorkshire Archaeological Society, 8–20.

Reece, R. 1987 *Coinage in Roman Britain*. London: Seaby.

Reynolds, P.J. 1979 *Iron Age farm: the Butser experiment*. London: British Museum.

Richardson, J. 2011 Bronze Age Cremations, Iron Age and Roman Settlement and Early Medieval Inhumations at the Langeled Receiving Facilities, Easington, East Riding of Yorkshire. *Yorkshire Archaeological Journal* **83**, 59–100.

Richmond, I.A. 1932 Review of Corder and Kirk *Journal of Roman Studies* **22**, 255.

Richmond, I.A. 1933 *The Roman pavements at Rudston*. Malton: Roman Malton and District Committee. Report, 6.

Richmond, I.A. 1963 *Roman Britain*. Harmondsworth: Penguin Books.

Richmond, I.A. 1968 *The Roman pavements from Rudston, East Riding*. Hull: Hull Museum Publication.

Rigby, V., Freestone, I., Humphrey, M.S. and Middleton, A. 1998 Thoughts on Pottery of the First Millennium BC found in East Yorkshire. In P. Halkon (ed.) *Further light on the Parisi*. Hull: University of Hull Department of History, East Riding Archaeological Research Trust, 36–40.

Rigby, V. 2004 Pots in Pits. The British Museum Yorkshire settlements project 1988–92. *East Riding Archaeologist* **11**.

Riley, D.N. 1982 *Aerial Archaeology in Britain*. Aylesbury: Shire.

Riley, D.N., Buckland, P.C. and Wade, J. 1995 Excavations and aerial reconnaissance at Littleborough on Trent, Nottinghamshire. *Britannia* **25**, 253–284.

Rivet, A.L.F. and Smith, C. 1979 *The Place names of Roman Britain*. London: Batsford.

Roberts, I. (ed.) 2005 *Ferrybridge Henge: The Ritual Landscape*. Leeds: West Yorkshire Archaeological Services.

Roberts, I., Deegan A. and Berg, D. 2010 *Understanding the Cropmark Landscapes of the Magnesian Limestone*. Wakefield: West Yorkshire Archaeology Service.

Robbins, G. 1999 Research and regionality; South Yorkshire as an example. In B. Bevan (ed.) *Northern Exposure: interpretative devolution and the Iron Ages in Britain*. Leicester: Leicester Archaeology Monographs **4**, 43–49.

Robinson, J.F. 1978 *The Archaeology of Malton*. Leeds: Yorkshire Archaeological Society.

Rodwell, W. 1980 *Temples, churches, and religion: recent research in Roman Britain: with a gazetteer of Romano-Celtic temples in continental Europe*. Oxford: British Archaeological Reports British Series **77**.

Roe, A. and Lawton, I.G. 2009, A Romano-British landscape at Moor Lane, Stamford Bridge. *East Riding Archaeologist* **12**, 70–87.

Rolfe, J.C. 1952 *Ammianus Marcellinus Res Gestae*. Cambridge: Loeb Classical Library.

Rowland, S. 2012 *The archaeology of the Easington to Paull Gas Pipeline*. Lecture to East Riding Archaeological Society, 18th April 2012 (unpublished).

Schadla-Hall T 1989 *Tom Sheppard: Hull's Great Collector*. Beverley: Highgate Publications Ltd.

Score, V. (ed.) 2011 *Hoards, Hounds and Helmets: A Conquest-period Ritual Site at Hallaton, Leicestershire*. Leicester: Leicester Archaeology Monograph 21.

Seetah, K. 2004 *The Hasholme logboat. Butchered cattle bones from the boat*. www.ironmasters. hull.ac.uk

Seetah, K. 2005 Multidisciplinary approach to Romano-British cattle butchery. In M. Maltby (ed.) *Integrating zooarchaeology*. Oxford: Oxbow Books, 111–118.

Sewpaul, N. forthcoming *The production, consumption and redistribution of animals and animal products in Late Iron Age and Romano-British North-East England*. University of Bradford Phd Thesis in progress.

Sheppard, J. 1966 *The draining of the marshlands of south Holderness and the Vale of York*. Hull: East Yorks. Local History Society.

Sheppard, T. 1902 Notes on the ancient model of a boat and a warrior crew found at Roos, in Holderness. *Transactions of the East Riding Antiquarian Society* **9**, 62–74.

Sheppard, T. 1903 Additional notes on the Roos Carr images. *Transactions of the East Riding Antiquarian Society* **10**, 76–79.

Sheppard, T. 1905 *Roman villa at Harpham*. Hull: Hull Museums Publications.

Sheppard, T. 1912a *The lost towns of the Yorkshire Coast*. London: Brown.

Sheppard, T. 1912b Some glimpses of Old Hull in the light of recent excavations. *Transactions of the Hull Scientific and Field Naturalists's Society* **4**. 187–204.

Sheppard, T. 1932 *Record of Additions* Hull Museum Publications (**169–180**) 178, 193.

Sherley-Price, L. 1972 *Bede: A History of the English Church and People*. Harmondsworth: Penguin Classics.

Sherlock, S.J. 2012 *Late prehistoric settlement in the Tees valley and North-East England*. Hartlepool: Tees Archaeology Monogaph Series 5.

Sills, J.A. and Kinsley, G. 1978 Grimsby, Weelsby Avenue. *Lincolnshire History and Archaeology* **13**, 77–8.

Sills, J.A. and Kinsley, G. 1979 Grimsby, Weelsby Avenue. *Lincolnshire History and Archaeology* **14**, 69.

Sills, J.A. and Kinsley, G. 1990 An Iron Age bronze foundry at Weelsby Avenue, Grimsby. *Lincolnshire History and Archaeology* **25**, 49–50.

Sills, J. 2011(a) Iron Age coin. In C. Fenton Thomas (ed.) *Where Sky and Yorkshire and Water Meet: The Story of the Melton Landscape from Prehistory to the Present*. York: On-Site Archaeology Monograph 2, 198–199.

Sills, J. 2011(b) Comments on Driffield hoard coins http://gilliscoins.com/reference/driffield_hoard/comments02.htm

Simmons, I. 1977 The Iron Age and Roman coasts around the Wash. In F.H. Thompson (ed.) *Archaeology and coastal change*. London: Society of Antiquaries, 56–73.

Sitch, B.J. 1987 *Faxfleet B, a Romano-British site near Broomfleet, North Humberside*. MA Thesis, University of Durham.

Sitch, B.J. 1989 A small Roman port at Faxfleet near Broomfleet. In P. Halkon (ed.) *New Light on the Parisi. Recent discoveries in Roman East Yorkshire*. Hull: ERAS University of Hull School of Adult and Continuing Education, 10–15.

Sitch, B.J. 1990 Faxfleet B, a Romano-British site near Broomfleet. In S. Ellis and D. Crowther (eds) *Humber Perspectives*. Hull: Hull University Press, 159–171.

Sitch, B.J. 1993 Thomas Sheppard. The Morfitts Of Atwick and Allen Coin Number 223. *Yorkshire Archaeological Journal* **65**, 11–21.

Sitch, B.J. 1998 Recent research on Roman coins from the East Riding. In P. Halkon (ed.) *Further Light on the Parisi. Recent research in Iron Age and Roman East Yorkshire*. Hull: University of Hull Department of History, East Riding Archaeological Research Trust, 41–46.

Sitch, B.J. 2006 The Roman coins. In M. Millett (ed.) *Shiptonthorpe: archaeological studies of a Roman roadside settlement*. Leeds: Yorkshire Archaeological Report, 90–125.

Slack, P.E. 1951 Report on a Roman Villa at Brantingham, E. Yorks. *Yorkshire Archaeological Journal* **37** (148) 514–20.

Smith, A.1990 The summer season of excavation at Winestead. *ERAS News* **34** – The newsletter of the East Riding Archaeological Society, 7.

Smith, B.M. 2002 *A Palaeoecological study of Raised Mires in the Humberhead Levels*. Oxford: British Archaeological Reports British Series **336**.

Smith, D.J. 2005 *Roman mosaics at Hull*. 3rd edition revised by Martin Foreman. Hull: Hull Museum and Art Galleries.

Smith, J.T. 1997 *Roman Villas*. London: Routledge.

Smith, P. and Kahlia, G. 1992 Identification of infanticide in archaeological sites: a case study from the late Roman early Byzantine periods at Ashkelon Israel. *Journal of Archaeological Science* **19** 667–75.

Smith, R.A. 1928 The pre-Roman remains at Scarborough, *Archaeologia* **77**, 179–200

Smith, W. 1923 *Ancient springs and streams of the East Riding of Yorkshire*. London: Brown.

Snetterton-Lewis, V. 2006 Iron nails. In M. Millett (ed.) *Shiptonthorpe, East Yorkshire. Archaeological Studies of a Romano-British roadside settlement*. Yorkshire Archaeological Report **5**. Leeds: Roman Antiquities Section Yorkshire Archaeological Society and East Riding Archaeological Society, 233–34.

Spradley-Kurowski, K., Millett, M., MacLean, M., Mills, P., Price J. and Willis S. The Small Finds. In P. Halkon, M. Millett, H. Woodhouse (eds) *Hayton, the archaeology of an Iron Age and Roman landscape in East Yorkshire*. Yorkshire Archaeological Report, Yorkshire Archaeological Society.

Spratt, D. 1981 Prehistoric Boundaries in the North Yorkshire Moors, in G. Barker (ed.) *Prehistoric Communities in Northern England*. Sheffield: University of Sheffield, 87–105.

Spratt, D. 1989 T*he linear earthworks of the Tabular Hills, North-East Yorkshire*. Sheffield: University of Sheffield.

Stacey, R. 2004 Evidence for the use of birch-bark tar from Iron Age Britain. *PAST – The newsletter of the Prehistoric Society* **47** (July 2004). http://www.le.ac.uk/has/ps/past/past47.html

Stallibrass, S. 1987 The animal bones. In M. Millett and S. McGrail, The archaeology of the Hasholme logboat. *Archaeological Journal* **144**, 69–155.

Stallibrass, S. and Thomas, R. 2008 (eds) *Feeding the Roman Army: The Archaeology of Production and Supply in NW Europe*. Oxford: Oxbow Books.

Stead, I.M. 1965 *The La Tène cultures of eastern Yorkshire*. York: The Yorkshire Philosophical Society.

Stead, I.M. 1968 An Iron Age hillfort at Grimthorpe, Yorkshire. *Proceedings of the Prehistoric Society* **34**, 148–190.

Stead, I.M. 1973 Part 1: The excavation. In J. Liversidge, I.M. Stead, and D.J. Smith, Brantingham Roman Villa: Discoveries in 1962. *Britannia* **4**, 84–106.

Stead, I.M. 1979 *The Arras Culture*. York: Yorkshire Philosophical Society.

Stead, I.M. 1980 *Rudston Roman Villa*. Leeds: Yorkshire Archaeological Society.

Stead, I.M. 1988. Chalk figurines of the Parisi. *Antiquaries Journal* **68**, 9–29.

Stead, I.M. 1990 Whitcombe, burial 9, the grave goods, in G.M. Aitken and G.N Aitken, Excavations at Whitcombe, 1965–1967, *Proceedings Dorset Natural. History and Archaeological Society* **112**, 73–75.

Stead, I.M. 1991 *Iron Age cemeteries in East Yorkshire*. London: English Heritage.

Stead, I.M. 1996 *Celtic art in Britain before the Roman conquest*. Harvard: Harvard University Press.

Stead, I.M. 2006 *British Iron Age Swords and Scabbards*. London: British Museum Press.

Stead, I.M., Bourk, J., Bothwell, D. 1986 *Lindow Man: the body in the bog*. London: British Museum Press.

Steedman K. 1991 A Late Iron Age settlement at Home Farm, Sewerby. *CBA Forum. Annual Newsletter of CBA Yorkshire*, 10–14.

Stephens, M., and Ware, P. 1995 New Rugby Club, Old Malton. *Roman Antiquities Section Bulletin* **12**. Leeds: Roman Antiquities Section, Yorkshire Archaeological Society, 12–15.

Stephens, M. 2004 *Land south of Glen Garth, Town Street, Hayton, East Riding of Yorkshire. Archaeological excavations assessment report*. Malton: MAP Archaeological Consultancy.

Stephens, M., Ware, P. and Ottaway, P. 2012 *Roman Pottery Kiln, Norton Community Primary School, Malton, North Yorkshire*. Malton: MAP Archaeological Practice Ltd.

Stevenson, J. and Johnson, C. 2004 Brisley Farm. The last Iron Age warriors of Kent. In J. May (ed.) *Current Archaeology* **191**, 490–494.

Stillingfleet, E. 1846 Account of the opening of some barrows on the Wolds of Yorkshire. Proceedings of the Archaeological Institute held at York, 26–32.

Stoertz, C. 1997 *Ancient Landscapes of the Yorkshire Wolds*. Swindon: Royal Commission on Historical Monuments of England.

Strang, A.1997 Explaining Ptolemy's Roman Britain. *Britannia* **28**, 1–30.

Stratton, S. 2005 *Analysis of Roman metal detected artefacts from Hayton*. Unpublished BA Hons Dissertation, University of Hull.

Stückelberger, A. and Graßhoff, G. 2006 *Ptolemaios Handbuch der Geographie*. Basel: Schwabe Verlag.

Sullivan, J.P. (Trans.) 2011 *Petronius:The Satyricon*. London: Penguin Classics, 21–67.

Swan, V. 1984 *The pottery kilns of Roman Britain*. London: RCHME.

Swan, V. 1992 Legio VI and its men: African legionaries in Britain *Journal of Roman Pottery Studies* **5**, 1–33.

Swan, V. 2002 The Roman pottery of Yorkshire in its wider historical context. In P. Wilson and J. Price (eds) *Craft and Industry in Roman Yorkshire and the North*. Oxford: Oxbow Books, 35–81.

Swan, V. and Monaghan, J. 1993 Head pots: a North African tradition in Roman York. *Yorkshire Archaeological Journal* **65**, 21–38.

Swift, E. 2003 *Roman Dress Accessories*. Princes Risborough: Shire Publications.

Swift, E. 2011 Personal ornament. In L. Allason-Jones (ed.) *Artefacts in Roman Britain. Their purpose and use*. Cambridge: Cambridge University Press, 194–219.

Sykes, B.G. 2006 *Blood of the Isles*. London: Bantam Press.

Taylor, J. 1995 Surveying small towns: the Romano-British roadside settlement at Shiptonthorpe, East Yorkshire. In A.E. Brown (ed.) *Roman small towns in eastern England and beyond*. Oxford: Oxbow Monograph 52, 39–52.

Taylor, J. 1996 *Iron Age and Roman landscapes in the East Midlands: a case study in integrated survey*. Unpublished PhD Thesis, University of Durham.

Taylor, J. 1999 The Holme on Spalding Moor Plots. In Halkon, P. and Millett, M. 1999. *Rural Settlement and industry: Studies in the Iron Age and Roman Archaeology of lowland East Yorkshire*. Yorkshire Archaeological Report **4**. Leeds: Yorkshire Archaeological Society, 17–42.

Taylor J. 2007 *An Atlas of Roman rural settlement in England*. London: CBA Research Report 151.

Thayer, W. 2005 *The Geography of Claudius Ptolemy*. http://penelope.uchicago.edu/Thayer/E/Gazetteer/Periods/Roman/_Texts/Ptolemy/2/2*.html

Thew, N. and Wagner, P. 1991 The molluscan evidence from Garton Station and Kirkburn. In I. Stead, *Iron Age cemeteries in East Yorkshire*. London: English Heritage, 148.

Thompson, T. 1824 *A history of the church and priory of Swine*. Hull: Thomas Topping.

Thompson Watkin, W. 1884 The Roman forces in Britain. *Archaeological Journal* **41**, 244–271.

Thoresby, R. 1715 *Ducatus Leodiensis: or, The topography of the ancient and populous town and parish of Leedes, and parts adjacent in the Westriding of the County of York*. London: Atkins.

Thurnham, J. 1871 On the ancient British barrows, especially those of Wiltshire and the adjoining counties, part 2, round barrows. *Archaeologia* **43**, 285–544.

Tibbles, S.E. 2000 *A Re-Appraisal of a Romano-British Tile Dump Excavated at Beck View Road, Beverley, East Yorkshire*. Certificate in Archaeology project. University of Hull.

Tilley, C. 1994 *A Phenomenology of landscape*. London: Berg.

Timby, J. 1993 Sancton I Anglo-Saxon cemetery: excavations carried out between 1976 and 1980. *Archaeological Journal* **150**, 243–365.

Tomlin R.S.O. 1969 Numerus supervenientium Petuariensium. In J.S. Wacher *Excavations at Brough-on-Humber*, 1958–61, London: Society of Antiquaries Research Report 25, 74–5.

Tomlin R.S.O. 2002 Writing to the gods. In A.E. Cooley *Becoming Roman, writing Latin?* International Roman Archaeology Conference Series, JRA Supplementary Series 48, 165–181.

Tooley, M.J. 1974 Sea-level changes during the last 9000 years in north-west England, *Geographical Journal* **140**, 18–42.

Toynbee, J. 1964 *Art in Britain under the Romans*. Oxford: Clarendon Press

Tufi, S.R.1983 Yorkshire. *Corpus Signorum Imperii Romani Great Britain* **1**. Oxford: Published for the British Academy by the Oxford University Press.

Tully G.D. 2005 A Fragment of a Military Diploma for Pannonia found in Northern England? *Britannia* **36** 375–82.

Turnbull, P. and Fitts, L. 1988 The politics of Brigantia. In J. Price and P.R. Wilson (eds) *Recent Research in Roman Yorkshire*. Oxford: British Archaeological Reports British Series **193**, 377–387.

Turner J. 1987. The pollen analysis. In M. Millett, and S. McGrail (eds) The Archaeology of the Hasholme logboat, *Archaeological Journal* **144**, 85–88.

Turney, C.S.M., Baillie, M., Palmer, J. and Brown, D. 2006 Holocene climatic change and past Irish societal response. *Journal of Archaeological Science* **33**, 34–38.

Tweddle, J.C. 2001. Regional vegetation history. In Bateman M.D., P.C. Buckland, C.D. Frederick and N.J. Whitehouse (eds) *The Quaternary of East Yorkshire and North Lincolnshire Field Guide*. London: Quaternary Research Association, 35–46.

Valentin, H. 1957 Glazialmorphologische Untersuchungen in Ostengland. Ein Beitrag zum Problem der letzten Vereisung im Noordseeraum. Berlin: Abhandlungen der Geografische Institut der Freien Universitat 4, 10–86.

Valentin, H. 1971 Land loss in Holderness in J. A. Steers (ed.) *Applied coastal geomorphology*. London: MacMillan, 116–37.

Van Arsdell, R.D. 1989 *Celtic Coinage of Britain*. London: Spink.

Van de Noort, R. 2004 *The Humber Wetlands. The Archaeology of a dynmic landscape*. Bollington: Windgather Press.

Van de Noort, R. and Ellis, S. 1995 *Wetland Heritage of Holderness: an archaeological survey*. Hull: Humber Wetlands Project, University of Hull and English Heritage.

Van De Noort R. and Ellis, S. 1997 (eds) *Wetland Heritage of the Humberhead levels: an archaeological survey*. Hull: Humber Wetlands Project, University of Hull and English Heritage.

Van de Noort, R. and Ellis, S. (eds) 1999 *Wetland Heritage of the Vale of York*. Hull: Humber Wetlands Project, University of Hull and English Heritage.

Van de Noort, R. and Ellis, S. (eds) 2000 *Wetland Heritage of the Hull Valley: Humber Wetlands Project*. Hull: University of Hull and English Heritage.

Van De Noort, R., Chapman H., and Collis, J. 2007 *Sutton Common: the excavation of an Iron Age 'Marsh-fort'*. York: CBA Research Report.

Van der Plicht, J. 2005 Radiocarbon, the calibration curve and Scythian chronology. In E. Marian Scott, A. Alekseev, G. Zaitseva (eds) *Impact of the Environment on Human Migration in Eurasia*. NATO Science Series: IV: Earth and Environmental Sciences. Netherlands: Springer, 45–65.

Van Driel-Murray, C. 1999 'And did those feet in ancient times'...Feet and shoes as a material projection of the self. In P. Baker, C. Forcey, S. Jundi and R. Witcher (eds). TRAC 98: Proceedings of the Eighth Annual Theoretical Roman Archaeology Conference, Leicester 1998. Oxford: Oxbow, 131–140.

Van Driel-Murray, C. 2006 Leather: the Roman footwear. In M. Millett *Shiptonthorpe, East Yorkshire. Archaeological Studies of a Romano-British roadside settlement*. Yorkshire Archaeological Report **5**. Leeds: Roman Antiquities Section Yorkshire Archaeological Society and East Riding Archaeological Society. 240–244.

Van Geel, B., Buurman, J. and Waterbolk, H.T. 1996 Archaeological and palaeoecological indications of an abrupt climate change in The Netherlands, and evidence for climatological teleconnections around 2650 BP. *Journal of Quaternary Science* **11**, 451–460.

Varndell, G. Thwing, East Yorkshire: Late Bronze Age gold penannular ring. Treasure Annual Report 2003. London: Department for Culture, Media and Sport, Cultural Property Unit, 19.

Wacher, J. 1969 *Excavations at Brough on Humber, 1958–61*. London: Society of Antiquaries Research Report **25**.

Wacher, J. 1975 *The Towns of Roman Britain*. Berkley: University of California Press.

Wacher, J. 1995 *The Towns of Roman Britain* (2nd edition). London: Batsford.

Wacher, J. 2000 *A portrait of Roman Britain*. London and New York: Routledge.

Wagner, P.1999 The Skelfrey Beck section. In P. Halkon, and M. Millett, 1999 *Rural Settlement*

and industry: Studies in the Iron Age and Roman Archaeology of lowland East Yorkshire.
Yorkshire Archaeological Report **4**, Yorkshire Archaeological Society. Leeds, 170.

Wagner, P. 2004 The molluscan evidence. In V. Rigby (ed.) Pots in Pits. The British Museum
Yorkshire Settlements Project 1988–92. *East Riding Archaeologist* **11**, 82–90.

Walters, B. 2009 Roman villas in Britain: Farms, temples, or tax-depots? *Current Archaeology*
230, 30–36.

Watts, D. 1998 *Religion in late Roman Britain: forces of change.* London: Routledge.

Watts, L., Jones, A, Rahtz, P. 2000 The Roman villa at Blansby Park, Pickering: excavations at
the Park Gate Roman site in 2000. *Yorkshire Archaeological Journal* **75**, 15–56.

Watts, V., Insley, J. and Gelling, M. 2004 *The Cambridge Dictionary of English place-names.*
Cambridge University Press, Cambridge.

Webster, G. 1969 The future of villas studies. In A.L.F. Rivet *The Roman Villa in Britain.*
London: Routledge and Kegan Paul, 246.

Webster, G. 1989. Deities and Religious Scenes on Romano-British Pottery. *Journal of Roman
Pottery Studies* **2**, 1–19.

Wellbeloved, C. 1881 *A hand-book to the antiquities in the grounds and museum of the Yorkshire
Philosophical Society.* York: John Sampson.

Wellesley K. 2007 *Tacitus – The Histories* (Translation) London: Penguin Books.

Wenham, L.P. 1968 *The Romano-British cemetery at Trentholme Drive, York.* London HMSO.

Wenham, L.P. 1974 *Derventio – (Malton) Roman Fort and Civilian Settlement.* Huddersfield:
Cameo Books.

Wenham, L.P. and Heywood, B. 1997 *The 1968 to 1970 excavations in the vicus at Malton,
North Yorkshire.* Leeds: Yorkshire Archaeological Report **3**.

Whimster, R. 1981 *Burial practices in Iron Age Britain.* Oxford: British Archaeological Reports
90.

Whitehouse, N.J., 2004. Mire ontogeny, environmental and climatic change inferred from fossil
beetle successions from Hatfield Moors, eastern England. *The Holocene* **14**, 79–93.

Whiting, C.E. 1936 Excavations on Sutton Common, 1933, 1934 and 1935. *Yorkshire
Archaeological Journal* **33**, 57–80.

Whitwell, J.B. 1988 Late Roman settlement on the Humber and Anglian beginnings. In J.
Price and P.R. Wilson, with C.S. Briggs and S.J. Hardman (eds) *Recent research in Roman
Yorkshire. Studies in honour of Mary Kitson Clark.* Oxford: British Archaeological Reports
British Series **193**, 49–73.

Whyman, M. and Howard, A. 2005 *Archaeology and Landscape in the Vale of York.* York: York
Archaeological Trust.

Wild, J.P. 2002 The textile industries of Roman Britain. *Britannia* **33**, 1–42.

Williams, J.H.C. 2002 Iron Age Coin finds. Treasure Annual Report 2001. London: Department
for Culture, Media and Sport.

Williams, J.H.C. 2004 Driffield, East Yorkshire (addenda): 20 Iron Age gold staters (2003 T401)
Treasure Annual Report 2003. London: Department for Culture, Media and Sport.

Williamson, D. 1987 *A Roman Villa at Bishop Burton.* Unpublished Certificate in Archaeology
project, Department of History, University of Hull.

Willis, S. 1996 The Romanization of Pottery Assemblages in the East and North-East of England
during the First Century AD: A Comparative Analysis. *Britannia* **27**, 179–221.

Willis, S. (forthcoming)The samian. In Halkon, P., Millett, M. Woodhouse, H. (eds) *Hayton, the archaeology of an Iron Age and Roman landscape in East Yorkshire*. Yorkshire Archaeological Report, Yorkshire Archaeological Society.

Willmott, T. 2001 *Birdoswald Roman Fort*. Stroud: The History Press.

Wilson, F. 2006 *The significance of copper alloy metal working in Iron Age East Yorkshire*. Unpublished BA Dissertation University of Hull.

Wilson, F., Wilson I., Myers G. and Mackey, R. 2006 Excavations at Chapel Garth, Arram, *Prehistory Research Section Bulletin* 43, Leeds: Yorkshire Archaeological Society, 44–45.

Wilson, P.R. 1989 (ed.) Crambeck Roman Pottery Industry. Leeds: Roman Antiquities Section, Yorkshire Archaeological Society, 43–91.

Wilson, P.R. 1991 Aspects of the Yorkshire Signal Stations. In V.A. Maxfield and M.J. Dobson (eds) Roman Frontier Studies1989. Proceedings of the XVth International Congress of Roman Frontier Studies. Exeter: University of Exeter Press, 142–147.

Wilson, P.R. 2002 *Cataractonium: Roman Catterick and its hinterland. Excavations and research 1958–1997*. Council for British Archaeology Research Reports128/129.

Wilson, P.R. 2003 The Roman Towns of Yorkshire: 30 years on in P. Wilson (ed.) *The Archaeology of Roman Towns. Studies in honour of John S. Wacher*. Oxford: Oxbow Books, 258–269.

Wilson, P.R.2006 A Yorkshire Fort and Small Town: Roman Malton and Norton reviewed. *Yorkshire Archaeological Journal* 78, 35–60.

Wilson, P.R. 2009 The Roman expansion in Yorkshire reconsidered. In A. Morillo, N. Hanel and E. Martín (eds) *Limes XX Estudios Sobre la Frontera Romana Madrid*, 103–111.

Wilson, P.R. 2011 Northern England. In E.M. Chapman., F. Hunter, P. Booth, P. Wilson, S.Worrell, and R.S.O. Tomlin (eds) Roman Britain in 2010 *Britannia* 42, 319–466.

Winton, H. 1998 The cropmark evidence for prehistoric and Roman settlement in West Lincolnshire. In R. Bewley (ed.) *Lincolnshire's Archaeology from the air*. Lincoln: Occasional Papers in *Lincolnshire History and Archaeology* 11, 47–69.

Witts, P. 2005 *Mosaics in Roman Britain: stories in stone*. Stroud: Tempus Publishing.

Wood, C. 1860 (exhibit note) Proceedings of the Society of Antiquaries of London 2nd Series (i) 1859–61, 263.

Woodward, A. 1992 *Shrines and Sacrifice*. London: Batsford/English Heritage.

Wrathmell, S. and Nicholson, A. 1990 *Dalton Parlours: Iron Age Settlement and Roman Villa*. Wakefield: West Yorkshire Archaeology Service.

Wright, E.V. 1990 An East Yorkshire retrospective. In S. Ellis and D. Crowther (eds) *Humber Perspectives*. Hull: Hull University Press, 71–88.

Wright, E.V., Hedges, R.E.M., Bayliss, A. and Van De Noort, R. 2001 New AMS dates for the North Ferriby boats – a contribution to dating prehistoric seafaring in north-western Europe. *Antiquity* 75, 726–34.

Wright, R.P. 1950 Roman Britain in 1949. Sites explored. *Journal of Roman Studies* 40, Parts 1 and 2, 92–118.

Wright, R.P. and Hassall M.W.C. 1971 Roman Britain in 1970. II. Inscriptions, *Britannia* 2, 291.

Yonge, C.M. 1960, Oysters. *The New Naturalist*. London: Collins.

Yorkshire Philsophical Society Annual Report 1853.

INDEX